$v = \sqrt{600} = \sqrt{6(100)} =$

THE GOLD STANDARD
DAT PAT & GS-1

Perceptual Ability Test [PAT]
and GS Full-length Practice Test [GS-1]

Book IV of IV

Gold Standard Contributors
• 4-Book GS DAT Set •

Brett Ferdinand BSc MD-CM
Karen Babia BS Arch
Brigitte Bigras BSc MSc DMD
Ibrahima Diouf BSc MSc PhD
Amir Durmić BSc Eng
Adam Segal BSc MSc
Da Xiao BSc DMD
Naomi Epstein BEng
Lisa Ferdinand BA MA
Antonio Nicodemo MSc PhD
Jeanne Tan Te
Kristin Finkenzeller BSc MD
Heaven Hodges BSc
Sean Pierre BSc MD
James Simenc BS (Math), BA Eng
Jeffrey Chen BSc
Timothy Ruger MSc PhD
Petra Vernich BA
Alvin Vicente BS Arch

DMD Candidates

E. Jordan Blanche BS
[Harvard School of Dental Medicine]
Stephan Suksong Yoon BA
[Harvard School of Dental Medicine]

$ET = Ek + Ep = 1/2mv2 + mgh$

glutamate recept
floating bridges
epithelial-mesen
subatomic partic

Gold Standard Illustrators
• 4-Book GS DAT Set •

Daphne McCormack
Nanjing Design
· Ren Yi, Huang Bin
· Sun Chan, Li Xin
Fabiana Magnosi
Harvie Gallatiera
Rebbe Julie Jurilla BSc MBA
Jonathan Jurilla MEd-ESL

floating bridges
subatomic particles
brain functions
receptors Helico bacteria

RuveneCo

The Gold Standard DAT was built for the US DAT.

 The Gold Standard DAT is identical to Canadian DAT prep <u>except</u> QR and ORG. Also, you must practice soap carving for the complete Canadian DAT.

 The Gold Standard DAT is identical to OAT prep <u>except</u> PAT, which is replaced by OAT Physics; see our Gold Standard OAT book for Physics review and OAT practice test.

Be sure to register at www.DAT-prep.com by clicking on GS DAT Owners and following the directions for Gold Standard DAT Owners. Please Note: benefits are for 1 year from the date of online registration, for the original book owner only and are not transferable; unauthorized access and use outside the Terms of Use posted on DAT-prep.com may result in account deletion; if you are not the original owner, you can purchase your virtual access card separately at DAT-prep.com.

Visit The Gold Standard's Education Center at www.gold-standard.com.

Address all inquiries, comments, or suggestions to the publisher. For Terms of Use go to: www.DAT-prep.com

RuveneCo Inc
Gold Standard Multimedia Education
559-334 Cornelia St
Plattsburgh, NY 12901
E-mail: learn@gold-standard.com
Online at www.gold-standard.com

DAT™ is a registered trademark of the American Dental Association (ADA). OAT™ is a registered trademark of the Association of Schools and Colleges of Optometry (ASCO). The Dental Aptitude Test (DAT) program is conducted by the Canadian Dental Association (CDA). Ruveneco Inc and Gold Standard Multimedia Education are neither sponsored nor endorsed by the ADA, ASCO, CDA, nor any of the degree granting institutions that the authors have attended or are attending. Printed in China.

Table of Contents

EXAM SUMMARY

The Dental Admission Test (DAT) consists of 280 multiple-choice questions distributed across quite a diversity of question types in four tests. The DAT is a computer-based test (CBT). This exam requires approximately five hours to complete - including the optional tutorial, break, and post-test survey. The following are the four subtests of the Dental Admission Test:

1. Survey of the Natural Sciences (NS) – 100 questions; 90 min.
   - General Biology (BIO): 40 questions
   - General Chemistry (CHM): 30 questions
   - Organic Chemistry (ORG): 30 questions

2. Perceptual Ability Test (PAT) - 90 questions; 6 subsections; 60 min.
   - Apertures: 15 questions
   - Orthographic or View Recognition: 15 questions
   - Angle Discrimination: 15 questions
   - Paper Folding: 15 questions
   - Cube Counting: 15 questions
   - 3-D Form Development: 15 questions

3. Reading Comprehension (RC) – 50 questions; 3 reading passages; 60 min.

4. Quantitative Reasoning (QR) – 40 questions; 45 min.
   - Mathematics Problems: 30 questions
   - Applied Mathematics/Word Problems: 10 questions

You will get six scores from: (1) BIO (2) CHM (3) ORG (4) PAT (5) QR (6) RC.

You will get two additional scores which are summaries:
    (7) Academic Average (AA) = BIO + CHM + ORG + QR + RC
    (8) Total Science (TS) = BIO + CHM + ORG

Common Formula for Acceptance:

GPA + DAT score + Interview = Dental School Admissions*

*Note: In general, Dental School Admissions Committees will only examine the DAT score if the GPA is high enough; they will only admit or interview if the GPA + DAT score is high enough. Some programs also use autobiographical materials and/or references in the admissions process. Different dental schools may emphasize different aspects of your DAT score, for example: PAT, BIO, TS, AA. The average score for any section is approximately 17/30; the average AA for admissions is usually 18-20 depending on the dental school; the AA for admissions to Harvard is around 22-23; the 100th percentile is usually 25 meaning that virtually 100% of the approximately 13 000 students who take the DAT every year have an AA less than 25. Only a handful of students score 25/30. Our two student contributors scored 27/30 (AA).

The DAT is challenging, get organized.

dat-prep.com/dat-study-schedule

1. How to study:

1. Study the Gold Standard (GS) books and videos to learn
2. Do GS Chapter review practice questions
3. Consolidate: create and review your personal summaries (= Gold Notes) daily

2. Once you have completed your studies:

1. Full-length practice test
2. Review mistakes, all solutions
3. Consolidate: review all your Gold Notes and create more
4. Repeat until you get beyond the score you need for your targeted dental school

3. Full-length practice tests:

1. ADA practice exams
2. Gold Standard DAT exams
3. TopScore Pro exams
4. Other sources if needed

4. How much time do you need?

On average, 3-6 hours per day for 3-6 months

WARNING: Study more or study more efficiently. You choose. The Gold Standard has condensed the content that you require to excel at the DAT. We have had Ivy League dental students involved in the production of the Gold Standard series so that pre-dent students can feel that they have access to the content required to get a score satisfactory at any dental school in the country. To make the content easier to retain, you can also find aspects of the Gold Standard program in other formats such as:

Is there something in the Gold Standard that you did not understand? Don't get frustrated, get online.

dat-prep.com/forum

Good luck with your studies!

Gold Standard Team

GOLD STANDARD
MULTIMEDIA EDUCATION

DAT-Prep.com

DENTAL
SCHOOL ADMISSIONS

PART I

IMPROVING ACADEMIC STANDING

1.1 Lectures

Before you set foot in a classroom you should consider the value of being there. Even if you were taking a course like 'Basket Weaving 101', one way to help you do well in the course is to consider the <u>value</u> of the course to **you**. The course should have an *intrinsic* value (i.e. 'I enjoy weaving baskets'). The course will also have an *extrinsic* value (i.e. 'If I do not get good grades, I will not be accepted...'). <u>Motivation</u>, a <u>positive attitude</u>, and an <u>interest in learning</u> give you an edge before the class even begins.

Unless there is a student 'note-taking club' for your courses, your <u>attendance record</u> and the <u>quality of your notes</u> should both be as excellent as possible. Be sure to choose a seat in the classroom that ensures you will be able to hear the professor adequately and see whatever she may write. Whenever possible, do not sit close to friends!

Instead of chattering before the lecture begins, spend the idle moments quickly reviewing the previous lecture in that subject so you would have an idea of what to expect. Try to <u>take good notes</u> and <u>pay close attention</u>. The preceding may sound like a difficult combination (especially with professors who speak and write quickly); however, with practice you can learn to do it well.

And finally, do not let the quality of teaching affect your interest in the subject nor your grades! Do not waste your time during or before lectures complaining about how the professor speaks too quickly, does not explain concepts adequately, etc. When the time comes, you can mention such issues on the appropriate evaluation forms! In the meantime, consider this: despite the good or poor quality of teaching, there is always a certain number of students who **still** perform well. You must strive to count yourself among those students.

1.2 Taking Notes

Unless your professor says otherwise, if you take excellent notes and learn them inside out, you will *ace* his course. Your notes should always be <u>up-to-date</u>, <u>complete</u>, and <u>separate</u> from other subjects.

To be safe, you should try to type or write everything! You can fill in any gaps by comparing your notes with those of your friends. You can create your own shorthand symbols or use standard ones. The following represents some useful symbols:

$\lvert \cdot \rvert$	*between*
$=$	*the same as*
$\neq$	*not the same as*
$\therefore$	*therefore*
Δ	*difference, change in*
cf.	*compare*
$\overline{c}$ or w	*with*
$\overline{c}$out or w/o	*without*
esp.	*especially*
$\because$	*because*
i.e.	*that is*
e.g.	*for example*

Many students rewrite their notes at home. Should you decide to rewrite your notes, your time will be used efficiently if you are paying close attention to the information you are rewriting. In fact, a more use- ful technique is the following: during class, write your notes only on the right side of your binder. Later, rewrite the information from class in a <u>complete</u> but <u>condensed</u> form on the left side of the binder (*this condensed form should include mnemonics, which we will discuss later*).

Some students find it valuable to use different colored pens. Juggling pens in class may distract you from the content of the lecture. Different colored pens would be more useful in the context of rewriting one's notes.

Of course, typing can be more efficient but time should still be set aside to actively condense and organize notes after class. If the professor has supplied handouts, ideally you would condense those notes as well to include only the most important information or content that you find challenging to remember.

1.3 The Principles of Studying Efficiently

If you study efficiently, you will have enough time for extracurricular activities, movies, etc. The bottom line is that your time must be used efficiently and effectively.

During the average school day, time can be found during breaks, between classes, and after school to quickly review notes in a library or any other quiet place you can find on campus. Simply by using the available time in your school day, you can keep up to date with recent information.

You should design an individual study schedule to meet your particular needs. However, as a rule, a certain amount of time every evening should be set aside for more in-depth studying. Weekends can be allotted for special projects and reviewing notes from the beginning.

On the surface, the idea of regularly reviewing notes from the beginning may sound like an insurmountable task that would take forever! The reality is just the opposite. After all, if you continually study the information, by the time midterms approach you would have seen the first lecture so many times that it would take only moments to review it. On the other hand, had you not been reviewing regularly, it would be like reading that lecture for the first time!

You should study wherever you feel most <u>comfortable</u> and <u>effective</u> (i.e., library, at home, etc.). Should you prefer studying at home, be sure to create an environment, which is conducive to the task at hand.

Studying should be an active process to <u>memorize</u>, <u>synthesize</u>, and <u>understand</u> a given set of material. Memorization and comprehension are best achieved by the **elaboration** of course material, **attention, repetition,** and practicing **retrieval** of the information. All these principles are carried out in the following techniques.

1.4 Studying from Notes and Texts

Successful studying from either class notes or textbooks can be accomplished in three simple steps:

- **Preview the material:** Read all the relevant headings, titles, and sub-titles to give you a general idea of what you are about to learn. You should never embark on a trip without knowing where you are going!

- **Read while questioning:** <u>Passive studying</u> is when you sit in front of a book and just read. This can lead to boredom, lack of concentration, or even worse - difficulty remembering what you just read! <u>Active studying</u> involves reading while actively questioning yourself. For example, how does this fit in with the 'big picture'? How does this relate to what we learned last week? What cues about these words or lists will make it easy for me to memorize them? What type of question would my professor ask me? If I was asked a question on this material, how would I answer?

- **Recite and consider:** Put the notes or text away while you attempt to <u>recall </u>the main facts. Once you are able to recite the important information, <u>consider</u> how it relates to the entire subject.

<u>N.B.</u> If you ever sit down to study and you are not quite sure with which subject to begin, always start with either the most difficult subject or the subject you like least (usually they are one and the same!).

1.5 Study Aids

The most effective study aids include practice exams, mnemonics and audio MP3s.

Practice exams (*exams from previous semesters*) are often available from the library, upper level students, online or directly from the professor. They can be used like maps, which guide you through your semester. They give you a good indication as to what information you should emphasize when you study; what question types and exam format you can expect; and what your level of progress is.

Practice exams should be set aside to do in the weeks and days before 'the real thing.' You should time yourself and do the exam in an environment free from distractions. This provides an ideal way to uncover unexpected weak points.

Mnemonics are an effective way of memorizing lists of information. Usually a word, phrase, or sentence is constructed to symbolize a greater amount of information (i.e. LEO is A GERC = Lose Electrons is Oxidation is Anode, Gain Electrons is Reduction at Cathode). An effective study aid to active studying is the creation of your own mnemonics.

Audio MP3s can be used as effective tools to repeat information and to use your time efficiently. Information from the left side of your notes (*see 1.2 Taking Notes*) or your summarized typed notes including mnemonics, can be dictated and recorded. Often, an entire semester of work can be summarized in one 90-minute recording.

Now you can listen to the recording on an MP3 player or an iPod while waiting in line at the bank, or in a bus or with a car stereo on the way to school, work, etc. You can also listen to recorded information when you go to sleep and listen to another one first thing in the morning. You are probably familiar with the situation of having heard a song early in the morning and then having difficulty, for the rest of the day, getting it out of your mind! Well, imagine if the first thing you heard in the morning was: "Hair is a modified keratinized structure produced by the cylindrical down growth of epithelium..."! Thus MP3s become an effective study aid since they are an extra source of repetition.

Some students like to **record lectures**. Though it may be helpful to fill in missing notes, it is not an efficient way to repeat information.

Some students like to use **study cards** (flashcards) on which they may write either a summary of information they must memorize or relevant questions to consider. Then the cards are used throughout the day to quickly flash information to promote thought on a course material. Smartphone apps, like the ones designed by Gold Standard, can make flashcards more interactive.

1.5.1 Falling Behind

Imagine yourself as a marathon runner who has run 25.5 km of a 26 km race. The finishing line is now in view. However, you have fallen behind some of the other runners. The most difficult aspect of the race is still ahead.

In such a scenario, some interesting questions can be asked: Is now the time to drop out of the race because 0.5 km suddenly seems like a long distance? Is now the time to reevaluate whether or not you should have competed? Or is now the time to remain faithful to your goals and to give 100%?

Imagine one morning in mid-semester, you wake up realizing you have fallen behind in your studies. What do you do? Where do you start? Is it too late?

You should see the situation as one of life's challenges. Now is the worst time for doubts, rather, it is the time for action. A clear line of action should be formulated such that it could be followed.

For example, you might begin by gathering all pertinent study materials like a complete set of study notes, relevant text(s), sample exams, etc. As a rule, to get back into the thick of things, notes and sample exams take precedence. Studying at this point should take a three pronged approach: i) a regular, consistent review of the information from your notes from the beginning of the section for which you are responsible (i.e., *starting with the first class*); ii) a regular, consistent review of course material as you are learning it from the lectures (*this is the most efficient way to study*); iii) regular testing using questions given in class or those contained in sample exams. Using such questions will clarify the extent of your progress.

It is also of value, as time allows, to engage in extracurricular activities, which, you find helpful in reducing stress (e.g., sports, piano, creative writing).

2.1 Introduction

The application process to most dental schools includes interviews. Only a select number of students from the applicant pool will be given an offer to be interviewed. The dental school interview is, as a rule, something that you achieve. In other words, after your school grades, DAT scores and/or references, and autobiographical materials have been reviewed, you are offered the ultimate opportunity to put your best foot forward: a personal interview.

Depending on the dental school, you may be interviewed by one, two or several interviewers (i.e., panel or committee interview). You may be the only interviewee or there may be others (i.e., a group interview). There may be one or more interviews lasting from 20 minutes to two hours. Some dental schools are introducing the multiple mini-interview (MMI) which includes many short assessments in a timed circuit. Despite the variations among the technical aspects of the interview, in terms of substance, most dental schools have similar objectives. These objectives can be arbitrarily categorized into three general assessments: (i) your personality traits, (ii) social skills, and (iii) knowledge of dentistry as a profession.

Personality traits such as maturity, integrity, compassion, originality, curiosity, self-directed learning, intellectual capacity, confidence (not arrogance!), and motivation are all components of the ideal applicant.

These traits will be exposed by the process of the interview, your mannerisms, and the substance of what you choose to discuss when given an ambiguous question. For instance, bringing up specific examples of academic achievement related to school and related to self-directed learning would score well in the categories of intellectual capacity and curiosity, respectively. Nevertheless, highlighting significant insights about support to and interaction with patients in say, a recent involvement in community service might set you apart from equally qualified candidates as more emotionally matured and compassionate.

Motivation is a personality trait, which may make the difference between a high and a low or moderate score in an interview. A student must clearly demonstrate that he or she has the energy and eagerness to survive (typically) four long years of dental school and beyond! If you are naturally shy or soft-spoken, you will have to give special attention to this category. In other instances, a student must display the desire to learn and the zest to think critically in a problem-based learning framework.

Social skills such as leadership, ease of communication, ability to relate to others and work effectively in groups, volunteer work, cultural and social interests, all constitute skills that are often viewed as critical for future dentists. It is not sufficient to say in an interview: "I have good social skills"! You must display such skills via your interaction with the interviewer(s) and by discussing specific examples of situations that clearly portray your social skills.

Knowledge of dental medicine includes at least a general understanding of what the field of dentistry involves, the curriculum you are applying to, and knowledge of common dental issues like the dental amalgam controversy, consumer safety issues, oral cancer, latest technologies used in dental procedures, special needs services, the health care system, and ethical decision-making issues involving patient autonomy, confidentiality, and practice values. It is striking to see the number of students who apply to dental school each year whose knowledge of dentistry is limited to headlines and popular TV shows! It is not logical for someone to dedicate their lives to a profession they know little about.

Doing volunteer work in a hospital or a community clinic is a good start. Alternatively, job shadowing at a private dental office or a relative who is an orthodontist can help expose you to the daily goings-on of a dental career. The key is to get a good grasp of the profession in diverse settings – from the public health care delivery system to private practice to dental specialties. Here are some more suggestions: (i) keep up-to-date with the details of dentistry-related controversies in the news. You should also be able to develop and support opinions of your own; (ii) skim through a dental journal at least once; (iii) read dental articles in a popular science magazine (i.e., Scientific American, Discover, Popular Science, etc.); (iv) keep abreast of changes in dental school curricula in general and specific to the programs to which you have applied. You can access such information online or at most university libraries and by writing individual dental schools for information on their programs; (v) get involved in a laboratory research project.

2.2 Preparing for the Interview

If you devote an adequate amount of time for interview preparation, the actual interview will be less tense for you and you will be able to control most of the content of the interview.

Reading from the various sources mentioned in the preceding sections would be helpful. Also, read over your curriculum

vitae and/or any autobiographical materials you may have prepared. Note highlights in your life or specific examples that reflect the aforementioned personality traits, social skills or your knowledge of dental medicine. Zero in on qualities or stories that are important, memorable, interesting, amusing, informative or "all of the above"! Once in the interview room, you will be given the opportunity to elaborate on the qualities you believe are important about yourself. Be ready to respond to an interviewer should they ask you: "What do you want to know about us?" In many cases, students tend to concentrate on preparing their most brilliant answers to various interview questions that they tend to overlook another means for the admission committee to gauge an applicant's sincere interest in the course and the university itself – by letting the applicant himself or herself ask and/or clarify essential information about the school and how the program could ultimately help advance a successful career in dentistry.

Once you have received the invitation, do not lose time to get to know the dental college with which you will be having the interview. Go online or call and inquire about the structure of the interview (e.g., one-on-one, group, MMI, etc.). Ask them if they can tell you who will interview you. Many schools have no qualms volunteering such information. Now you can determine the person's expertise by either asking or looking through staff members of the

different faculties or dental specialties at that university or college. A periodontist, an academician, and a general practitioner all have different areas of expertise and will likely orient their interviews differently. Thus you may want to read from a source, which will give you a general understanding of their specialty.

Choose appropriate clothes for the interview. Every year some students dress for a dental school interview as if they were going out to dance! Dentistry is still considered a conservative profession; you should dress and groom yourself likewise. First impressions are very important. Your objective is to make it as easy as possible for your interviewer(s) to imagine you as a dentist.

Do practice interviews with people you respect but who can also maintain their objectivity. Let them read this entire chapter on dental school interviews. They must understand that you are to be evaluated *only* on the basis of the interview. On that basis alone, they should be able to imagine you as an ideal candidate for a future dentist.

2.3 Strategies for Answering Questions

Always remember that the interviewer controls the *direction* of the interview by his questions; you control the *content* of the interview through your answers. In other words, once given the opportunity, you should speak about the topics that are important to you; conversely, you should

avoid volunteering information that renders you uncomfortable. You can enhance the atmosphere in which the answers are delivered by being polite, sincere, tactful, well-organized, outwardly oriented and maintaining eye contact. Motivation, intellectual interest, and a positive attitude must all be evident.

As a rule, there are no right or wrong answers. However, the way in which you justify your opinions, the topics you choose to discuss, your mannerisms and your composure all play important roles. It is normal to be nervous. It would be to your advantage to channel your nervous energy into a positive quality, like enthusiasm.

Do not spew forth answers! Take your time - it is not a contest to see how fast you can answer. Answering with haste can lead to disastrous consequences as what happened to this student in an actual interview:

Q: *Have you ever doubted your interest in dentistry as a career?*

A: *No! Well . . . ah . . . I guess so. Ah . . . I guess everyone doubts something at some point or the other . . .*

Retractions like that are a bad signal, but it illustrates an important point: there are usually no right or wrong answers in an interview; however, there are right or wrong ways of answering. Through this example we can conclude the following: listen carefully to the question, try to relax, and think before you answer!

Do not sit on the fence! If you avoid giving your opinions on controversial topics, it will be interpreted as indecision, which is a negative trait for a prospective dentist. You have a right to your opinions. However, you must be prepared to defend your point of view in an objective, rational, and informative fashion. It is also important to show that,

despite your opinion, you understand both sides of the argument. If you have an extreme or unconventional perspective and if you believe your perspective will not interfere with your practice of dentistry, you must let your interviewer know that.

Imagine a student who is uncomfortable with the idea of cosmetic dentistry as a legitimate medical practice. If asked about her opinion on cosmetic dentistry, she should clearly state her opinion objectively, show she understands the opposing viewpoints, and then use data to reinforce her position. If she feels that her opinion would not interfere with her objectivity when practicing dentistry, she might volunteer: "If I were in a position where my perspective might interfere with an objective management of a patient, I would refer that patient to another dentist."

Carefully note the reactions of the interviewer in response to your answers. Whether the interviewer is sitting on the edge of her seat wide-eyed or slumping in her chair while yawning, you should take such cues to help you determine when to continue, change the subject, or when to stop talking. Also, note the more subtle cues. For example, gauge which topic makes the interviewer frown, give eye contact, take notes, etc.

Lighten up the interview with a well-timed story. A conservative joke, a good analogy, or anecdote may help you relax and make the interviewer sustain his interest. If it is done correctly, it can turn a routine interview into a memorable and friendly interaction.

It should be noted that because the system is not standardized, a small number of interviewers may ask overly personal questions (i.e., about relationships, religion, etc.) or even questions that carry sexist tones (e.g., *What would you do if you got pregnant while attending dental school?*). Some questions may be frankly illegal. If you do not want to answer a question,

simply maintain your composure, express your position diplomatically, and address the interviewer's <u>real</u> concern (i.e., *Does this person have the potential to be a good dentist?*). For example, you might say in a non-confrontational tone of voice: "I would rather not answer such a question. However, I can assure you that whatever my answer may have been, it would in no way affect either my prospective studies in dentistry or any prerequisite objectivity I should have to be a good dentist."

2.4 Sample Questions

There are an infinite number of questions and many different categories of questions. Different dental schools will emphasize different categories of questions. Arbitrarily, ten categories of questions can be defined: ambiguous, medically related, academic, social, stress-type, problem situations, personality-oriented, based on autobiographical material, miscellaneous, and ending questions. We will examine each category in terms of sample questions and general comments.

Ambiguous Questions:

* *   *Tell me about yourself.*

   How do you want me to remember you?

   What are your goals?

   There are hundreds if not thousands of applicants, why should we choose you?

Convince me that you would make a good dentist.

Why do you want to study dentistry?

COMMENTS: These questions present nightmares for the unprepared student who walks into the interview room and is immediately asked: "Tell me about yourself." Where do you start? If you are prepared as previously discussed, you will be able to take control of the interview by highlighting your qualities or objectives in an informative and interesting manner.

Dentistry/Health Care Questions:

What are the pros and cons to our health care system?

If you had the power, what changes would you make to our health care system?

How are dentists responsible for educating the general public about oral health?

Do dentists make too much money?

Is it ethical for medical practitioners to strike?

What is the difference between the Hippocratic Oath and the Dentist's Pledge?

How important is dentistry in relation to the health profession in general?

Do you know of any controversial bill concerning dental health care that was recently passed in Congress?

COMMENTS: The health care system, esthetic dentistry, confidentiality, patient autonomy, health insurance, and other ethical issues are very popular topics in this era of technological advances, skyrocketing health care costs, and ethical uncertainty. A well-informed opinion can set you apart from most of the other interviewees.

Questions Related to Academics:

Why did you choose your present course of studies?

What is your favorite subject in your present course of studies? Why?

Would you consider a career in your present course of studies?

Can you convince me that you can cope with the workload in dental school?

How do you study/prepare for exams?

Do you engage in self-directed learning?

What is Problem-Based Learning or PBL?

How do you feel about the online delivery format in dental education?

COMMENTS: Dental schools like to see applicants who are well-disciplined, committed to dentistry as a career, and who exhibit self-directed learning (i.e., such a level of desire for knowledge that the student may seek to study information independent of any organized infrastructure). Beware of any glitches in your academic record. You may be asked to give reasons for any grades they may deem substandard. On the other hand, you should volunteer any information regarding academic achievement (i.e., prizes, awards, scholarships, particularly high grades in one subject or the other). At some point, you may also be asked to discuss aspects that you mentioned in your personal statement.

Questions Related to Social Skills or Interests:

Give evidence that you relate well with others.

Give an example of a leadership role you have assumed.

Have you done any volunteer work?

Have you engaged in any sports?

What are the prospects for a lasting peace in Afghanistan? Libya? The Sudan? The Middle-East?

COMMENTS: Questions concerning social skills should be simple for the prepared student. If you are asked a question that you cannot answer, say so. If you pretend to know something about a topic in which you are completely uninformed, you will make a bad situation worse.

Stress-Type Questions:

How do you handle stress?

What was the most stressful event in your life? How did you handle it?

The night before your final exam, your father has a heart-attack and is admitted to a hospital, what do you do?

COMMENTS: The ideal dentist has positive coping methods to deal with the inevitable stressors of a dental practice. Stress-type questions are a legitimate means of determining if you possess the raw material necessary to cope with dental school and dentistry as a career. Some decide to introduce stress <u>into</u> the interview and see how you handle it. For example, they may decide to ask you a confrontational question or try to back you into a corner (e.g., You do not know anything about dentistry, do you?). Alternatively, the interviewer might use silence to introduce stress into the interview. If you have completely and confidently answered a question and silence falls in the room, <u>do not</u> retract previous statements, mutter, or fidget. Simply wait for the next question. If the silence becomes unbearable, you may consider asking an intelligent question (e.g., a specific question

regarding their curriculum).

Questions on Problem Situations:

You are about to administer anesthesia to a sixteen-year-old patient. She suddenly expresses apprehension about the procedure and confesses that she is pregnant. She begs you to keep the information in utmost confidentiality. Would you still inform the girl's parents?

How would you deal with a group member who does not submit his assigned tasks for a small group project?

You have a very nervous patient who is about to undergo a dental treatment. What would you do to ease the anxiety?

Your patient is at the top of his career. How do you tell him that he has oral cancer?

COMMENTS: As for the other questions, listen carefully and take your time to consider the best possible response. Keep in mind that the ideal dentist is not only knowledgeable, but is also <u>compassionate</u>, <u>empathetic</u>, and is objective enough to understand <u>both sides</u> of a dilemma. Be sure such qualities are clearly demonstrated.

Personality-Oriented Questions:

If you could change one thing about yourself, what would it be?

How would your friends describe you?

What do you do with your spare time?

What is the most important event that has occurred to you in the last five years?

If you had three magical wishes, what would they be?

What are your best attributes?

COMMENTS: Of course, most questions will assess your personality to one degree or the other. However, these questions are quite direct in their approach. Forewarned is forearmed!

Questions Based on Autobiographical Materials:

COMMENTS: Any autobiographical material you may have provided to the dental school is fair game for questioning. You may be asked to discuss or elaborate on any point the interviewer may feel is interesting or questionable.

Miscellaneous Questions:

Should the federal government reinstate the death penalty? Explain.

What do you expect to be doing 10 years from now?

How would you attract dentists to rural areas?

Why do you want to attend our dental school?

What other dental schools have you applied to?

Have you been to other interviews?

COMMENTS: You will do fine in this grab-bag category as long as you stick to the strategies previously iterated.

Ending Questions:

What would you do if you were not accepted to a dental school?

How do you think you did in this interview?

Do you have any questions?

COMMENTS: The only thing more important than a good first impression is a good finish in order to leave a positive lasting impression. They are looking for students who are so committed to dentistry that they will not only re-apply to dental school if not accepted, but they would also strive to improve on those aspects of their application that prevented them from being accepted in the first attempt. All these questions should be answered with a quiet confidence. If you are given an opportunity to ask questions, though you should not flaunt your knowledge, you should establish that you are well-informed. For example: "I have read that you have changed your curriculum to a more patient-oriented and self-directed learning approach. I was wondering how the dental students are getting along with these new changes." Be sure, however, not to ask a question unless you are genuinely interested in the answer.

2.4.1 Interview Feedback: Questions, Answers and Feedback

Specific interview questions can be found online for free at studentdoctor.net and futuredoctor.net. Dr. Ferdinand reproduced and captured the intense experience of a medical school interview on video which, of course, is very similar to the content, process and interaction of a dental school interview. "The Gold Standard Medical School Interview: Questions, Tips and Answers + MMI" DVD was filmed live in HD on campus in front of a group of students. A volunteer is interviewed in front of the class and the entire interview is conducted as if it were the real thing. After the interview, an analysis of each question and the mindset behind it is discussed in an open forum format. If you are not sure that you have the interviewing skills to be accepted to dental school, then it is a must-see video.

$$A + B = ?$$

DAT-Prep.com

UNDERSTANDING THE DAT

PART II

THE STRUCTURE OF THE DAT

1.1 Introduction

The Dental Admission Test (DAT) is required by all dental schools in the United States and its territories, for applicants seeking entry into the D.M.D. program (Doctor of Dental Medicine), or its equivalent the D.D.S. (Doctor of Dental Surgery). The test is standardized by the American Dental Association (ADA) through its Department of Testing Services and is available throughout the year by testing appointments in Prometric Test Centers around the US, Guam, Puerto Rico, the US Virgin Islands, and Canada.

In most instances, the weight given to DAT scores in the admissions process varies from school to school. However, results in the different sections of the test tend to be used in a way similar to your university GPA (i.e. your academic standing). Some schools consider the Academic Average and Total Science scores as significant criteria in their selection of candidates. Others combine the PAT with the Academic Average and Total Science scores, and a few others give as much emphasis to the Reading Comprehension score. Consult programs directly about their evaluation guidelines.

1.1.1 When to Take the DAT

Taking the DAT requires registering with the ADA and meeting their eligibility requirements. Usually, applicants have successfully completed at least one year of undergraduate studies, including the prerequisite courses in biology, general chemistry, and organic chemistry at the time of application. Note that the majority of the applicants complete two or more years of college before taking the DAT.

Upon approval of your application, the Department of Testing Services (DTS) will notify you, through email or letter, of the procedure in securing a testing appointment with the Prometric Contact Center. As a registered examinee, you will have the next twelve months from your application and payment to confirm a testing date.

Prospective students commonly arrange for their DAT roughly a year before their intended matriculation into dental school. However, varying circumstances may call for careful planning when choosing the appropriate time for you to take this exam. The following are common factors to consider:

1. The Admissions Cycle

Most dental schools begin reviewing applications around June, the majority of successful candidates start receiving acceptance letters as early as the 1st of December. Getting over the DAT hurdle well ahead of the submission deadlines will put you in a more favorable position in several ways: you will have ample time to procure any supplemental materials that the schools might request; you will have a less stressful time preparing for your interview; and, you would have a better chance of belonging to the initial bulk of the entering classes.

Many schools observe a rolling admissions process - they continue to accept applications until all vacant spots are filled. Applicants with remarkable credentials who wait until the last minute may miss admission into their schools of preference if the number of early applicants who satisfactorily meet the entry requirements quickly closes the enrollment seats.

2. Course Requirements

Dental colleges usually impose certain curricular prerequisites as part of their entry requirements. Some applicants opt to take their DAT a year before completing any required coursework. They can then focus on improving their GPAs in the remaining semesters. Others take the opposite route. You should weigh which schedule would work best for you. In any case, be sure to check the individual schools regarding their rules and criteria for DAT scores – some might consider scores received three years before the date of your application, while others may only look at scores from two years ago.

3. Contingent Results

If you are not satisfied with your DAT score, the ADA permits you to retake the exam 90 days later. As a precaution, you should provide some allowance for such an event.

1.1.2 Retaking the DAT

To reiterate, an applicant who is unsatisfied with his or her DAT scores must wait 90 days before retesting. If approved, students are permitted to retake the DAT once per twelve-month period. Results of the four most recent DATs taken, as well as the total number of attempts, are reported on the official score reports. Admissions committees may consider either the best, or the most recent marks. There is currently no limit as to the number of times to take the DAT.

For the most up-to-date guidelines on registration, scheduling and pertinent information about the DAT, consider consulting your undergraduate advisor and accessing the following:

US:
www.ada.org/dat.aspx
Canada:
www.cda-adc.ca/en/dental_profession/dat/index.asp
Prometric Centers:
www.prometric.com/ADA

1.2 The Format of The DAT

Part of doing well in a standardized test includes being familiar with the format of the actual exam, what it covers, and what skills and level of knowledge are being assessed. Accurate information of this sort helps identify your study needs and as a result, allows you to judge which prep materials and courses would help to address your weak areas.

The Dental Admission Test measures your general academic aptitude, understanding of scientific information, and visual discrimination. Memory, comprehension, and problem solving are essential cognitive skills needed for this exam.

The DAT is a timed computer-based test divided into four sections. All questions are in multiple choice format with four or five options per question. You are to work on only one section at a time. A timer is visible on the upper right hand corner of the computer screen. If you are unsure of your answer on a specific item, you may click the "Mark" button. You can then review your marked and/or incomplete responses if you have enough time left. Otherwise, a message that says "The time limit for this test has expired" will appear and you will have to move on to the next segment of the test.

REMEMBER

Once you exit a test section, you cannot go back to it.

The test center administrator provides two laminated note boards and two low-odor, fine-tip permanent markers. The laminated sheets are 8.5" x 11" in size with one side in the form of graph paper and the other side just a blank page. Should you require additional pieces, you only need to raise your hand so that the test center administrator will replace them with new ones. No scratch paper is permitted within the testing area during the exam.

The following table shows the sequence of the different DAT test sections:

Optional Tutorial	
Time	15 minutes
Survey of Natural Sciences	
Time	90 minutes
Number of Questions	100
Perceptual Ability Test	
Time	60 minutes
Number of Questions	90
Optional Break	
Time	15 minutes
Reading Comprehension Test	
Time	60 minutes
Number of Questions	50
Quantitative Reasoning Test	
Time	45 minutes
Number of Questions	40
Optional Post-Test Survey	
Time	15 minutes

The Natural Sciences on the DAT collectively include biology, general and organic chemistry at introductory university levels. The subject material is apportioned as follows:

Biology	40 items
General Chemistry	30 items
Organic Chemistry	30 items

Some pages contain an Exhibit button that allows you to open a new window showing the periodic table.

The Perceptual Ability Test or PAT comes after the Survey of Natural Sciences. It is comprised of the following six areas:

Apertures	15 figures; 5 answer choices each
View Recognition	15 problem sets; 4 answer choices each
Angle Discrimination	15 patterns; 4 answer choices each
Paper Folding	15 problem sets; 5 answer choices each
Cube counting	15 questions; 5 answer choices each
3D Form Development	15 problem sets; 4 answer choices each

Keep in mind that using pencils, fingers, and note boards as measuring devices are prohibited during this section.

You can choose whether or not to take the 15-minute break. If you choose to take it, the timer will continue to monitor the minutes remaining on the upper right hand corner of the computer screen. Once 15 minutes has elapsed, the test will resume automatically. If you decide to continue without any break, you can click the "End" button and you will be immediately directed to the Reading Comprehension (RC) section.

The RC Test presents three passages of about 1,500 words each. An average of 16 to 17 questions accompanies every reading text. The computer screen displays on the same page the individual question on the upper half of the page and the corresponding reading passage in a scrollable box on the lower half of the page.

The Quantitative Reasoning Test (QRT) is the last exam section of the DAT. It covers Number Operations, Algebra, Geometry, Trigonometry, Probability and Statistics, and Applied Mathematics problems. In this particular section only, a basic four-function calculator appears on the computer screen.

Overall, you will have a total of 4 hours and 15 minutes without the three optional portions of the test or 5 hours if you go through each segment. The Canadian DAT has a slightly different format, which we will present in the next section.

1.2.1 The Canadian DAT

The Dental Aptitude Test in Canada is a paper and pencil exam that assesses general academic knowledge, comprehension of scientific information, two and three dimensional visual perception, and manual dexterity. It can be taken either in English or in French, depending on which is required by the school where you are applying. Of the ten accredited Canadian dental schools, only the Université de Montréal and the Université Laval in Quebec offer the dental program in French at present. On the other hand, the University of Toronto and the University of Western Ontario accept scores from the American DAT while McGill University no longer includes the DAT scores in their admissions criteria.

Unlike the American DAT, which can be scheduled almost any time of the year in more than 70 Prometric locations, the Canadian DAT is administered only twice a year. The test is normally conducted on a Saturday in November and in February at test centers in the ten Canadian dental schools and thirteen additional sites across Canada. The Canadian Dental Association (CDA) also gives consideration to candidates who cannot take the exam on a Saturday schedule for religious reasons.

Commonly, candidates who plan to matriculate into dental school within one year write the November exam. Most retakers and those applying a year farther, attempt the February DAT. Some schools recognize DAT results obtained five years prior to the application while others, two or three years.

1.2.2 Content and Sequence of the Canadian DAT

Both the English and the French DAT have identical test sections: Survey of Natural Sciences, Perceptual Ability Test, and Manual Dexterity Test. However, only the English DAT contains the Reading Comprehension Test. Additionally, the Manual Dexterity Test is an optional portion of the DAT. At this time, the University of British Columbia, the University of Toronto, the University of Dalhousie, and the University of Western Ontario do not require the Manual Dexterity Test Score. Applicants are, therefore, advised to base their options of the exams according to the qualifications set by the dental program(s) to which they seek acceptance.

The typical order of the test sections in the English Canadian DAT is as follows:

1. Manual Dexterity Test

In this section, you will be given a cylindrical bar of soap of about 15 cm long and a pattern, which specifies the shape of the two

The Canadian DAT Testing Schedule	
Manual Dexterity Test (MDT)	
Time	30 minutes
Carving Pattern	1
Section Break*	
Survey of Natural Sciences	
Time	60 minutes
Questions	70
Stretch Break*	
Perceptual Ability Test	
Time	60 minutes
Questions	90
Section Break*	
Reading Comprehension Test	
Time	50 minutes
Questions	50

* The duration of each section break depends on the invigilators, although these typically last between 5 to 15 minutes. No formal lunch break is provided.

ends and the middle portions of the soap – for example, square, triangle, or fluted. You will have five minutes to study the figure during which you will not be allowed to do anything to the soap. Once the 30-minute carving time starts, YOU CAN NO LONGER REPLACE YOUR SOAP, so be careful not to chip any edges when cutting it; or worse, break the soap itself. You are permitted to use surgical gloves, but you must supply your own. You can also request for a pencil to mark your soap.

Four areas serve as the basis in scoring the carved pattern:

1. **Pattern reproduction** – completeness and accuracy of measurements

2. **Planes** – flatness and smoothness

3. **Angles** – sharpness and accuracy of lines, corners, and angles

4. **Sectional relationship** – symmetry and orientation

2. Survey of Natural Sciences

The Natural Sciences section covers only Biology and General Chemistry and none of the Organic Chemistry component found in the American DAT. The breakdown of the test items is as follows:

Biology	40 items
General Chemistry	30 items

3. Perceptual Ability Test

The Perceptual Ability Test consists of angle discrimination, form development, cube counting, orthographic projections and apertures.

4. Reading Comprehension Test (English DAT only)

Similar to the RC Test in the American DAT, this section presents three reading passages of 1,500 words in length and an average of 16 to 17 questions each. However, the time limit is 10 minutes shorter with a total of 50 minutes for all 50 RC questions in the Canadian DAT.

Because this is a paper test, you can mark, highlight, and/or write notes on the test booklet. All answers, however, must be written on the answer sheet.

General Comparison of the American and Canadian DAT		
	American DAT	**Canadian DAT**
Name of the Test	• Dental Admission Test	• Dental Aptitude Test
Testing Method	• Computer	• Paper
Total Test Time	4 hours and 15 minutes and 3 15-minute optional breaks	Approximately 4 hours; breaks in between sections
Total Number of Questions	280 questions	210 questions + MDT for the English DAT; 160 questions + MDT for the French DAT
Survey of Natural Sciences	100 questions; 90 minutes 1) Biology (40) 2) General Chemistry (30) 3) Organic Chemistry (30)	70 questions; 60 minutes 1) Biology (40) 2) General Chemistry (30)
Perceptual Ability Test	90 questions; 60 minutes 1) apertures 2) view recognition 3) angle discrimination 4) paper folding 5) cube counting 6) 3D form development	90 questions; 60 minutes 1) apertures 2) angle discrimination 3) cubes 4) form development 5) orthographic projections
Reading Comprehension	50 questions; 60 minutes • 3 reading passages	50 questions; 50 minutes (English DAT) • 3 reading passages
Quantitative Reasoning	40 Questions; 45 minutes	NONE
Manual Dexterity (Soap Carving)	NONE	30 minutes (optional)*
Administering Body	American Dental Association	Canadian Dental Association
Test Frequency	Almost any time throughout the year	Every November and February
Official Practice Materials	• 1 full-length Practice Test (available in print and web based format) • 1 Sample Test (available as free download in PDF format from the ADA website)	• DAT Preparation Kit (includes materials for the MDT and DAT Preparation Manual with sample tests); consider practicing with at least 20 CDA soaps
*Consult with the dental school where you are applying before choosing to disregard this section.		

1.3 English as a Second Language (ESL)

Many ESL students will need to pay extra attention to the Reading Comprehension Test of the DAT. Although specific advice for all students will be presented in the sections that follow, extra tips are discussed for ESL students in Section 3.2.3 of the Reading Comprehension part of this book series.

Having said that, DAT scores are subjected to a statistical analysis to check that each question is fair, valid and reliable. Test questions in development are scrutinized in order to minimize gender, ethnic or religious bias, and to affirm that the test is culturally fair.

Depending on your English skills, you may or may not benefit from an English reading summer course. Certainly, you have the option of deciding whether or not you would want to take such a course for credit.

1.4 How the DAT is Scored

The DAT reports eight standard scores. The first six scores are from the individual tests themselves, i.e. biology, general chemistry, organic chemistry, perceptual ability, reading comprehension, and quantitative reasoning. The multiple choice questions are first scored right or wrong resulting in a raw score. Note that wrong answers are worth the same as unanswered questions so ALWAYS ANSWER ALL THE QUESTIONS even if you are not sure of certain answers. The raw score is then converted to a scaled score ranging from 1 (lowest) to 30 (highest). A test section that is skipped will be scored 1. This is neither a percentage nor a percentile. The test is not based on a curve. Essentially, DAT performance is measured using an ability-referenced system. Based on standard scores, an individual examinee's abilities (i.e. knowledge and problem solving skills) are directly compared to that of the other DAT examinees'. It is not possible to accurately replicate this scoring system at home.

The remaining two scores are Total Science and Academic Average. The Total Science score is the standard score for the 100 questions in the Survey of Natural Sciences as a whole – NOT THE AVERAGE OF THE STANDARD SCORES of the Science subtests. This is derived from the sum of your raw scores each in biology, general chemistry, and organic chemistry. The total score is then converted to a standard score for Total Science. In contrast, a score in the Academic Average is the rounded average of the standard scores from the reading comprehension (RC), quantitative reasoning (QR), biology (BIO), general chemistry (CHM), and organic chemistry (ORG) tests. Here is an example of an Academic Average calculation:

QR – 19
RC – 21
BIO – 22
CHM – 21
ORG – 20

TOTAL: 103 ÷ 5 = 20.6; rounded up to the nearest whole, the Academic Average for these scores would be 21.

Standards for interviews or admissions may vary for the individual scores, Total Science and the Academic Average. For example, one particular dental school may establish a cutoff (minimum) of 17 for all sections. In other cases, admissions committees assess candidates against a mean of DAT scores in a particular batch of applicants; therefore, the range can vary from year to year. Contact individual programs for specific score requirements.

The DAT may include a small number of questions, called pretest questions, which will not be scored. These questions are trial questions which may be used in the future. If you see a question that you think is off the wall, unanswerable or inappropriate for your level of knowledge, it could well be one of these questions, so never panic! And of course, answer every question because guessing may provide a 25% chance of being correct while not answering provides a 0% chance of being correct!

1.4.1 Average, Good, and High DAT Scores

Because the DAT employs an ability-referenced measurement, there are no established cutoff scores, or Pass and Fail marks. Rather, the standard score indicates your test performance relative to all the students who did the same test on the same day. This means that the national average of 17 on the scored sections is not always a guarantee for acceptance in a dental program. In most instances, what is considered "average" depends on the entering batch of a particular academic year. This could range from as low as 16 to as high as 22 in the Academic Average and 14 to 22 in the Perceptual Ability Test. Likewise, a "good" score may be good enough for admittance to one dental school but below the cutoff of another. The best way to find out is to consult the websites of the dental institutions to which you intend to apply.

Your main aim is to achieve the scores that will put you on a competitive footing among all the other applicants. Statistics of enrollees entering dental school in 2011 report a majority with scores around 19 to 20 in the Academic Average, PAT, and Total Science. Section scores of 21 and above are generally perceived to be highly competitive.

Source: Predoctoral Dental Applicants and Enrollees Graphs published online by ADEA (American Dental Education Association).

1.4.2 When are the Scores Released?

Right after completing the DAT, an unofficial score report is immediately generated at the Prometric Test Center. This report will then be audited for accuracy and verified by the Department of Testing Services. Official scores are forwarded within three to four weeks to the dental schools, which are indicated in the DAT application of the examinee. The ADA also sends the scores to the appropriate standardized application service such as the Associated American Dental Schools Application Service (AADSAS) or the Texas Medical and Dental Schools Application Service (TMDSAS) in case the specified dental schools participate in any one of these services. Scores are then posted to the examinee's dental school application and then forwarded to the respective faculties within one week. In such a case, you can confirm the proper submission of your official DAT scores by logging into your ADEA AADSAS application.

Requests of additional copies and/or recipients mean additional fees and transmittal time. For more details about this process, please check the ADA website.

1.4.3 DAT Scores in Canada

Similar to the American DAT, scores from the Canadian DAT are reported as standard scores ranging from 1 to 30. The test is based on the number of correct answers and does not penalize wrong answers. However, a blank answer sheet will be reported as zero. Therefore, DO NOT LEAVE ANY QUESTION UNANSWERED, even if you only have to guess.

A standard score of 15 is considered the national average. However, since there are only a few dental schools operating in Canada, admissions tend to be quite competitive. Any score above 20 would be ideal.

Total Science is the weighted average from the Biology and Chemistry scores; Academic Average is the arithmetic mean of the scores in Biology, Chemistry and Reading Comprehension. The Manual Dexterity or Carving Test uses a criterion-referenced measurement, i.e., scores are scaled on a complete or perfect mastery of a defined set of skills at one end and the complete absence of those skills at the other end. In order to be graded for this section, the carving must be two-thirds complete and correct. Otherwise, an incomplete or incorrect pattern will be penalized. The perfect score for this section is 30.

About six to eight weeks from the testing date, CDA mails the official DAT transcripts to the examinee (student transcript) and up to five schools that are specified in the DAT registration form. The student copy contains a detailed explanation of the test scores. Requests for additional copies after registration entail additional fees. Check the CDA website for detailed information.

THE RECIPE FOR DAT SUCCESS

2.1 The Important Ingredients

- Time, Motivation
- Read from varied sources/Check SDN and premed101 websites for advice (read essential sources; familiarize with the actual test content and the skills demanded)
- A review of the basic DAT sciences

DAT-Specific Information

- The Gold Standard DAT Books
- optional: The Gold Standard Natural Sciences DVDs, smartphone apps/ flashcards, MP3s or online programs (DAT-prep.com)

- optional: speed reading/comprehension course if necessary

DAT-Specific Problems

- Gold Standard (GS) chapter review problems in the book and online
- Gold Standard DAT tests (full lengths GS-1 and GS-2; GS free mini)
- Official DAT Practice Test (Web-based or Print format) and Sample Test Items (free download in PDF format from the ADA website)
- TopScore Pro: 3 full length practice DATs

2.2 The Proper Mix

1) Study regularly and start early. Creating a study schedule is often effective. Adhering to it is even more productive. Even the best study plans will unlikely yield the scores that you want if you do not follow your own preparation regimen. A lot of material needs to be covered and you will need sufficient time to review. Starting early will highlight your weak areas and give you ample time

to remedy them. This will also reduce your stress level in the weeks leading up to the exam and may make your studying easier. Make sure that you get a good grasp of what each section of the test is designed to assess.

Depending on your English skills and the quality of your science background, a good rule of thumb is: 3-6 hours/day of study for 3-6 months.

2) Keep focused and enjoy the material you are learning. Forget all past negative learning experiences, so you can open your mind to the information with a positive attitude. Given an open mind and some time to consider what you are learning, you will find most of the information tremendously interesting. Motivation can be derived from a sincere interest in learning and by keeping in mind your long-term goals.

3) Preparation for the Sciences: The Gold Standard (GS) DAT books are the most comprehensive review guides for the DAT ever to be sold in bookstores. Thus the most directed and efficient study plan is to begin by reviewing and understanding the science sections in the GS. While doing your science survey, you should take notes specifically on topics that are marked Memorize or Understand on the first page of each chapter. Your notes - we call them Gold Notes (!!) - should be very concise (no longer than one page per chapter). Every week, you should study from your Gold Notes at least once.

As you are incorporating the information from the science review, do the practice problems in the books and/or those included in the free chapter review questions online at DAT-prep.com. This is the best way to more clearly define the depth of your understanding and to get you accustomed to the questions you can expect on the DAT.

4) Preparation for the PAT: This section in the DAT requires a keen eye for details. Developing this skill starts with acquiring visualization techniques and applying them in several practice problem sets until you get used to seeing the different angles and dimensions of various figures. Go through the GS PAT chapters and familiarize yourself with the six subsections of the test. As you go along with your review, you will be able to adapt our techniques and strategies to identify the correct options.The more practice, the more you are likely to sharpen your perceptual acuity.

5) Preparation for Reading Comprehension: Begin by reading the advice and techniques given in GS RC. Time yourself and practice, practice, practice with various resources for this section as needed (in the book, online at DAT-prep.com, TopScore, and of course, the ADA materials). You should be sure to understand each and every mistake you make so as to ensure there will be improvement.

6) Preparation for Quantitative Reasoning: Similar to your preparation for the section on the Sciences, take note of the scope and demands of the test, which are listed on the first page of GS QR. Your aim is to determine your deficiencies and work on the foundations that will help address these.

7) Do practice exams. Ideally, you would finish your science review in The Gold Standard text and/or the science review DVDs at least a couple of months prior to the exam date. Then each week you can do a practice exam under simulated test conditions and thoroughly review each exam after completion. Scores in practice exams should improve over time. Success depends on what you do between the first and the last exam. You can start with ADA's DAT Sample Test Items then continue with the GS and TopScore practice exams and then complete the DAT Practice Test from ADA. You should do practice exams as you would the actual test: in one sitting within the expected time limits. Doing practice exams serves two important purposes in your preparation. First, it will increase your confidence and allow you to see what is expected of you. It will make you realize the constraints imposed by time limits in completing the entire test. Second, it will allow you to identify the areas in which you may be lacking.

Some students can answer all DAT questions quite well if they only had more time. Thus you must time yourself during practice and monitor your time during the test. On average, you will have a little less than a minute per question for Natural Sciences, a little over 30 seconds per question for the PAT, 20 minutes per passage and its accompanying questions for the RC, and 1.1 minutes per question for QR. In other words, every 30 minutes, you should check to be sure that you have completed an approximate number of questions for that section; for example, 34 questions or more in the first 30 minutes for Science, 70 or more in the next, and so on. If not, then you always guess on "time consuming questions" in order to catch up and, if you have time at the end, you return to properly evaluate the questions you skipped. Set aside at least the equivalent of a full day to review the explanations for EVERY test question. Do NOT dismiss any wrong answer as a "stupid mistake." You made that error for a reason, so you must work that out in your mind to reduce the risk that it occurs again. You can reduce your risk by test-proofing answers (i.e. spending 5-10 seconds being critical of your response) and by considering the following questions:

1. Why did you get the question wrong (or correct)?

2. What question-type or passage-type gives you repeated difficulty?

3. What is your mindset when looking

at a particular visual figure?

4. Did you monitor your time during the test?

5. Are most of your errors at the beginning or the end of the test?

6. Did you eliminate answer choices when you could?

7. For the Reading Comprehension Test, did you effectively scan for the detail questions? Did you comprehend the fundamental concepts presented in each passage?

8. Was your main problem a lack of content review or a lack of practice?

9. In which specific science or QR content areas do you need improvement?

10. Have you designed a study schedule to address your weaknesses?

8) Remember that the DAT will primarily measure your basic knowledge and understanding of concepts. Evidently, a lot of material in the GS books must simply be memorized; for example, some very basic science equations, rules of logarithms, trigonometric functions, the phases in mitosis and meiosis, naming organic compounds and many, many basic science facts. Nonetheless, for the most part, your objective should be to try to understand, rather than memorize, the biology, chemistry, and math material you review. This may appear vague now, but as you immerse yourself in the review chapters and practice material, you will more clearly understand what is expected of you.

9) Relax once in a while! While the DAT requires a lot of preparation, you should not forsake all your other activities. Try to keep exercising, maintain a social life and do things you enjoy. If you balance work with things that relax you, you will study more effectively overall.

2.3 It's DAT Time!

1) On the night before the exam, try to get a good night sleep. The DAT can be physically draining and it is in your best interest to be well rested when you do the exam.

2) Avoid last minute cramming. On the morning of the exam, do not begin studying ad hoc. You will not learn anything effectively, and noticing something you do not know or will not remember might reduce your confidence and lower your score unnecessarily. Just get up, eat a good breakfast, consult your Gold Notes (the top level information that you personally compiled) and go do the exam.

3) Eat breakfast! You need the food energy to get through the exam.

4) If you are taking an afternoon schedule, eat a light lunch. Avoid greasy food that will make you drowsy. You do not want to feel sleepy while taking the test. A chocolate bar or other sweet highly caloric food could, however, be very useful during the break when you may be tired for the last section. The 'sugar low' will hit you only after you have completed the exam when you do not have to be awake!

5) Make sure you answer all the questions! You do not get penalized for incorrect answers, so always choose something even if you have to guess. If you run out of time, pick a letter and use it to answer all the remaining questions. The ADA performs statistical analyses on every test so no one letter will give you an unfair advantage. Just choose your "lucky" letter and move on!

6) Pace yourself. Do not get bogged down trying to answer a difficult question. If the question is very difficult, mark it, guess, move on to the next question and return later if you have enough time remaining.

7) Remember that some of the questions may be thrown out as inappropriate, used solely to calibrate the test or trial questions. If you find that you cannot answer some of the questions, do not despair. It is possible they could be questions used for these purposes.

8) Do not let others psyche you out! Some people might be leaving an earlier exam saying, 'It went great. What a joke!' Ignore them. Often these types may just be trying to boost their own confidence or to make themselves look good in front of their friends. Just focus on what you have to do and tune out the other examinees.

9) Relax during the short break. You need the time to recuperate and rest.

10) Before reading the RC passage, some students find it more efficient to quickly read the questions first. In this way, as soon as you read something in the passage which brings to mind a question you have read, you can answer immediately. Otherwise, if you read the text first and then the questions, you may end up wasting time searching through the text for answers.

11) Read the text and questions carefully! Often students leave out a word or two while reading, which can completely change the sense of the problem. Pay special attention to words in italics, CAPS, bolded, or underlined. You will certainly find the word "EXCEPT" in CAPS in a question on the real DAT!

12) You must be both diligent and careful with the way you choose the correct answer because you will not be given extra time to make corrections when time expires.

13) Consider your choice of clothing on test day. Be ready for too much heat or an overzealous air conditioning unit.

14) Some problems involve algebraic manipulation of equations and/or numerical calculations. Be sure that you know what all the variables in the equation stand for and that you are using the equation in the appropriate circumstance. In chemistry and QR, the use of dimensional analysis will help you keep track of units and solve some problems where you might have forgotten the relevant equations.

15) The final step in problem solving is to ask yourself: is my answer reasonable? This is where your intuition serves as a guide. But to be frank, 'intuition' in the context of the DAT is really learned through the experience of a comprehensive review and completing many practice problems and tests.

We, at The Gold Standard, will do our best - on paper and online - to guide you through the content and strategies you can use to be successful. Let's continue . . .

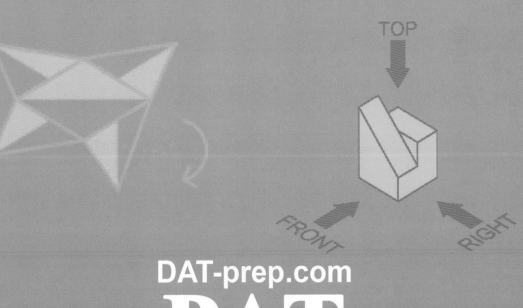

TOP

FRONT

RIGHT

DAT-prep.com
PAT
PERCEPTUAL ABILITY

Memorize	Understand	Not Required
The Paper Folding Quadrant The Gold Standard Cube Formula	* The Purpose of the Test * Three-dimensional Objects * Three-dimensional (3D) and Two-dimensional (2D) Views * Rules, Concepts and Skills Required for Each Subsection	* Formal training or academic course

DAT-Prep.com

Introduction ▧▮▮▮

This section is a test of your visual acumen rather than formal knowledge. Nevertheless, understanding the concepts involved in the six subtests of the PAT is paramount to your successful performance in this test.

Additional Resources

Free Online Forum

1.1 The Importance of the PAT Score

The Perceptual Ability Test (PAT) is the only section in the DAT that does not require academic knowledge or training. It is designed to be used as a predictor of an applicant's performance in the preclinical operative skills and restorative dentistry practical laboratory classes. The ability to perceive small differences is also important in selecting candidates for dental schools that require eye-to-hand fine motor coordination in their curriculum.

Just as perceptual aptitude is not typically correlated with general grade point average (GPA) in dental school, the PAT score is likewise NOT included in the computation of the DAT academic average score. The importance of your performance in this test varies from school to school wherein the minimum requirement can be as low as 16 to as high as 20. Needless to say, the best way to determine the extent of your preparation for the PAT is to consult directly with the institution to which you are applying.

1.2 How to Prepare for the Perceptual Ability Test

Preparing for the PAT is somewhat different from the rest of the DAT sections as it is more about perceptual *ability* rather than knowledge. Your ability to visualize patterns and mentally manipulate 2D and 3D objects will be measured in at least four of the subtests. Central to your approach is a clear understanding of the concepts governing each subsection, and primary in your general preparation for the PAT is getting acquainted with the content and structure of the test.

1.2.1 The Format and Content of the PAT

As already mentioned, six divisions comprise this exam. They are presented in the test in the following order: apertures, view recognition, angle discrimination, paper folding, cube counting, and 3D form development. In total, you will be given 60 minutes to complete 90 questions – which are further divided to15 questions per subsection. This means that you will have 40 seconds to answer each question.

However, keep in mind that not all six parts require equal amounts of time. You might find some sections to be more challenging and thus more time-consuming than the others. For example, most DAT candidates find the apertures and view recognition to be the most difficult; hence, they would allot approximately 15 minutes for each of these two subsections and then divide the remaining time accordingly in answering the other four subsections. Since the PAT is administered as a single segment – meaning, there are no section breaks – an alternative strategy would be to skip the questions that you think will require relatively more time for you to complete. You can then go back to these questions once you have worked your way through the whole section. Remember that an "easy" question counts just as equally as a "hard" question. Also, knowing that you have completed at least all of the "easy" questions will give you more peace of mind as you spend the rest of the allotted time working on the harder questions.

The Six PAT Subsections	
Apertures	You will be presented with a 3-D object and you must determine through which of the five openings this object can pass.
View Recognition	Two projections of an object will be presented in each question. You are to determine the third.
Angle Discrimination	Each question will show four angles labeled 1 - 4. You are required to rank them from the smallest to the largest.
Paper Folding	A series of folds – usually two to three times – on a piece of paper will be illustrated in each question. One or more holes will then be punched at specific locations of the paper. Your task is to mentally unfold the paper and determine the resulting pattern of holes.
Cube Counting	For every two to four questions, you will be shown a stack of cubes. You will be asked to imagine that the stack as a whole is painted on all sides except for the bottom. You are to determine how many cubes have a particular number of sides painted.
Pattern Folding	A flat, unfolded pattern is presented in a question. You will have to choose the correct 3D figure that it represents once folded.

1.2.2 Practice, Practice, Practice

As with most undertakings that call for skills development, repetition is the key to success. Many candidates, at least in the beginning, will often find themselves running out of time in the PAT section. But with constant practice, you can train your brain to visualize these patterns and objects. Complete the first to second practice tests at a comfortable pace and record the precise time it took you to finish an entire subsection. This will give you a clear idea of your current level in terms of skills and speed. From there, you can create a more realistic study schedule for the PAT, and even the DAT as a whole.

For every practice set, go through each question and understand not only why an option is correct, but also why the other answer choices are wrong. Oftentimes in the actual test, you will arrive at the correct answer by eliminating the wrong ones first. Eventually, you will be able to perceive these problems much quicker and more efficiently.

It is also imperative that you do not stress out in this section. The PAT requires the most visualization out of all the sections in the DAT. If you are anxious and tired, you will not be able to solve the problems efficiently.

Finally, take note that you are not allowed to bring any item into the testing room: NO calculators, rulers, and pencils. You will be provided with a dry erase board and a marker, but you will not be permitted to use your fingers or the note boards as measuring devices during this section.

1.2.3 Living the PAT

If the PAT is supposed to test your real life visual skills, then let real life improve your PAT performance. Whether you are indoors or outdoors right now, look around. There are angles everywhere. There are objects behind other objects: notice that even though you can't see all of the objects behind, you can make logical inferences about their shapes.

Look at a cup. Notice the linear vertical lines that make out its outline. Notice how the top - which you know is really circular - seems more and more elliptical as you lower the angle of your view.

Can you pick out any acute or obtuse angles within your field of view? Which ones are clearly smaller than others? What allows you to know this to be true?

Paper folding (hole punching) and pattern folding do not appear as naturally as some of the other sections. If you are struggling with either of these two sections, you should try to actually do the folding in "real life" at least a few times. It would be especially meaningful if you tried it for an actual problem where you were having difficulty imagining the correct answer. Going through the process might help you to visualize the answer in a new way.

Looking at complex 3D objects from different angles is a normal part of life. Thinking about the edges, outlines, shapes, etc. as you are looking at objects does not come naturally. Try it in your free time, or when you are waiting in line somewhere, just as a temporary exercise to prepare for the PAT.

The more that you do PAT problems, the more you can see PAT in your surroundings. This sharpens your "instinct" for this section of the DAT.

In the succeeding pages, we will review each of the subsections specified by the ADA for the Perceptual Ability Test, as well as techniques for the respective topics. Each chapter comes with a set of exercises that will help reinforce your understanding and skills. Additional PAT chapter review questions and explanations are also available online at DAT-prep.com.

Understand

* The Six Standard Views
* Mirror Outlines of 3D Objects
* Aperture Rules

DAT-Prep.com

Introduction ▋▋▋▋

An aperture generally refers to an opening or a hole. This explains why Apertures in the PAT is also known as the Keyhole or the Key and Hole section. In this section, an aperture is the shape of an opening to a pathway, through which a three-dimensional object fits exactly and therefore, passes through without leaving any gaps.

In other words, an aperture of a three-dimensional object does not only have the same shape but also corresponds to the exact scale of the object. This basically tests your visual keenness to measure and differentiate irregularly shaped objects, as well as perceive their subtle details.

Additional Resources

Free Online Forum

2.1 About the Aperture Test

The first subsection of the Perceptual Ability Test is called "Apertures" or "Aperture Passing." Its more popular name among DAT candidates is "Keyhole." Each question in this test presents a three-dimensional object as the main reference (the "key"), followed by a choice of five outlines, representing possible passages ("holes") into which the object can go through in a single continuous motion.

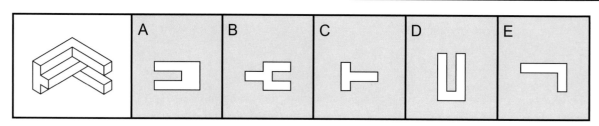

Figure PAT 2.1: Sample **Aperture** question that appears on the DAT. The correct answer is **A.**

The purpose of this subsection is to test a candidate's ability to visualize the two-dimensional view of a given object from three directions: the top, front, and right. This entails mentally rotating, turning, and flipping an object; the main objective of which is to identify the aperture that would match one of these three visualized 2D outlines of the object and perform the insertion with perfect ease.

2.2 Understanding Three-dimensional Objects and Views

One essential point that you need to understand is that a three-dimensional object has a total of six standard views namely the top, the bottom, the front, the rear or back, and the right and left sides as illustrated in Figures PAT 2.2 and 2.2-A.

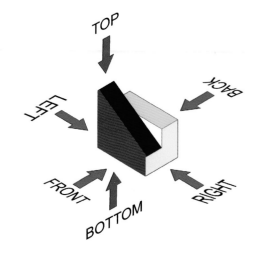

Figure PAT 2.2: The six sides (TOP, BOTTOM, FRONT, BACK, RIGHT, LEFT) in three-dimensional view.

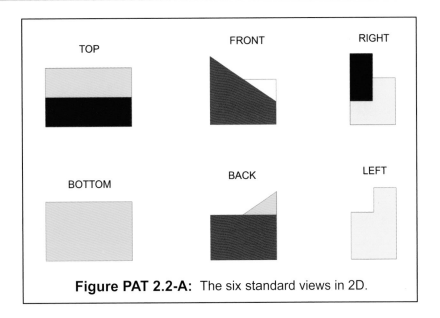

Figure PAT 2.2-A: The six standard views in 2D.

Slopes are some of the commonly confusing shapes to gauge from a two-dimensional perspective. They usually appear as rectangles or squares from certain points of view. See section 2.2.3 for a detailed discussion of understanding irregular shapes in 2D.

In this specific PAT subsection, however, each view is assumed to mirror the outline of its opposite side (top-bottom, front-back and right side-left side). If you focus on the outlines of the six standard views, the total height and width of the top and bottom are essentially the same.

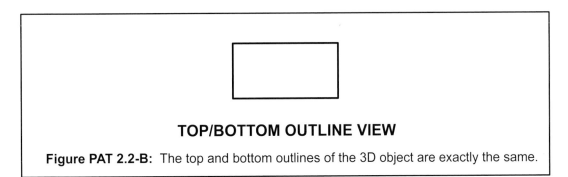

TOP/BOTTOM OUTLINE VIEW

Figure PAT 2.2-B: The top and bottom outlines of the 3D object are exactly the same.

The back view is just the flip side of the front view, as is the case with the right and left views. Their only differences would be the angle from where one side is viewed.

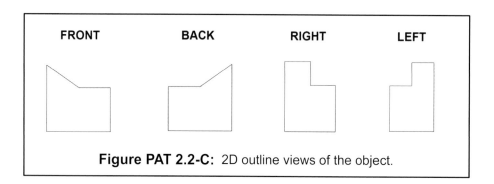

Figure PAT 2.2-C: 2D outline views of the object.

Hence, visualizing accurately the three basic outlines (top, front, and right) of a given 3D model is the most important skill that you should develop for the PAT Aperture test.

From this point onwards, we will refer to only three essential views: the top/bottom, the front/back, and the right/left views. Now let's try exploring a more complicated looking object.

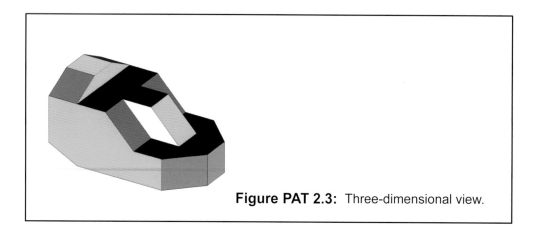

Figure PAT 2.3: Three-dimensional view.

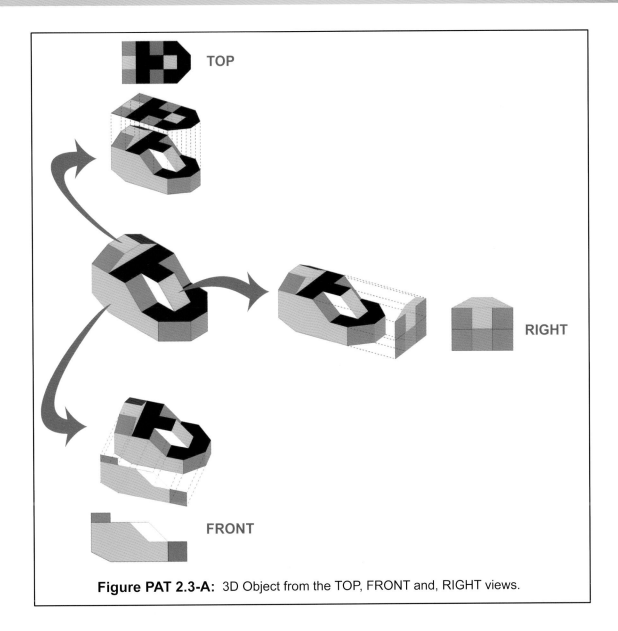

Figure PAT 2.3-A: 3D Object from the TOP, FRONT and, RIGHT views.

This time, try to either draw or imagine the outlines of the top, front, and right views. These outlines represent the shapes of the openings into which the object can pass through. Just remember that any of these apertures could be presented in the test in an upside down or flipped position. Nevertheless, the basic outline of a certain view never changes.

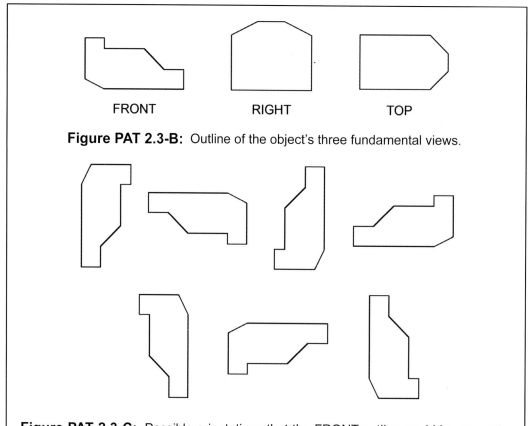

FRONT   RIGHT   TOP

Figure PAT 2.3-B: Outline of the object's three fundamental views.

Figure PAT 2.3-C: Possible orientations that the FRONT outline could be presented in the test. Take some time to review each option above so that it begins to become part of the way you think when reviewing answer choices during the exam.

This time, let's try assessing a 3D object without any color and see if you can now comfortably determine its top, front and right outlines.

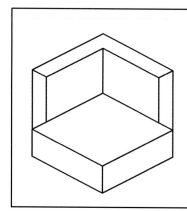

Figure PAT 2.4: 3D object in black and white as it could appear in a real exam question. Can you visualize the top, front, and right outline views of this object?

N.B. Your imagination is a muscle. All of our exercises have been carefully chosen to help you flex that muscle. So please take your time, focus and give a full effort with each exercise before reviewing the answers. This is your path to improvement.

A critical aspect in evaluating Figure PAT 2.4 is understanding how the L-shaped component is attached behind the box.

Your first clue is the way its edges are drawn relative to the edges of the box.

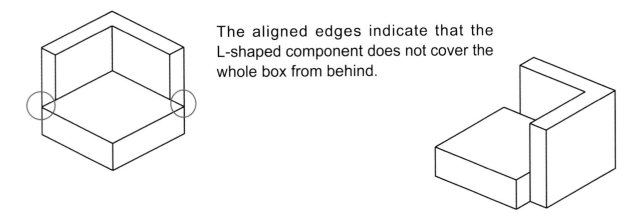

The aligned edges indicate that the L-shaped component does not cover the whole box from behind.

Alternate Scenario

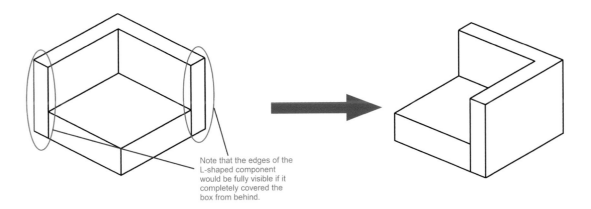

Note that the edges of the L-shaped component would be fully visible if it completely covered the box from behind.

Now let's start examining the three fundamental views of Figure PAT 2.4 and determine the shape of its outline. In order

to aid us in distinguishing each view, let's assign colors to the parts corresponding to a specific side.

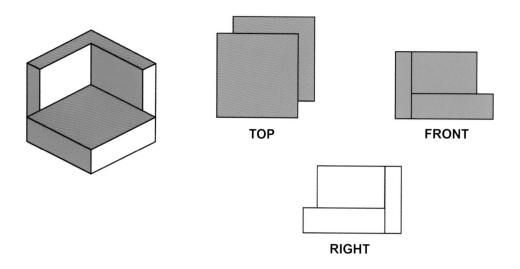

Based on these three basic views, the object's outlines would look like the following:

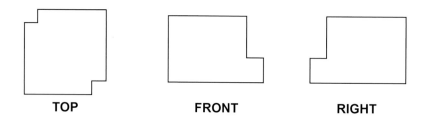

While several strategies may be applied with the Apertures section, **FOCUSING ON THE OUTLINES** of the object itself and on its three basic views is the most fundamental approach in determining the correct aperture for a 3D object.

Now let's do some short exercises to make sure that you have understood and can now focus on the three basic outlines of 3D objects. Draw the TOP, FRONT, and RIGHT outline views of each given object in the appropriate spaces provided. If, at this point, you find that drawing their opposite views – that is, the bottom, back and left, respectively – help you visualize the outlines better, you are free to do so.

1.

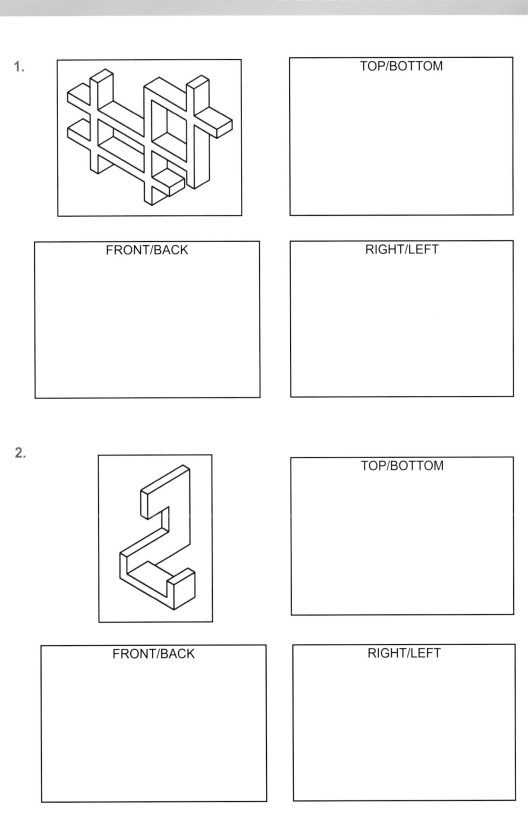

TOP/BOTTOM

FRONT/BACK

RIGHT/LEFT

2.

TOP/BOTTOM

FRONT/BACK

RIGHT/LEFT

3.

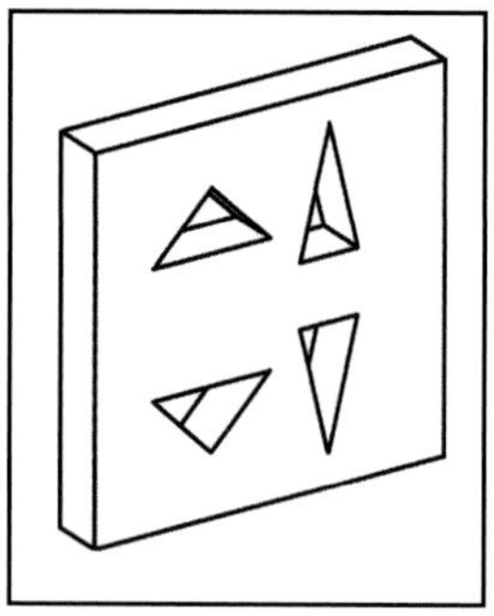

TOP/BOTTOM

FRONT/BACK

RIGHT/LEFT

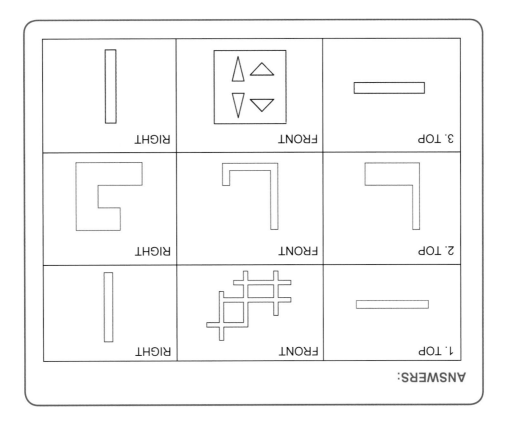

Now that we have narrowed down the important views and outlines to consider (TOP, FRONT, and RIGHT) when determining the correct apertures of a given object, let's start evaluating specific 3D objects in detail using these three fundamental views. Familiarizing yourself with the different views of various objects, especially the confusing ones, will make visualizing on the PAT not only so much easier but also so much faster.

2.2.1 Cylinders

Cylinders have three significant parts: two flat ends (also called *bases*) and one curved surface. The important thing to remember about cylinders is that their flat ends, which can be circular or elliptical in shape, will always show a rounded outline from a 180-degree view (see Figure PAT 2.6) while the curved surface, straight edges (see Figure PAT 2.7).

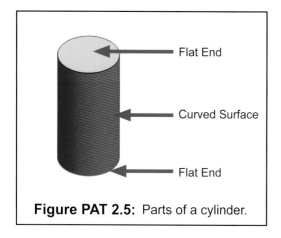

Figure PAT 2.5: Parts of a cylinder.

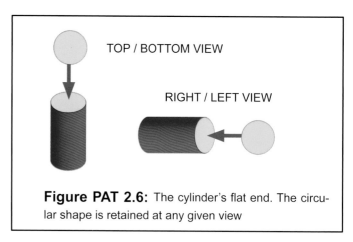

Figure PAT 2.6: The cylinder's flat end. The circular shape is retained at any given view

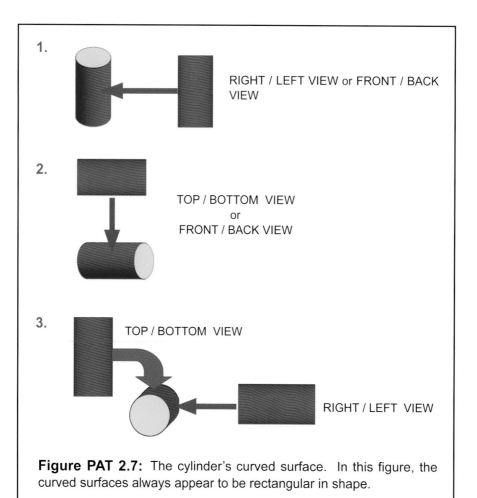

Figure PAT 2.7: The cylinder's curved surface. In this figure, the curved surfaces always appear to be rectangular in shape.

Looking at Figure PAT 2.7, you would observe that the shape of a curved surface stays proportionally the same in two views when in upright position (the front/back and right/left views) and in horizontal position (the top/bottom and front/back views). Even from an oblique view of the cylinder, only the orientation changes – vertical from the top/bottom view and horizontal from the right/left view – but the rectangle shape basically stays the same.

Inversely, the base always stays rounded in shape and from only one view, which could be the top/bottom, the right/left view, or the front/back view depending on how the cylinder is positioned.

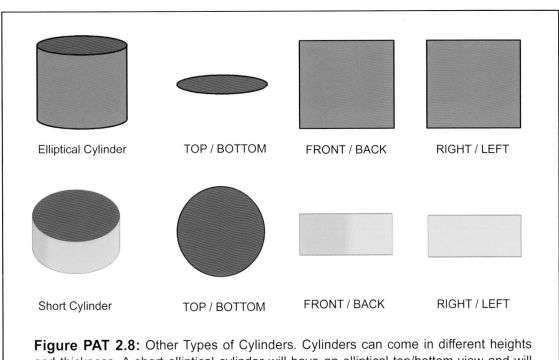

Elliptical Cylinder   TOP / BOTTOM   FRONT / BACK   RIGHT / LEFT

Short Cylinder   TOP / BOTTOM   FRONT / BACK   RIGHT / LEFT

Figure PAT 2.8: Other Types of Cylinders. Cylinders can come in different heights and thickness. A short elliptical cylinder will have an elliptical top/bottom view and will appear square-shaped when viewed from the front or back. A disk cylinder will have a top/bottom view of a circle and a wide rectangle for its front/back and right/left views.

The cylinder shape will be presented in the actual test in a variety of sizes and orientations. They can also be shown as the main surface of an object or as one of the components. The best way to deal with this shape is to first, determine the correct contours of its bases and curved surface in the three fundamental views. Next, you need to gauge their respective dimensions. Finally, critical to these visualizations is to stay focused on the outlines of the different views.

Let's take a look at two Aperture questions featuring this three-dimensional shape. Again, remember that you can effectively determine the correct answers if you stay focused on the outlines of the object's three basic views.

Choose the correct aperture to each object:

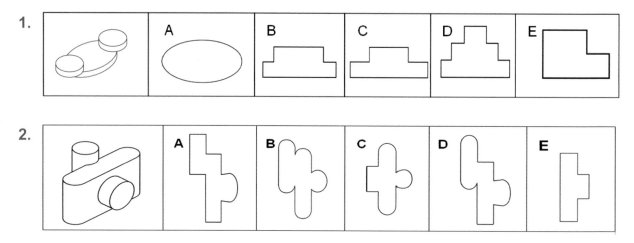

ANSWERS:

1. B. The 3D object in this question is composed of three cylinders: two small circular parts and one elliptical main surface. This should be easy to answer if you can easily recall that the curved surfaces of cylinders always show straight edges.

In this question, all three cylinders have the same orientation – that is, the top/bottom views show the bases of the two small parts as rounded and the bigger component as elliptical while the curved surfaces show up as short rectangles for the smaller circles and a wide rectangle for the elliptical one from the front/back and right/left views.

This means that A is the only aperture that shows the top/bottom view. At first glance, A is obviously incorrect. Because the two circular cylinders are attached passed the edges of the elliptical cylinder, the circular shapes should be visible on the top/bottom outline. However, A shows only the elliptical shape; therefore, it is wrong. This narrows down the choices to B, C, D, and E.

Since the remaining options all show straight edges, you can start visualizing the front/back and the right/left views and outlines.

Please cover the solution while you are considering your answer.

* For clarification purposes, we have included the Top/ Bottom view in the illustration.

From Figure PAT 2.9, we gather that all the shapes from the front/back and right/left views are rectangular. You can now eliminate D because it shows a square outline on top of the figure. E is also off the mark.

B and C show the object's outline from the right/left view. Both figures outline a

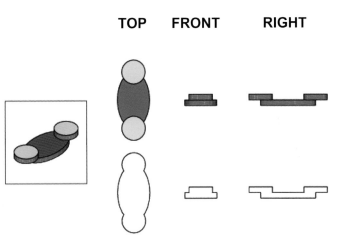

TOP   FRONT   RIGHT

Figure PAT 2.9: Three Fundamental Views of Object 1.

rectangular shape of the short cylinder on top and another (wider) rectangular outline of the elliptical cylinder below it. The only difference between these two options is that the rectangular outline on top is wider in B and narrower in C. Your ability to spot these proportions in an object's outline as a whole will be tested quite often in the PAT Apertures questions. The correct answer here is B based on its scale and proportion to the given figure.

2. C. The 3D object in this question is also comprised of three cylinders – this time, of different sizes, shapes, and orientations. These can be confusing to the untrained eye. However, distinguishing such differences as reflected on their various views and outlines is a skill that is frequently tested on the PAT; hence, you should practice working and visualizing similar types of questions as much as you can to help you overcome this challenge.

Looking at the given figure, the attachment on the left is a long cylinder in the upright position. The main surface is a narrow elliptical – also in the upright position, and the protrusion on the right is a short, circular cylinder in the horizontal position. This means that the top/bottom view will show the shapes of a circle, an oblong, and a rectangle, respectively. (Remember that the circular protrusion is horizontally positioned from the main elliptical object. Hence it would show its curved surface – rectangular – from the top or bottom view.) This eliminates A and B.

On the other hand, the front view will show three different sizes of rectangles. The right side view is tricky: it will indeed show the circular protrusion on the center of the elliptical cylinder. However, because it is a solid protrusion and not a hole, this will be negligible from the outline view (see Figure PAT 2.10). The main surface (the elliptical object) will now appear as a rectangle while the long cylinder attachment will only have a small square as its visible part on top of the rectangle. This will now prove E is an incorrect choice.

Between C and D, you only need to evaluate the correct placement of the circle, the oblong, and the rectangle from the top view. Based on the outline view on Figure PAT 2.10, C is the best answer.

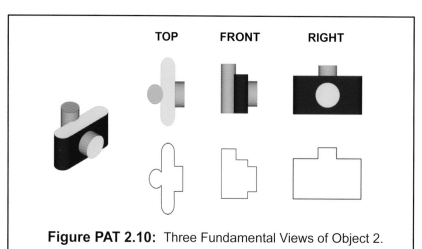

Figure PAT 2.10: Three Fundamental Views of Object 2.

2.2.2 Spheres

This shape seldom appears on the actual DAT, but it would be worth knowing that because a sphere is globular in shape, it thus appears as a circle at any angle.

Figure PAT 2.11: 3D and outline views of the sphere. Take note that the shape remains circular from any of the three fundamental views.

2.2.3 Slopes

Familiarizing yourself with the different types of slopes and curves is one of the most important aspects of your preparation for this PAT subsection. These shapes frequently appear as protrusions, angled cuts, and/or attachments in an object. They are quite confusing when presented in combination with other shapes. They are also mostly found on the difficult questions of the PAT Apertures in order to gauge your visual scrutiny of details.

The following are some of the most common types, which you might encounter on the actual test. Again, the outlines of the top, front, and right views should be your main focus.

1. Convex Slopes

With slopes that curve outward, you have to be keen on how the curved and straight edges appear in the two-dimensional view of specific sides.

In Figure PAT 2.12, note how the arc on the slope's upper edge appears straight while the lower edge is curved from the top view. The right view shows the reverse.

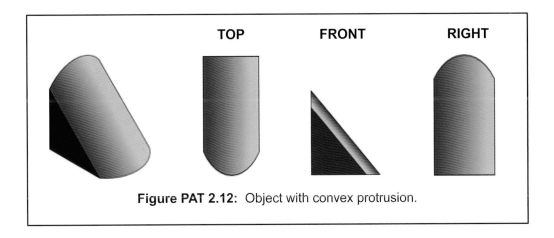

| TOP | FRONT | RIGHT |

Figure PAT 2.12: Object with convex protrusion.

The front view is another area that requires close attention. The triangular base (i.e. flat surface) of the object will definitely appear; but you must also remember that the curvature of the convex slope protrudes outward. Hence this bulge will be visible from the front or back view. The question is, what shape will it manifest?

Now a convex protrusion is very much like the curved surface of a cylinder. As illustrated in section 2.2.1, curved surfaces always appear with flat edges in the two-dimensional views. Therefore, this will show as a linear layer on top of the trian-gle's hypotenuse, making the front-back outline a larger triangle than the actual size of the base.

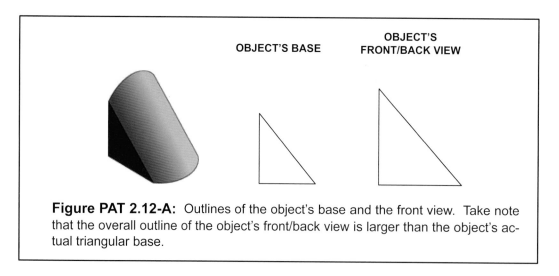

OBJECT'S BASE

OBJECT'S FRONT/BACK VIEW

Figure PAT 2.12-A: Outlines of the object's base and the front view. Take note that the overall outline of the object's front/back view is larger than the object's actual triangular base.

Of course, convex slopes can come in various forms. In Figure PAT 2.13, the top and right views yield square outlines because the upper and lower edges of the slope are both straight. Being able to spot these details and differences are vital in choosing an object's correct aperture in the exam.

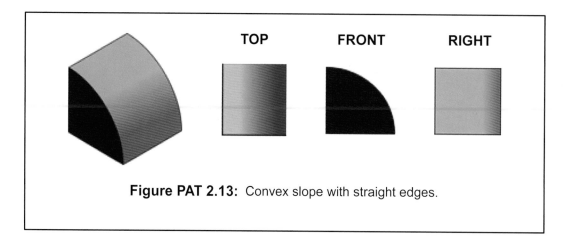

TOP　　**FRONT**　　**RIGHT**

Figure PAT 2.13: Convex slope with straight edges.

2. Concave Slopes

Contrary to convex slopes, objects with concave components have depressions (i.e. "if it goes in like a cave, it's concave"). They DO NOT show bulges in any view. Instead, the concave surface may be completely invisible to at least one view.

Hence, they are mostly irrelevant in visualizing the outline views of an object. The most fundamental approach, in this case, is to be attentive to the basic contour of the object's edges.

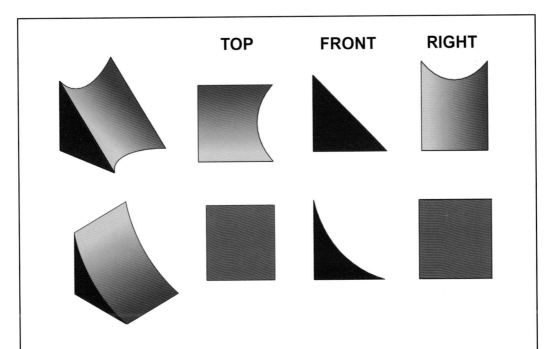

Figure PAT 2.14: Top, Front, and Right Views of Objects with Concave Parts. Take note how the curvatures appear in the different views.

3. Linear Slopes

With objects that have linear edges on their slopes, the DAT often uses these in the PAT Apertures questions to test your eye on proportions. This is primarily because the height or the length of an object can vary, depending on the degree of the inclination. The steeper the slope, the more area of the slanting surface becomes visible on a 180 degree view. The lower the inclination, the lesser area shows up, making the object look shorter in a particular two-dimensional view.

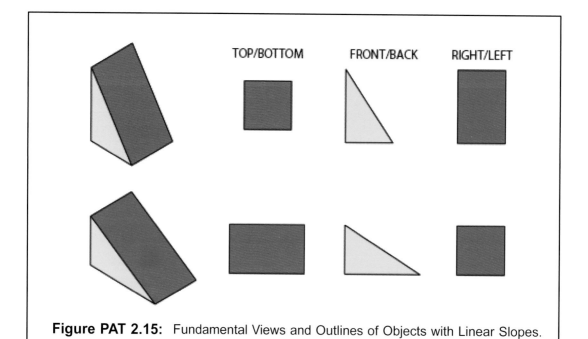

Figure PAT 2.15: Fundamental Views and Outlines of Objects with Linear Slopes. A steeper tilt shows a taller right/left view while a lower inclination forms a shorter one.

You must realize by now that the actual length of the slanting surface cannot be a reliable basis in judging an object's height in the 2D views. Similar to the second model in Figure PAT 2.15, an object with a mild slope can appear shorter from the right view even if the slanting surface may be longer.

One "trick" that will keep you from getting confused is to concentrate on the outline of the mirroring views. As explained in section 2.2, in this particular PAT subsection, each view will always have the same dimensions as its opposite side. In Figure PAT 2.16 for example, you can get the exact picture of the right view by estimating the height and width of the left outline. You can do the same procedure in determining the top view.

Now you have another strategy that you can utilize for the Apertures test (!): if you find a shape or an object to be confusing, you can move your sight to the opposite views and see if you could figure out the correct outline that you are looking for.

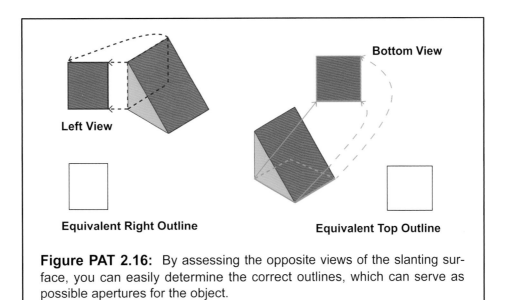

Figure PAT 2.16: By assessing the opposite views of the slanting surface, you can easily determine the correct outlines, which can serve as possible apertures for the object.

The pyramid and the star are another set of 3D objects that are confusing because of the sloping parts. Just keep in mind that a pyramid will always have the triangle shape on all its sides (front-back and top-bottom views). However, the top view in a classic "square" pyramid will be a square – just like its base, which is the bottom view.

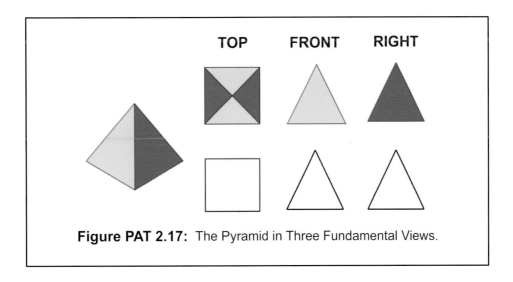

Figure PAT 2.17: The Pyramid in Three Fundamental Views.

Please note that there are other *rare* bases for pyramids which could be triangular, rectangular or which could have more than 4 corners.

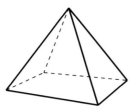

rectangular-based
pyramid

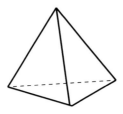

triangular-based
pyramid

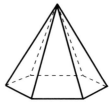

hexagonal-based
pyramid

With star-shaped objects, the top-bottom view takes the form of the star. The two other views (front and right) have straight edges, with the height and width depending on the object's depth.

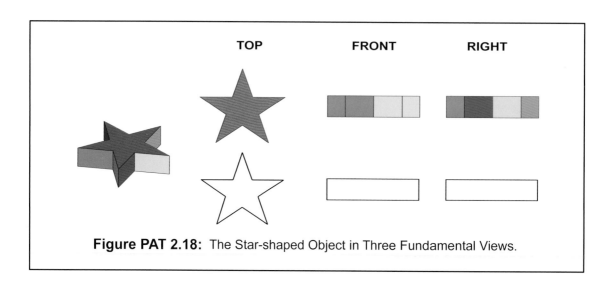

Figure PAT 2.18: The Star-shaped Object in Three Fundamental Views.

4. Angled Cuts

Angled cuts work practically the same way as the linear slopes. The "cut" shows up only on one of the fundamental views – usually the front view – of the object. Again, the trick is to consider the opposite outlines of the three fundamental views in order to determine the precise dimensions of the correct aperture.

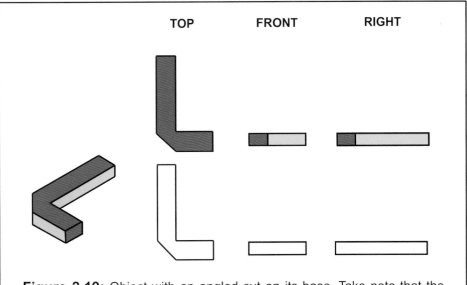

TOP   FRONT   RIGHT

Figure 2.19: Object with an angled cut on its base. Take note that the slope does not show on the two views (front/back and right/left).

Now let's test the extent of your understanding and visual skills in assessing 3D objects in the Apertures test so far. The following are three typical questions that you will encounter in the PAT section. You can time yourself on every question in order to get a clear idea of your current level.

You have 40 seconds to complete each question in the PAT section, so you can give yourself 2 minutes to choose your answers for the 3 questions below. The three fundamental views and their outlines are provided in the answer key which follows on the next page.

If at the end of this short exercise, you still find the different objects to be confusing, please access the Lessons section of dat-prep.com for further explanations and exercises.

1.

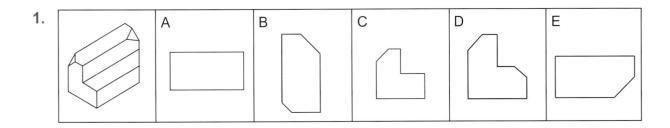

2.

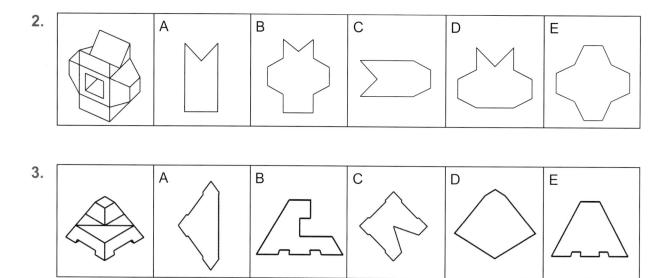

3.

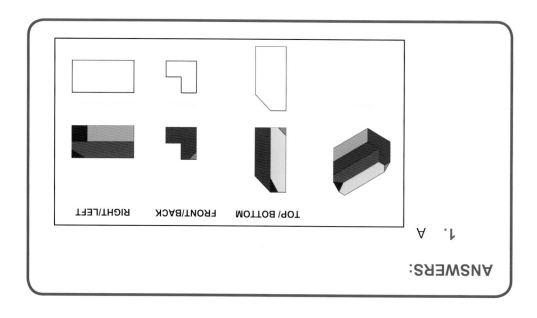

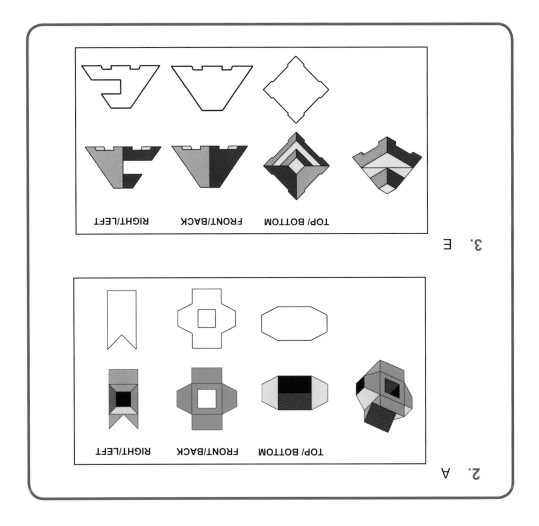

3. E

RIGHT/LEFT FRONT/BACK TOP/BOTTOM

2. A

RIGHT/LEFT FRONT/BACK TOP/BOTTOM

The next critical aspect of your preparation for the PAT Apertures is getting acquainted with its specific rules, which we will discuss in detail in the next section.

2.3 Understanding the Rules for PAT Apertures

Of the six subsections of the Perceptual Ability Test, only the Apertures have specific rules that dictate the manner by which you select the answer to each question. It is thus very important that you fully understand them and incorporate these into your strategies.

Rule 1. Before performing the insertion into an aperture, the irregularly shaped object may be rotated in any direction. The object may be entered through the aperture on a side not shown in the question.

This rule requires your knowledge and understanding of the six standard views and the three essential outlines as discussed in section 2.2. Moreover, while the rule does say that the object can be rotated in "any" direction, this is rather confusing because the solid object can only be inserted through the aperture in one of the three directions namely the top (or bottom), the front (or back) and the right (or left) sides. This is highly related to rule no. 2.

Rule 2. Once the object is introduced to the opening, it should pass completely through the hole without further rotating the object in any direction.

The most important thing to remember with this rule is that the correct aperture is always the exact shape of the object's outline. Rule number 3 explains this further.

Rule 3. Both the three-dimensional object and its corresponding aperture are drawn to the same scale. It may be possible for one of the answer choices to have the correct shape yet be too small or too big for the object. However, the differences are large enough to be seen by the naked eye.

Pay attention to proportions! The actual DAT stresses proportions more than anything else for this subsection. As soon as you set your eyes on the 3D object given in the question, start visualizing the outline of its three fundamental views. Make sure that one of these views corresponds to one of the "keyholes" presented. Do not forget that protruding elements are also part of the outline.

Most test center administrators are quite strict about enforcing the rules. Some students have managed to use their marker or a finger as rough "rulers" to assess proportions. Of course, we cannot recommend such a technique.

Rule 4. No irregularities are hidden in any portion of the object. In case the figure has indentations, the hidden portion would be symmetric with the visible part.

In section 2.2, we have discussed that each view is assumed to mirror the outline of its opposite side. While a hole or a protrusion on one side of the view would usually be reflected on its reverse part, there are cases, such as with the concave slopes and the angled cuts in section 2.2.3 for example, when the irregular portion may prove irrelevant in considering the outline of the object. Figure PAT 2.22 makes a very simple illustration of this rule.

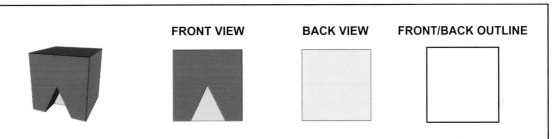

FRONT VIEW   **BACK VIEW**   **FRONT/BACK OUTLINE**

Figure PAT 2.22: Despite the indentation on the front part of the object, the square outline of the front view remains symmetrical to its back view.

Rule 5. For each question, only one aperture matches the exact shape and size of one of the two-dimensional views of the object.

This rule may be quite obvious, but several questions on the DAT have two almost identical answer choices. Your ability to spot the tiny details such as the exact shape of one of the edges and the direction of the slants is a critical skill that must be developed.

2.3.1 Applying the Rules

Now that we have analyzed each rule in this PAT subsection, let us try applying them with the following example:

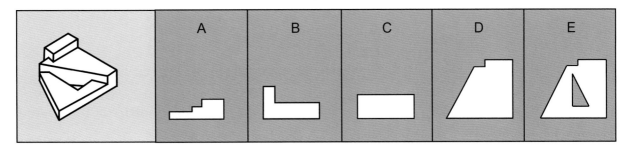

Step 1. Find the outlines of the object from the three fundamental views.

There are three sides of the object that are visible: the TOP, FRONT and RIGHT SIDE VIEWS as shown in Figure 1. Remember that you need not worry about the hidden sides since according to Rule 4, no irregularities are hidden in the object. If ever the figure would have symmetric indentations, the hidden portion would be symmetric with the visible part (See figure 2).

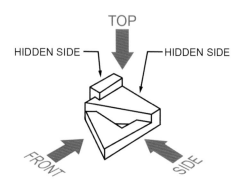

Figure 1

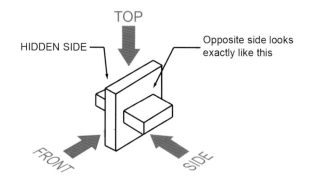

Figure 2. Symmetrical Object

Imagine how the object looks like when viewed from the three different points. This is to distinguish the outlines of the object. Do not get confused by the other parts of the object. Focus on the outlines.

Figure 3 shows the object from Figure 1 when viewed from each point.

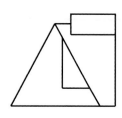  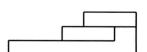

Fig. 3a. Top View   **Fig. 3b. Front View**   **Fig. 3c. Right Side View**

Figure 3

Figure 4 shows the outlines only of the object when viewed from each point.

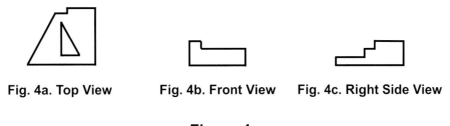

Fig. 4a. Top View **Fig. 4b. Front View** **Fig. 4c. Right Side View**

Figure 4

Step 2. Find the correct aperture from the given options.

Let us start by trying the outline of the side view. Only one choice from the **side** view's outline may fit – this is aperture A.

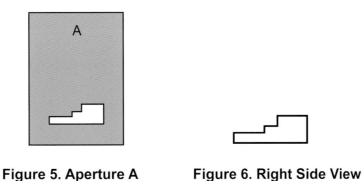

Figure 5. Aperture A **Figure 6. Right Side View**

Aperture A (Figure 5) looks exactly like the side view outline (Figure 6) but obviously smaller, so this is not the correct answer according to Rule 3.

Next let us try the **front** view outline. Only one choice fits – this is aperture B.

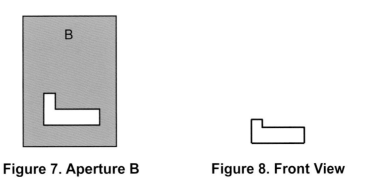

Figure 7. Aperture B **Figure 8. Front View**

Aperture B (Figure 7) looks close to the front view outline (Figure 8) but there is obviously a slight difference in the upper left part, so this is still not the correct answer.

Let us try the last option, which is the **top** view outline. Two possible choices seem to match the top view outline. These are apertures D and E.

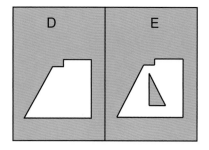

Figure 9. Aperture D and E

Figure 10. Top View

The top view outline shows a hole in the center but regardless of whether a hole is there or not, the object will fit to both apertures D and E. You might argue that in this question, two answers are possible. This is not possible because Rule 5 clearly states that only one aperture is correct for each object. In a case like this, the aperture that can accommodate all the features

of the object should be the answer. Therefore, the best answer is E.

Remember that the object can pass through aperture E if the bottom is inserted first. If aperture E is oriented in a reversed direction as illustrated in Figure 11, the object will still pass through the aperture if the top is inserted first.

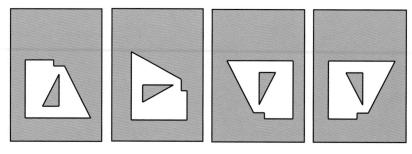

Figure 11. Aperture E is still the correct answer if it looks like any of these.

Both of these two options of aperture E may also be rotated in any direction. Re-

member therefore, that some or all of the choices in the actual test may be rotated.

REMINDER: Everything should be done as quickly as possible with approximately 40 seconds to answer each question.

Now let's try with a few more exercises to help you apply the different strategies and rules, which we have discussed in this chapter.

2.4 Mini Exercises

1. This object is made up of basic shapes and requires you to pay attention to proportions.

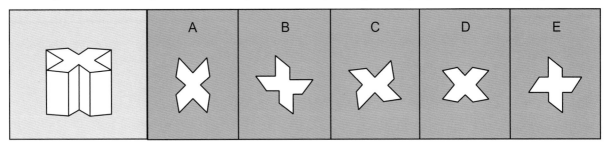

2. This object has attachments or components with basic shapes but requires you to consider the rotated or mirrored view.

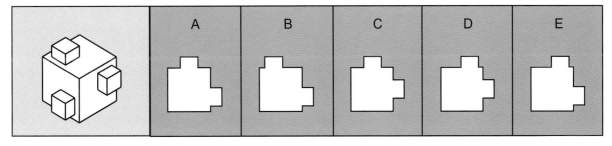

3. The shape of the object looks complex, and the options require you to pay attention to the proportions, as well as consider the rotated or mirrored views.

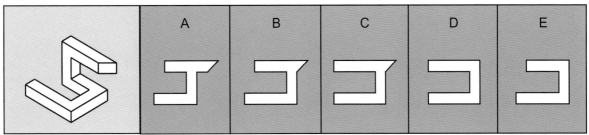

4.

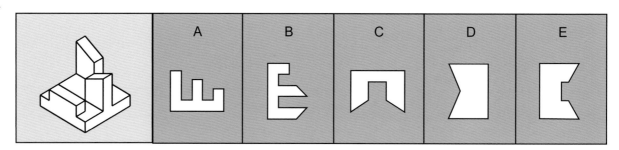

5.

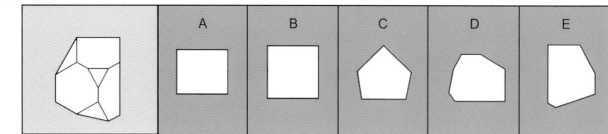

1. Answer: A

The aperture in this question resembles the letter X. You need to concentrate on this basic shape, which is the largest surface of the 3D figure. Only A and D most resemble the letter X. The only difference between the two is that option D is smaller in size and its inner edges are smaller compared to the figure. Instantly, you know that A is the right answer.

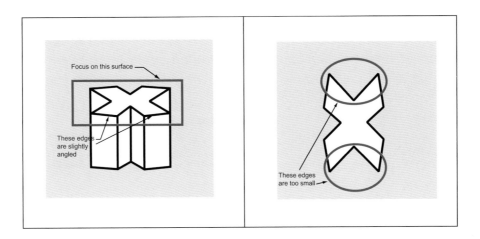

2. Answer: E

All of the options are viewed from a single direction: the left view (mirror image of the right side view). The main differences between the given apertures are the distances of the attached small cubes, so you only need to focus on these. Notice that the cubes are not centered but are placed near the edges of the big cube.

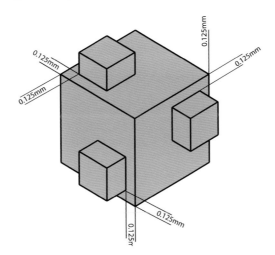

By comparing each option to the 3D figure, you will easily identify that A is wrong because the small cube on top is positioned at the center. Options C and D are also incorrect because the cubes on the side are both located at the center. The upper cube of B is way too far from the edge adjacent to the face where the side cube is located; thus, incorrect. This leaves option E as the right answer.

3. Answer: B

All of the choices in this question are viewed from one direction: the top view. You can simply proceed to comparing each option to the 3D figure. Option A has shorter components therefore, wrong. B follows the outline of the object's top view: the upper arm is shorter than the lower arm; the pointed edge is shown. B is the correct answer.

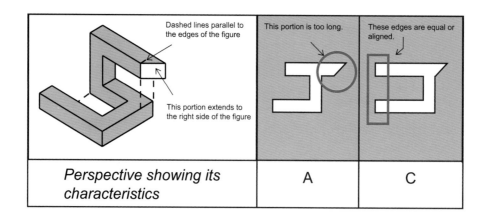

Options C and D are both incorrect because all portions of the aperture are aligned or equal in length. E does not have the angled extension and therefore, incorrect.

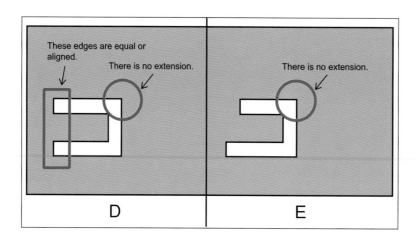

4. Answer: E

This is a complicated looking figure so you need to study it carefully. Take note of the height of the components, which are like towers; the distance of these towers from one another; and the thickness of the square base.

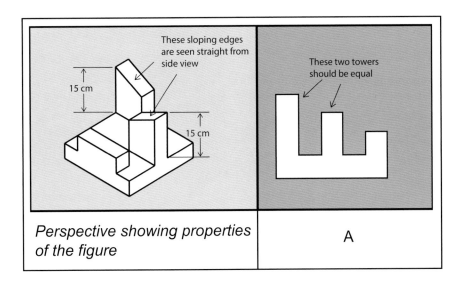

These sloping edges are seen straight from side view 15 cm 15 cm	These two towers should be equal
Perspective showing properties of the figure	A

The best strategy here is the process of elimination. Option A is viewed from the left side. However, it shows the wrong aperture because the two taller towers should be equal in height. B is also incorrect because the sloping edges should be seen as straight from the right side view. Option C might have the correct taller towers from the front view, but the small tower/protrusion is not considered. Thus it is wrong. The sloping edges in option D are too wide, which makes this a wrong answer as well. The only option left is E (taken from the front view and rotated 90 degrees clockwise) and thus the correct answer.

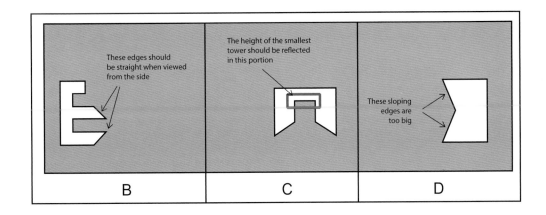

B	C	D
These edges should be straight when viewed from the side	The height of the smallest tower should be reflected in this portion	These sloping edges are too big

5. Answer: B

This is another complicated figure, which would approximately represent the rock-like figure that often appears in the keyhole section of the recent DATs. This 3-D object, however, is simpler than the 10-sided figures that many candidates reported to have encountered in the real exam. Nevertheless, what makes this object quite complex is the difficulty of identifying which planes belong to the top, front and right side views -unless you are familiar with axonometric projection. This type of visualization sounds intimidating; but a very simplistic way of describing it is enclosing a figure in a glass cube. A common type of axonometric projection is called isometric projection, wherein the 3 axes of space look equally foreshortened. See Glass Cube illustrations.

Using this visualization will help clarify the possible shapes of a figure's top, front and right side view. Now let's use this projection as our "glass cube technique". Three

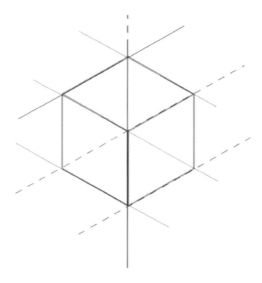

Example of an Isometric or "Glass Cube" Projection

views are projected here: the top, front and the right side views. Always remember that the horizontal side of an object is actually represented by a 30-degree angle line. And so, whenever we see a 30-degree angle at the bottom side, always consider it as the horizontal base of your object.

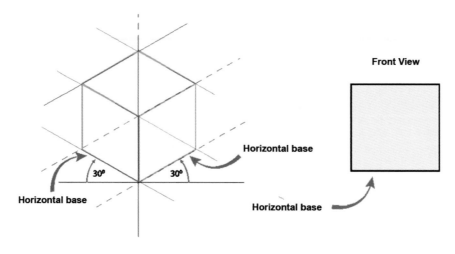

Following the natural reading process - that is, we start from left to right - let us locate the leftmost axis where the horizontal base and the vertical edge of our object meet and position our glass cube in this manner:

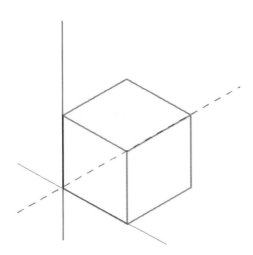

To determine the top, front and right views of the figure in this question, we need to likewise determine the end points of the object. These points will lead us to the different views that we are looking for because these are where our lines should cross.

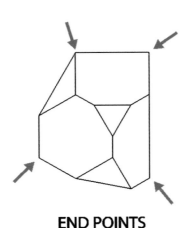

END POINTS

Now applying our glass cube technique, we need to trace those end points. So we end up with this:

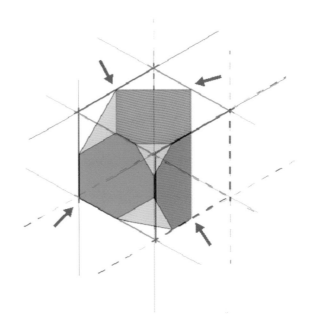

With this projection, the process of elimination may now work. Options A and E are out. The holes may be possibly rectangular, but it cannot be a square because the length and the width of the image are not equal. E is also out - none of the top, front or right side has that kind of trapezoidal shape. Option D looks exactly like the outline of the figure; but surely, neither side would fit through this shape. This leaves us with B and C. The top view resembles the pentagram of option C. Unfortunately, the lower left and right sides are not parallel. In the illustration, the two sides of the image may actually end up as parallel. This leaves us with option B. All corners of the image fit into the square shape.

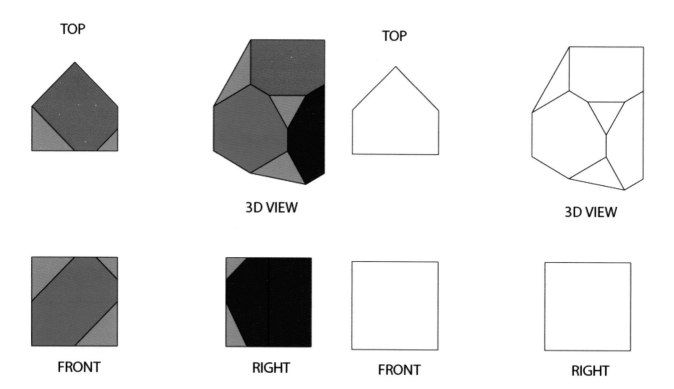

TOP   TOP

3D VIEW   3D VIEW

FRONT   RIGHT   FRONT   RIGHT

GOLD STANDARD WARM-UP EXERCISES

CHAPTER 2: Apertures

The following questions represent one of the six subsections in the Perceptual Ability Test of the DAT. While this serves as a review of the discussions in this chapter, the level of difficulty of each question closely parallels the actual test.

You have 10 minutes to complete this portion of the DAT Mini Test; the actual test is 60 minutes.

Please time yourself accordingly.

> **BEGIN ONLY WHEN YOUR TIMER IS READY**

1.

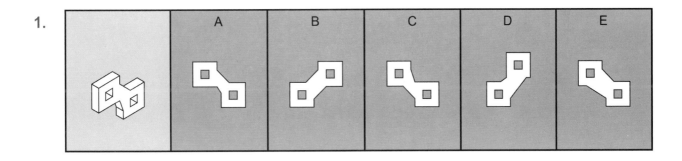

2.

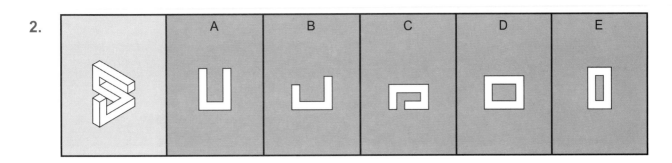

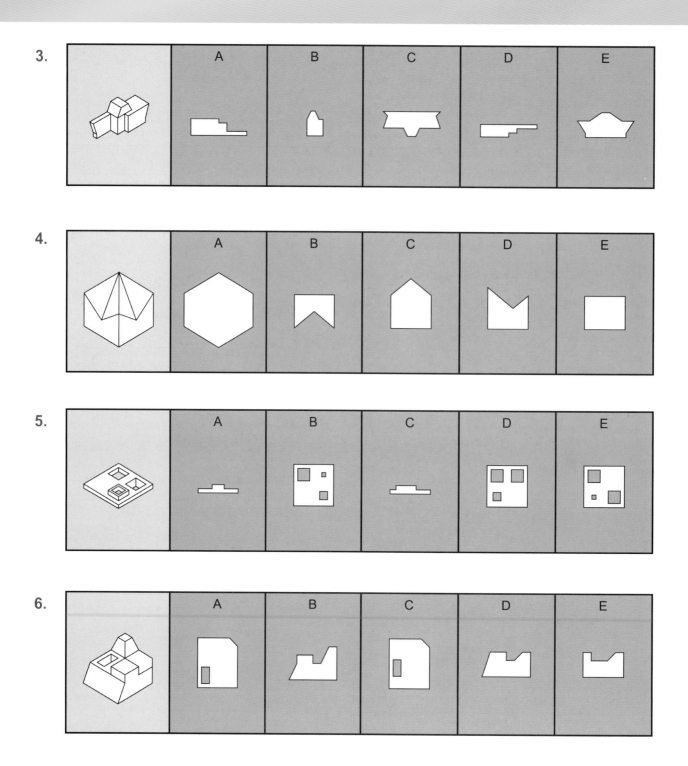

3. | | A | B | C | D | E |

4. | | A | B | C | D | E |

5. | | A | B | C | D | E |

6. | | A | B | C | D | E |

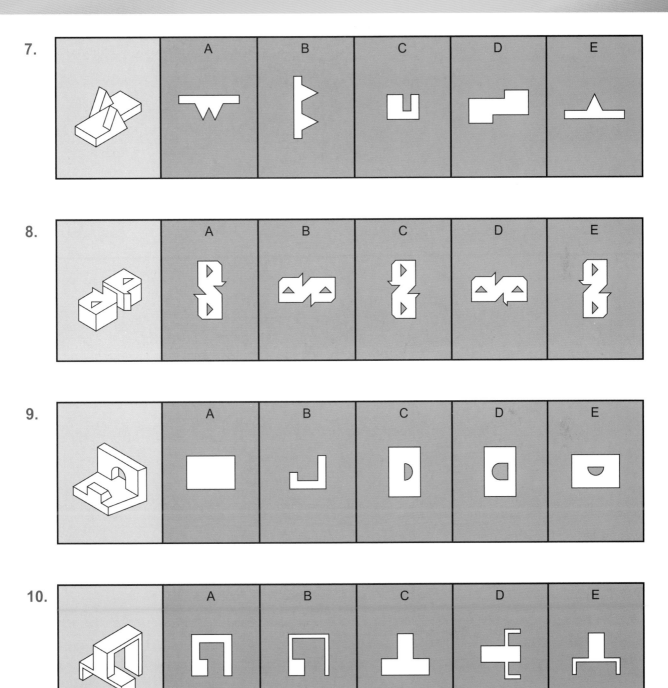

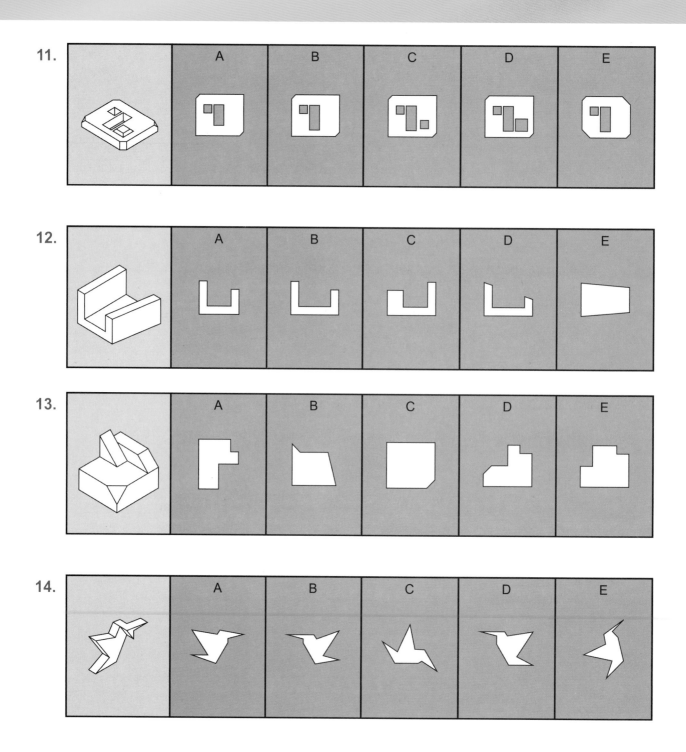

15.

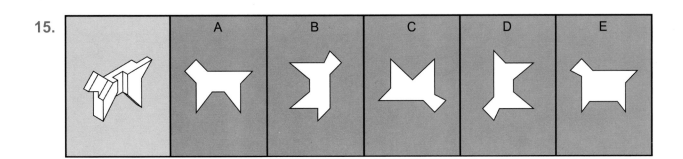

| | A | B | C | D | E |

If time remains, you may review your work. If your allotted time is complete, please proceed to the Answer Key.

GS ANSWER KEY

CHAPTER 2

1.	C		9.	C
2.	E		10.	D
3.	A		11.	B
4.	E		12.	C
5.	B		13.	A
6.	C		14.	E
7.	A		15.	D
8.	E			

* Explanations can be found in the Lessons section at www.dat-prep.com.

Go online to DAT-prep.com for additional chapter review Q&A and forum.

Go online to DAT-prep.com for additional chapter review Q&A and forum.

GOLD NOTES

ORTHOGRAPHIC PROJECTION

Chapter 3

Understand

* Orthographic Projection
* The Projection Grid
* Hidden Lines

DAT-Prep.com

Introduction

An orthographic projection is a representation of a three-dimensional object in flat or two-dimensional perspectives: usually the top, front and right side (end) views. The top view would often indicate the width and depth of the object; the front view, its height and width; and the end view, its depth and height. This second section of the PAT is essentially a view recognition test - the views are orthographic projections. For practical reasons, students commonly refer to this section as the TFE (Top/Front/End) Section.

In the drawing, solid lines represent the edges hence the object's skeletal shape. Dotted lines signify a hidden edge, also known as a hidden line, denoting that either a folded or an extended part of the object exists but becomes invisible from a two-dimensional view. Therefore, this section demands your scrutiny to compare, contrast, and to logically match the adjacent solid and dotted lines.

Additional Resources

Free Online Forum

Most DAT candidates refer to the View Recognition test as the Top/Front/End (TFE) section. In this PAT subsection, three-dimensional objects are represented in their detailed two-dimensional forms through the three standard views, namely the top view, front view, and end view (this time, the "right view" is identified as the "end view").

This test assesses your ability to analyze the two-dimensional views of a 3D object so that you can mentally reconstruct the object in its entirety. Each question will show two out of the three possible projections of the 3D object. Your task is to determine the missing view.

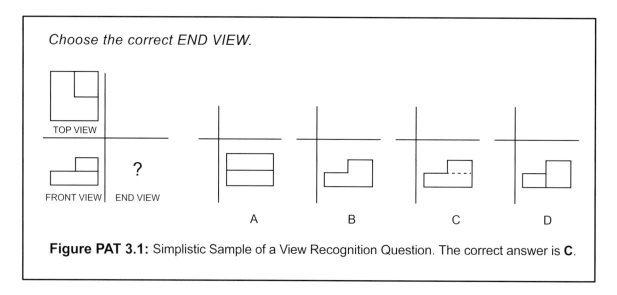

Choose the correct END VIEW.

Figure PAT 3.1: Simplistic Sample of a View Recognition Question. The correct answer is **C**.

Visualizations in the View Recognition test are very much similar to the Apertures section. Both require your acute perception of the three fundamental views. The main difference is that with View Recognition, you must now consider the details – not just the outlines – of the objects including the holes and the edges of surfaces, which may not be directly visible in a particular view because they are behind another surface. These hidden details are indicated by dotted lines. Solid lines, on the other hand, signify edges that can be directly seen from that specific view.

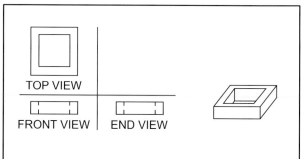

Figure PAT 3.2: Top, Front, and End Views of an Object with Hidden Edges. The dotted lines on the front and end views represent the intersections of the surfaces of the square cavity behind the outer surfaces of the object.

3.2 Understanding Orthographic Projection

A common approach to this test involves matching the lines in each of the given views to the lines or edges of the correct figure among the answer choices. Adopting this method entails a clear understanding of how the three different views in the drawing relate to the actual 3D object that they symbolize. Let us start by getting a good grasp of what View Recognition is really all about.

Technically, view recognition is known as *orthographic projection*. Orthographic projection is a means of drawing an object as viewed in at least three different directions in order to help a person visualize what the individual parts look like. The most common views presented in orthographic drawings are the top, front, and end (right side) views. A better way to comprehend the principles of orthographic projection is to imagine an object being placed in a glass cube with its surface reflected (i.e. projected) onto the crystal faces of the cube.

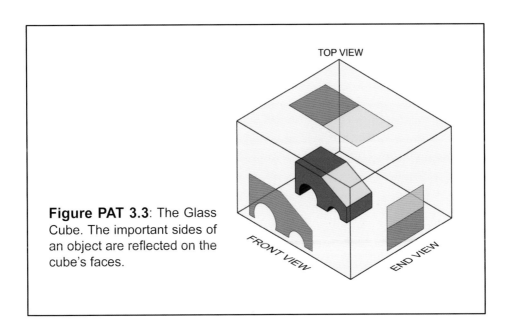

Figure PAT 3.3: The Glass Cube. The important sides of an object are reflected on the cube's faces.

Imagine unfolding the cube so that the three views of the object can now be seen on the same plane.

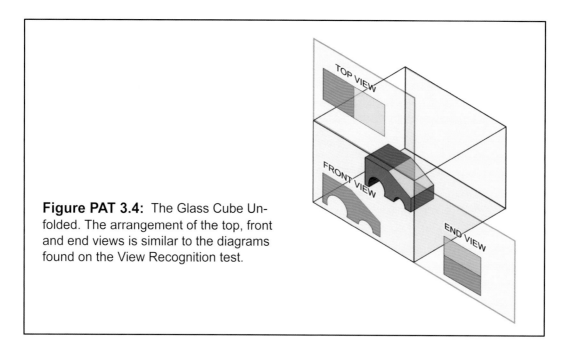

Figure PAT 3.4: The Glass Cube Unfolded. The arrangement of the top, front and end views is similar to the diagrams found on the View Recognition test.

Now that the glass cube is unfolded, the three views should be able to exhibit the following characteristics:

1. The **front view** shows the **width** and **height** dimensions of the object.
2. The **top view** shows the **width** and **depth** dimensions of the object.
3. The **end view** shows the **height** and **depth** dimensions of the object.
4. **Each view** is relatively **aligned to the other views**: the top view parallels vertically with the front view and share the same width dimension, in the same manner that the front view aligns horizontally with the end view and share the same height dimension.

Paying attention to the proportions of the figures from the given views and the answer choices is indeed a logical approach to this test. Oftentimes, options will only vary in the sizes or lengths of an edge or a line. You should thus reinforce this technique with a systematic procedure in interpreting the orthographic representations. We will discuss some of these in the succeeding sections.

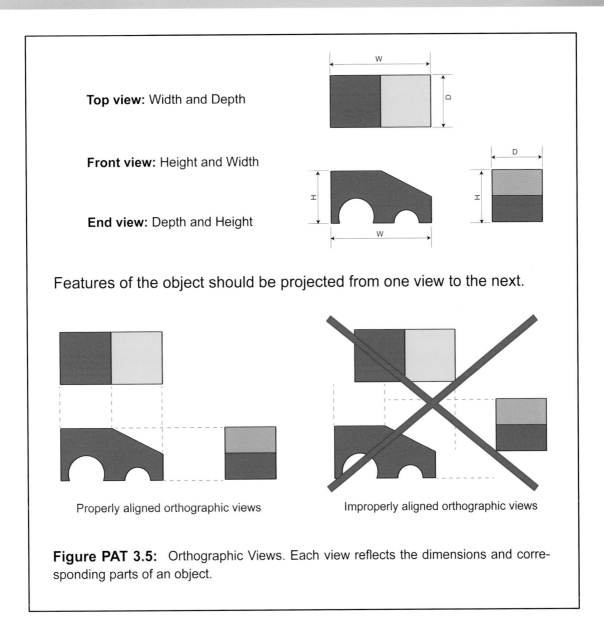

Top view: Width and Depth

Front view: Height and Width

End view: Depth and Height

Features of the object should be projected from one view to the next.

Properly aligned orthographic views

Improperly aligned orthographic views

Figure PAT 3.5: Orthographic Views. Each view reflects the dimensions and corresponding parts of an object.

3.3 How to Find the Missing Views

Identifying one of the orthographic (two-dimensional) views presented in the test necessitates recognizing the shape of the actual three-dimensional object. This skill takes time and regular, structured practice to develop. Nonetheless, one effective method that you can adopt is constructing a projection grid of the two given views in order to determine the form of the third view.

This method requires that you draw construction lines that will function as your guide in establishing the features of the missing view. All lines from the intersections and corners of the two views must be extended on the missing spot of the quadrant.

Please note that this method is quite helpful to start building your visual skills for the TFE section. However, this approach may not work on many of the problems. Your end goal should be focused on developing the ability to mentally construct the 3-D image of the object in order to determine the third view.

1. To find the FRONT VIEW

Extend all vertical lines from the top view and all horizontal lines from the end view, including those from the dotted lines, and allow them to cross each other on the front view. Spot the intersections and mark them.

1. All solid and dotted lines and intersections projected downwards should be aligned with any tips, edges and intersections of the object on the front view.

2. All horizontal solid and dotted lines as well as intersections projected from the end view, which may intersect with the vertical lines from the top, can be the significant corners and intersections of the front view.

3. Angled lines viewed from the top may also be a hint for an inclination on the front view.

4. Hidden edges or lines covered by any solid line may no longer be viewed as dotted lines but as a solid line from the front view.

TOP VIEW

?

FRONT VIEW   END VIEW

Figure PAT 3.6

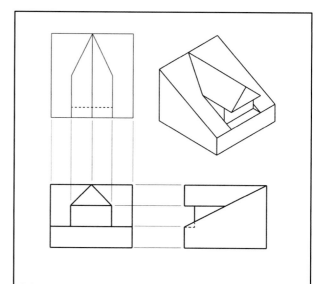

Figure PAT 3.6-A: Sketch the top and side views and make projections as shown.

Keep in mind that the front view, among the three 2D views, shows the most characteristics of an object. Usually, this view contains the least amount of hidden lines.

2. To find the TOP VIEW

In doing the projections for the top view, it is necessary that you mark the main intersections by locating the lines from the front to the end view. For example, mark only the intersection created by the center and outermost lines from the front with that of the end view.

1. Rotate the end view 90 degrees counterclockwise.

2. Vertical lines – both solid and dotted lines – from the front view should be projected upwards. Intersection points should also be extended as vertical lines in the projection.

3. All solid and dotted lines, as well as intersections from the end view should be projected horizontally to the left.

4. The intersections created from these lines should serve as your guide in determining the corners and edges of the top view.

5. Most lines from the inner portion of the end view figure become hidden on the top view. Lines coming from the right area of the end view become the upper portion of the top view.

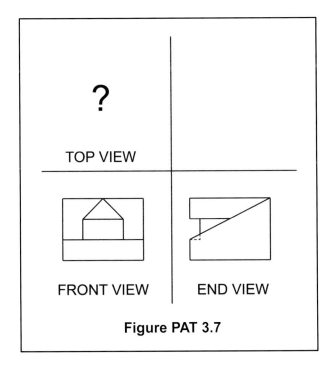

Figure PAT 3.7

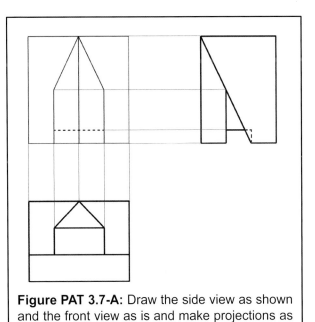

Figure PAT 3.7-A: Draw the side view as shown and the front view as is and make projections as shown.

3. To find the END VIEW

1. Rotate the top view 90 degrees clockwise.

2. The upper part of the top view will now become the right part of the end view.

3. The intersections of the vertical lines from the rotated top view and the horizontal lines from the front view are crucial.

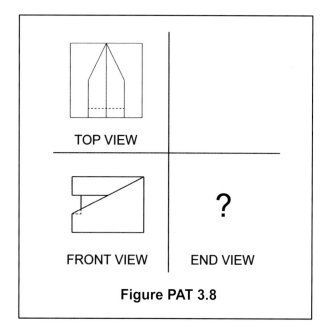

Figure PAT 3.8

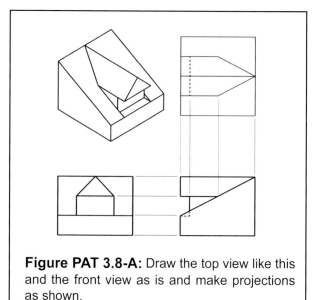

Figure PAT 3.8-A: Draw the top view like this and the front view as is and make projections as shown.

Please note that this method may take time in the beginning. The key is to practice consistently so that you will eventually become comfortable with the various steps and concepts of creating projections. In the meantime, let's try applying this approach to the sample question from Figure 3.1.

Choose the correct END VIEW.

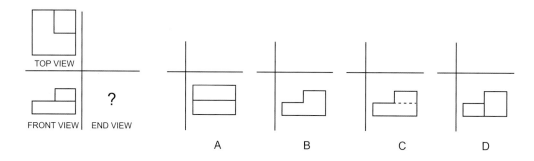

From the given views, the top figure shows that within the square is a smaller square located on the upper right. On the front view, the smaller rectangle, also located at the upper right, is about half the size of the bigger rectangle.

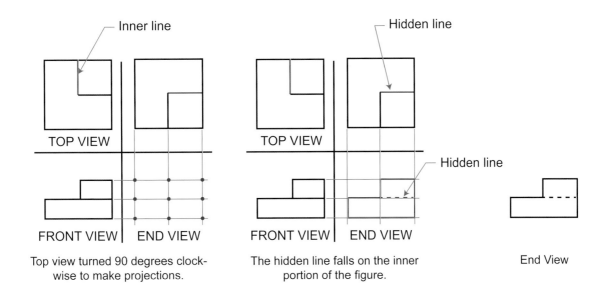

Top view turned 90 degrees clockwise to make projections.

The hidden line falls on the inner portion of the figure.

End View

Given the top and front views, you can start making projections to get the end view. First, turn the top view 90 degrees clockwise. Use construction lines for projections (blue lines are from the top view and red lines are from the front). Take note that all vertical lines on the top view and all horizontal lines on the front view should be projected. The intersections of these lines would be the significant points or corners of the end view.

Carefully eliminate irrelevant intersections by verifying from the front and top views. You should also consider any inner vertical or horizontal lines on the top and front views – these should be hidden from the end view. In this case, it is the green-colored line.

3.3.2 The Hidden Lines

Sometimes, an object will have a component or a feature located at the back, so this becomes invisible from the front view. To indicate the presence of this feature, dotted lines are used in its place.

Hidden lines are one of the most confusing details to visualize in the test. One way to deal with them is to remember that they represent one of three things:

1. the edge view of a hidden surface (see Figure PAT 3.1)

2. an intersection of two surfaces that is behind another surface (see Figure PAT 3.2)

3. the outer edge of a curved surface that is hidden (see Figure PAT 3.6).

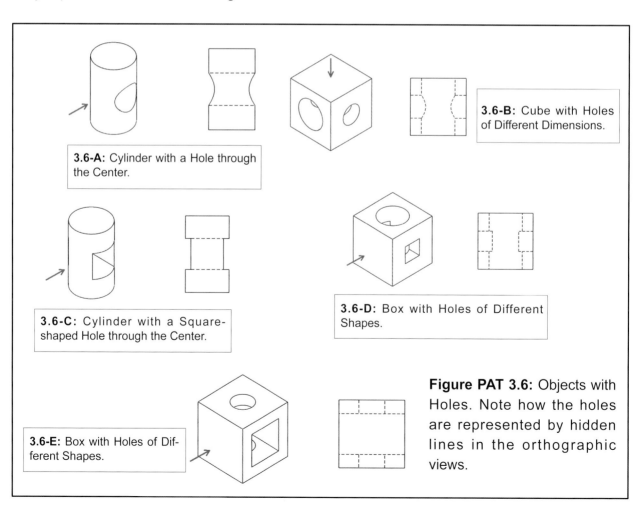

3.6-A: Cylinder with a Hole through the Center.

3.6-B: Cube with Holes of Different Dimensions.

3.6-C: Cylinder with a Square-shaped Hole through the Center.

3.6-D: Box with Holes of Different Shapes.

3.6-E: Box with Holes of Different Shapes.

Figure PAT 3.6: Objects with Holes. Note how the holes are represented by hidden lines in the orthographic views.

3.3.3 Visualizing Three-Dimensional Objects in Two-Dimensional Views

You can also think of the View Recognition test as the opposite of the Apertures test. The former requires you to visualize the three-dimensional form of the given 2D views while the latter compels you to do the opposite.

Both PAT subsections, on the other hand, share the same concepts and principles governing the 3D objects and their corresponding 2D views. Judging the distances of the object's components and the shapes of sloping surfaces are critical sections to review for both tests: their shapes and the placement of their edges tend to vary on certain views.

For example, a circle viewed from the top should have straight edges both from the front and the end views, but retains its rounded shape from the top view. Likewise, a protrusion situated at the back portion of the object will appear on top of the object's surface in the 2D front view (see the FRONT VIEW of the object in Figure PAT 3.1). If you find these details confusing, you should go back and review sections 2.2 to 2.2.3 of Chapter 2.

During the early stage of your preparation for the PAT, take time and try to visualize the views of the 3D object as they are projected into the top, front, and end views. It also helps to mentally map out the top-front-end views of everyday objects whenever possible to get your eyes and mind used to visualizing 3D objects in their 2D views and vice versa.

3.4 Mini Exercises

1. Choose the correct END VIEW.

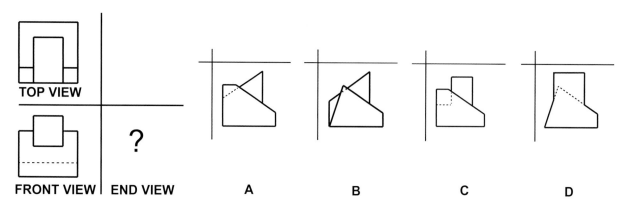

2. Choose the correct FRONT VIEW.

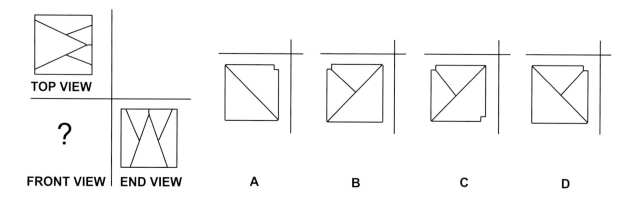

3. Choose the correct FRONT VIEW.

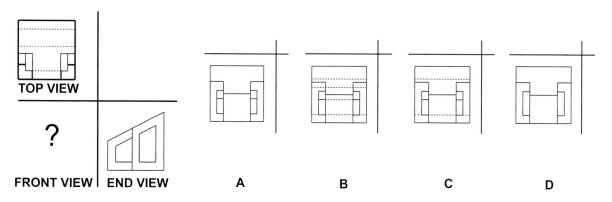

4. Choose the correct FRONT VIEW.

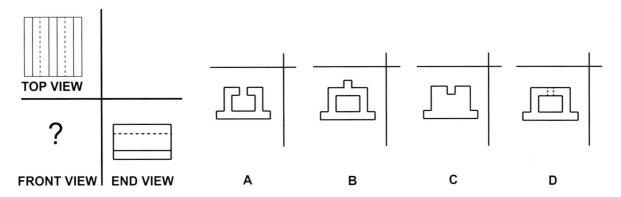

5. Choose the correct TOP VIEW.

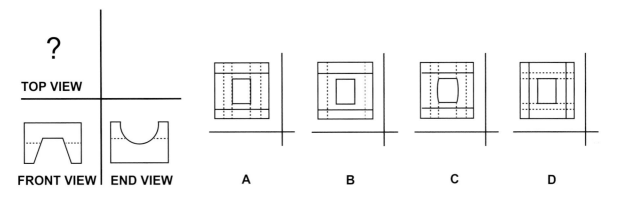

Explanations for the mini exercises can be accessed by clicking Lessons in the top Menu when you are logged into www.dat-prep.com.

GOLD STANDARD WARM-UP EXERCISES

CHAPTER 3: Orthographic Projection

The following questions represent one of the six subsections in the Perceptual Ability Test of the DAT. While this serves as a review of the discussions in this chapter, the level of difficulty of each question closely parallels the actual test.

You have 10 minutes to complete this portion of the DAT Mini Test; the actual test is 60 minutes.

Please time yourself accordingly.

BEGIN ONLY WHEN YOUR TIMER IS READY

1. Choose the correct TOP VIEW.

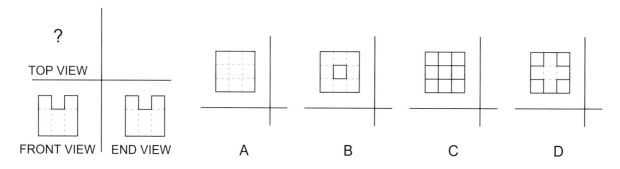

2. Choose the correct END VIEW.

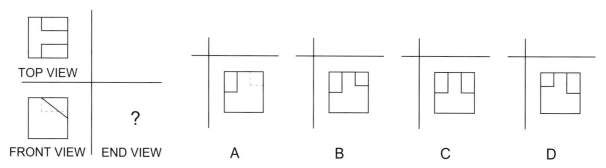

3. Choose the correct FRONT VIEW.

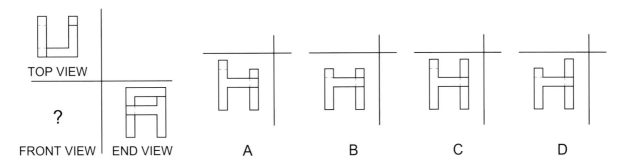

4. Choose the correct END VIEW.

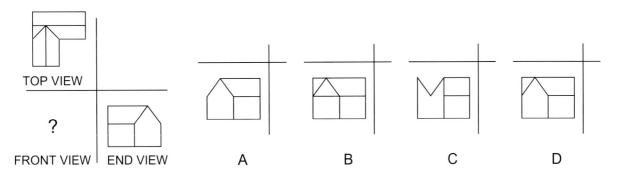

5. Choose the correct FRONT VIEW.

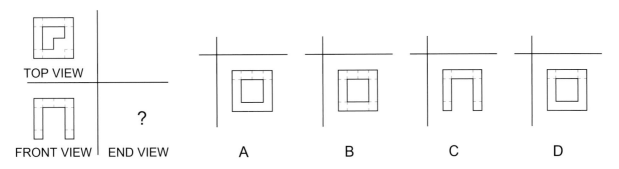

6. Choose the correct END VIEW.

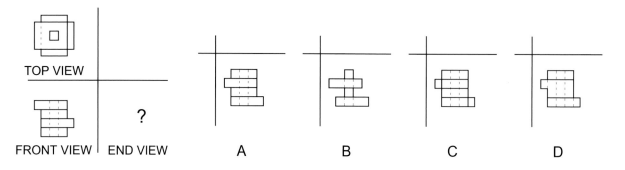

7. Choose the correct TOP VIEW.

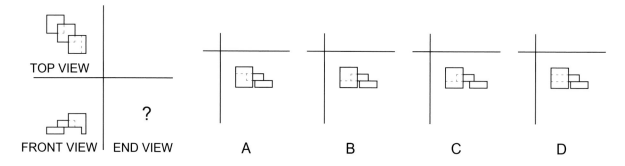

8. Choose the correct END VIEW.

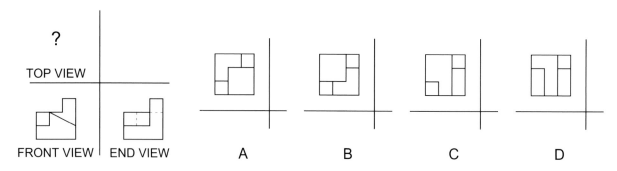

9. Choose the correct END VIEW.

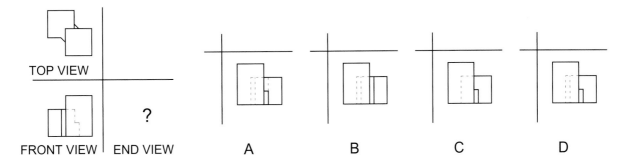

10. Choose the correct FRONT VIEW.

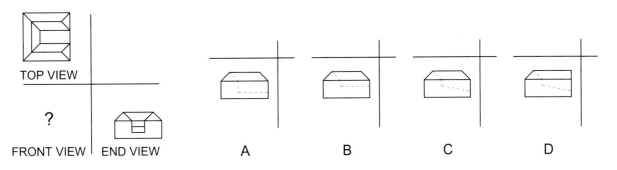

11. Choose the correct TOP VIEW.

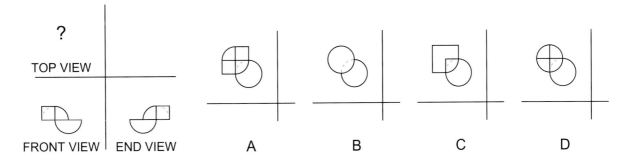

12. Choose the correct TOP VIEW.

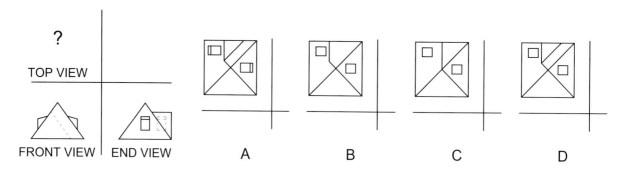

13. Choose the correct END VIEW.

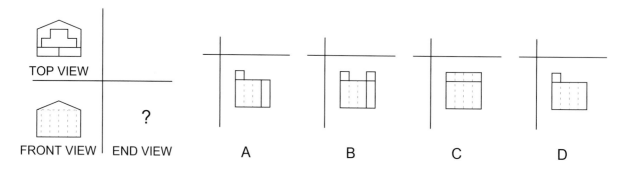

14. Choose the correct END VIEW.

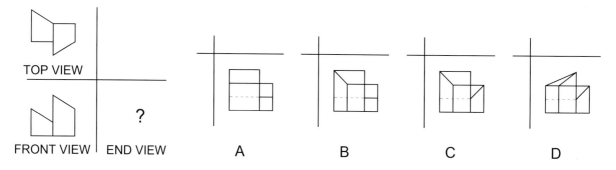

15. Choose the correct TOP VIEW.

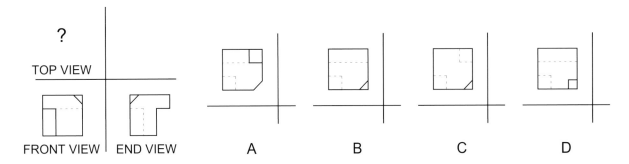

If time remains, you may review your work. If your allotted time is complete, please proceed to the Answer Key.

GS ANSWER KEY

CHAPTER 3

1.	C	9.	D	
2.	B	10.	C	
3.	A	11.	A	
4.	A	12.	D	
5.	D	13.	A	
6.	A	14.	C	
7.	A	15.	B	
8.	B			

* Explanations can be found in the Lessons section at www.dat-prep.com.

Go online to DAT-prep.com for additional chapter review Q&A and forum.

Go online to DAT-prep.com for additional chapter review Q&A and forum.

GOLD NOTES

ANGLE
DISCRIMINATION
Chapter 4

Understand

* Key Strategies for Acute and Obtuse Angles

DAT-Prep.com

Introduction

An angle is the space between two lines that intersect at a common endpoint, called *the vertex*. Angles become smaller when the lines are brought closer to each other and become larger when moved farther away. The Angle Discrimination Section tests your ability to rank the angles of the figures from the smallest to the largest. This section is more commonly referred to as Angle Ranking.

Additional Resources

Free Online Forum

4.1 About the Angle Discrimination Test

Angle Discrimination is the third subsection in the DAT PAT test that examines your visual reasoning and spatial abilities. This test consists of 15 multiple choice questions, which ask examinees to identify the relative sizes of four interior angles from the smallest to the largest. This is the reason why most candidates refer to this PAT subsection as "angle ranking."

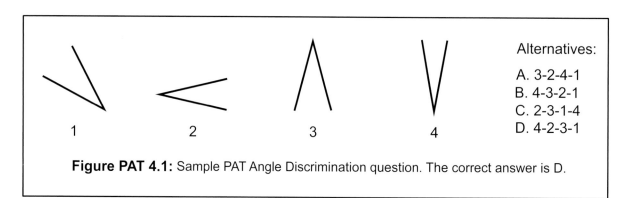

Alternatives:

A. 3-2-4-1
B. 4-3-2-1
C. 2-3-1-4
D. 4-2-3-1

Figure PAT 4.1: Sample PAT Angle Discrimination question. The correct answer is D.

4.2 How to Prepare for this PAT Section

For the purpose of clarity, let us first briefly describe the different parts of an angle.

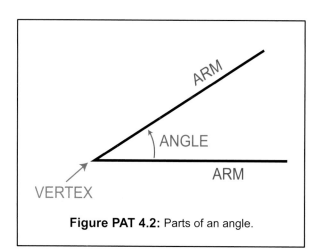

Figure PAT 4.2: Parts of an angle.

The two straight lines of an angle are called the *arms*. The point where these two arms intersect is called the *vertex*. The space between the vertex and the two arms is considered as the *angle*. The angle shown in the diagram represents the interior angle which is the smaller of the two possible angles between 2 arms. Thus the interior angle must always be less than 180°, which would be a straight line. This DAT PAT section is only concerned with interior angles.

There are several kinds of angles, but the most important ones with which you should be familiar in this test are the acute

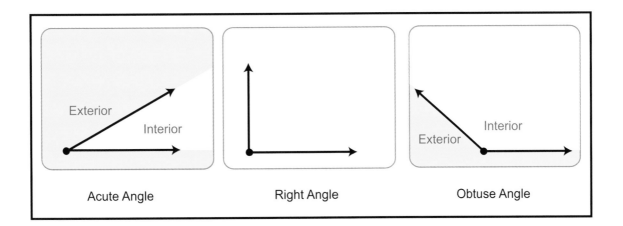

(smaller than 90°) and obtuse (greater than 90° but less than 180°) angles. The key here is to frequently practice looking at the slight differences involving these two types of angles: the "darker" the vertex of an acute angle, the smaller its angle; the nearer an angle to becoming a straight line, the bigger its angle.

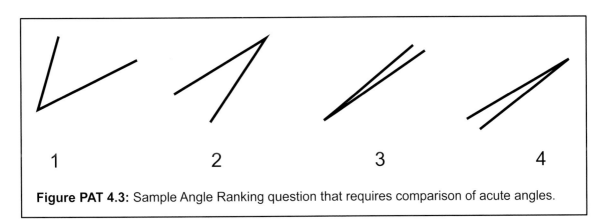

Figure PAT 4.3: Sample Angle Ranking question that requires comparison of acute angles.

In Figure PAT 4.3, angles 3 and 4 are obviously the closest possible choices for the smallest angle. If you examine their vertices, you would notice that angle 3 has a darker vertex than angle 4. This is because when the two arms of an angle are drawn closer to each other, the white space between them lessens, making the vertex look darker. In Angle 4, more white space is visible because the arms are far-ther apart. This makes Angle 3 the smallest among the four angles.

On the other hand, for questions involving obtuse angles, you would want to look for the figure that nearly resembles a straight line to determine the largest angle. The smallest angle would have its two arms closest to each other.

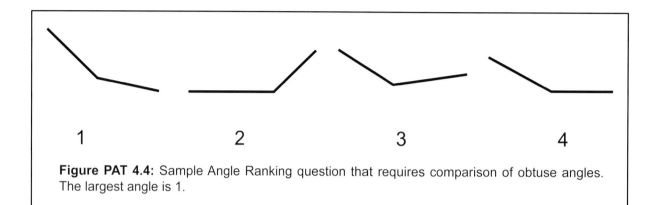

Figure PAT 4.4: Sample Angle Ranking question that requires comparison of obtuse angles. The largest angle is 1.

Of course, if this is your first encounter with angle ranking questions, you might find the initial attempts to be quite difficult – just like any other new endeavor. But like most of the DAT sections, consistent practice (in the book and online at DAT-prep. com) is paramount to your success in this test.

The point of frequently doing these exercises is for you to try as many techniques as you can so that you would finally settle on the one strategy that will not only make you visually keen with angles, but also help you increase your speed in answering the questions. In other words, you need to train your eyes to QUICKLY SPOT the minute differences between at least two closely similar angles.

Now let's discuss specific strategies that you can adopt for this PAT subsection.

4.3 Strategies

1. Process of Elimination

Remember that your main task in this test is to rank the angles from the smallest to the largest for all 15 Angle Discrimination questions. Thus identifying these two extremes should be your first strategy. Often, at least one of the two, either the smallest or the largest, would be easy to identify. This will make eliminating some of the options easier. For example, if the smallest angle is represented in one or two of the answer choices, you can instantly discard the remaining choices. Then check if the largest angle is represented in the answer choices you have considered. You can occasionally determine the correct answer at this point.

Quite often, you will find yourself down to two angles that are difficult to compare. Generally, you need to focus on the intersections (the vertex) of the angles, not on their lines. Likewise, try not to stare at the angles for too long. Doing this will only make all the angles look like they are all of the same size.

In other cases, you may need to use different techniques depending on how the angles are presented in a question.

2. Extend a horizontal line

When comparing obtuse angles, one method that you can temporarily do, in the beginning, is to place your hand or a piece of paper on one of the arms of the angle. Please note though that touching the computer screen during the actual test is prohibited; hence, you should eventually move from this "physical" method to purely visualizations. In any case, the objective is to create a base – a horizontal point of reference – so that you can compare, this time, from the outer angles.

Taking Figure PAT 4.5 as an example, the two obtuse angles might be difficult to compare because they are positioned in different directions. In this instance, (mentally) extending a line on one of the arms tends to make the outer angles clearer and easier to gauge. Angle 1 shows a farther distance from the horizontal line, which indicates that it has a smaller angle than Angle 2.

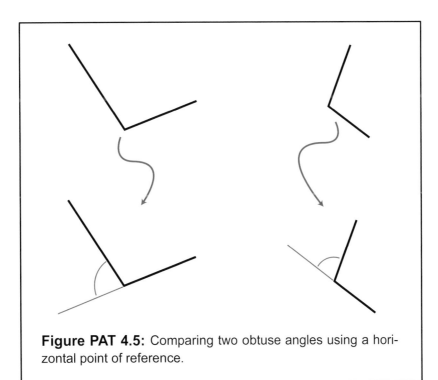

Figure PAT 4.5: Comparing two obtuse angles using a horizontal point of reference.

3. Create an isosceles triangle

Another option is to mentally adjust the image provided to create an isosceles triangle which has two arms that are equal in length. Then, compare the base of these triangles; the longer the base, the bigger the angle. In some questions, it is not necessary to extend any arms because all of the arms of all of the given angles are of the same length. In such cases, creating the base is even simpler.

There are also a number of popular strategies that have either been originated or popularized by former DAT candidates. The following methods are the most well-known up to the date of this publication.

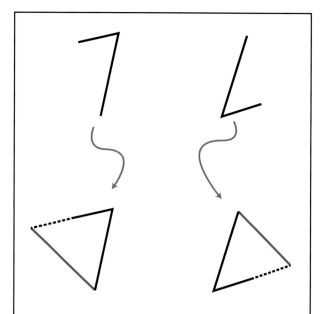

Figure PAT 4.6: Mentally converting similar angles into isosceles triangles can accentuate the differences by focusing on their bases. The smaller base points to the smaller angle which, in this case, is on the right. This technique is reliable if the arms of the triangles are of equal lengths.

4.3.1 Other Useful Techniques

1. The "Hill" Technique

This technique was designed by Justin Orlandini (a graduate of Temple University School of Dentistry), popularly referred to as Orlo on the Student Doctor Network DAT forum (www.studentdoctor.net). It has earned a great number of commendations from candidates who have improved their Angle Ranking scores after using the said technique.

To use this method, you have to visualize one side of the angle as the ground and the other side as a hill. Then imagine you are riding a bicycle you want to safely ride down that hill. For acute angles, you should be looking from the outside of the angle: the safest hill to ride down, which is not as steep, will be the smallest angle. The steepest hill to ride down will be the largest angle.

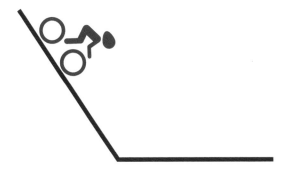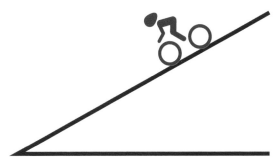

For obtuse angles, you should be looking from the inside of the angle: the safest hill (closest to 180 degrees) to ride down will be the largest angle. The steepest hill to ride down will be the smallest angle.

Let it roll: If you do not like the imagery of riding a bike downhill during an exam (!!), you can imagine a ball rolling down the hill. If it rolls slowest when the angle is acute, then it is smallest, and vice-versa for an obtuse angle.

2. The Laptop Technique

This technique was also designed by Justin Orlandini. It involves visualizing each angle as an open laptop. Select the longer arm as the base of the laptop and the shorter arm as the screen. Imagine that the base of the laptop is flat on the table in front of you. The laptop (angle) that is easiest to close is the smallest angle.

3. The Rapid Eye Technique

This is a technique devised since 2010 by Ross Conner (University of Colorado School of Dental Medicine, Class of 2015). Most candidates recommend this technique when estimating closely related angles. You need to focus on the interior portion of the angle then quickly move your eyes back and forth from one to the other of the two closest angles. Ross Conner has also put up a number of videos on YouTube, discussing the details of this technique.

4. Get Back and Glance

This technique combines 2 observations that some candidates have had: (1) when they back away from the computer screen, they can get a better impression of the problem; and (2) they only need a few seconds to decide which is the biggest and which is the smallest angle – even when choosing between 2 very similar angles. This method relies more on instinct than logical decision-making. The truth is, some students are able to use this skill with little practice and get great scores; whereas, other students need practice and relaxation techniques to tap into this "reflex".

5. Caution

Both the given angles and the options on the PAT can be misleading and can cause faulty reasoning. Beware of different forms of perceptual interferences such as oblique positioning and different lengths of arms of the given angles. These can affect your visual sensibility.

It is essential to understand that the length of an angle's arm is independent of its angular measurement. Once again, constant practice and exposure to various angle ranking problems can greatly enhance your ability to move from one angle to another with sharp eyes. You can take 20-25 minutes every day practicing DAT-style problems. Again, the point is to try to use different techniques and determine which is easier and faster for you to use.

Ideally, you would genuinely attempt each of the strategies during practice. After some experience, you will find a combination of strategies that works best for you.

4.4 Mini Exercises and Explanations

At this point, you would want to apply some of the techniques for yourself on some DAT-style Angle Ranking questions. Before you do so, let us first discuss one sample question before taking on the mini exercises.

Rank the following angles from the smallest to the largest:

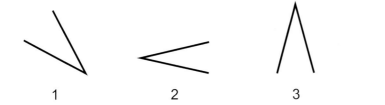

1   2   3   4

Alternatives:

A. 3-2-4-1
B. 4-3-2-1
C. 2-3-1-4
D. 4-2-3-1

The correct answer is **D**.

As discussed earlier, it is usually best to pick the largest angle first and then the smaller one or the reverse. This is because the smallest and largest angles get noticed quickly.

We can see that the largest angle is 1 and the smallest is 4. Now look for the choices that start with 4 and end with 1. Any other options that do not start or end with these can never be the right answer. In our given example, A and C should be excluded from the alternatives.

The next task is to find what the second and third angles are. Some questions on the PAT show obvious differences between angles 2 and 3. Most, however, are

"too close to call." Angles are generally perceived as the hardest section because the angles are so close and difficult to distinguish. This section can be highly instinctual and there is just no magic bullet. Hence do not spend too much time glaring at the angles for an extra 15-30 seconds as this will be even more visually confusing. Since you are dealing with acute angles here, look for the darker vertex – which is 2. The correct answer is thus D.

Though the process of elimination can be very helpful at times, of course there will be challenging questions where the answer choices are designed to confuse you. This is why having experience with different strategies will allow you to pull a specific tool out of the toolbox when you need it most.

4.4.1 Mini Exercises

This section requires you to evaluate the four INTERIOR angles and rank each item from SMALL to LARGE in terms of degrees. From the alternatives, select the one with the correct order.

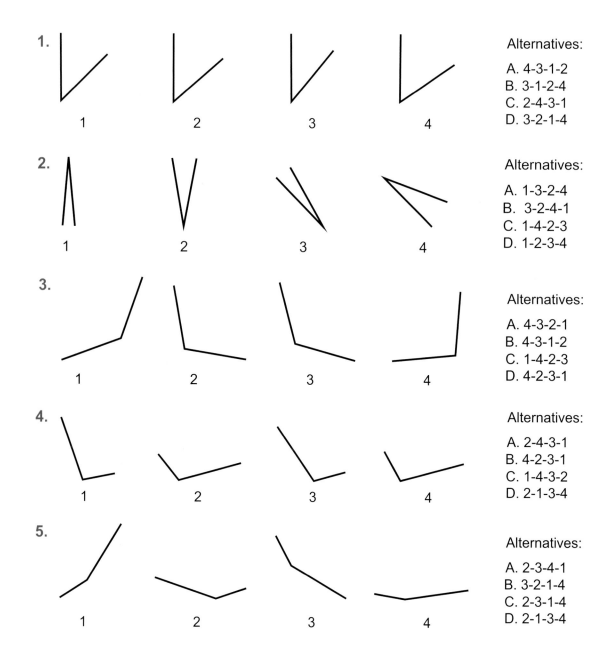

1.

    1   2   3   4

Alternatives:

A. 4-3-1-2
B. 3-1-2-4
C. 2-4-3-1
D. 3-2-1-4

2.

    1   2   3   4

Alternatives:

A. 1-3-2-4
B. 3-2-4-1
C. 1-4-2-3
D. 1-2-3-4

3.

    1   2   3   4

Alternatives:

A. 4-3-2-1
B. 4-3-1-2
C. 1-4-2-3
D. 4-2-3-1

4.

    1   2   3   4

Alternatives:

A. 2-4-3-1
B. 4-2-3-1
C. 1-4-3-2
D. 2-1-3-4

5.

    1   2   3   4

Alternatives:

A. 2-3-4-1
B. 3-2-1-4
C. 2-3-1-4
D. 2-1-3-4

4.4 Mini Exercises and Explanations

1. Answer: B

By focusing on the intersection of the two lines, you will know which angle is smaller than the other. In this item, number 3 seems to be the smallest. So you can readily eliminate options A and C. Next you need to compare angles 1 and 2. Angle 1 is clearly smaller, so the sequence should be 3-1-2-4. The correct answer is B.

2. Answer: A

If all angles on the question were acute such as in this case, you can look for the darkest angle to determine the smallest among the figures. This means that the two lines are so close to one another, making the angle look darker.

In this question, the first angle is the smallest. You can now get rid of choice B. Among the remaining angles, 4 is the biggest so you can discard option C now. If you are still having a hard time determining the smaller angle, compare the openings (you can only do this if the lines of both angles are equal in length). Number 3 is smaller than 2, yielding the sequence 1-3-2-4. Thus the correct answer is A.

3. Answer: D

Angles 2 and 3 are similar in direction; so are 1 and 4. Between 2 and 3, 2 is smaller whereas 4 is smaller than 1. With this information, option C is eradicated from the choices. Next to number 4 should be 2. From here, you can instantly decide that D is the right answer.

4. Answer: C

Similar to question 3, compare first the similarly positioned angles. Between 2 and 4, 4 is smaller, and then 1 is smaller than 3. Now compare 1 and 4 since they are the smaller angles. The angle in number 1 is smaller than 4. Next, angle 4 is smaller than angle 3. Therefore, the sequence should be 1-4-3-2, which is C.

5. Answer: C

With angles that are all obtuse, finding the largest angle first would be the easiest to do. You should be looking for the angle which is closest to a straight line. In this item, angle 4 is the biggest. You can then narrow down your choices to B, C and D, which have 4 as the biggest angle. Now compare 2 and 3 since all of the remaining choices start with these two. Notice that number 2 is more bent than 3. Finally, between 1 and 3, angle 3 is smaller. Hence, the correct sequence is 2-3-1-4, which is choice C.

GOLD STANDARD WARM-UP EXERCISES
CHAPTER 4: Angle Discrimination

The following questions represent one of the six subsections in the Perceptual Ability Test of the DAT. While this serves as a review of the discussions in this chapter, the level of difficulty of each question closely parallels the actual test.

You have 10 minutes to complete this portion of the DAT Mini Test; the actual test is 60 minutes.

Please time yourself accordingly.

BEGIN ONLY WHEN YOUR TIMER IS READY

1.

1   2   3   4

Alternatives:

A. 4-2-3-1
B. 1-3-2-4
C. 2-1-3-4
D. 4-2-1-3

2.

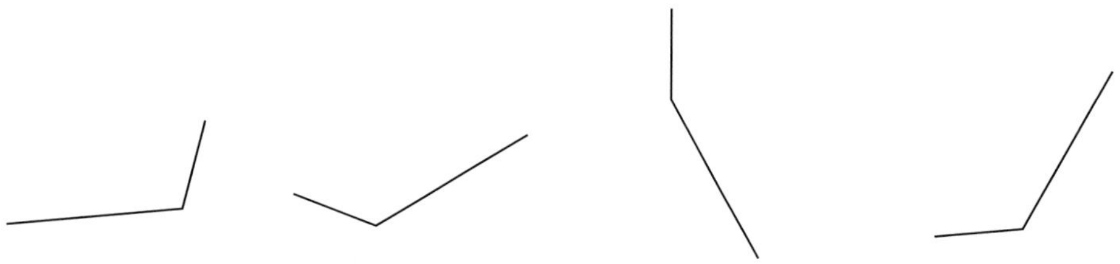

1   2   3   4

Alternatives:

A. 1-4-2-3
B. 3-4-2-1
C. 2-4-1-3
D. 4-1-3-2

3.

1   2   3   4

Alternatives:

A. 3-1-4-2
B. 2-1-4-3
C. 1-4-3-2
D. 4-2-3-1

4.

1   2   3   4

Alternatives:

A. 3-2-1-4
B. 2-3-1-4
C. 2-4-3-1
D. 3-1-4-2

5.

1   2   3   4

Alternatives:

A. 4-3-1-2
B. 1-2-3-4
C. 2-1-4-3
D. 3-1-2-4

6.

1   2   3   4

Alternatives:

A. 3-4-2-1
B. 2-4-1-3
C. 1-4-3-2
D. 4-3-2-1

7.

1   2   3   4

Alternatives:

A. 3-1-4-2
B. 4-1-3-2
C. 3-2-1-4
D. 1-4-3-2

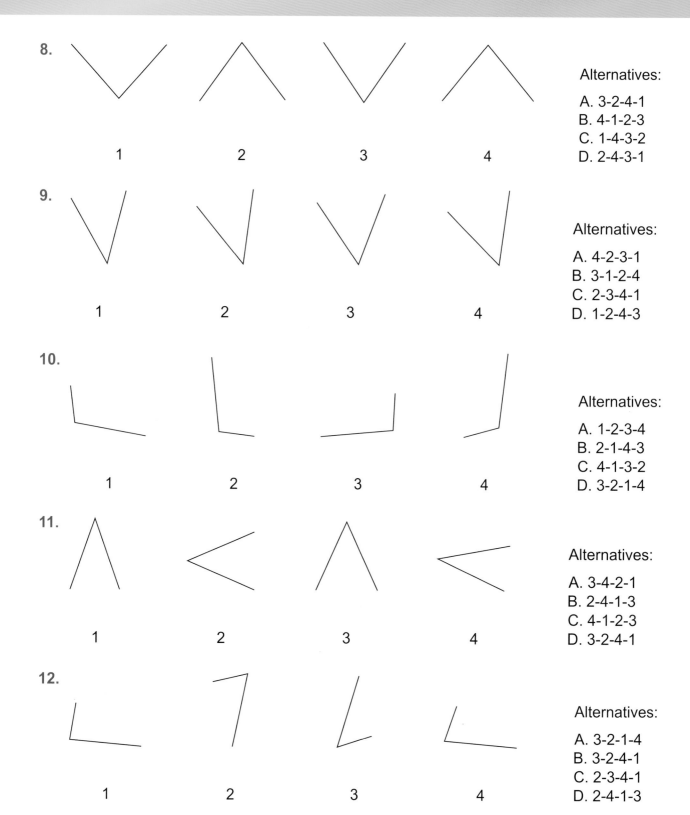

8.

1   2   3   4

Alternatives:

A. 3-2-4-1
B. 4-1-2-3
C. 1-4-3-2
D. 2-4-3-1

9.

1   2   3   4

Alternatives:

A. 4-2-3-1
B. 3-1-2-4
C. 2-3-4-1
D. 1-2-4-3

10.

1   2   3   4

Alternatives:

A. 1-2-3-4
B. 2-1-4-3
C. 4-1-3-2
D. 3-2-1-4

11.

1   2   3   4

Alternatives:

A. 3-4-2-1
B. 2-4-1-3
C. 4-1-2-3
D. 3-2-4-1

12.

1   2   3   4

Alternatives:

A. 3-2-1-4
B. 3-2-4-1
C. 2-3-4-1
D. 2-4-1-3

13.

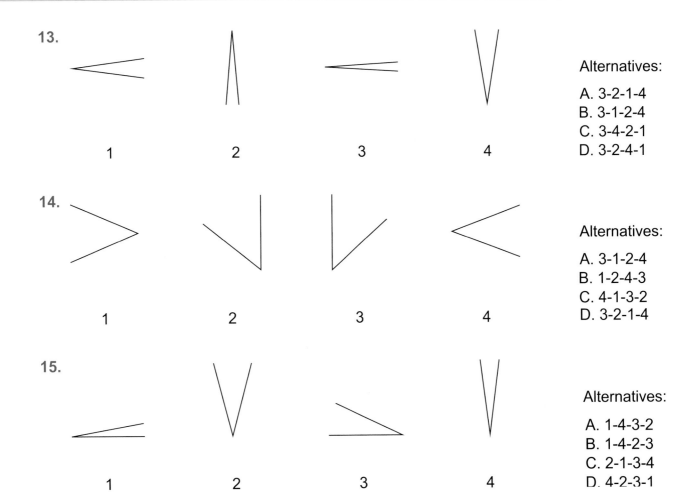

1 2 3 4

Alternatives:

A. 3-2-1-4
B. 3-1-2-4
C. 3-4-2-1
D. 3-2-4-1

14.

1 2 3 4

Alternatives:

A. 3-1-2-4
B. 1-2-4-3
C. 4-1-3-2
D. 3-2-1-4

15.

1 2 3 4

Alternatives:

A. 1-4-3-2
B. 1-4-2-3
C. 2-1-3-4
D. 4-2-3-1

If time remains, you may review your work. If your allotted time is complete, please proceed to the Answer Key.

GS ANSWER KEY

CHAPTER 4

1.	D		9.	D
2.	A		10.	D
3.	B		11.	C
4.	C		12.	B
5.	D		13.	A
6.	C		14.	C
7.	B		15.	A
8.	A			

* Explanations can be found in the Lessons section at www.dat-prep.com.

Go online to DAT-prep.com for additional chapter review Q&A and forum.

Go online to DAT-prep.com for additional chapter review Q&A and forum.

GOLD NOTES

♣ PAPER FOLDING
Chapter 5

Memorize	Understand	
The Hole Sequences in the Paper Folding Quadrants	* Folding Patterns * Linear and Diagonal Folds * Half Hole-punch	

DAT-Prep.com

Introduction ▐▐██

A folded paper that is punched with a hole in it will create a pattern of more than one hole when unfolded. The Paper Folding Section, also known as the Hole Punching Section, entails considering a square sheet of paper on a flat surface; observing how it is folded and by how many times; looking at the spot where a hole is punched; and then, visualizing the resulting pattern of the holes once the paper is fully spread. This section essentially examines your ability to foresee where the holes end up in the paper.

Additional Resources

Free Online Forum

5.1 About the Paper Folding Test

The Paper Folding test is commonly referred to as the "hole punching" section. It primarily measures your ability to mentally manipulate three-dimensional diagrams.

Similar to the other PAT subsections, this test includes 15 multiple-choice questions. Each item presents a pattern of a square piece of paper being folded and eventually hole-punched in specific places. You will need to mentally unfold the paper in order to determine the answer choice with the correct placement of holes.

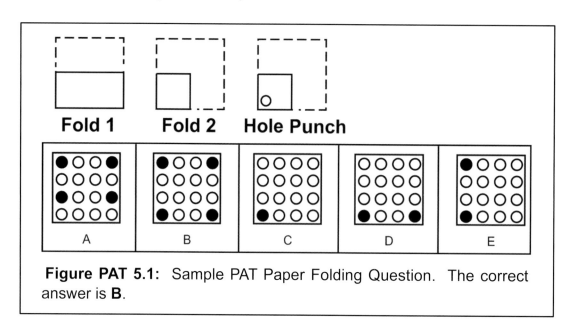

Figure PAT 5.1: Sample PAT Paper Folding Question. The correct answer is **B**.

Basic in your review for this PAT subsection is to understand how a paper is folded. In each question, the sequence of the folding pattern is shown similar to Figure PAT 5.2.

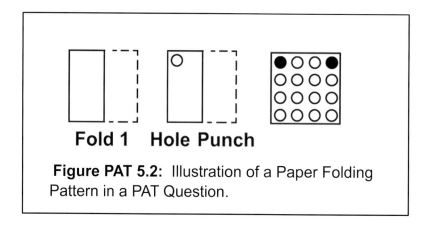

Figure PAT 5.2: Illustration of a Paper Folding Pattern in a PAT Question.

The solid outline on each square represents the position of the folded paper while the broken lines indicate the portion of the paper before it was folded. It is important to note that the paper is neither turned nor twisted after each fold. Now let's look at this procedure from an isometric view.

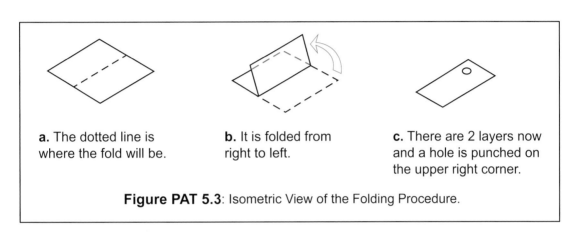

a. The dotted line is where the fold will be.

b. It is folded from right to left.

c. There are 2 layers now and a hole is punched on the upper right corner.

Figure PAT 5.3: Isometric View of the Folding Procedure.

Each question will then require you to identify the resulting pattern of the punched hole or holes from among five options. The most common method in answering these questions is to work the folding procedure backwards, starting with the paper with a hole already punched through it. From there, you would unfold the figure in the reverse sequence. For each step, mentally locate the portion of the paper where the hole or holes should now take their places.

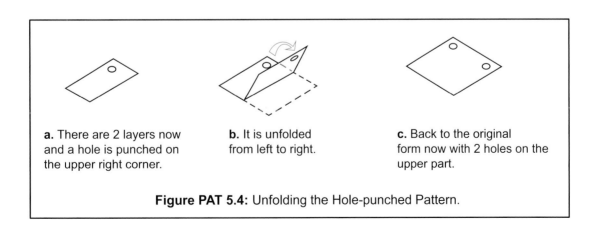

a. There are 2 layers now and a hole is punched on the upper right corner.

b. It is unfolded from left to right.

c. Back to the original form now with 2 holes on the upper part.

Figure PAT 5.4: Unfolding the Hole-punched Pattern.

Besides knowing the paper folding procedure in this test, understanding the patterns involved in the various questions is also important.

5.2 Understanding the Paper Folding Pattern

The Paper Folding test is essentially about patterns and symmetry. The fundamental premise is that in every piece of square paper given in the questions, there are potentially 16 holes that can be punched. These holes are evenly distributed by four in four smaller squares or quadrants (see Figure PAT 5.5). From this arrangement, we can assign a sequence number for each hole that describes its specific location within the quadrants.

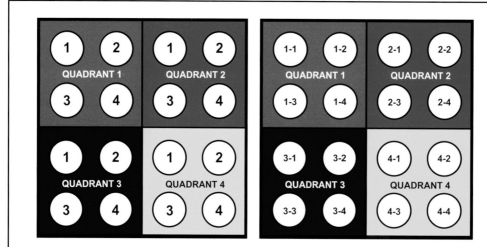

Figure PAT 5.5: Gold Standard Paper Folding Quadrants and the Sequence of Holes.

The first numeral in our sequence number represents the quadrant where the hole belongs. The second numeral is the location of the hole within the quadrant. Hence they are organized as follows:

Quadrant 1	Quadrant 2	Quadrant 3	Quadrant 4
1-1: Hole Number 1 of Quadrant 1	2-1: Hole Number 1 of Quadrant 2	3-1: Hole Number 1 of Quadrant 3	4-1: Hole Number 1 of Quadrant 4
1-2: Hole Number 2 of Quadrant 1	2-2: Hole Number 2 of Quadrant 2	3-2: Hole Number 2 of Quadrant 3	4-2: Hole Number 2 of Quadrant 4
1-3: Hole Number 3 of Quadrant 1	2-3: Hole Number 3 of Quadrant 2	3-3: Hole Number 3 of Quadrant 3	4-3: Hole Number 3 of Quadrant 4
1-4: Hole Number 4 of Quadrant 1	2-4: Hole Number 4 of Quadrant 2	3-4: Hole Number 4 of Quadrant 3	4-4: Hole Number 4 of Quadrant 4

Formalizing the order of the holes like this eventually makes visualizing the different paper folding patterns easier and more precise. Now that we have established a basic sequence of the holes, we can now focus on the folding action itself.

5.2.1 Folding Patterns

While a piece of paper can be folded in numerous possible ways, these can actually be classified in just two general folding systems: the linear and the diagonal.

1. The Linear Fold

A linear manner of folding can be horizontal or vertical. In any of these procedures, the sequence of holes in each quadrant remains intact. This means that any of the 16 hole-sequences can appear in the resulting hole-punching pattern.

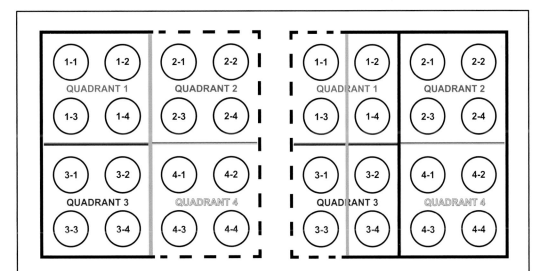

Figure PAT 5.6-A: Examples of Vertical Linear Folds. The tangerine line indicates where the vertical fold is made on the paper.

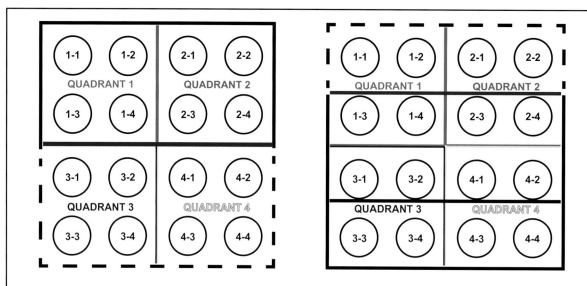

Figure PAT 5.6-B: Two Examples of Horizontal Linear Folds. The purple line indicates the part of the paper where the horizontal fold is made.

2. The Diagonal Fold

In contrast to the linear fold, a diagonal fold causes some hole sequences to be eliminated from certain possible hole-punching patterns UNLESS the punch is made on the fold itself (see discussion in section 5.2.2). A diagonal fold leaning to-wards the upper right edge of the paper makes the hole sequences 2-2, 2-3, 3-2, and 3-3 irrelevant (see Figure 5.7-A). The one leaning towards the upper left edge of the paper discounts hole sequences 1-1,1-4, 4-1, and 4-4 (see Figure 5.7-B).

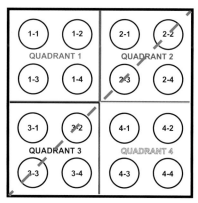

Figure PAT 5.7-A: Diagonal Fold Leaning to the Right.

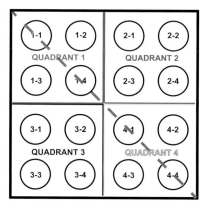

Figure PAT 5.7-B: Diagonal Fold Leaning to the Left.

5.2.2 The Symmetrical Pattern of Hole Punches

Another approach to this section is to think of each fold as a line of symmetry – that is, a hole punched on one side of the fold will be reflected on the other side of the line upon unfolding. In many cases, however, this system may not be as simple as it sounds.

Not all holes are punched on a "full" layer (see Figure PAT 5.2). Some holes are punched on the fold itself, such as demonstrated in Figure PAT 5.8, making the hole look sliced in half. Nevertheless, the line of symmetry will still apply in this kind of punch: a "half-punch" will generate its symmetrical half and yield one whole punched hole (not two) in the process.

There are 2 layers
and 1 hole punched.

Total number
of holes is still 1.

1 hole is punched through 2 layers of paper, but the punch is made on the fold.

Figure PAT 5.8: The Half Hole-Punch. A hole is made on the fold itself.

Moreover, whenever a hole is punched along the fold itself, it immediately highlights the exact location of that hole from the quadrants. For example, in Figure PAT 5.8, the hole-punch is made on Hole 2-3; hence the answer is a hole on that very spot itself. Taking note of this as you try to visualize the resulting pattern of the paper folds will highly aid in distinguishing the correct answer choice in case you find yourself stuck on two closely similar options during the actual test.

Several questions on the DAT PAT also combine the linear and diagonal folds. Keeping track of the overlapping layers of paper in each fold is thus very important. Some holes are punched through several layers while others are punched through a single layer. Practicing with an actual piece of paper in the beginning would help. Eventually though, you will need to adopt a strategy that will wean you off the physical manipulations. We will discuss this strategy in the next section.

5.2.3 The Importance of Counting the Layers

Being able to quickly determine the number of holes produced by the punches helps you narrow down the answer choices in a time-efficient manner. To give you a clearer idea, let's take the following sample problem as a concrete reference.

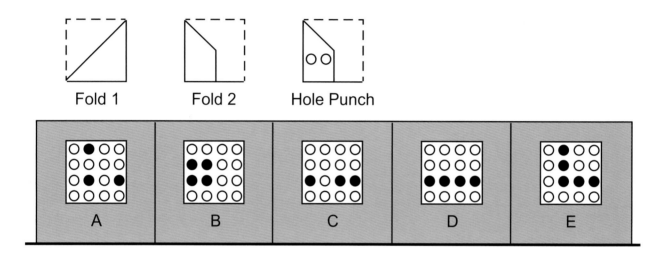

Fold 1   Fold 2   Hole Punch

A   B   C   D   E

The first thing that you should do to answer this question is to count the number of layers from the first fold (Fold 1) to the last (Fold 2). To accurately track the folding sequence, it may help to draw a dotted line, representing the previous layer that is now hidden from view.

Fold 1 makes 2 layers.

2 Layers

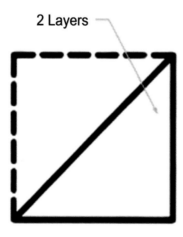

Now because Fold 1 makes a second fold, you might think that Fold 2 will simply yield another 2 layers. BE CAREFUL – this is not as simple as you might think. Take note that after the paper was folded to the left on Fold 2, Quadrant 1 of the paper remains 2 layers while the upper left half of Quadrant 3 is 2 layers and the lower right half, 4 layers.

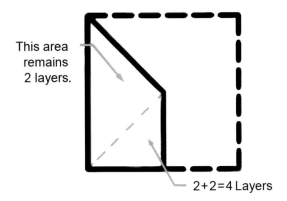

This area remains 2 layers.

2+2=4 Layers

Next, observe that one of the holes is punched on the fold itself.

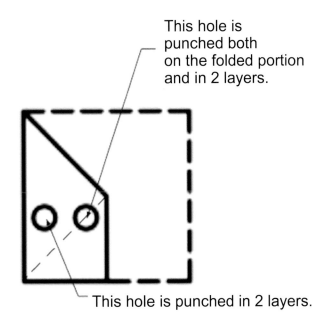

This hole is punched both on the folded portion and in 2 layers.

This hole is punched in 2 layers.

The first hole, in the 3-1 location, is punched on a two-layer area. This means that this hole will be symmetrically reflected on the opposite side of the paper, specifically Hole 4-2. You can also think of this in mathematical terms: multiply the number of holes by the number of layers to get the total number of punched holes produced in a fold. You can now be certain that there should be at least 2 punched holes in the resulting pattern.

The second hole, on the other hand, requires some careful analysis. The hole is punched on the 3-2 location and it also falls on two areas:

1. the 2 layers from Fold 2: 2 layers multiplied by 1 hole makes 2 holes

2. the fold itself from Fold 1, which is now hidden: as discussed in section 5.2.2, a punch made on the hole itself makes only 1 hole

In total, the resulting pattern should have 5 holes. The only option with 5 holes is E, making it the best answer.

Alternatively, you can figure out the resulting hole-punched pattern using the 4-quadrant diagram. The following figures show how the hole-punches on the 3-1 and 3-2 spots create the 5-hole, L-shaped pattern from our sample problem.

Fold 1: Diagram Showing Possible Patterns of Symmetrical Hole-sequences Produced by the Diagonal Fold.

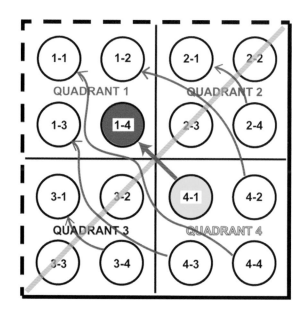

From the figure Fold 1, you will note that the following hole-sequences are expected to possibly create symmetrical patterns:

- 2-4 and 2-1
- 4-2 and 1-2
- 4-1 and 1-4
- 4-4 and 1-1
- 4-3 and 1-3
- 3-4 and 3-1

This time, figure Fold 2 shows the possible symmetrical hole-punched patterns generated by the vertical fold to the left. Take note that a three-point combina-

tion is created on 3 patterns:

- 4-1, 3-2, and 1-4
- 4-3, 3-4, and 1-3
- 4-4, 3-3, and 1-1

This is due to the overlapping layers of the diagonal fold on the first instance and the vertical fold on the second. On the other hand, take note that the following patterns from the diagonal fold on Fold 1 are also possible to show up on Fold 2:

- 2-4 and 2-1
- 4-2 and 1-2

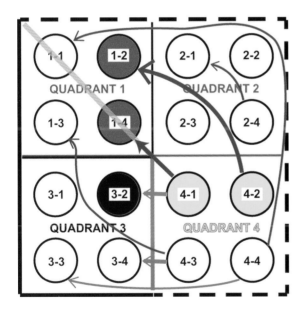

Fold 2: Diagram Showing Possible Patterns of Symmetrical Hole-sequences Produced by the Vertical Fold.

Now you can be certain that hole-sequences 3-2, 4-1, and 1-4 are part of the resulting pattern. On the other hand, take note that Hole 3-1 has already overlapped with Hole 3-4 during the diagonal fold. The vertical fold of the paper going to the left did not move this overlapping spot. Instead, the original 3-1 spot is now replaced by the overlapping holes of 4-2 and 1-2. This results to a final pattern that includes hole-sequences 1-2, 1-4, 3-2, 4-1, and 4-2.

To summarize, these are some of the strategies that you can use with the hole-punching PAT subsection:

1. Counting the layers brought about by the folds:

   • Count the number of layers on every fold
   • Separately count the number of layers for each hole-punch
   • Draw dashed lines to indicate hidden lines and edges

> To determine the number of holes created by a punch, multiply the number of holes by the number of layers where it is punched.

2. If the hole-punch is on the fold itself, immediately note the hole's location from the four quadrants.

3. Note the direction of the fold because this suggests the trend of the holes. Make sure you are familiar with the positions of the holes from the quadrants.

> Remember that the hole-punches follow a symmetrical pattern. Make sure to pay attention to the retained layer of the punched holes as well as the mirror locations of the hole-sequences.

At this point, you might find the concepts and strategies that we have discussed here to be either confusing or difficult to visualize. The trick is to do as many exercises as possible. Your goal in the beginning is not to ace each and every question but to understand what makes your answers incorrect. In the process, you would hopefully find the approach that works best for you.

If you need further help in visualizing the different folds, we have prepared a series of videos at www.dat-prep.com, which you can access when you register as a Gold Standard DAT PAT book owner.

5.4 Mini Exercises

Choose the correct pattern that results from the following folding sequences:

1.

Fold 1   Fold 2   Hole Punch

A   B   C   D   E

2.

Fold 1   Fold 2   Hole Punch

A   B   C   D   E

3.

Fold 1   Fold 2   Fold 3   Hole Punch

A   B   C   D   E

4.

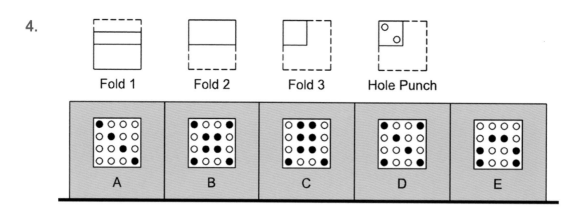

Fold 1   Fold 2   Fold 3   Hole Punch

A   B   C   D   E

5.4.1 Answer Key and Explanations

1. Answer: E

Closely follow the folding of the paper, especially the number of layers on each fold. Fold 1 creates 2 layers. At this point, take note also that the diagonal fold is made along the lines of holes 2-1 and 2-4.

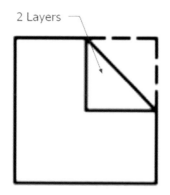

2 Layers

Fold 2 generates 3 areas, each with a differing number of layers. The upper left half of Quadrant 1 is 1 layer, its lower

right half is 3 layers, and the whole area of Quadrant 3 is 2 layers. The hole-punch was made on the upper right spot of Quadrant 1 (the 1-2 location), so we will not worry about Quadrant 3 from here on.

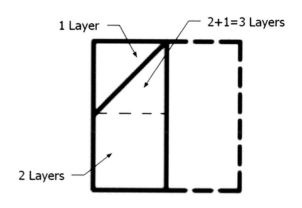

1 Layer — 2+1=3 Layers

2 Layers

Two folds are made but only one hole is punched on the entire paper, and it is on a folded area. Remember that when a hole is punched on a folded portion, it will create just 1 hole.

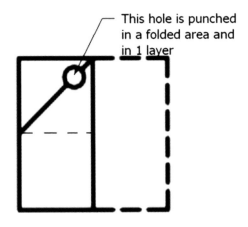

This hole is punched in a folded area and in 1 layer

3 layers (on half of the 1-2 location) multiplied by a half-hole is 1.5; add, 1 layer (on the other half of the 1-2 location) multiplied a half hole is .5. There should be a total of 2 punched holes. You can easily delete option D.

Next, take note that we earlier identified the Fold 1 to have been made on the line that includes holes 2-1 and 2-4. This time, notice that the hole was punched on the 2-1 spot (only in reverse since the paper was folded going to the left on Fold 2). If you unfold the paper, the hole on the folded part is located at the upper left of Quadrant 2, which is hole 2-1. This spot is symmetrical to the hole 1-2 of Quadrant 1. Therefore, the correct answer is E.

2. Answer: B

In this question, sketching the hidden edges of the folds would greatly help in determining the number of layers. Plot the 4 quadrants with their corresponding hole-sequences if you have to.

Carefully observe the number of layers where each hole is punched. The hole-punch on the 1-4 spot has 3 layers while the bottom hole (on the 3-1 spot) is punched in 2 layers. Using the layer-counting strategy, the following formula would prove that the total number of holes in the resulting pattern should be 5:

3 layers × 1 hole = 3
2 layers × 1 hole = 2
3 + 2 = 5 holes

Only option B has 5 holes, so it is the correct answer.

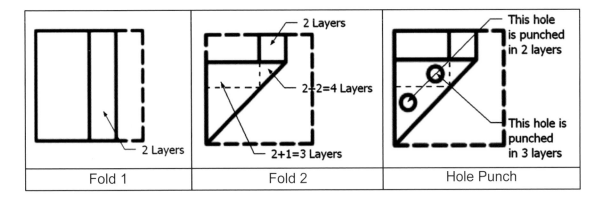

| Fold 1 | Fold 2 | Hole Punch |

3. Answer: A

Your knowledge of the hole-sequences in the quadrants will be highly useful in this question. Drawing dashed lines will also aid you in knowing the precise number of layers where the holes are punched.

Take note that the paper is folded three times. First look at the upper hole (on the 3-2 spot) and trace back the number of layers on this hole-punch from Fold 1 (2

layers) to Fold 2 (1 layer added) to Fold 3 (2 layers added). Hole-punch on the 3-2 spot is therefore 5-layered.

Now trace back the layers on the lower hole (on the 3-3 spot) from Fold 1 (none) to Fold 2 (1 layer) to Fold 3 (2 layers added). This hole-punch has 3 layers. You should then be looking for a folding pattern with 8 holes. Easily, you would know that the correct answer is A.

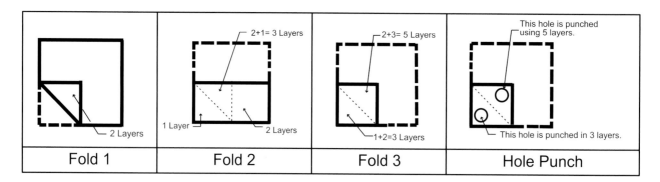

4. Answer: C

In answering this question, it is important to remember the direction of the folding. This way, you would not get confused in counting the number of layers in each area.

Similar to question 3, the paper is folded three times. First, determine the number of layers on the upper hole (on the 1-1 spot): Fold 1 (none), Fold 2 (1 layer), Fold 3 (1 layer added). This hole-punch has 2 layers.

The lower hole (on the 1-4 spot) has 2 layers on Fold 1, 1 layer added on Fold 2, and 3 layers added on Fold 3. Thus the lower hole-punch has 6 layers. The pattern that we will be looking for should have a total of 8 holes. This narrows down your answer choices to B and C.

Now let's go back to the upper hole-punch and evaluate the symmetrical patterns of the holes. (It would be good to draw a diagram of the 4 quadrants here.)

Take note that because the paper is already folded on Fold 1, Holes 1-1 and 1-2, 2-1 and 2-2 are instantly eliminated from the pattern of the upper hole-punch ONLY. You will note later that Holes 1-2 and 2-1 will still show up for the lower hole-punch.

In the meantime, you can only start on Fold 2: the hole-sequence that lands on this spot is 3-3. On Fold 3, Hole 4-4 joins the layer.

Next, let's evaluate the lower hole-punch. On Fold 1, the symmetrical Holes 1-2 and 1-4 make up the 2 layers. On Fold 2, Hole 3-2 goes with the third layer. On Fold 3, 3 symmetrical holes - Holes 2-1, 2-3, and 4-1- should be included.

The correct pattern should include Holes 1-2, 1-4, 2-1, 2-3, 3-2, 3-3, 4-1 and 4-4. The right answer is C.

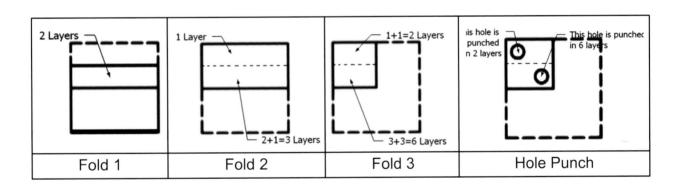

| Fold 1 | Fold 2 | Fold 3 | Hole Punch |

GOLD STANDARD WARM-UP EXERCISES

CHAPTER 5: Paper Folding

The following questions represent one of the six subsections in the Perceptual Ability Test of the DAT. While this serves as a review of the discussions in this chapter, the level of difficulty of each question closely parallels the actual test.

You have 10 minutes to complete this portion of the DAT Mini Test; the actual test is 60 minutes.

Please time yourself accordingly.

BEGIN ONLY WHEN YOUR TIMER IS READY

1.

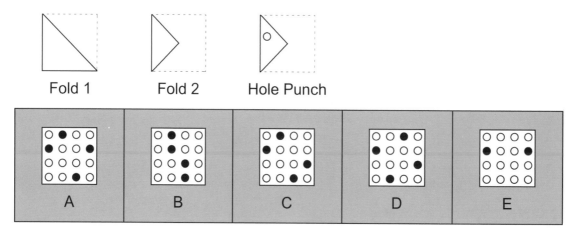

Fold 1   Fold 2   Hole Punch

A   B   C   D   E

2.

Fold 1   Fold 2   Hole Punch

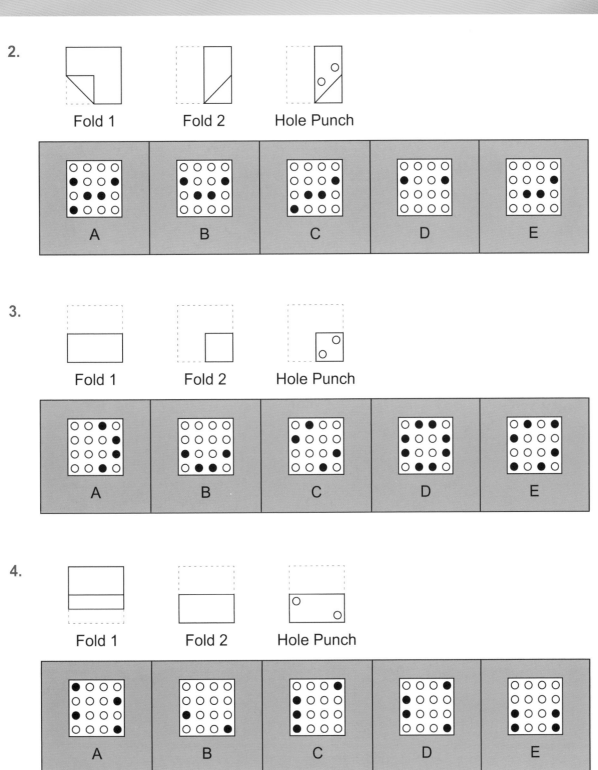

A	B	C	D	E

3.

Fold 1   Fold 2   Hole Punch

A	B	C	D	E

4.

Fold 1   Fold 2   Hole Punch

A	B	C	D	E

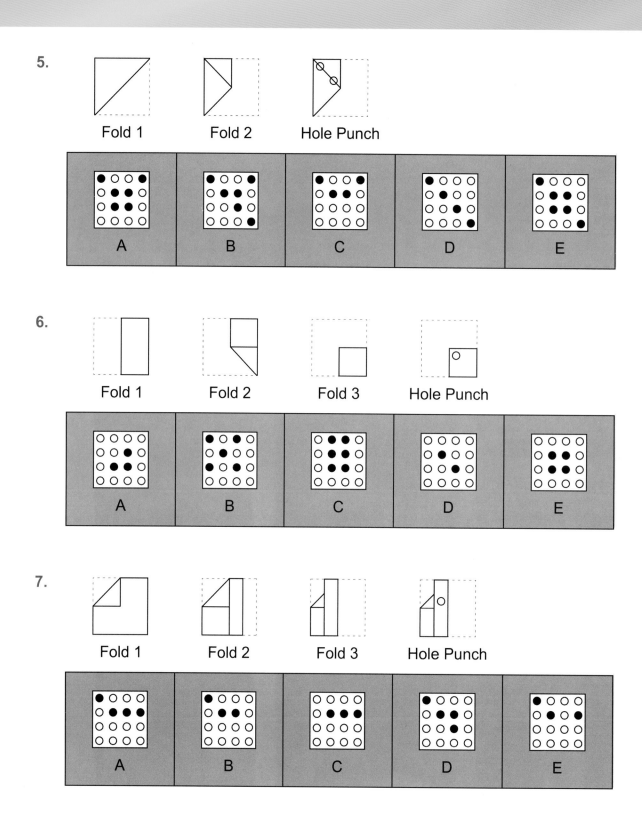

8.

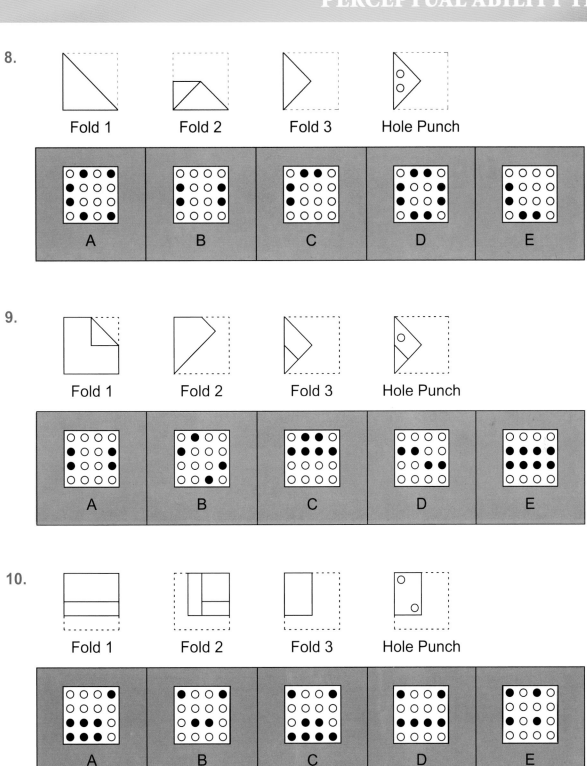

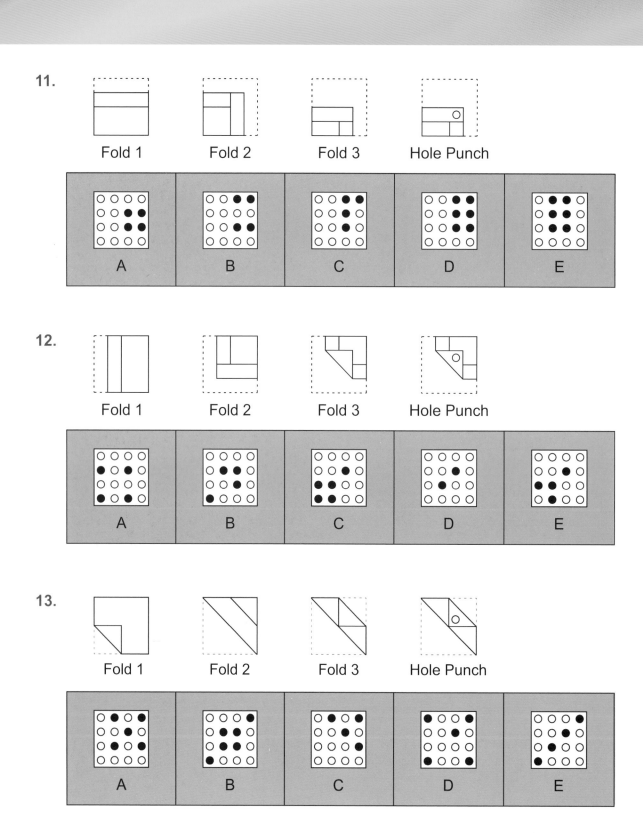

14.

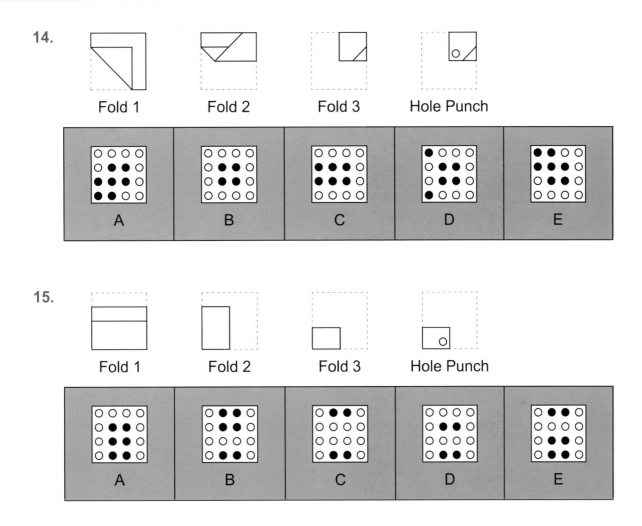

15.

GS ANSWER KEY

CHAPTER 5

1.	C	9.	B
2.	A	10.	A
3.	D	11.	D
4.	C	12.	C
5.	B	13.	E
6.	E	14.	A
7.	A	15.	B
8.	D		

* Explanations can be found in the Lessons section at www.dat-prep.com.

Go online to DAT-prep.com for additional chapter review Q&A and forum.

Go online to DAT-prep.com for additional chapter review Q&A and forum.

GOLD NOTES

♣ CUBE COUNTING
Chapter 6

Memorize	Understand	
* The Gold Standard Cube Counting Formula	* Three Assumptions of the Cube Formations * Examples of Cubes with 1 to 5 Exposed Sides	

DAT-Prep.com

Introduction ▮▮▮▮

A cube is a three-dimensional object with six square faces. Cube counting involves assessing three-dimensional cubes of the same size, stacked in a certain formation, and thereafter, painted on all sides except the base, which rests on a surface.

When cubes are piled over or behind another, some may become invisible behind or under the other cubes. Nonetheless, you should include the painted surfaces of these hidden cubes when counting. This section obviously challenges your thorough attention to details.

Additional Resources

Free Online Forum

6.1 About Cube Counting

The fifth subsection of the PAT consists of 15 multiple-choice questions that involve cube-counting. Formations of stacked cubes are presented, followed by two to four questions that ask you to identify the total count of cubes, which have a particular number of sides painted.

In Figure 1, how many cubes have two of their exposed sides painted?

A. 1 cube
B. 2 cubes
C. 3 cubes
D. 4 cubes
E. 5 cubes

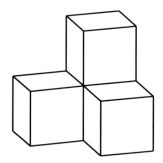

Figure PAT 6.1: Simplistic Sample Figure and Cube Counting Question in the PAT. The correct answer is **A**.

You are to imagine that each figure in the test is constructed by bonding identical cubes together. Thereafter, the cubes are painted on all of their exposed surfaces, excluding the bases. The number of painted sides per cube can range from zero to five.

6.2 Understanding the Cube Formations

Most candidates find this PAT subsection to be relatively easy because the questions merely involve simple counting and a keen eye for details. Nevertheless, you have to keep in mind that some cubes may be "invisible" – that is, they are piled either behind or under other cubes. Essentially, there are three assumptions of cube formations:

1. A cube that serves as a base supporting another cube on top of it may be hidden from view if there are four other cubes attached to it. This type of cube is usually found "inside" the stacks. At other times, it is located at the back of the pile.

2. The stack of cubes is assumed to be continuous where there are no gaps in between.

3. There are no floating cubes.

6.3 Cube Counting Strategies

It is important to note that for every model given in this test, the corresponding set of questions follows a chronological sequence that starts by asking for the smallest number to the most number of cubes with their X number of sides exposed. Continuing from our sample question in Figure PAT 6.1, these are the complete set of questions pertaining to the figure:

1. In Figure 1, how many cubes have two of their exposed sides painted?

   A. 1 cube
   B. 2 cubes
   C. 3 cubes
   D. 4 cubes
   E. 5 cubes

2. In Figure 1, how many cubes have four of their exposed sides painted?

   A. 1 cube
   B. 2 cubes
   C. 3 cubes
   D. 4 cubes
   E. 5 cubes

3. In Figure 1, how many cubes have five of their exposed sides painted?

   A. 1 cube
   B. 2 cubes
   C. 3 cubes
   D. 4 cubes
   E. 5 cubes

This means that when evaluating the cube formations, beginning with the inner portion and the bottom of the figure would be quite logical since these are the areas where you would find most of the cubes with only 1 exposed side painted.

Visualize the hidden cubes and determine how many other cubes connect to it. Focus on the number of cubes attached rather than the cube itself. Using the dry erase board provided in the test center, sketch the figure and mark the cubes with the number of exposed sides, which you have already identified. You can also designate numbers on cubes from the bottom front to the upper rear cubes, depending on your preference to avoid confusion.

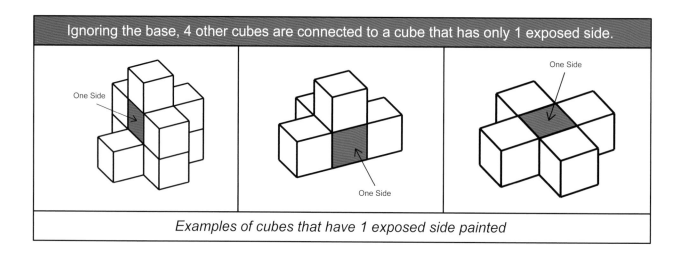

Ignoring the base, 4 other cubes are connected to a cube that has only 1 exposed side.

One Side

One Side

One Side

Examples of cubes that have 1 exposed side painted

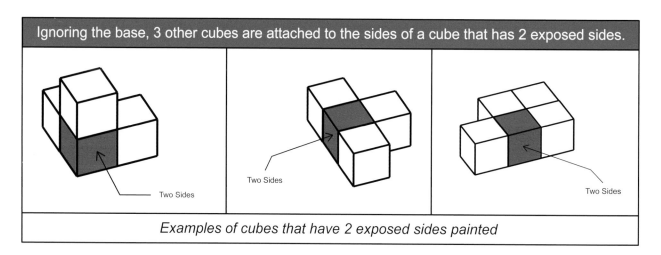

Ignoring the base, 3 other cubes are attached to the sides of a cube that has 2 exposed sides.

Two Sides

Two Sides

Two Sides

Examples of cubes that have 2 exposed sides painted

Ignoring the base, 2 other cubes are connected to the sides of a cube that has 3 exposed sides.

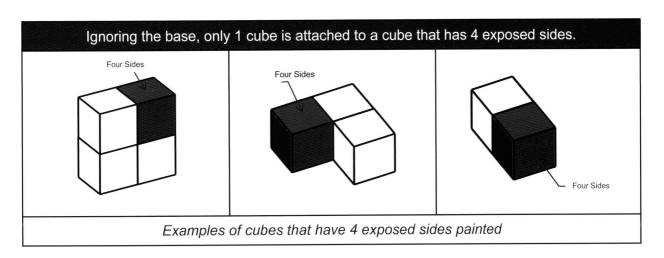

Three Sides

Three Sides

Three Sides

Examples of cubes that have 3 exposed sides painted

Ignoring the base, only 1 cube is attached to a cube that has 4 exposed sides.

Four Sides

Four Sides

Four Sides

Examples of cubes that have 4 exposed sides painted

A cube that has 5 of its exposed sides painted should be found on top without any cube connected to it except the one acting as its base.

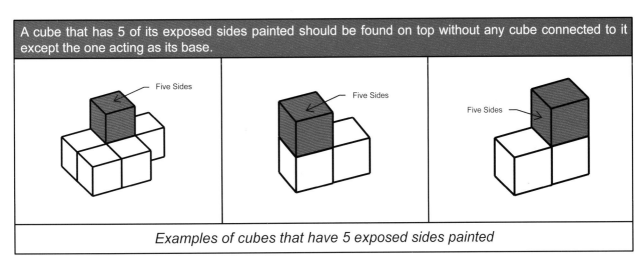

Five Sides

Five Sides

Five Sides

Examples of cubes that have 5 exposed sides painted

6.3.1 The Gold Standard Cube Counting Formula

Using a simple mathematical principle, you can simply scan each cube and calculate the sides that can be painted. We know that a cube can only have six sides. But because the bottom of these cubes rests on a parallel plane (remember the third assumption: no floating cubes), you should always consider just five sides when you calculate the number of sides exposed.

Now determine the number of other cubes surrounding a cube. Subtract these from 5 (representing the five sides of the cube that can be possibly exposed or attached to). The difference is the number of sides painted.

6 sides of a regular cube – 1 side (its base) = 5 exposed sides to consider
Number of cubes attached = n

$5 - n$ = number of exposed sides painted

6.3.2 The Tally Method

A popular cube counting technique among DAT candidates is the 'tally' method. This requires you to literally write and keep a tally as you track which cubes have a particular number of their sides painted. To make this technique even more efficient, you will need to review the total cube count as your final step. The following will illustrate how the tally method works.

On the note board that will be provided to you in the real exam, draw a chart that looks like this:

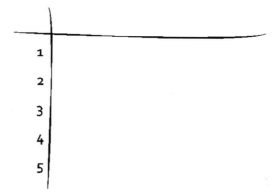

For easier reference, we will call this chart your "tally-note". The numbers 1 to 5 represent the number of painted faces in a cube. Some recommend to include the number 0 in the note to indicate the cubes that do not get painted at all. However, the DAT never contains questions asking for the number of cubes that do not have any of its sides painted.

Before you start figuring out which cubes have a certain number of sides painted, you need to count all the individual cubes and write your answer on top of your tally-note. You will need this information during your last step. Let's take this problem as an example:

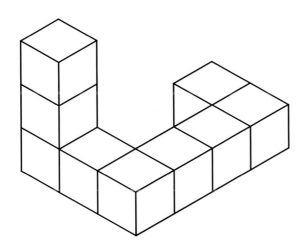

This cube formation has a total of 9 individual cubes.

1. Write down the number 9 on top of your tally-note:

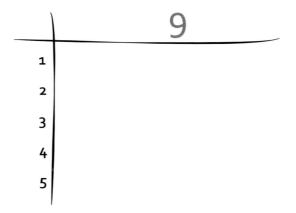

2. Next, examine each cube and figure out how many of its faces are painted. As a convention, let us start from the top left then proceed downwards, then to the next column until we reach the last cube at the back. Now, remember that top cubes without any neighboring cube on their sides are always the easiest to determine. They have all 5 of their faces painted. In the example, we have one top cube. Now we go to our

tally-note and put a mark next to number 5:

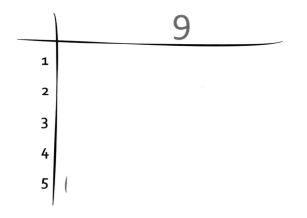

3. The next cube down, just like the topmost cube, does not have any other cube attached on its sides except on its top and its bottom. Recalling one of our illustrations in Section 6.3, a cube that has only 1 cube attached to it, other than on its base, will have 4 of its faces painted. So now, we put a mark next to number 4 in our tally-note.

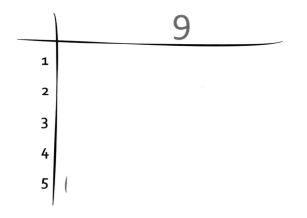

4. For cubes 3 to 8, you will notice that each one of them has 2 other cubes attached. Using the Gold Standard cube counting formula ($5 - n$ = number of exposed sides painted), this means that cubes 3 to 8 all have 3 painted sides. Our tally-note will now show a total of 6 marks next to number 3.

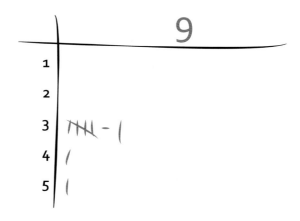

5. The last block obviously has four painted sides and so, you need to add a second mark next to number 4.

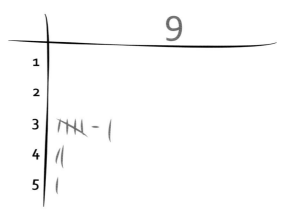

6. Now add the individual tallies, sum them up ,and compare with your original count of 9 cubes:

$$
\begin{array}{r|l}
 & 9 \\
\hline
1 & \\
2 & \\
3 & \text{卌} - | = 6 \\
4 & || \quad\; = 2 \\
5 & | \quad\;\; = 1 \\
\hline
 & \quad\;\; 9
\end{array}
$$

The final step may look unnecessary because the process appear so simple to waste a few more seconds doing basic addition. But in the actual test, block formations are much more complicated than our sample illustration here. Tallying the blocks as the last step in order to compare and confirm the total number of blocks will prove invaluable. If your manual count does not match the sum of your tallies, that means something must be wrong with your answers.

6.4 Mini Exercises

PROBLEM A

1. In Figure A, how many cubes have two of their exposed sides painted?

    A. 1 cube
    B. 2 cubes
    C. 3 cubes
    D. 4 cubes
    E. 5 cubes

2. In Figure A, how many cubes have four of their exposed sides painted?

    A. 1 cube
    B. 2 cubes
    C. 3 cubes
    D. 4 cubes
    E. 5 cubes

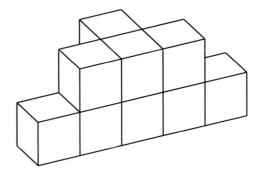

Figure A

PROBLEM B

3. In Figure B, how many cubes have two
   of their exposed sides painted?

   A. 1 cube
   B. 2 cubes
   C. 3 cubes
   D. 4 cubes
   E. 5 cubes

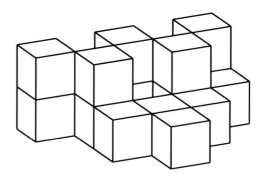

Figure B

4. In Figure B, how many cubes have three
   of their exposed sides painted?

   A. 1 cube
   B. 2 cubes
   C. 3 cubes
   D. 4 cubes
   E. 5 cubes

5. In Figure B, how many cubes have four
   of their exposed sides painted?

   A. 1 cube
   B. 2 cubes
   C. 3 cubes
   D. 4 cubes
   E. 5 cubes

6.4.1 Answer Key and Explanations

1. Answer: C

Keep in mind that when looking for cubes that have 2 of their exposed sides painted, you should identify those cubes that have 3 other cubes attached to it. These are mostly located at the inner portion of the figure. The 3 cubes are colored red in the diagram for easy viewing. The correct answer is C.

2. Answer: E

For cubes that have more exposed sides painted, lesser number of cubes are attached to it. This question asks for cubes having 4 of their exposed sides painted hence search for cubes located at the outer portion or the edges of the figure. There are 5 cubes that have 4 of their exposed sides painted. Therefore, the correct answer is E.

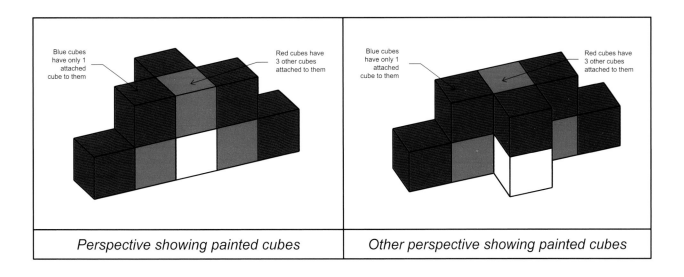

Blue cubes have only 1 attached cube to them

Red cubes have 3 other cubes attached to them

Blue cubes have only 1 attached cube to them

Red cubes have 3 other cubes attached to them

| Perspective showing painted cubes | Other perspective showing painted cubes |

3. Answer: B

This question requires that you look for the number of cubes that have 2 of their exposed sides painted. These cubes are frequently positioned at the bottom or in between cubes. There are only 2 red cubes in the figure, which means that the correct answer is B.

4. Answer: E

If the question asks for the number of cubes with 3 of their sides exposed, look for cubes having 2 cubes attached. In this case, all green cubes are located at the bottom of the figure. There are a total of 5 green cubes that have 3 exposed sides painted. Thus, the correct answer is E.

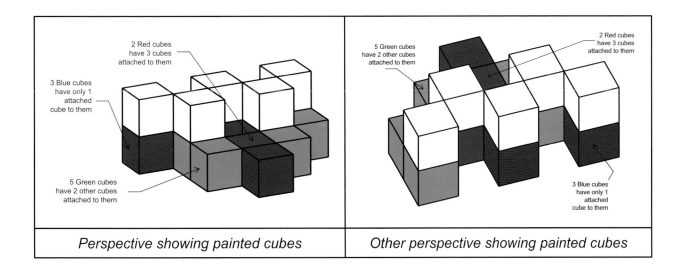

2 Red cubes have 3 cubes attached to them

3 Blue cubes have only 1 attached cube to them

5 Green cubes have 2 other cubes attached to them

5 Green cubes have 2 other cubes attached to them

2 Red cubes have 3 cubes attached to them

3 Blue cubes have only 1 attached cube to them

| Perspective showing painted cubes | Other perspective showing painted cubes |

5. Answer: C

This question asks for the total number of cubes that have 4 of their exposed sides painted. Bear in mind that only 1 cube should be attached to this cube excluding the base. They are typically situated at the edge or at the corner of the figure. Hence, the correct answer is C because there are only 3 cubes having 4 of their sides exposed.

GOLD STANDARD WARM-UP EXERCISES

Chapter 6: Cube Counting

The following questions represent one of the six subsections in the Perceptual Ability Test of the DAT. While this serves as a review of the discussions in this chapter, the level of difficulty of each question closely parallels the actual test.

You have 10 minutes to complete this portion of the DAT Mini Test; the actual test is 60 minutes.

Please time yourself accordingly.

> **BEGIN ONLY WHEN YOUR TIMER IS READY**

Problem A

1. In Figure A, how many cubes have two of their exposed sides painted?

    A. 1 cube
    B. 2 cubes
    C. 3 cubes
    D. 4 cubes
    E. 5 cubes

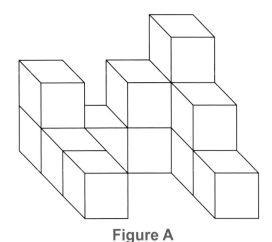

Figure A

2. In Figure A, how many cubes have three of their exposed sides painted?

    A. 1 cube
    B. 2 cubes
    C. 3 cubes
    D. 4 cubes
    E. 5 cubes

3. In Figure A, how many cubes have four of their exposed sides painted?

    A. 1 cube
    B. 2 cubes
    C. 3 cubes
    D. 4 cubes
    E. 5 cubes

Problem B

4. In Figure B, how many cubes have three of their exposed sides painted?

    A. 1 cube
    B. 2 cubes
    C. 3 cubes
    D. 4 cubes
    E. 5 cubes

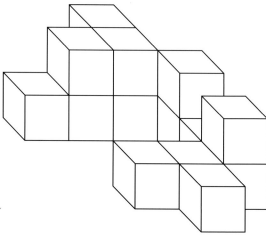

Figure B

5. In Figure B, how many cubes have four of their exposed sides painted?

    A. 1 cube
    B. 2 cubes
    C. 3 cubes
    D. 4 cubes
    E. 5 cubes

Problem C

6. In Figure C, how many cubes have two of their exposed sides painted?

   A. 1 cube
   B. 2 cubes
   C. 3 cubes
   D. 4 cubes
   E. 5 cubes

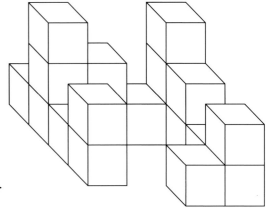

Figure C

7. In Figure C, how many cubes have four of their exposed sides painted?

   A. 1 cube
   B. 2 cubes
   C. 3 cubes
   D. 4 cubes
   E. 5 cubes

8. In Figure C, how many cubes have five of their exposed sides painted?

   A. 1 cube
   B. 2 cubes
   C. 3 cubes
   D. 4 cubes
   E. 5 cubes

Problem D

9. In Figure D, how many cubes have two of their exposed sides painted?

    A. 1 cube
    B. 2 cubes
    C. 3 cubes
    D. 4 cubes
    E. 5 cubes

10. In Figure D, how many cubes have four of their exposed sides painted?

    A. 1 cube
    B. 2 cubes
    C. 3 cubes
    D. 4 cubes
    E. 5 cubes

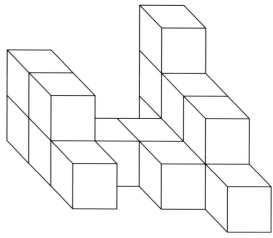

Figure D

Problem E

11. In Figure E, how many cubes have one of their exposed sides painted?

    A. 1 cube
    B. 2 cubes
    C. 3 cubes
    D. 4 cubes
    E. 5 cubes

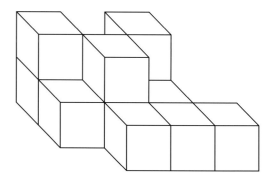

Figure E

12. In Figure E, how many cubes have three
of their exposed sides painted?

    A. 1 cube
    B. 2 cubes
    C. 3 cubes
    D. 4 cubes
    E. 5 cubes

13. In Figure E, how many cubes have
five of their exposed sides painted?

    A. 1 cube
    B. 2 cubes
    C. 3 cubes
    D. 4 cubes
    E. 5 cubes

Problem F

14. In Figure F, how many cubes have two
of their exposed sides painted?

    A. 1 cube
    B. 2 cubes
    C. 3 cubes
    D. 4 cubes
    E. 5 cubes

15. In Figure F, how many cubes have
four of their exposed sides painted?

    A. 1 cube
    B. 2 cubes
    C. 3 cubes
    D. 4 cubes
    E. 5 cubes

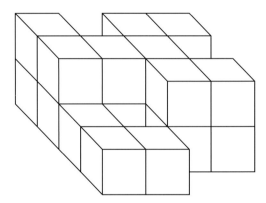

Figure F

If time remains, you may review your work. If your allotted time is complete, please proceed to the Answer Key.

GS ANSWER KEY

CHAPTER 6

1.	E
2.	B
3.	D
4.	D
5.	E
6.	D
7.	D
8.	D

9.	A
10.	E
11.	A
12.	D
13.	C
14.	D
15.	D

* Explanations can be found in the Lessons section at www.dat-prep.com.

Go online to DAT-prep.com for additional chapter review Q&A and forum.

GOLD NOTES

3D FORM DEVELOPMENT

Chapter 7

Understand

* The Folding Pattern
* Significant Parts of the Unfolded Figure

DAT-Prep.com

Introduction

Form Development requires mentally constructing the unfolded pattern of a three-dimensional object into its formed shape. Different flat patterns represent various figures, which can include a shaded dice, a diamond, and any irregular shape.

Just as the other preceding sections in the PAT, the 3D Form Development section tests your ability to spot fine differences but this time, actively perceiving an object spatially and in multiple probable forms.

Additional Resources

Free Online Forum

7.1 About 3D Form Development

The last subsection of the PAT is the 3D Form Development test – also known as Pattern Folding. Each question presents a flat pattern. You are to imagine folding it into a three-dimensional figure, which can turn out to be a dice, a cube, or an irregularly-shaped object.

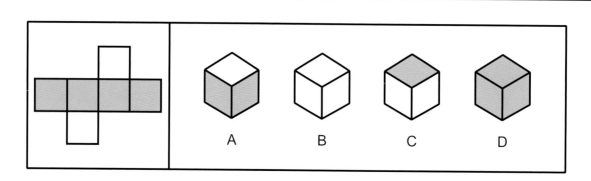

Figure PAT 7.1: Sample Pattern Folding Question on the PAT. One of the figures in the four options (A, B, C, or D) can be formed from the flat pattern shown on the left. The correct answer is **A.**

This test aims to measure your spatial skills: the ability to mentally manipulate 3D figures. Take note that the orientation of the 3D figures may vary in each question, so you need to be visually sharp on such details.

7.2 How to Prepare for this Subsection

Most candidates find this part of the PAT to be quite difficult. Some patterns can be very complex, and solving them can take so much time. Generally, you should get familiar with common geometric figures like the circle, triangle, square and rectangle. Try to explore the differences in their shapes and how each one would look like if viewed from various directions. Distinguishing trapezoids from parallelograms and other irregular shapes in 3D views also makes a good foundation in building your skills in 3D form development.

Identifying the significant parts of an unfolded pattern and understanding how a figure is folded are likewise paramount to your preparation for this test. Usually, the base is the largest portion of the figure. It is located at the center of the unfolded object but falls on the bottom once folded. Keep in mind that the direction of the fold should be inward. The base can also have the most number of components attached to it.

7.2.1 Numbering the Parts

Sometimes, sketching helps you visualize the object better. You may also designate numbers to represent the surfaces of the unfolded figure. This way, you can mark and remember which side is connected to another.

Let us try applying a numbering system on the following sample question.

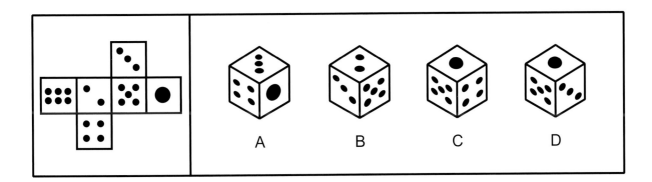

Start by looking for two surfaces that are not placed beside each other. These are parts that are located at least one side apart from each other. Looking at the flat pattern, these are 1 and 2 (the numbering used here corresponds to the number of circles found in a component), 3 and 4, and 5 and 6. If you see any of these sides beside each other in any of the answer choices, you can eliminate those options. Looking at the given options in the question, A should be discounted from the alternatives because the components having 3 and 4 circles are shown to be next to each other. So now we are left with only three options.

The next step is to find the correct answer by mentally folding the flat pattern. First, you can assign a reference side or a base. The reference side is where all the components should converge and it should end up at the bottom since the fold should be done inward.

Let's start evaluating option B. We are looking at a cube with a top having 2 circles. Looking at the image on the left, the bottom should be the component containing only 1 circle (remember that the opposite side of 2 is 1). For easier reference, let's call this part "Surface 1". Let us fold it one part at a time using the isometric view.

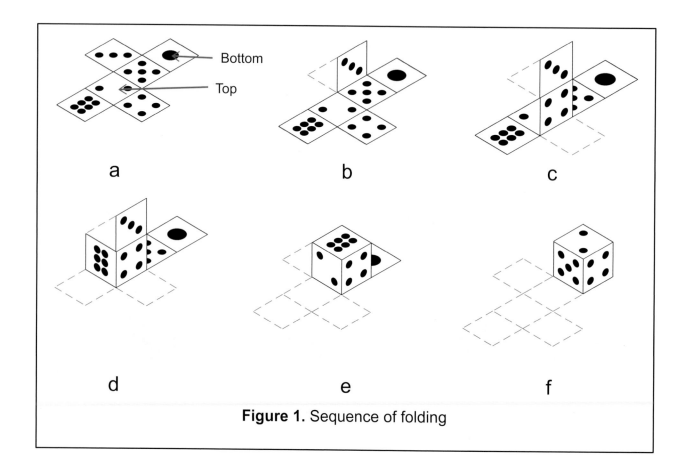

Figure 1. Sequence of folding

Figure 1f shows how the 3D object looks like after being fully folded. None of the options matches it. This does not automatically mean however that choice B is incorrect because we have not seen the other side yet. It is therefore important to know how the object appears from all sides.

If we rotate choice B to see the other side, it will look like Figure 2. B is, indeed, not the correct answer.

We are now down to two choices (C and D). This time, you can try finding the correct answer either mentally or by making sketches. Figure 3 shows the possible views of the object with Surface 1 on top.

Looking at C and D, the only option that matches Figure 3d is D. The correct answer therefore is D.

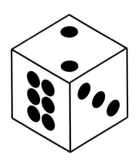

Figure 2

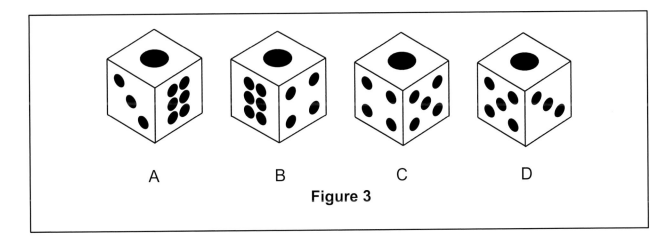

Figure 3

Now let's take a more complex-looking pattern.

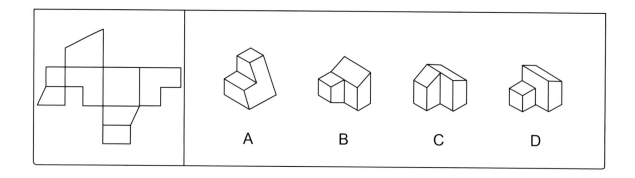

First, number each part of the flat pattern. Then choose a base for the object: it should be the largest part of the pattern and should have the most number of components attached to it. In this case, it is Surface 5.

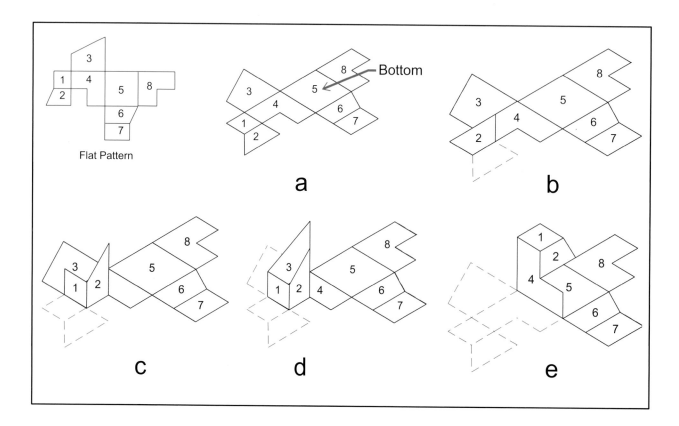

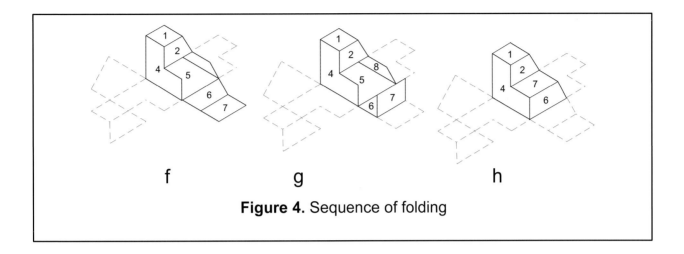

Figure 4. Sequence of folding

Figure 4h reflects how the 3D object looks like after the folds are completed. However, we cannot see a match among the options. We should then explore how the object would look like from all directions.

If we are going to rotate our folded object 90 degrees clockwise, it will look like Figure 5b.

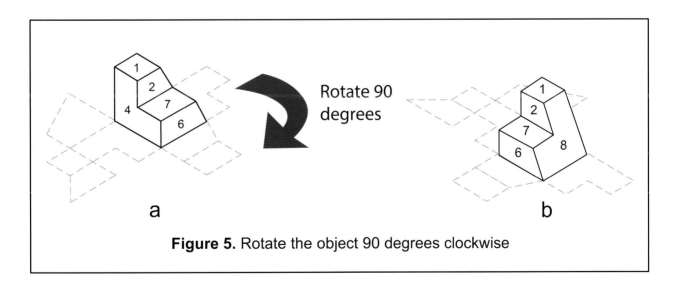

Figure 5. Rotate the object 90 degrees clockwise

Figure 5b is identical to choice A. Therefore, the correct answer is A.

There are also patterns that have at least two identical parts. With such patterns, you should keep in mind that identical parts are most often located opposite each other once the pattern is folded. In Figure 6a, we can see that the parts numbered 2 and 6 are identical. After several folds, it will look like Figure 6f.

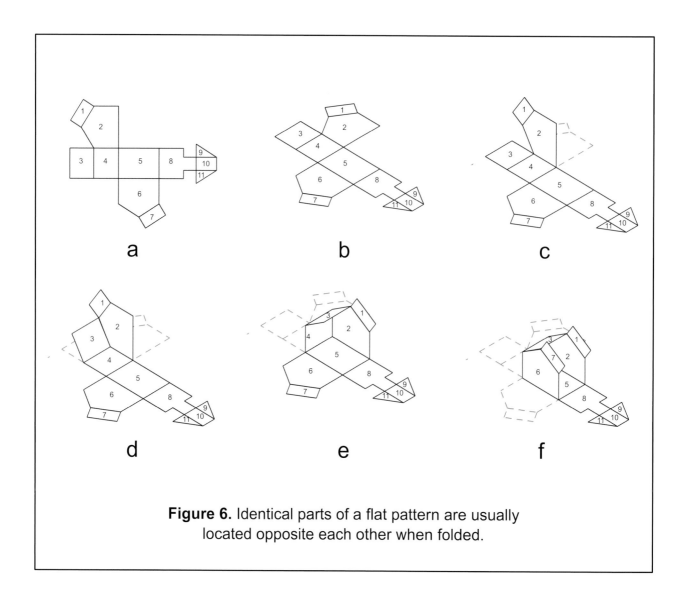

Figure 6. Identical parts of a flat pattern are usually located opposite each other when folded.

After a few more folding, the finished product and correct answer can be any of the images in Figure 7.

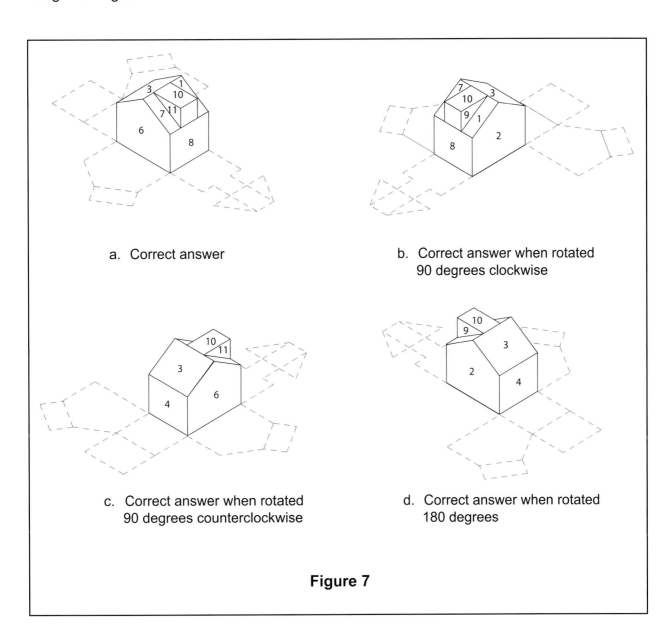

a. Correct answer

b. Correct answer when rotated 90 degrees clockwise

c. Correct answer when rotated 90 degrees counterclockwise

d. Correct answer when rotated 180 degrees

Figure 7

Several techniques have been popularized in tackling the 3D Pattern Folding test. You do not need to master all of them but it would be worth trying them out. You can modify some of them or even discover your own techniques in the process. What is most important is for you to find a method that makes you more efficient in answering the questions.

Nevertheless, here are some known strategies for this PAT subsection:

1. Side-counting Technique

This technique is commonly used for irregular shapes. First, count all the sides of each irregular shape from the flat figure. Then count the number of sides of the 3D shape from the answer choices. You can then use the process of elimination by discounting, one at a time, the choices that do not match the number of sides from the given flat figure.

2. Comparing Substructures in the Most Pronounced Shape

This technique involves mainly looking for the largest irregular shape in the given flat figure. Examine the largest irregular shape by its width and length. Then check if the selected irregular shape from the flat figure is represented in the answer choices. Compare the obvious differences and proceed with the elimination technique if needed.

3. Top-Front-End Technique

Practicing with as many questions as you can using this technique is important because this can be tricky. You can start by looking at two projections: top and front, front and end, or top and end. The most common – and the easiest – projection to look at is the front view, and then you can determine its top and end view. The Top-Front-End technique is suitable for dice, shaded cubes, and shaded irregular shapes. When you first see the given figure, be quick to find where your eyes should focus. Look for the widest and highest dimensions to be able to determine essential characteristics to be used as points of reference. Eliminating the wrong answers will then become easy for you.

For dice figures, you can also use the number of points on each side as the point of reference to identify the correct answer. For shaded figures, you can use the shaded region as a point of reference to determine the correct 3D form from the answer choices.

The following section contains five "mini" exercises on which you can try applying the approaches and techniques, which we have discussed so far. Even as early as now, timing yourself during these short exercises would prove beneficial. Note the time it took you to answer one question. This will give you a clearer view of your current level of performance in the test.

7.4 Mini Exercises

1.

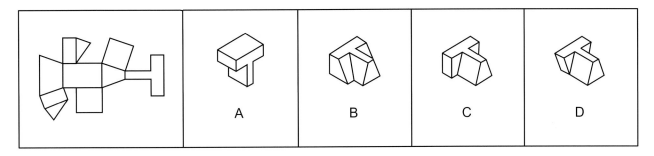

2.

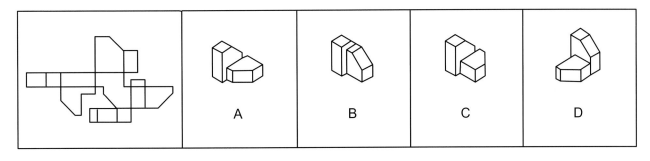

3.

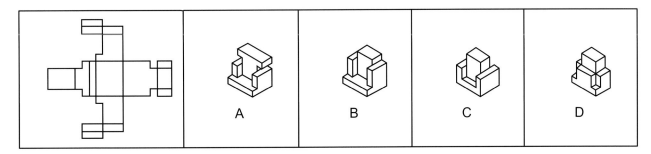

4.

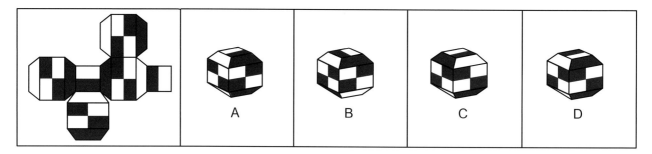

5.

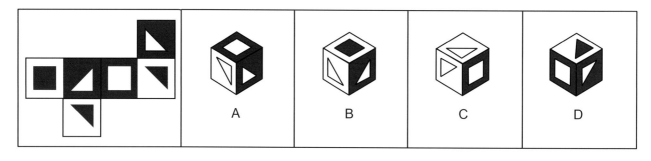

7.4.1 Answer Key and Explanations

1. Answer: D

The figure in this question has a total of 10 components or surfaces. Different types of shapes are also spotted within the figure. There are big and small rectangles, triangles, two kinds of trapezoids and a T-shaped component. Given these characteristics, you can check which option is correct. A depicts 2 T-shaped components hence incorrect. B, on the other hand, has 3 kinds of trapezoids instead of just 2. C has 2 kinds of trapezoids, but the triangular components are not seen. Thus the correct answer is D.

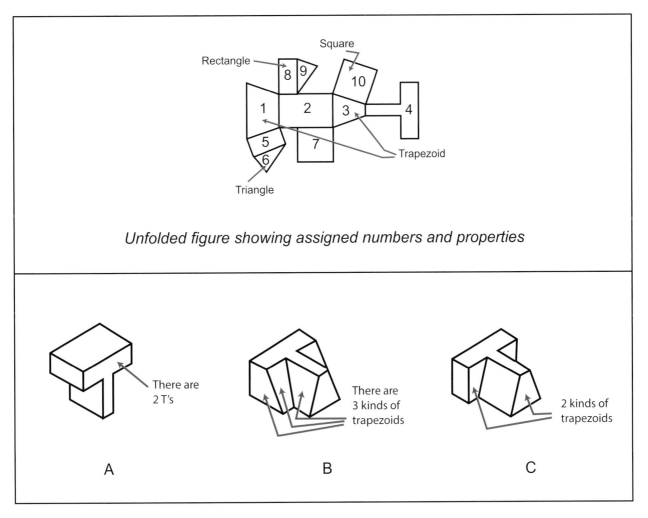

Unfolded figure showing assigned numbers and properties

2. Answer: A

The unfolded figure here has unique components such as Surfaces 4 and 5.

Surface 5 can be used as the base of the 3D figure. With these properties, you can already compare it with the given choices. The correct answer is A.

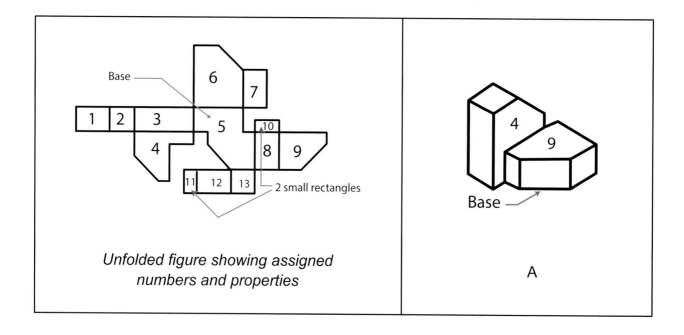

Unfolded figure showing assigned numbers and properties

A

3. Answer: B

The figure in this question shows differing shapes like L, T and various sizes of rectangles. You can directly compare each option based on these observations. A is obviously wrong because it has a different T-shaped side. B is the correct answer because the L and T-shaped surfaces are evident. Both C and D are wrong because C does not have the L or T-shaped component while D has more than 16 components.

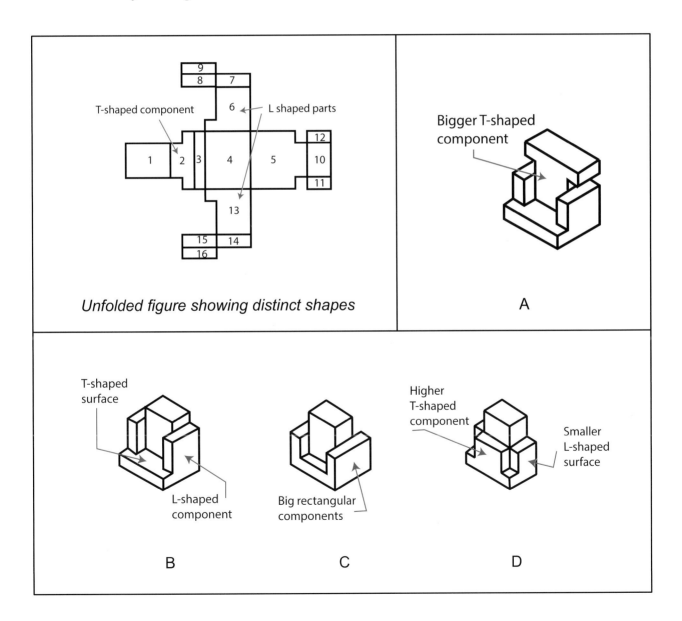

Unfolded figure showing distinct shapes

A

B   C   D

4. Answer: C

Remember that shaded figures are usually folded downwards. You also need to take note of the adjacent or connecting planes of the figure. Take note of the shaded rectangles that should be connected when folded as well as the orientation of these shadings. A and D have the rectangular shading aligned with the shaded trapezoid, and this is wrong. B also has a different shading arrangement compared to the unfolded figure. Thus the correct answer is C.

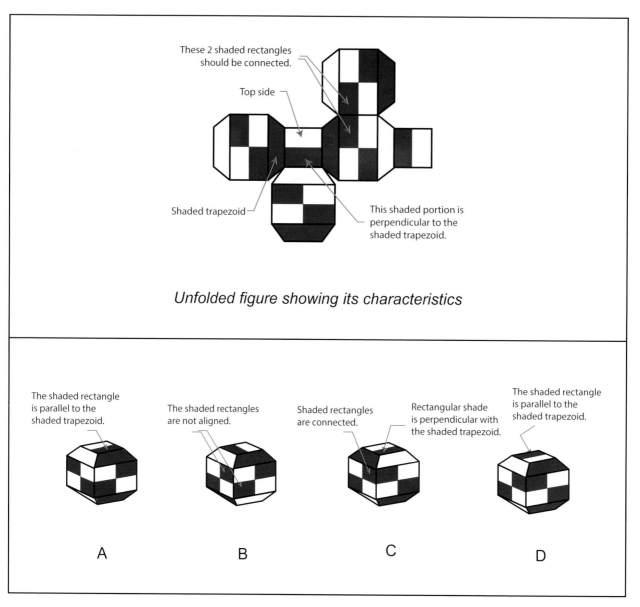

These 2 shaded rectangles should be connected.

Top side

Shaded trapezoid

This shaded portion is perpendicular to the shaded trapezoid.

Unfolded figure showing its characteristics

The shaded rectangle is parallel to the shaded trapezoid.

A

The shaded rectangles are not aligned.

B

Shaded rectangles are connected.

Rectangular shade is perpendicular with the shaded trapezoid.

C

The shaded rectangle is parallel to the shaded trapezoid.

D

5. Answer: D

This test item may look difficult at first glance, but this is actually quite easy. What matters here is the position of the shaded sides since this is basically just a cube. You would observe that each of options A, B and C has a white side with a white triangle. These are totally wrong and therefore, the correct answer is D.

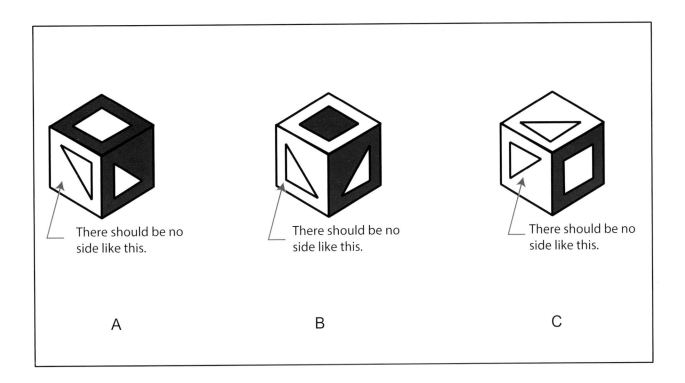

There should be no side like this.

There should be no side like this.

There should be no side like this.

A

B

C

GOLD STANDARD WARM-UP EXERCISES
Chapter 7: 3D Form Development

The following questions represent one of the six subsections in the Perceptual Ability Test of the DAT. While this serves as a review of the discussions in this chapter, the level of difficulty of each question closely parallels the actual test.

You have 10 minutes to complete this portion of the DAT Mini Test; the actual test is 60 minutes.

Please time yourself accordingly.

BEGIN ONLY WHEN YOUR TIMER IS READY

1.

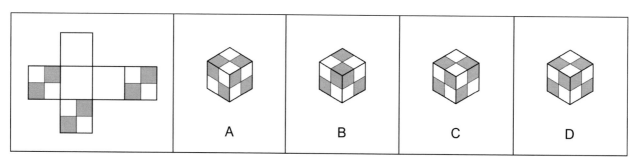

2.

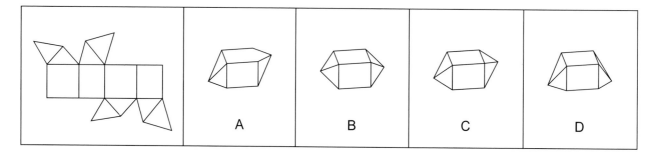

3.

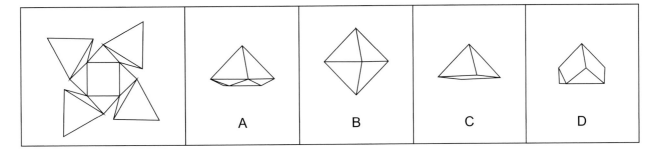

4.

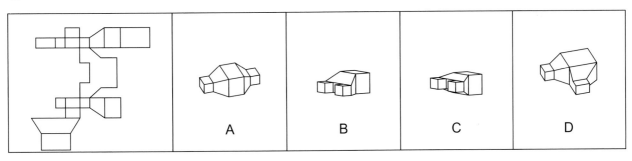

5.

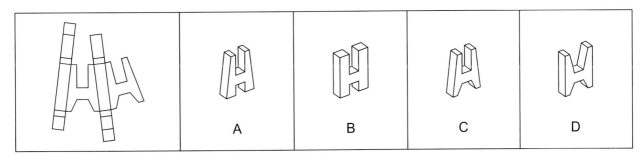

6.

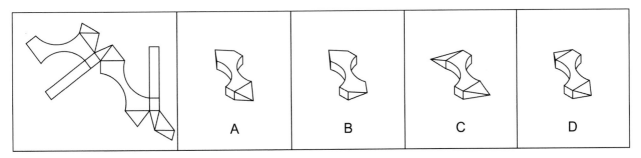

7.

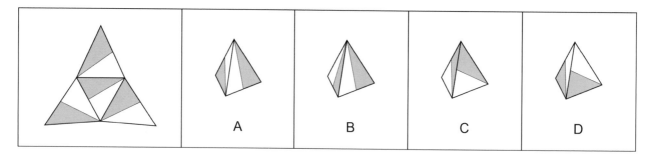

8.

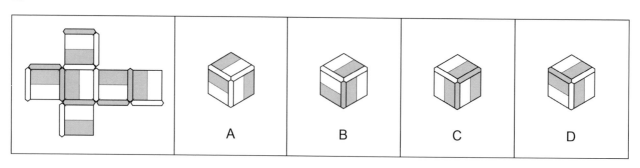

9.

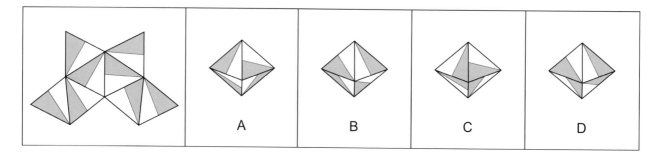

10.

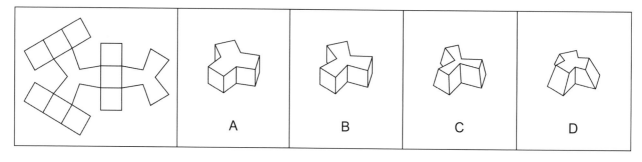

11 .

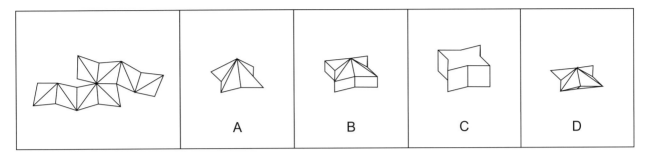

12.

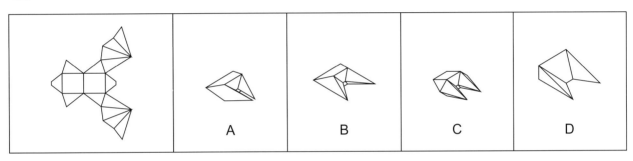

13.

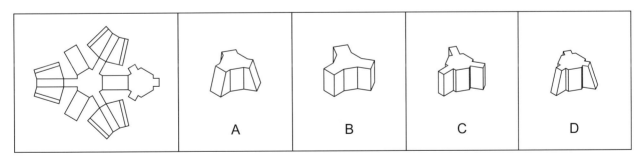

14.

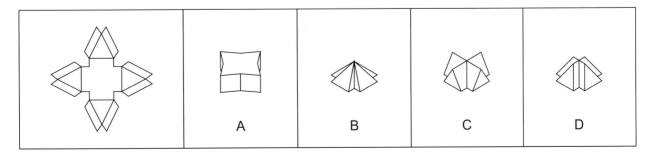

15.

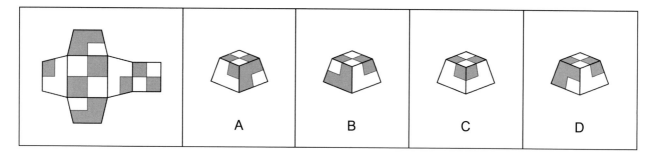

If time remains, you may review your work. If your allotted time is complete, please proceed to the Answer Key.

GS ANSWER KEY

CHAPTER 7

1.	D	9.	C
2.	C	10.	B
3.	A	11.	D
4.	B	12.	C
5.	C	13.	D
6.	D	14.	D
7.	B	15.	A
8.	A		

* Explanations can be found in the Lessons section at www.dat-prep.com.

Go online to DAT-prep.com for additional chapter review Q&A and forum.

Go online to DAT-prep.com for additional chapter review Q&A and forum.

GOLD NOTES

GOLD STANDARD
MULTIMEDIA EDUCATION

Gold Standard DAT
PRACTICE TEST

GS-1

THE GOLD STANDARD DAT

Introduction

Prior to attempting this practice test, section 2.3 from this book - Understanding the DAT - should be reviewed.

The following full-length practice Gold Standard (GS) DAT is designed to challenge you and to teach you at a whole new level. You will need to take the tools you have learned and build new structures and create new paths to solving problems. **Please consider using your computer's on-screen default calculator (with the same four basic functions described in QR 1.2).** The problems will range from very simple to very challenging, but they will all be very helpful for your DAT preparation. Do not be afraid of making mistakes - it is part of the learning process. The student who makes the most mistakes has the greatest learning potential!

Timing is critical. Many students do not complete various sections of the exam. If you decide to do a few problems from time to time then you have never practiced for the DAT. An almost five-hour exam is a rigorous event. It requires practice that simulates exam conditions. An important aspect of the latter is timing. Practice according to the prescribed exam schedule.

Upon finishing the exam, the next challenge is the equally important thorough review. Mistakes, and even correct answers for which some doubt existed, should be examined without time restrictions for maximum learning benefit.

You are not alone! You have access to a free interactive forum at dat-prep.com/forum so you can discuss any question from your practice exam with other students or even with the authors. You can share your experience, learn, complain, contribute or gain some new tips.

Dental Admission Test	
Survey of Natural Sciences	90 minutes
Perceptual Ability Test	60 minutes
Reading Comprehension Test	60 minutes
Quantitative Reasoning Test	45 minutes

Preparing for the Tests

You will need a watch or timer for this practice test. During the actual administration, a basic calculator will be provided on-screen during the Quantitative Reasoning section. Any calculations or notations can also be made on the laminated note boards using fine-tip permanent markers, both of which will be provided by the testing center upon request (scrap paper is not permitted).

These exam sheets are perforated so that you can tear your sheets out gently and systematically. Place the front of the book flat on a table and open to the pages just after the full-length exam and Answer Documents. Tear along the perforation.

The page numbers reflect the exam section to which the page belongs. For example, GS-NAT SCI-3 is the 3rd page of the Natural Sciences Test of the GS DAT. Begin pulling out pages while paying close attention to the page numbers. Once the complete exam is removed, you will require a stapler. Now you can use the Answer Document.

PERIODIC TABLE OF THE ELEMENTS

1 H 1.008																	2 He 4.003
3 Li 6.941	4 Be 9.012											5 B 10.81	6 C 12.011	7 N 14.007	8 O 15.999	9 F 18.998	10 Ne 20.179
11 Na 22.990	12 Mg 24.305											13 Al 26.982	14 Si 28.086	15 P 30.974	16 S 32.06	17 Cl 35.453	18 Ar 39.948
19 K 39.098	20 Ca 40.08	21 Sc 44.956	22 Ti 47.90	23 V 50.942	24 Cr 51.996	25 Mn 54.938	26 Fe 55.847	27 Co 58.933	28 Ni 58.70	29 Cu 63.546	30 Zn 65.38	31 Ga 69.72	32 Ge 72.59	33 As 74.922	34 Se 78.96	35 Br 79.904	36 Kr 83.80
37 Rb 85.468	38 Sr 87.62	39 Y 88.906	40 Zr 91.22	41 Nb 92.906	42 Mo 95.94	43 Tc (98)	44 Ru 101.07	45 Rh 102.906	46 Pd 106.4	47 Ag 107.868	48 Cd 112.41	49 In 114.82	50 Sn 118.69	51 Sb 121.75	52 Te 127.60	53 I 126.905	54 Xe 131.30
55 Cs 132.905	56 Ba 137.33	57 *La 138.906	72 Hf 178.49	73 Ta 180.948	74 W 183.85	75 Re 186.207	76 Os 190.2	77 Ir 192.22	78 Pt 195.09	79 Au 196.967	80 Hg 200.59	81 Tl 204.37	82 Pb 207.2	83 Bi 208.980	84 Po (209)	85 At (210)	86 Rn (222)
87 Fr (223)	88 Ra 226.025	89 **Ac 227.028	104 Unq (261)	105 Unp (262)	106 Unh (263)												

*	58 Ce 140.12	59 Pr 140.908	60 Nd 144.24	61 Pm (145)	62 Sm 150.4	63 Eu 151.96	64 Gd 157.25	65 Tb 158.925	66 Dy 162.50	67 Ho 164.930	68 Er 167.26	69 Tm 168.934	70 Yb 173.04	71 Lu 174.967
**	90 Th 232.038	91 Pa 231.036	92 U 238.029	93 Np 237.048	94 Pu (244)	95 Am (243)	96 Cm (247)	97 Bk (247)	98 Cf (251)	99 Es (254)	100 Fm (257)	101 Md (258)	102 No (259)	103 Lr (260)

This GS-1 exam has 100 multiple choice questions.
Biology: 1-40; General Chemistry: 41-70; and Organic Chemistry: 71-100

> **Please do not begin until your timer is ready.**

1. Which of the following represents a genetic mutation in which bases are added or deleted in numbers other than multiples of three?

   A.   Inversion
   B.   Duplication
   C.   Frame shift
   D.   Translocation
   E.   Point mutation

2. All of the following are functions of the human spleen EXCEPT one. Which one is the EXCEPTION?

   A.   Produces platelets
   B.   Filters damaged red blood cells
   C.   Filters bacteria
   D.   Stores erythrocytes
   E.   Stores antigen presenting cells

3. Which of the following statements is true concerning inspiration?

   A.   The internal pressure is positive with respect to the atmosphere.
   B.   The diaphragm and accessory muscles relax.
   C.   It is a passive process.
   D.   The thoracic cage moves inward, while the diaphragm moves downward.
   E.   The phrenic nerve is stimulated.

4. PKU disease is a recessive autosomal genetic condition. DNA isolated from parents reacted with normal specific and abnormal specific probes in the following manner:

	normal specific	abnormal specific
mother	reaction	reaction
father	no reaction	reaction

   A male offspring of the couple represented in the table above could potentially be which of the following?
   I.   PKU disease positive
   II. PKU disease negative, PKU gene carrier
   III. PKU disease negative, PKU gene non-carrier

   A.   I only
   B.   I and II only
   C.   I and III only
   D.   II and III only
   E.   I, II and III

5. A conjoint and open vascular bundle will be observed in the transverse section of which of the following?

   A.   Monocot twig
   B.   Monocot root
   C.   Monocot stem
   D.   Dicot root
   E.   Dicot stem

6. Match and choose the correct option:

I. Cuticle	i. guard cells
II. Bulliform cells	ii. single layer
III. Stomata	iii. waxy layer
IV. Epidermis	iv. empty colorless cell

- A.   I-i, II-iv, III-iii, IV-ii
- B.   I-i, II-ii, III-iii, IV-iv
- C.   I-iii, II-iv, III-i, IV-ii
- D.   I-iii, II-ii, III-i, IV-iv
- E.   I-iii, II-ii, III-iv, IV-i

7. The mechanism by which blastomeres differentiate into germ cells is referred to as:

- A.   induction.
- B.   determination.
- C.   specialization.
- D.   differentiation.
- E.   neurulation.

8. Prokaryotic organisms make up the:

- A.   protists.
- B.   protists and eubacteria.
- C.   archaebacteria and protists.
- D.   archaebacteria, eubacteria, and protists.
- E.   eubacteria and archaebacteria.

9. Calcitonin lowers calcium levels in blood by inhibiting the action of:

- A.   osteoclasts.
- B.   osteoblasts.
- C.   osteocytes.
- D.   osteons.
- E.   osteomeres.

10. All of the following are characteristics of most enzymes EXCEPT one. Which one is the EXCEPTION?

- A.   They affect the equilibrium of reaction.
- B.   They affect the rate of reaction.
- C.   They are specific to particular substrates.
- D.   They lower the energy of activation of a chemical reaction.
- E.   They are composed of simple or complex proteins.

11. Implantation of the developing embryo into the uterine lining occurs during:

- A.   fertilization.
- B.   cleavage.
- C.   blastulation.
- D.   gastrulation.
- E.   neurulation.

12. The antarctic tundra:

- A.   is characterized by deciduous needleleaf trees.
- B.   is characterized by evergreen needleleaf trees.
- C.   is divided by the tree line.
- D.   contains numerous species of reptiles.
- E.   is unforested because it is both cold and dry.

13. In which of the following blood vessels would PO_2 be the highest?

- A.   Hepatic portal system
- B.   Left pulmonary artery
- C.   Renal vein
- D.   Inferior vena cava
- E.   Pulmonary vein

14. Filtration of plasma occurs in the Bowman's capsule of the nephron. What is the driving force for this initial filtration step in the kidney?

- A.   An ionic gradient formed by a countercurrent multiplier system
- B.   Blood pressure
- C.   A chemiosmotic gradient across the semipermeable tubular membrane
- D.   Contraction of smooth muscles surrounding the Bowman's capsule
- E.   Vacuoles in the podocytes

15. Consider the following table.

Table 1: Experimental data presenting the rates of protein degradation (Rxn rate) with varying concentration of trypsin and the enzyme inhibitor inhibitin.

Trial#	[trypsin] mmol/L	Rxn rate mmol$(Ls)^{-1}$	[inhibitin] mmol/L
1	5.6×10^{-4}	5.40	0
2	7.4×10^{-3}	5.45	3.6×10^{-6}
3	5.6×10^{-4}	1.98	7.2×10^{-6}
4	7.4×10^{-3}	2.02	1.1×10^{-5}
5	8.3×10^{-5}	0.04	1.4×10^{-5}

On statistical analysis, researchers confirmed that there was no significant difference between the rate of reaction determined for Trial # 1 and Trial # 2. The most likely explanation is:

A. the concentration of inhibitin was 0.

B. the concentration of inhibitin was significantly elevated.

C. the concentration of trypsin was significantly elevated.

D. the concentration of trypsin was significantly decreased.

E. the concentration of trypsin was 0.

16. Which of the following statements could be used to correctly describe the overall polymerase chain reaction (PCR)?

A. It is an anabolic reaction that breaks down new DNA strands.

B. It is an anabolic reaction that synthesizes new DNA strands.

C. It is a catabolic reaction that breaks down new DNA strands.

D. It is a catabolic reaction that synthesizes new DNA strands.

E. It is neither anabolic nor catabolic.

17. The medication AZT is an analog of thymidine which has an $-N_3$ group in the place of an $-OH$ at the 3' position of the sugar. Thus AZT will act to disrupt which process of the retrovirus HIV?

A. Transcription

B. Reverse transcription

C. Translation

D. Endocytosis

E. Exocytosis

18. The genetic basis of human blood types includes recessive (Z^O) and codominant alleles (Z^A and Z^B). Determine which of the following genotypes produce blood that agglutinates when combined with type O serum.

I. $Z^A Z^A$
II. $Z^A Z^B$
III. $Z^A Z^O$

A. I only

B. III only

C. I and II only

D. I and III only

E. I, II and III

19. Which of the following structures of the ear is responsible for maintaining a sense of equilibrium?

A. The organ of Corti

B. The vestibulo-cochlear apparatus

C. The semicircular canals

D. The Eustachian tube

E. The ossicles

20. Plasmodesmata:

A. are considered to be the desmosomes of plant cells.

B. connect to intermediate fibers of the cytoskeleton.

C. encircle cells like a belt.

D. connect actin fibers of one cell to the extracellular matrix of another.

E. connect the cytoplasm of one plant cell to that of another.

21. Exocytosis is directly associated with all of the following EXCEPT one. Which one is the EXCEPTION?

A. Porosomes

B. Chloride and calcium channels

C. Clathrin-coated vesicles

D. "Kiss-and-run" fusion

E. SNARE proteins

22. Which of the following observations would support the hypothesis that the movement of dopamine into a cell is mediated by a transporter protein in the plasma membrane?

A. A hypotonic cell bathed in dopamine leads to increased dopamine uptake by the cell.
B. A cell bathed in an isotonic dopamine solution has no net uptake of dopamine.
C. The rate of dopamine influx increases proportionally with the extracellular dopamine concentration.
D. The rate of dopamine influx reaches a plateau, despite increasing extracellular concentration.
E. Cyclic AMP concentration remains steady.

23. The early Earth was a harsh environment. The present day organisms that could possibly have survived that type of environment are:

A. eubacteria.
B. protobionts.
C. blue-green algae.
D. archeabacteria.
E. eukaryotic organisms.

24. A time versus population-size graph with exponential growth may be graphed with what shaped curve?

A. S
B. k
C. C
D. J
E. N

25. Consider the diagram below.

Prot = proteins which are the only ions which cannot cross the membrane *m*. Thus the membrane is semipermeable.

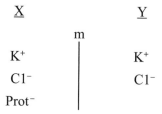

Assuming that the total concentrations of anions and cations on both sides of the membrane are initially equal, how would Cl⁻ ions be expected to act?

A. They would not move at all because no electrochemical gradient exists.
B. They would diffuse across the membrane from Y to X along its chemical gradient.
C. They would diffuse across the membrane from X to Y along the electrochemical gradient.
D. They would diffuse across the membrane from Y to X along its electrical gradient.
E. Cl⁻ ions from both sides of the membrane would diffuse across the membrane, but would stop net movement once the electrochemical gradient no longer existed.

26. After sexual maturation, the primordial germ cells in the testes are initially called:

A. spermatids and are haploid.
B. primary spermatocytes and are diploid.
C. primary spermatocytes and are haploid.
D. spermatogonia and are diploid.
E. spermatogonia and are haploid.

27. In which order of priority are the human body's nutrient stores utilized for energy production during fasting and subsequent starvation?

A. Glycogen, protein, fat
B. Fat, glycogen, protein
C. Glycogen, fat, protein
D. Fat, protein, glycogen
E. Protein, fat, glycogen

28. Which of the following hormones, found in the human menstrual cycle, are produced in the ovary?

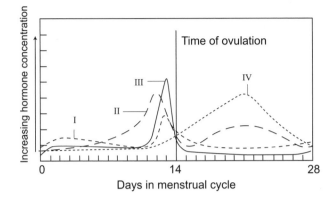

A. I and II
B. II and III
C. III and IV
D. I and III
E. II and IV

29. The K_m is the substrate concentration at which an enzyme-catalyzed reaction occurs at half its maximal velocity, $V_{max}/2$. What effect would a competitive reversible inhibitor be expected to have on V_{max} and K_m?

A. V_{max} would stay the same, but K_m would decrease.
B. V_{max} would stay the same, but K_m would increase.
C. K_m would stay the same, but V_{max} would decrease.
D. Both V_{max} and K_m would decrease.
E. Both V_{max} and K_m would increase.

30. Down's syndrome, in which $2N = 47$, is one of the most common forms of chromosomal abnormalities. This results from the failure of one pair of homologous chromosomes to separate during meiosis. During which of the meiotic phases would this likely occur?

A. Metaphase I
B. Metaphase II
C. Anaphase I
D. Anaphase II
E. Telophase

31. What sequence of bases would tRNA have, in order to recognize the mRNA codon CAG?

A. GTC
B. UAG
C. CAG
D. GCU
E. GUC

32. The difference between the bacterium Lactobacillus and the eukaryote Trichomonas is that Lactobacillus has no:

A. ribosomes.
B. cell wall.
C. plasma membrane.
D. lysosomes.
E. RNA.

33. Bile, a chemical which emulsifies fat, is produced by the:

A. liver.
B. gallbladder.
C. common bile duct.
D. pancreas.
E. duodenum.

34. During the dark phase of photosynthesis, the molecule that is oxidized and the molecule that is reduced, respectively, are:

A. NADP and water.
B. water and CO_2.
C. water and NADP.
D. $NADPH_2$ and CO_2.
E. CO_2 and water.

35. Which of the following are LEAST appropriately matched?

A. Reduction - gain of electrons
B. Anabolic reactions - expend energy
C. Exergonic reaction-catabolism
D. Endergonic reaction - anabolism
E. Activation energy - entropy

36. At what level(s) of protein structure could you expect to find hydrogen bonds?

A. Primary
B. Secondary
C. Tertiary
D. Only A and B
E. Only B and C

37. In cardiovascular physiology, ejection fraction (EF) represents which of the following?

    A.   Blood pressure / heart rate
    B.   Stroke volume × heart rate
    C.   Stroke volume / heart rate
    D.   Stroke volume × end diastolic volume
    E.   Stroke volume / end diastolic volume

38. Assuming that parasites and their hosts coevolve in an "arms race," we might deduce that the parasite is "ahead" if local populations are more capable of attacking the host population with which they are associated than other populations. Whereas the host may be "ahead" if local populations are more resistant to the local parasite than to other populations of the parasite. The preceding suggests that one result of interspecific interactions might be:

    A.   genetic drift within sympatric populations.
    B.   genetic drift within allopatric populations.
    C.   genetic mutations within sympatric populations.
    D.   genetic mutations within allopatric populations.
    E.   genetic mutations within migrating populations.

39. Each of the following statements are true regarding evidence consistent with the endosymbiotic theory EXCEPT one. Which one is the EXCEPTION?

    A.   Mitochondria and chloroplasts reproduce independently of their eukaryotic host cell.
    B.   Mitochondria and chloroplasts possess their unique DNA which is circular like prokaryotic DNA.
    C.   The thylakoid membranes of chloroplasts resemble the photosynthetic membranes of cyanobacteria.
    D.   The ribosomes of mitochondria and chloroplasts resemble those of prokaryotes in both size and sequence.
    E.   Animal cells do not have chloroplasts and plant cells do not have mitochondria.

40. The wrist bones are also referred to as which of the following?

    A.   Carpals
    B.   Metacarpals
    C.   Phalanges
    D.   Tarsals
    E.   Metatarsals

41. Using the information in the table, calculate the enthalpy change for the following process:

$$C_{graphite} \rightarrow C_{diamond}$$

Table 1

	Graphite	Diamond
Enthalpy of combustion to yield oxide (ΔH_c) kJ mol^{-1}	-393.3	-395.1

    A.   1.8 kJ mol^{-1}
    B.   −1.8 kJ mol^{-1}
    C.   1.0 kJ mol^{-1}
    D.   −1.0 kJ mol^{-1}
    E.   0 kJ mol^{-1}

42. H_2SO_3 acts as a Lewis acid probably because sulfurous acid:

    A.   is a proton donor.
    B.   donates a pair of electrons from another species.
    C.   reacts with NaOH which is a strong base.
    D.   possesses oxygen atoms.
    E.   accepts a pair of electrons from another species.

43. What is the percent by mass of oxygen in sulfurous acid (H_2SO_3)?

    A.   31.9%
    B.   19.7%
    C.   39.0%
    D.   58.5%
    E.   68.8%

44. 20 mL of 0.05 M Mg^{2+} in solution is desired. It is attempted to achieve this by adding 5 mL of 0.005 M $MgCl_2$ and 15 mL of $Mg_3(PO_4)_2$. What is the concentration of $Mg_3(PO_4)_2$?

A. $\dfrac{(0.015)}{\left[(.05)(.02)-(.005)(.005)\right]}$

B. $(0.015)\left[(0.05)(.02)\ -\ (.005)(.005)\right]$

C. $\left[\dfrac{(.05)(.02)-(.005)(.005)}{(0.015)}\right]$

D. $\dfrac{(0.045)}{\left[(.05)(.02)-(.005)(.005)\right]}$

E. $\dfrac{\left[(.05)(.02)-(.005)(.005)\right]}{(0.045)}$

45. What would be the pH of a 1.0 M solution of an unknown salt hydroxide given that the metal is monovalent and the K_b of the salt is 1.0×10^{-6}?

A. 11
B. 8.0
C. 7.5
D. 13.0
E. 14.0

46. A sample of white phosphorus (P_4) was reacted with excess Cl_2 gas to yield 68.75 grams of phosphorus trichloride. How many discrete P_4 molecules were there in the sample?

A. $\left[\dfrac{\left(\dfrac{69}{138}\right)}{4}\right](6.0\times10^{23})$

B. $\dfrac{\left[\dfrac{\left(\dfrac{69}{138}\right)}{4}\right]}{(6.0\times10^{23})}$

C. $\left[\dfrac{\left(\dfrac{69}{138}\right)}{8}\right](6.0\times10^{23})$

D. $\dfrac{(6.0\times10^{23})}{\left[\dfrac{\left(\dfrac{69}{138}\right)}{4}\right]}$

E. $\dfrac{(6.0\times10^{23})}{\left[\dfrac{\left(\dfrac{69}{138}\right)}{8}\right]}$

47. Which of the following is the strongest reducing agent?

Electrochemical reaction	$E°$ value (V)
$MnO_2 + 4H^+ + 2e^- \rightleftharpoons Mn^{2+} + 2H_2O$	+1.23
$Fe^{3+} + e^- \rightleftharpoons Fe^{2+}$	+0.771
$Cr^{3+} + e^- \rightleftharpoons Cr^{2+}$	−0.410

A. Cr^{3+}
B. Cr^{2+}
C. Mn^{2+}
D. MnO_2
E. Fe^{3+}

48. As the atomic number increases as one moves across the periodic table, the numerical value for electron affinity generally:

A. remains neutral though the electron affinity increases.

B. becomes more positive because of the decreasing effective nuclear charge.

C. becomes more negative because of the increasing effective nuclear charge.

D. becomes more positive because of the increasing atomic radius.

E. becomes more negative because of the increasing atomic radius.

49. HCl has a higher boiling point than either H_2 or Cl_2. The likely reason is that HCl:

A. exhibits weak dipole-dipole interactions, unlike H_2 and Cl_2.

B. has a greater molecular mass than either H_2 or Cl_2.

C. is less polar than either H_2 or Cl_2.

D. is a smaller molecule than H_2 and Cl_2.

E. is a strong acid.

50. Which of the following molecules can be involved in hydrogen bond formation but cannot form hydrogen bonds with molecules of its own kind?

A. C_2H_5OH

B. HCOOH

C. CH_3OCH_3

D. HF

E. H_3O^+

51. Reaction I was carried out in the dark and stopped before equilibrium was reached. The partial pressure of Cl_2 was found to be 35 atm and the mole fraction of HCl found to be 0.40. If the total pressure of the system is 100 atm, what is the partial pressure of H_2?

Reaction I

$$H_2 + Cl_2 \rightleftharpoons 2HCl$$

A. 10 atm

B. 25 atm

C. 65 atm

D. 75 atm

E. 85 atm

52. A fossil was discovered in the forests of Africa and when examined, it was found that it had a carbon-14 activity of 10.8 disintegrations per minute per gram (dpm g^{-1}). If the average activity of carbon-14 in a living organism is 43.0 dpm g^{-1}, approximately how many half-lives have passed since the death of the organism?

A. 8

B. 6

C. 4

D. 3

E. 2

53. Uranium ^{238}U is radioactive. One of the intermediates in its decay is obtained via 3 alpha emissions, 2 beta emissions and 3 gamma emissions. What is the identity of this intermediate?

A. $^{238}_{84}Po$

B. $^{232}_{88}Ra$

C. $^{226}_{84}Po$

D. $^{226}_{88}Ra$

E. $^{238}_{86}Po$

54. Given the following information:

$$2Fe \rightleftharpoons 2Fe^{2+} + 4e^- \qquad E° = +0.440 \text{ V}$$

$$O_2 + 2H_2O + 4e^- \rightleftharpoons 4OH^- \qquad E° = +0.401 \text{ V}$$

Determine the E° for the overall reaction:

$$2Fe(s) + O_2(g) + 2H_2O(l) \rightarrow 2Fe^{2+}(aq) + 4OH^-(aq)$$

A. +0.382 V

B. +0.841 V

C. −0.058 V

D. −1.702 V

E. −0.673 V

55. Given that the K_{sp} of FeX_2 is 5.0×10^{-16} where "X" is an unknown anion, what is its solubility in moles per liter?

A. 1.0×10^{-2}

B. 2.1×10^{-3}

C. 3.4×10^{-3}

D. 5.0×10^{-6}

E. 6.1×10^{-3}

56. Which of the following is a plausible structure for white phosphorus (P_4)?

A.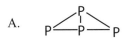

B.

C.

D.

E.

57. All of the following can be used to describe metals EXCEPT one. Which one is the EXCEPTION?

A. Excellent conductors of heat
B. Form positive ions by losing electrons
C. Ductile and malleable
D. Low ionization energy
E. Good conductors of electricity, but less well than metalloids

58. When s-block carbonates decompose, a gas is obtained which is heavier than air and does not support a lighted splint. What gas is it?

A. O_2
B. CO
C. CO_2
D. CO_3
E. C

59. Li_2O is often considered to be covalent in nature because of the unusually high electronegativity of lithium. Which of the following would be a plausible Lewis dot structure for the compound?

A. Li—Li—Ö
B. Li—Ö—Li
C. Li═O═Li
D. ·Li—Ö—Li·
E. ·Li—O—Li·

60. In the following electrolytic cell, which solution(s) could be used such that the electrode at A is the anode?

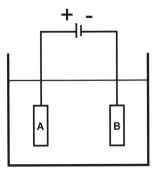

A. Molten NaCl
B. $CuSO_4$
C. $FeBr_2$
D. All of the above
E. None of the above

61. Given that the K_a of the indicator methyl-orange (HMe) is 4.0×10^{-4}, a solution of pH = 2 containing methyl-orange would be what color?

$$HMe \rightleftharpoons H^+ + Me^-$$
Red   Colorless   Yellow

A. Orange
B. Yellow
C. Colorless
D. Pink
E. Red

62. Consider the following reaction:

$$FeCl_2(aq) + H_2S(g) \rightarrow FeS(s) + 2HCl(aq)$$

When sulfur is precipitated, what type of reaction has occurred?

A. Oxidation-reduction
B. Neutralization
C. Disproportionation
D. Displacement
E. Double replacement

63. Which of the following electron configurations of atoms in neutral form corresponds to that of a Group II metal?

A. $1s^2, 2s^3$
B. $1s^2$
C. $1s^2, 2s^2, 2p^6, 3s^2$
D. $1s^2, 2s^2, 2p^2$
E. $1s^2, 2s^2, 2p^6, 3s^2, 3p^6, 3d^4, 4s^2$

64. What is the K_{a2} expression for hydrogen sulfide (H_2S) as an acid?

A. $[H^+][S^{2-}]$

B. $\dfrac{\left[H^+\right]\left[S^{2-}\right]}{\left[HS^-\right]}$

C. $[H^+]^2[S^{2-}]$

D. $\dfrac{\left[H^+\right]^2\left[S^{2-}\right]^2}{\left[HS^-\right]}$

E. $\dfrac{\left[2H^+\right]^2\left[2S^{2-}\right]}{\left[HS^-\right]}$

65. At a given temperature T in kelvin, the relationship between the three thermodynamic quantities including the change in Gibbs free energy (ΔG), the change in enthalpy (ΔH) and the change in entropy (ΔS), can be expressed as follows:

$$\Delta G = \Delta H - T\Delta S$$

The sublimation of carbon dioxide occurs quickly at room temperature. What might be predicted for the three thermodynamic quantities for the reverse reaction?

A. Only ΔS would be positive.
B. Only ΔS would be negative.
C. Only ΔH would be negative.
D. Only ΔG would be positive.
E. All 3 would be negative.

66. Water has a specific heat of 4.18 J/g•°C while glass (Pyrex) has a specific heat of 0.78 J/g•°C. If 40.0 J of heat is added to 1.00 g of each of these, which will experience the larger temperature increase?

A. They both will experience the same change in temperature because only the mass of a substance relates to the increase in temperature.
B. Neither would necessarily experience a temperature increase.
C. It would depend on the source of the heat added.
D. Water
E. Glass

67. 50 grams of glucose $(C_6H_{12}O_6)$ and 50 grams of sucrose $(C_{12}H_{22}O_{11})$ were each added to beakers of water (beaker 1 and beaker 2, respectively). Which of the following would be true?

A. Boiling point elevation for beaker 1 would be greater than the boiling point elevation for beaker 2.
B. Boiling point elevation for beaker 1 would be less than the boiling point elevation for beaker 2.
C. The same degree of boiling point elevation will occur in both beakers.
D. No boiling point elevation would be observed in either of the beakers.
E. Boiling point depression would occur in both beakers but to different degrees.

68. Which of the following would cause a gas to more closely resemble an ideal gas?

    A.   Decreased pressure
    B.   Decreased temperature
    C.   Decreased volume
    D.   Increased pressure
    E.   Increased volume

69. The data in Table 1 were collected for Reaction I:

Reaction I

$$2X + Y \rightarrow Z$$

Table I

Exp.	[X] in M	[Y] in M	Initial rate of reaction
1	0.050	0.100	2×10^{-4}
2	0.050	0.200	8×10^{-4}
3	0.200	0.100	8×10^{-4}

What is the rate law expression for Reaction I?

    A.   Rate = $k[X]^2[Y]$
    B.   Rate = $k[X]^2[Y]^2$
    C.   Rate = $k[X][Y]^2$
    D.   Rate = $k[X][Y]$
    E.   Rate = $k[2X][Y]$

70. What piece of laboratory equipment is best for accurately measuring the volume of a liquid?

    A.   Graduated cylinder
    B.   Erlenmeyer flask
    C.   Beaker
    D.   Evaporating dish
    E.   More than one of the above

71. Morphine is illustrated below.

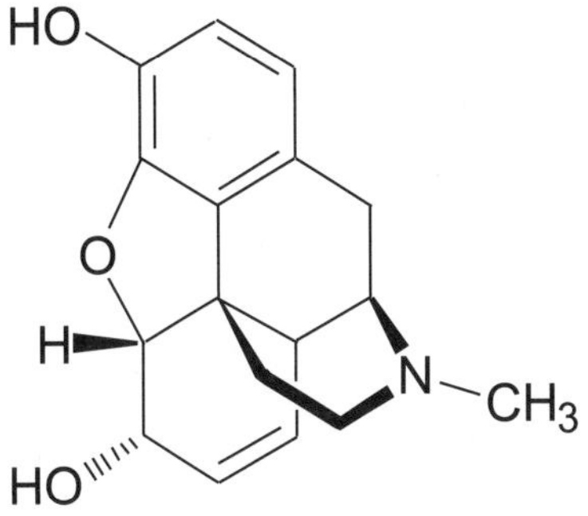

How many chiral carbons are there in morphine?

    A.   5
    B.   6
    C.   7
    D.   8
    E.   More than 8

72. Using 2 equivalents of the first and 1 equivalent of the second, respectively, which of the following pairs of compounds can be used to form the following tertiary alcohol?

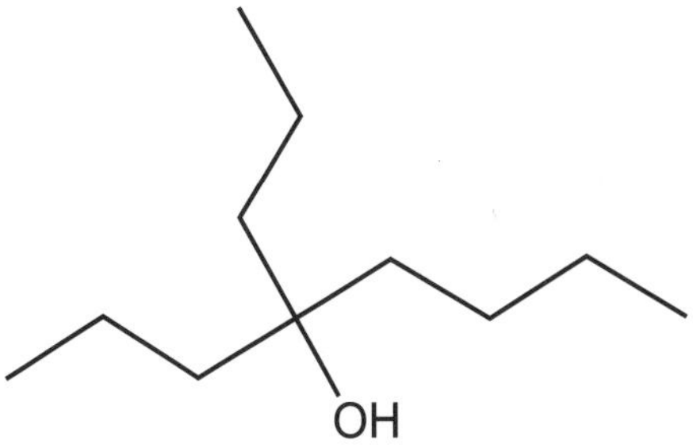

    A.   Propyl lithium and methyl butanoate
    B.   Butyl magnesium bromide and propyl butanoate
    C.   Butyl lithium and pentyl pentanoate
    D.   Pentyl magnesium chloride and propyl propanoate
    E.   Propyl magnesium bromide and hexyl pentanoate

73. Rank the following compounds from most to least basic:

I. $CH_3CH_2^-$
II. $CH_3CH_2O^-$
III. $CH_3CH_2NH_2$

A. I > II > III
B. II > III > I
C. III > II > I
D. II > I > III
E. I > III > II

74. Four compounds – allyl alcohol, benzoic acid, 2-butanone and butyraldehyde - were identified and stored in separate bottles. By accident, the labels were lost from the sample bottles. The following information was obtained via infrared spectroscopy and was used to identify and relabel the sample bottles.

Infrared absorption peaks (cm^{-1})

Bottle I	Bottle II	Bottle III	Bottle IV
1700 (sharp)	1710	1730 (sharp)	3333 (broad)
–	3500 – 3333 (broad)	2730	1030 (small)

Which of the following most accurately represents the contents of bottles I, II, III, and IV, respectively?

A. Butyraldehyde, 2-butanone, benzoic acid, allyl alcohol
B. Benzoic acid, butyraldehyde, allyl alcohol, 2-butanone
C. 2-Butanone, butyraldehyde, allyl alcohol, benzoic acid
D. 2-Butanone, benzoic acid, butyraldehyde, allyl alcohol
E. Benzoic acid, allyl alcohol, butyraldehyde, 2-butanone

75. What is the structure of formic acid?

A.

B.

C.

D.

E.

76. Phenols are soluble in a strongly basic sodium hydroxide solution, and insoluble in dilute sodium bicarbonate. Phenol has a pKa = 10.0. The introduction of an ortho bromine atom into the phenol would have the effect of:

A. lowering the pKa and thus decreasing the acidity of the phenol.
B. lowering the pKa and thus increasing the acidity of the phenol.
C. increasing the pKa and thus decreasing the acidity of the phenol.
D. increasing the pKa and thus increasing the acidity of the phenol.
E. no effect on the pKa nor the acidity of the phenol.

77. What is the product of the following acid catalyzed reaction?

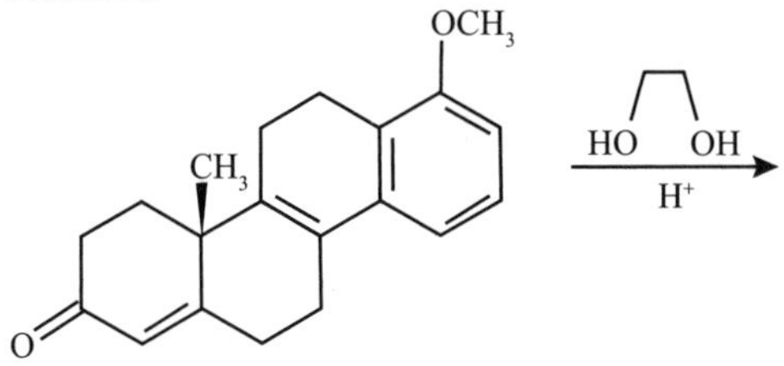

A.

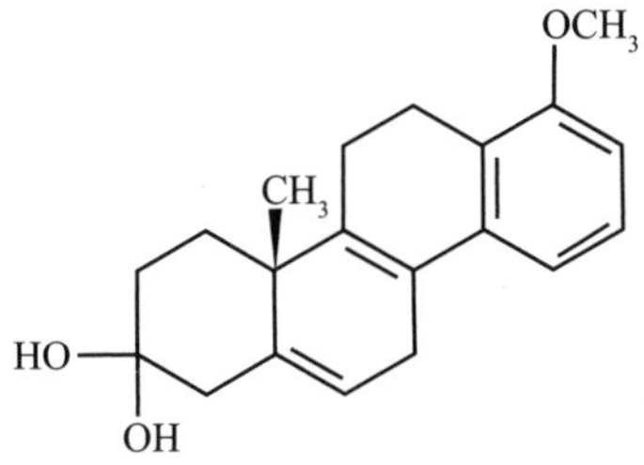

B.

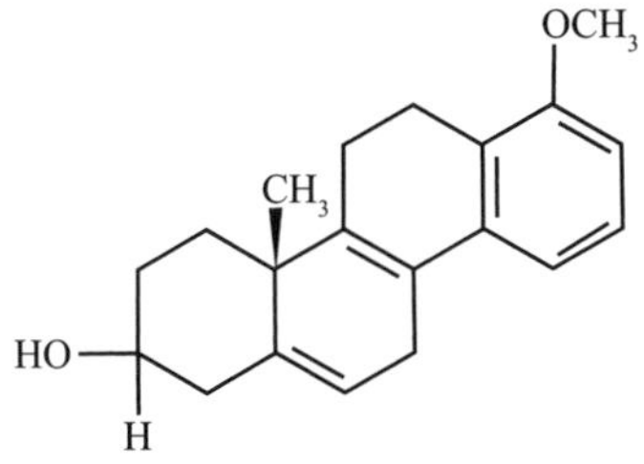

C.

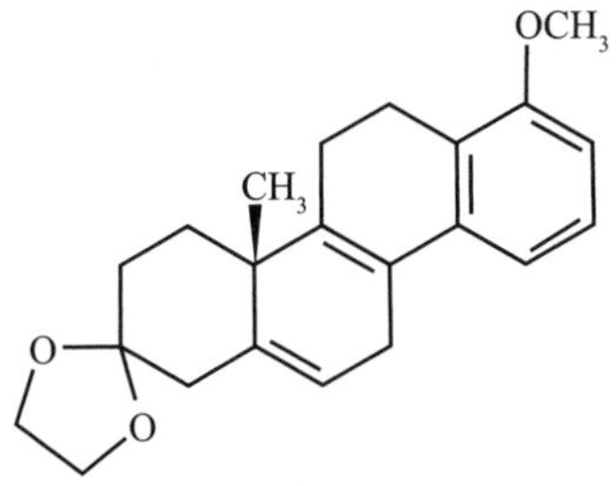

D.

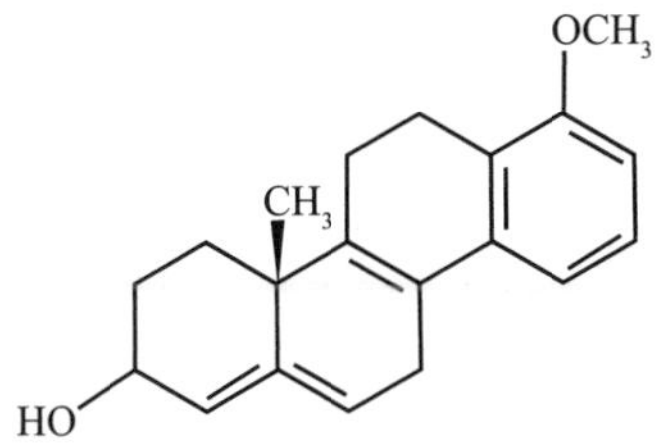

78. The efficiency of the distillation process in producing a pure product is improved by repeating the process, increasing the length of the column and avoiding overheating. All of the following can prevent overheating EXCEPT one. Which one is the EXCEPTION?

- A. Boiling chips
- B. Boiling slowly
- C. Adding a vacuum
- D. Adding a nucleophile
- E. Decreasing the vapor pressure

79. Cyclic ethers, or epoxides, are important chemical compounds that are composed of a 3–membered ring containing an oxygen atom and 2 carbon atoms. What are the bond angles in the epoxide ring?

- A. 109.5°
- B. 60°
- C. 108°
- D. 110°
- E. 120°

80. Which hydrogen(s) labeled below – directly bonded to a carbon – is (are) most acidic?

$$NH_2CH_2CH_2CH_2COOH$$
$$\quad 1 \quad 2 \quad 3 \quad 4$$

- A. 1
- B. 2
- C. 3
- D. 4
- E. 1, 2 and 3 are equally acidic.

81. Which of the following would explain the non-separation of cortisol from cortisone by gas-liquid chromatography (GLC)?

- A. The solid material in the column of the GLC, through which substances pass in their mobile phase, absorbs cortisol and cortisone equally well.
- B. Cortisol and cortisone have relatively high boiling points.
- C. Cortisol and cortisone have very similar melting points.
- D. Cortisol moves through the column of the GLC, through which substances pass in their mobile phase, at a much quicker rate than cortisone.
- E. Cortisone moves through the column of the GLC at a much quicker rate than cortisol.

82. Which of the following represents the amino acid methionine at its isoelectric point?

A. $CH_3-S-CH_2-CH_2-\overset{\overset{\displaystyle H}{|}}{\underset{\underset{\displaystyle NH_3^+}{|}}{C}}-COO^-$

B. $CH_3-S-CH_2-CH_2-\overset{\overset{\displaystyle H}{|}}{\underset{\underset{\displaystyle NH_3^+}{|}}{C}}-COOH$

C. $CH_4^+-S-CH_2-CH_2-\underset{\underset{\displaystyle NH_2}{|}}{C^-}-COOH$

D. $CH_4^+-S-CH_2-CH_2-\underset{\underset{\displaystyle NH_3^+}{|}}{C^-}-COO^-$

83. Consider the following schematic of a ^{1}H NMR:

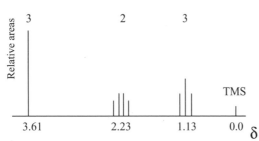

Which of the following compounds is most consistent with the ^{1}H NMR above?

A. C_4H_6O
B. $CH_3COCH_2OCH(CH_3)_2$
C. $CH_3CH_2COOCH_3$
D. $CH_3CH_2OCH_2CH_2CH_3$
E. $CH_3COCH_2OCH_3$

84. Choose the correct structure for:

$CH_3CH_2CH(CH_3)CH(CH(CH_3)_2)CH_2CH=C(CH_3)_2$

A.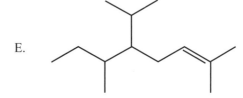

B.

C.

D.

E.

85. The solvent used to do an extraction should do all of the following EXCEPT one. Which one is the EXCEPTION?

A. It must be sparingly soluble in the liquid from which the solute is to be extracted.
B. It must readily dissolve the substance to be extracted.
C. It must react chemically with the solute to form a product.
D. It must be easily separated from the solute after extraction.
E. None of the above.

86. How many possible structural isomers are there for C_4H_8?

 A. 2
 B. 4
 C. 5
 D. 6
 E. 16

87. Which of the following statements is consistent with the acid-catalyzed dehydration of tertiary alcohols?

 A. Formation of the carbocation is a slow step.
 B. Protonation of the OH functional group is rapid and reversible.
 C. Deprotonation of the carbocation is a fast step.
 D. Cleavage of the C–O bond occurs in the rate determining step.
 E. All of the above

88. Consider the following reaction:

The preceding reaction can be classified most closely as which of the following?

 A. Enamine formation
 B. Decarboxylation reaction
 C. Enzymatic cleavage
 D. Sp-sp hybridization
 E. Imine formation

89. How many of the following compounds contain at least 1 chiral carbon and how many exhibit optical activity, respectively?

 A. 4 compounds possess at least 1 chiral carbon; 1 compound is optically active.
 B. 4 compounds possess at least 1 chiral carbon; 2 compounds are optically active.
 C. 2 compounds possess at least 1 chiral carbon; 1 compound is optically active.
 D. 2 compounds possess at least 1 chiral carbon; 2 compounds are optically active.
 E. 3 compounds possess at least 1 chiral carbon; 3 compounds are optically active.

90. Consider the following reaction:

$$(CH_3)_2C = CH_2 + HCl \rightarrow Product$$

Which of the following compounds best exemplifies the major organic product of the above reaction?

 A. $(CH_3)_2CHCH_2Cl$

 B. $(CH_3)_2 \underset{\underset{Cl}{|}}{C}CH_3$

 C. $CH_2 = \underset{\underset{Cl}{}}{\overset{\overset{Cl}{|}}{C}} - CH_2CH_3$

 D. $CH_3 - \underset{\underset{Cl}{|}}{\overset{\overset{Cl}{|}}{C}} - CH_2CH_3$

 E. $(ClCH_2)_2CHCH_3$

91. Acid catalysts such as *p*–toluensulfonic acid are often used to dehydrate alcohols. The role of the acid catalyst is to:

   A.   increase $\Delta G°$ and increase the activation energy for the dehydration reaction.

   B.   increase $\Delta G°$ and lower the activation energy for the dehydration reaction.

   C.   maintain $\Delta G°$ at the same value and lower the activation energy for the dehydration reaction.

   D.   lower $\Delta G°$ and increase the activation energy for the dehydration reaction.

   E.   lower $\Delta G°$ and lower the activation energy for the dehydration reaction.

92. Which of the following is the most accurate representation of the reaction coordinate diagram for the solvolysis of t–butyl bromide?

Note that [ ]* represents the intermediate.

A.

B.

C.

D.

93. The free energy changes for the equilibria *cis* ⇌ *trans* of 1,2–, 1,3–, and 1,4– dimethylcyclohexane are shown below.

I.

     A   B

II.

     A   B

III.

     A   B

The most stable diastereomer in each case would be:

   A.   IA, IIB, IIIA
   B.   IB, IIB, IIIB
   C.   IA, IIA, IIIA
   D.   IA, IIB, IIIB
   E.   IB, IIA, IIIB

94. What is the hybridization of C1 in coniine?

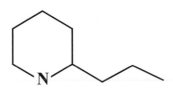

Coniine

   A.   sp
   B. sp^2
   C. sp^3
   D. sd^4
   E.   None of the above

95. Which of the following would be the least reactive diene in a Diels-Alder reaction?

A.

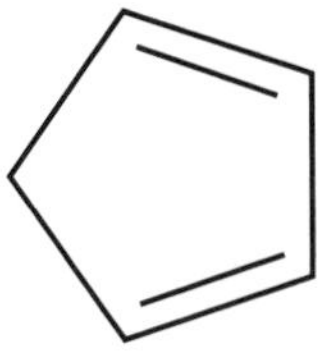

B.

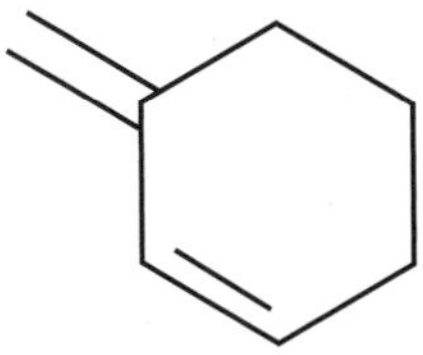

C.

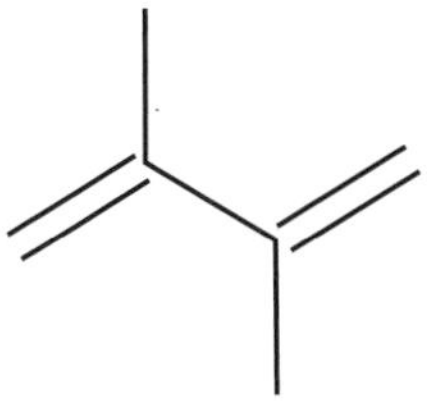

D.

E.

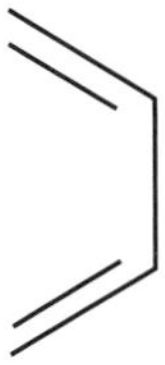

96. A student used a distillation apparatus to separate ethyl acetate from 1–butanol because of the difference in boiling points of these 2 compounds. This difference is most likely attributed to which of the following factors?

A.   Hydrogen bonding
B.   Bond hybridization
C.   Temperature scanning
D.   Increments of 5 degrees
E.   Resonance stabilization

97. All of the following are true regarding allene (C_3H_4) EXCEPT one. Which one is the EXCEPTION?

A.   The C–H bond angles are 120°.
B.   The hybridization of the carbon atoms are sp and sp^2.
C.   The bond angle formed by the three carbons is 180°.
D.   The central carbon of allene forms two sigma bonds and two pi bonds.
E.   Allene is a conjugated diene.

98. Which of the following is aromatic?

A.

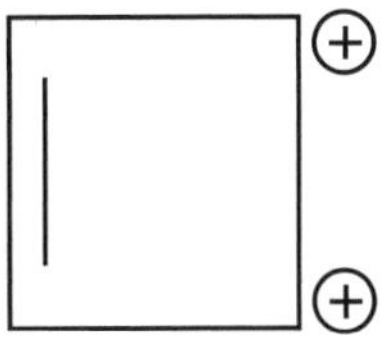

B.

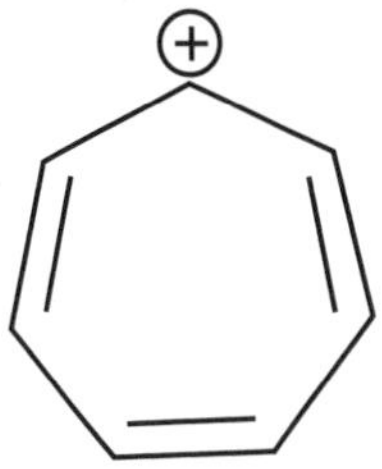

C.

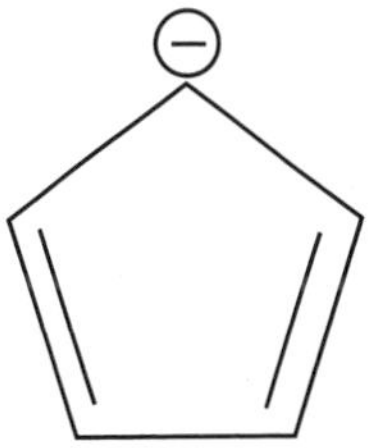

D.

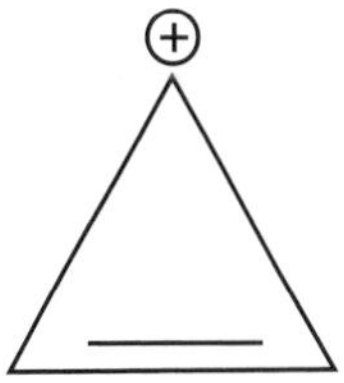

E.   All of the above

99. Which of the following represents the product from the reaction shown below?

$$\xrightarrow{\begin{array}{l} 1.\ CH_3COCl,\ AlCl_3 \\ 2.\ MeNH_2 \\ 3.\ NaBH_4 \end{array}}$$

A. (structure with NHMe and O)

B. (structure with MeHN and O)

C. (structure with O and NHMe)

D. (structure with NHMe)

E. (structure with Me, N, and O)

100. Each of the following structures is a resonance form of the molecule shown below EXCEPT one. Which one is the EXCEPTION?

A.

B.

C.

D.

E.

Perceptual Ability Test

Time limit: 60 minutes

Part 1

For questions 1 through 15:

This visualization test is composed of items modeled in the sample question below. A three-dimensional object is presented on the left, followed by five choices of apertures or openings.

The task is the same in each question. First, you have to mentally rotate the given object to see how it looks from different directions. Next, select the aperture from the five options that would allow the object to pass smoothly if the correct side were inserted first. Lastly, mark the letter of your choice on the answer sheet.

Rules:

1. The given object may be entered through the aperture from a direction that is different from the one shown in the question.

2. Once the object is introduced to the opening, it must pass completely through the hole without rotating the object in any direction.

3. Both the three-dimensional object and the corresponding apertures are drawn to the same scale. It may be possible for an aperture to have the correct shape yet be too small or too big for the object. However, the differences are large enough to be seen by the naked eye.

4. No irregularities are hidden in any portion of the object. In case the figure has symmetric indentations, the hidden portion would be symmetric with the visible part.

5. For each question, only one aperture matches the exact shape and size of one of the two-dimensional views of the object.

Example: (The answer to this example should not be marked on the answer sheet.)

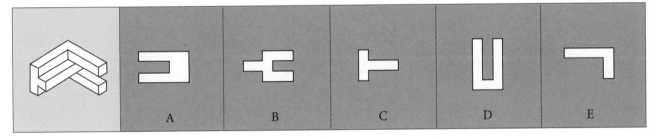

The correct answer is A.

For the object to pass all the way through the aperture, it has to be rotated first at 180 degrees from right to left and then, the side on the right is inserted first.

Please proceed to the questions.

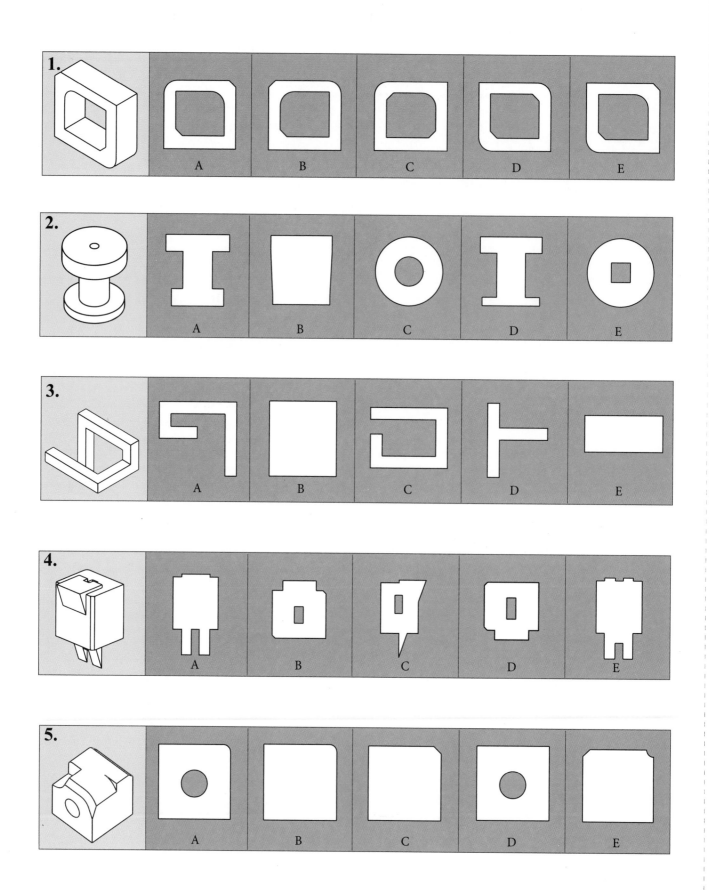

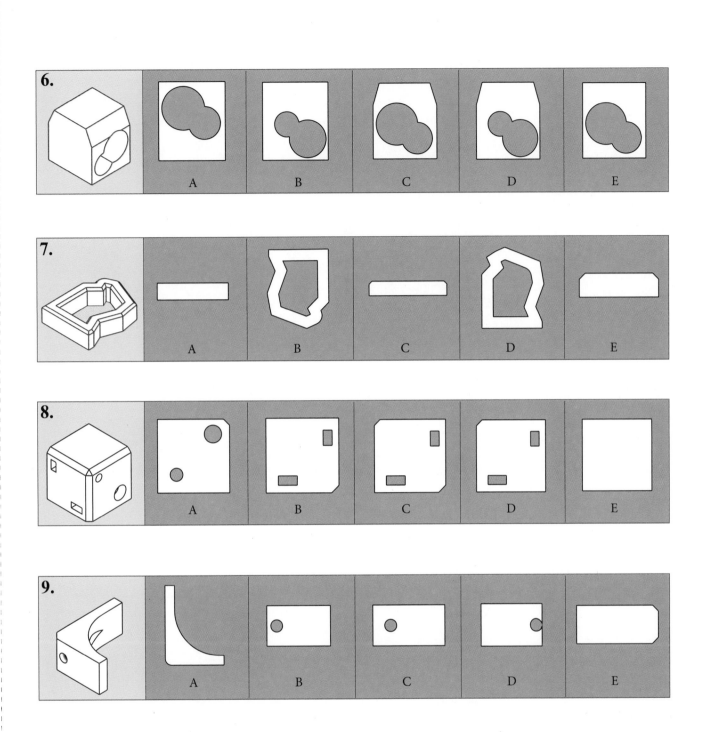

11.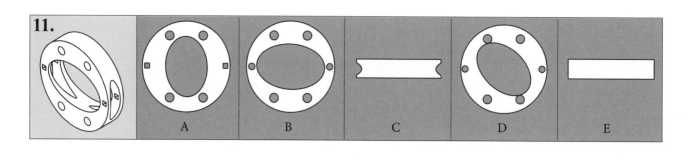

12.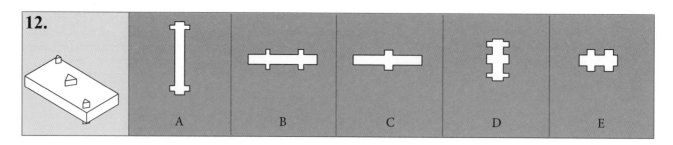

13.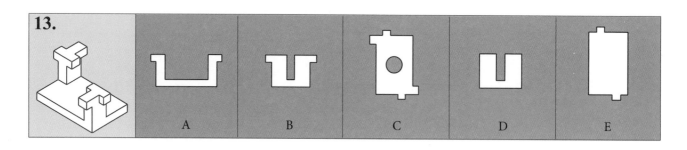

14.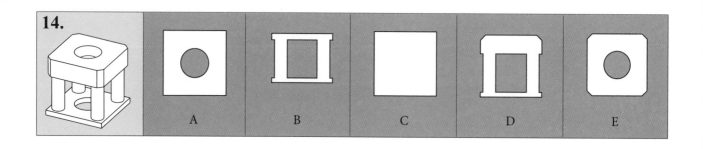

15.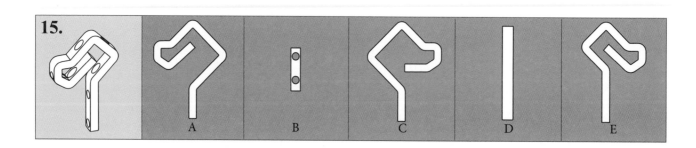

DO NOT STOP - READ DIRECTIONS FOR PART 2 AND CONTINUE

Part 2

For questions 16 through 30:

The following figure shows the top, front, and end views of a basic solid object. These are flat perspectives where only points along the parallel lines of the object's surface are shown. The projection looking DOWN on the object (TOP VIEW) is in the upper left-hand corner of the illustration. The projection looking at the object from the FRONT (FRONT VIEW) is in the lower left-hand corner. The projection looking at the object from the RIGHT side (END VIEW) is in the lower right-hand corner. The positions of these views are ALWAYS the same in each question and are also labeled accordingly.

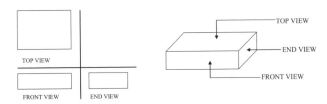

If the object had a hole in it, the views would look as such:

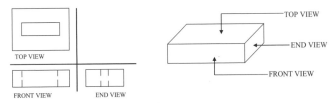

Points that are not visible on the surface of the object in a particular view are represented by DOTTED lines.

In the succeeding questions, two views are presented, followed by four options to complete the set. Pick the correct choice that corresponds to the missing view and mark it on the answer sheet.

Example: Choose the correct END VIEW.   (The answer to this example should not be marked on the answer sheet.)

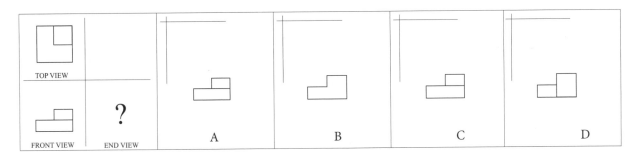

The correct answer is C.

The front view shows a smaller block on the base and no hole (because no dotted lines are shown). The top view shows that the block is a square and located on the upper left corner of the base. These characteristics correspond to the outline shown in option C if viewed from the right side of the object.

Please note that the problems given in the succeeding items do not always require you to choose the end view. The top view or front view may also be asked.

Please proceed to the questions.

16. Choose the correct TOP VIEW.

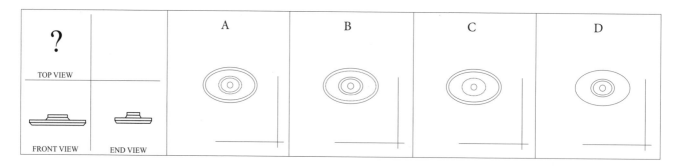

17. Choose the correct TOP VIEW.

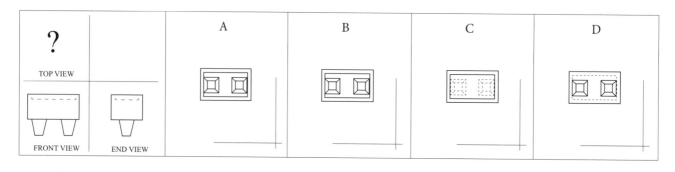

18. Choose the correct END VIEW.

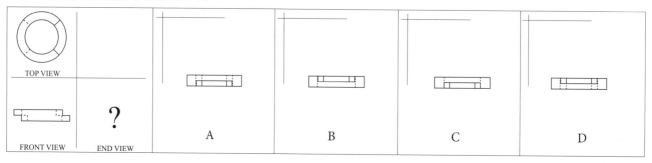

19. Choose the correct END VIEW.

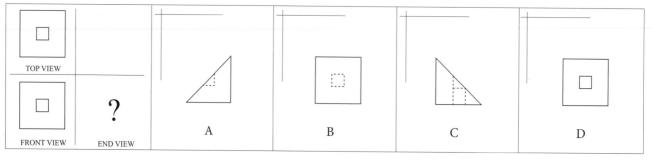

20. Choose the correct FRONT VIEW.

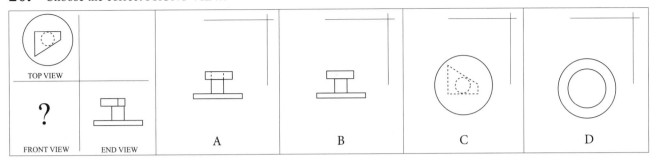

21. Choose the correct TOP VIEW.

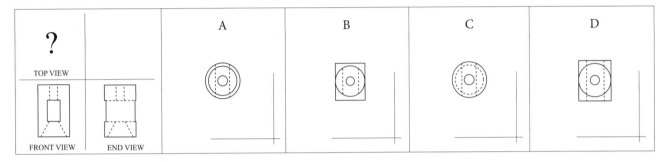

22. Choose the correct FRONT VIEW.

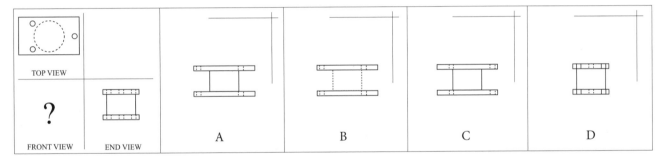

23. Choose the correct TOP VIEW.

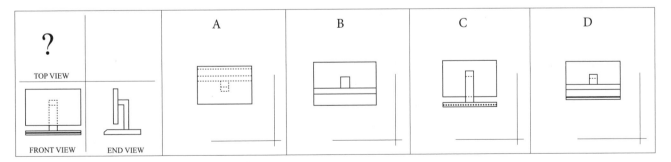

24. Choose the correct END VIEW.

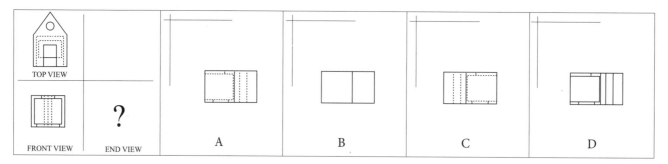

25. Choose the correct FRONT VIEW.

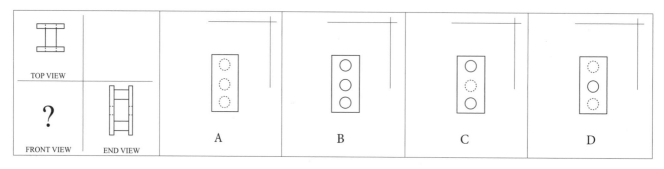

26. Choose the correct END VIEW.

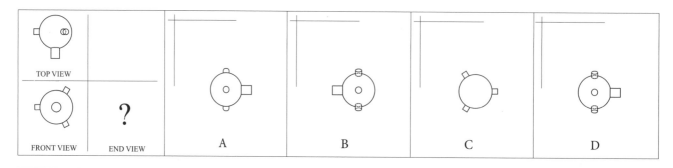

27. Choose the correct TOP VIEW.

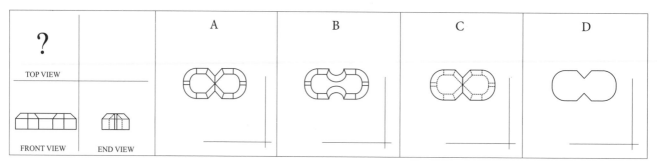

28. Choose the correct FRONT VIEW.

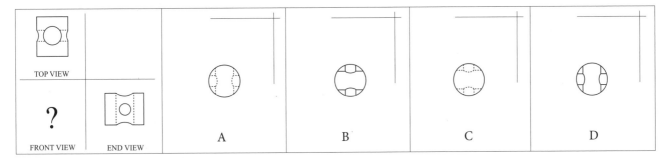

29. Choose the correct TOP VIEW.

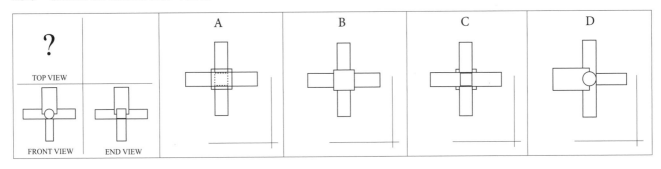

30. Choose the correct TOP VIEW.

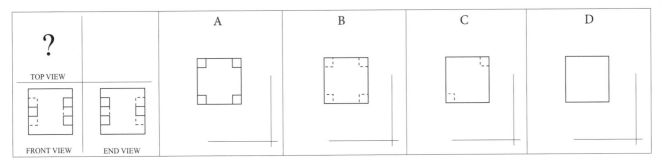

DO NOT STOP - READ DIRECTIONS FOR PART 3 AND CONTINUE

Part 3

For questions 31 through 45:

This section requires you to evaluate the four INTERIOR angles and rank each item from SMALL to LARGE in terms of degrees. From the alternatives, select the one with the correct order. Indicate your choice on the answer sheet.

Example:

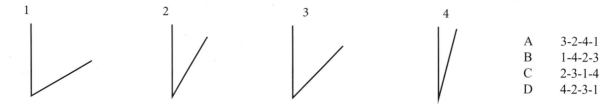

A	3-2-4-1
B	1-4-2-3
C	2-3-1-4
D	4-2-3-1

The correct answer is D.

The correct order of the angles from small to large is 4-2-3-1.

Please proceed to the questions.

31.

1   2   3   4

 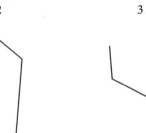 

A   3-1-4-2
B   2-3-1-4
C   2-1-3-4
D   1-3-4-2

32.

1   2   3   4

A   1-2-4-3
B   2-1-4-3
C   4-3-2-1
D   3-4-1-2

33.

1   2   3   4

A   2-1-3-4
B   1-2-4-3
C   3-2-1-4
D   4-3-1-2

34.

1   2   3   4

A   2-1-3-4
B   1-2-4-3
C   3-2-1-4
D   4-3-1-2

35.   1   2   3   4

A   1-4-2-3
B   1-2-3-4
C   4-1-3-2
D   1-2-4-3

36.   1   2   3   4

A   4-3-1-2
B   3-4-2-1
C   1-2-4-3
D   2-3-1-4

37.   1   2   3   4

A   1-3-4-2
B   2-3-1-4
C   2-1-4-3
D   3-2-1-4

38.   1   2   3   4

A   3-1-4-2
B   2-1-4-3
C   1-3-4-2
D   4-1-3-2

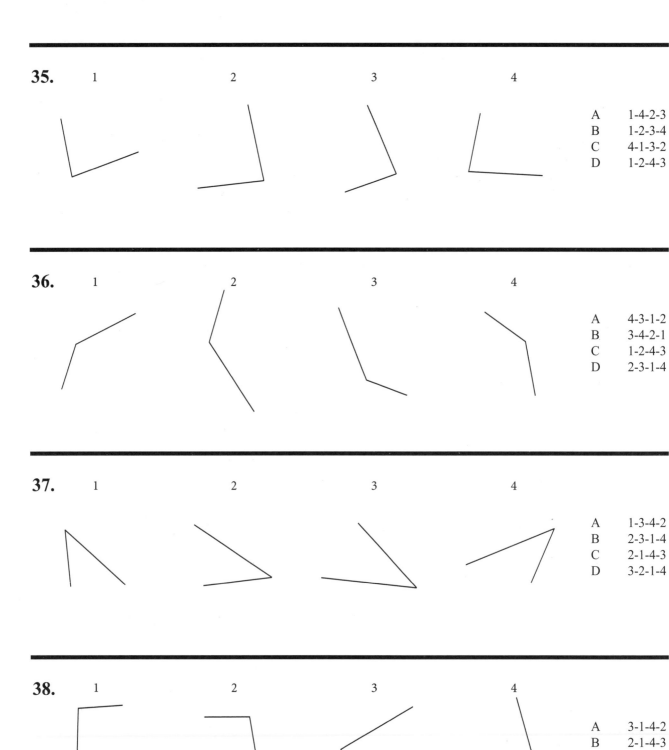

39.

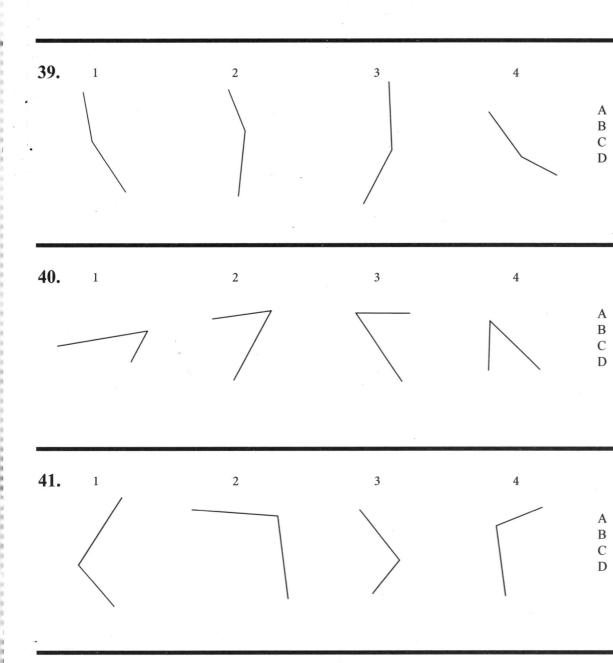

A	2-1-4-3
B	1-4-3-2
C	2-1-3-4
D	3-2-4-1

40.

1   2   3   4

A	1-2-4-3
B	1-4-3-2
C	4-1-2-3
D	3-4-2-1

41.

1   2   3   4

A	1-2-3-4
B	3-2-4-1
C	3-1-4-2
D	2-3-4-1

42.

1   2   3   4

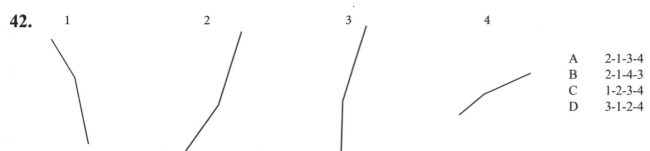

A	2-1-3-4
B	2-1-4-3
C	1-2-3-4
D	3-1-2-4

43.

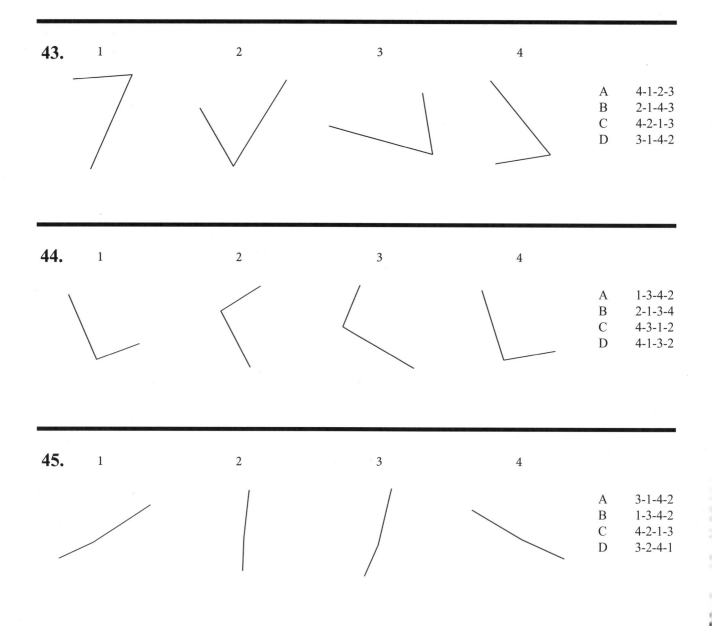

A	4-1-2-3
B	2-1-4-3
C	4-2-1-3
D	3-1-4-2

44.

A	1-3-4-2
B	2-1-3-4
C	4-3-1-2
D	4-1-3-2

45.

A	3-1-4-2
B	1-3-4-2
C	4-2-1-3
D	3-2-4-1

DO NOT STOP - READ DIRECTIONS FOR PART 4 AND CONTINUE

Part 4

For questions 46 through 60:

Each question in this section presents the following scenario:

A square-shaped paper is folded one or more times. The broken lines in the next figures represent the main outline of the paper; the solid lines signify the position of the paper as it is being folded. Take note that the paper is never turned or twisted. This means that the folded paper always stays within the boundaries of the original square.

Each question shows the paper folded multiple times. After the last fold, the paper is punched with a hole. Your task is to visualize unfolding the paper and identifying the position of the holes on the unfolded square. Only one pattern is correct for each question.

Example 1:(The answer to this example should not be marked on the answer sheet.)

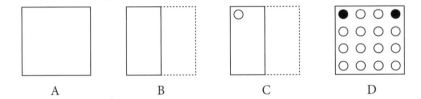

In Example 1, Figure A shows the unfolded paper. Figure B shows the paper now folded in half. Figure C shows where the hole is punched on the folded paper. Figure D shows the resulting pattern of the holes, indicated by the darkened circles, on the original square.

Example 2 shows how a question appears on the test.

Example 2:

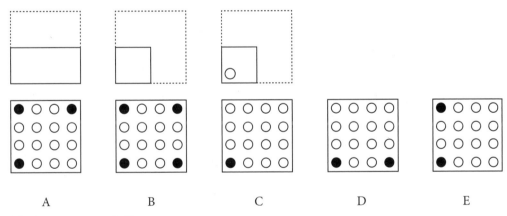

The correct answer is B.

The paper was four layers when punched, resulting to the holes placed in each of the four corners.

Please proceed to the questions.

46.

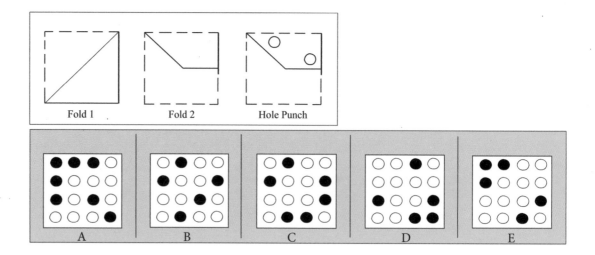

Fold 1   Fold 2   Hole Punch

A   B   C   D   E

47.

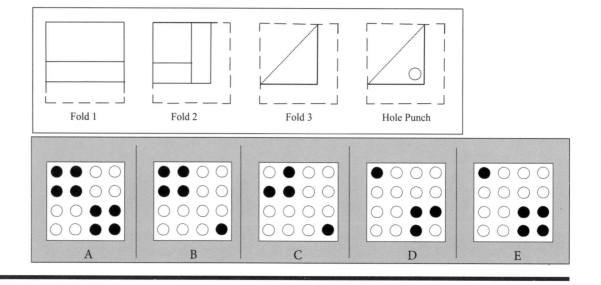

Fold 1   Fold 2   Fold 3   Hole Punch

A   B   C   D   E

48.

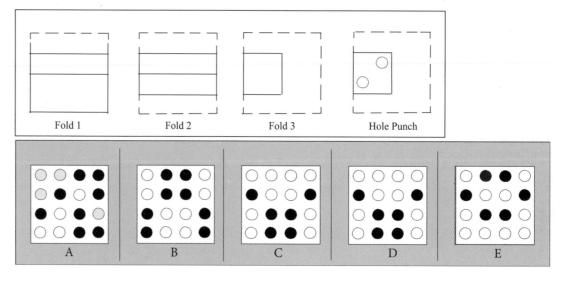

Fold 1   Fold 2   Fold 3   Hole Punch

A   B   C   D   E

49.

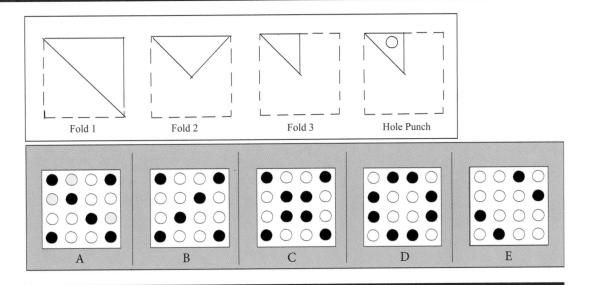

Fold 1   Fold 2   Fold 3   Hole Punch

A   B   C   D   E

50.

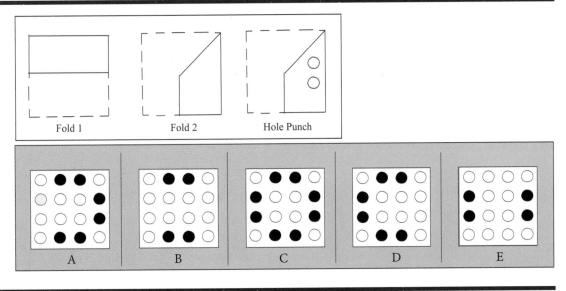

Fold 1   Fold 2   Hole Punch

A   B   C   D   E

51.

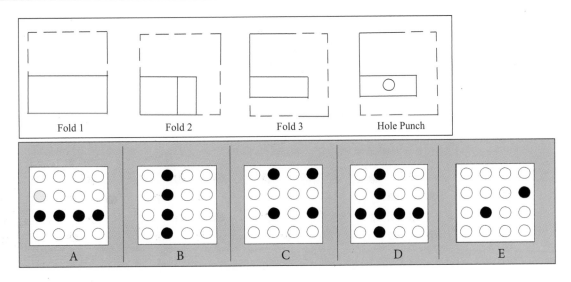

Fold 1   Fold 2   Fold 3   Hole Punch

A   B   C   D   E

52.

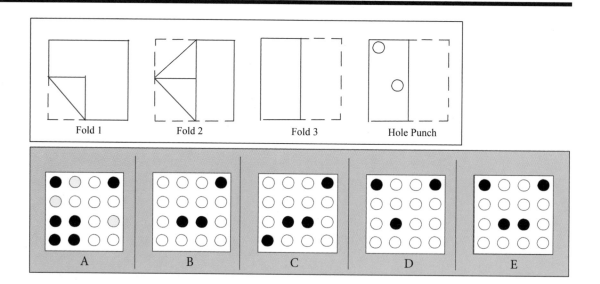

Fold 1   Fold 2   Fold 3   Hole Punch

A   B   C   D   E

53.

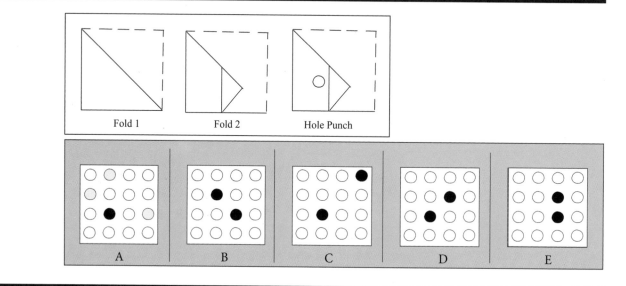

Fold 1   Fold 2   Hole Punch

A   B   C   D   E

54.

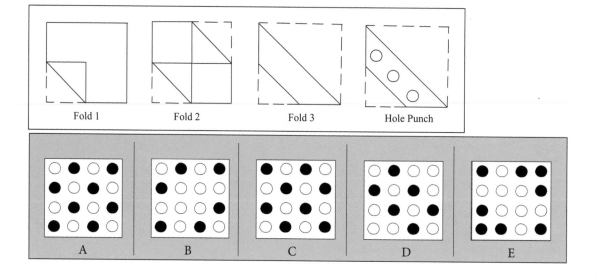

Fold 1   Fold 2   Fold 3   Hole Punch

A   B   C   D   E

55.

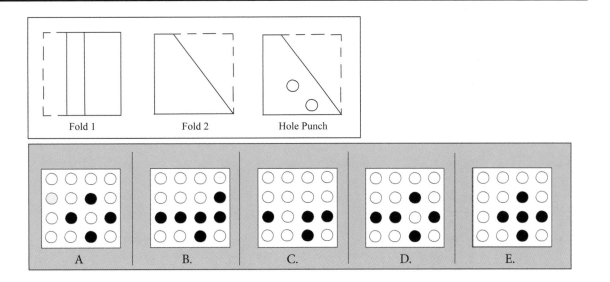

Fold 1   Fold 2   Hole Punch

A.   B.   C.   D.   E.

56.

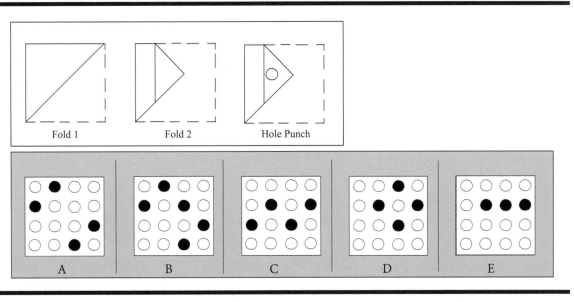

Fold 1   Fold 2   Hole Punch

A   B   C   D   E

57.

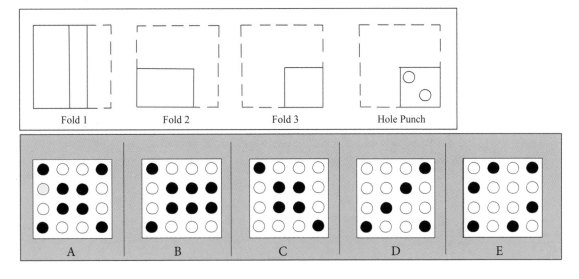

Fold 1   Fold 2   Fold 3   Hole Punch

A   B   C   D   E

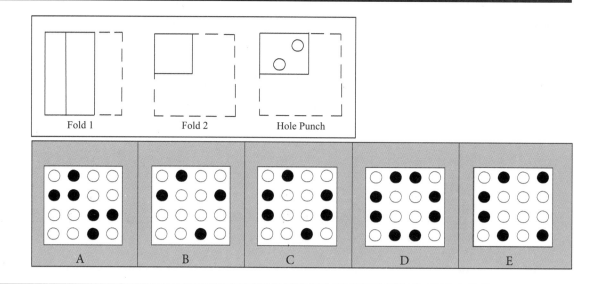

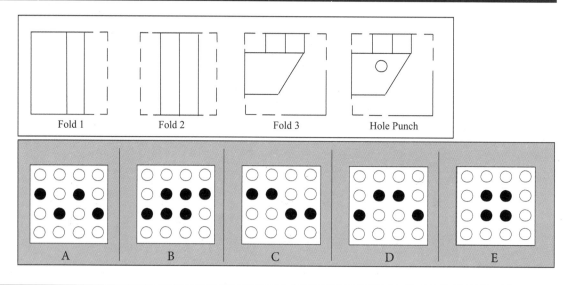

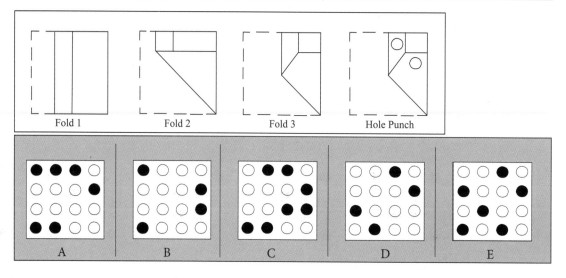

DO NOT STOP - READ DIRECTIONS FOR PART 5 AND CONTINUE

Part 5

For questions 61 through 75:

Each figure is constructed by stacking cubes on top of each other. Once they are stacked, all of the exposed surfaces, excluding the bottom surfaces, are painted. The number of painted sides per cube can range from zero to five. Do not forget that there are cubes "hidden" behind the other cubes.

For the questions in this section, you are required to evaluate each figure and conclude how many cubes have:

> only **one** of their sides painted.
> only **two** of their sides painted.
> only **three** of their sides painted.
> all **five** of their sides painted.

Remember: No problem will have zero (0) as the correct answer.

Example: (The answer to this example should not be marked on the answer sheet.)

In figure 1, how many cubes have two of their exposed
sides painted?

A.   1 cube
B.   2 cubes
C.   3 cubes
D.   4 cubes
E.   5 cubes

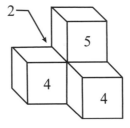

The correct answer is A.

There are four cubes in Figure 1. Three are visible, and one is hidden supporting the top cube. Two sides of the invisible cube are painted; five sides of the top cube are painted; and for each of the remaining two cubes, four of their sides are painted .

Note: The numbers in the cubes indicating the number of exposed sides shown in the sample (Figure 1) are not shown in the actual questions. However, it is important to remember that after the cubes are stacked together, each one is PAINTED ON ALL VISIBLE SIDES EXCEPT THE BOTTOM.

Please proceed to the questions.

PROBLEM A

61. In Figure A, how many cubes have two of their exposed sides painted?

    A. 1 cube
    B. 2 cubes
    C. 3 cubes
    D. 4 cubes
    E. 6 cubes

62. In Figure A, how many cubes have three of their exposed sides painted?

    A. 1 cube
    B. 3 cubes
    C. 4 cubes
    D. 5 cubes
    E. 6 cubes

63. In Figure A, how many cubes have four of their exposed sides painted?

    A. 1 cube
    B. 2 cubes
    C. 3 cubes
    D. 5 cubes
    E. 6 cubes

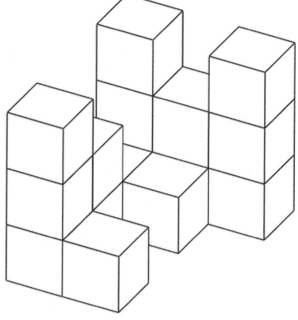

FIGURE A

PROBLEM B

64. In Figure B, how many cubes have one of their exposed sides painted?

    A. 1 cube
    B. 2 cubes
    C. 3 cubes
    D. 4 cubes
    E. 5 cubes

65. In Figure B, how many cubes have three of their exposed sides painted?

    A. 2 cubes
    B. 3 cubes
    C. 4 cubes
    D. 6 cubes
    E. 7 cubes

66. In Figure B, how many cubes have four of their exposed sides painted?

    A. 2 cubes
    B. 3 cubes
    C. 4 cubes
    D. 6 cubes
    E. 7 cubes

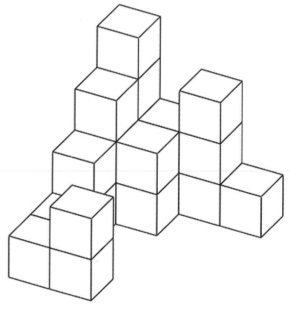

FIGURE B

PROBLEM C

67. In Figure C, how many cubes have two of their exposed sides painted?

A. 2 cubes
B. 3 cubes
C. 4 cubes
D. 5 cubes
E. 6 cubes

68. In Figure C, how many cubes have three of their exposed sides painted?

A. 1 cube
B. 2 cubes
C. 4 cubes
D. 6 cubes
E. 7 cubes

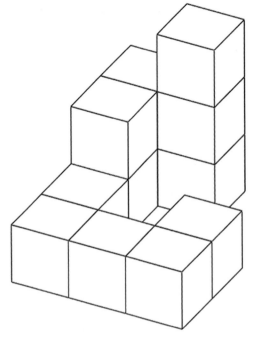

FIGURE C

PROBLEM D

69. In Figure D, how many cubes have two of their exposed sides painted?

A. 2 cubes
B. 3 cubes
C. 4 cubes
D. 6 cubes
E. 7 cubes

70. In Figure D, how many cubes have three of their exposed sides painted?

A. 2 cubes
B. 3 cubes
C. 5 cubes
D. 6 cubes
E. 7 cubes

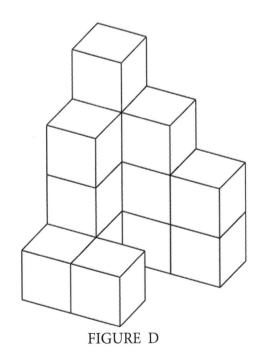

FIGURE D

PROBLEM E

71. In Figure E, how many cubes have two of their exposed sides painted?

    A. 1 cube
    B. 2 cubes
    C. 3 cubes
    D. 5 cubes
    E. 6 cubes

72. In Figure E, how many cubes have three of their exposed sides painted?

    A. 1 cube
    B. 2 cubes
    C. 3 cubes
    D. 4 cubes
    E. 5 cubes

73. In Figure E, how many cubes have four of their exposed sides painted?

    A. 1 cube
    B. 2 cubes
    C. 4 cubes
    D. 5 cubes
    E. 6 cubes

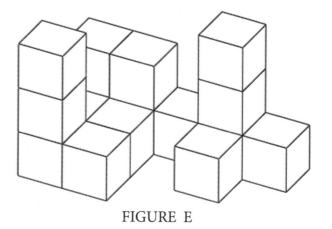

FIGURE E

PROBLEM F

74. In Figure F, how many cubes have two of their exposed sides painted?

    A. 1 cube
    B. 2 cubes
    C. 3 cubes
    D. 5 cubes
    E. 6 cubes

75. In Figure F, how many cubes have three of their exposed sides painted?

    A. 1 cube
    B. 3 cubes
    C. 4 cubes
    D. 6 cubes
    E. 7 cubes

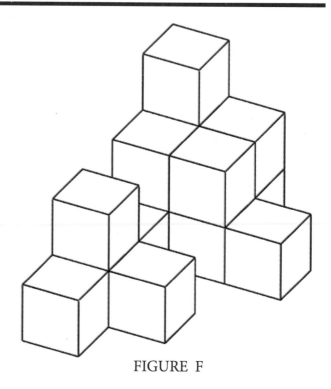

FIGURE F

DO NOT STOP - READ DIRECTIONS FOR PART 6 AND CONTINUE

Part 6

For questions 76 through 90:

Each question in this section will present a flat pattern, which will then be folded into a three-dimensional model. Four options of the resulting actual figure are given. Only one model is correct in every set.

Some figures will have shaded portions similar to the pattern shown in the example below. The shaded areas are not necessarily the "sides" of a figure. They can also be the top or the bottom of the figure.

Example: (Do not mark the answers to this example on your answer sheet.)

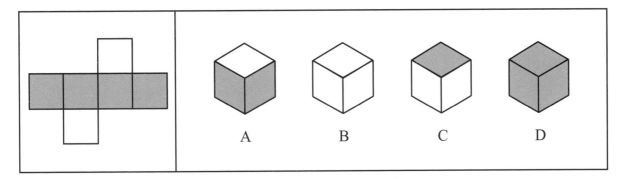

The correct answer is A.

From the given figures A, B, C, or D, the shaded parts obviously form as the sides of the box. The resulting model will then have all four sides shaded while the top and bottom will be white. This makes A the best answer.

Please proceed to the questions.

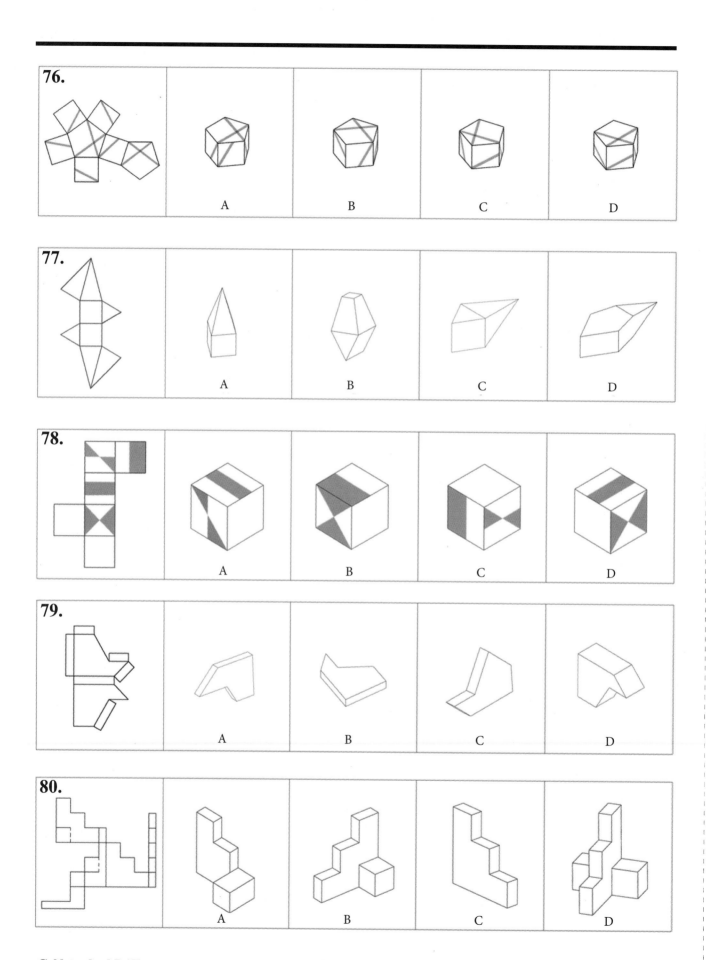

76.
A B C D

77.
A B C D

78.
A B C D

79.
A B C D

80.
A B C D

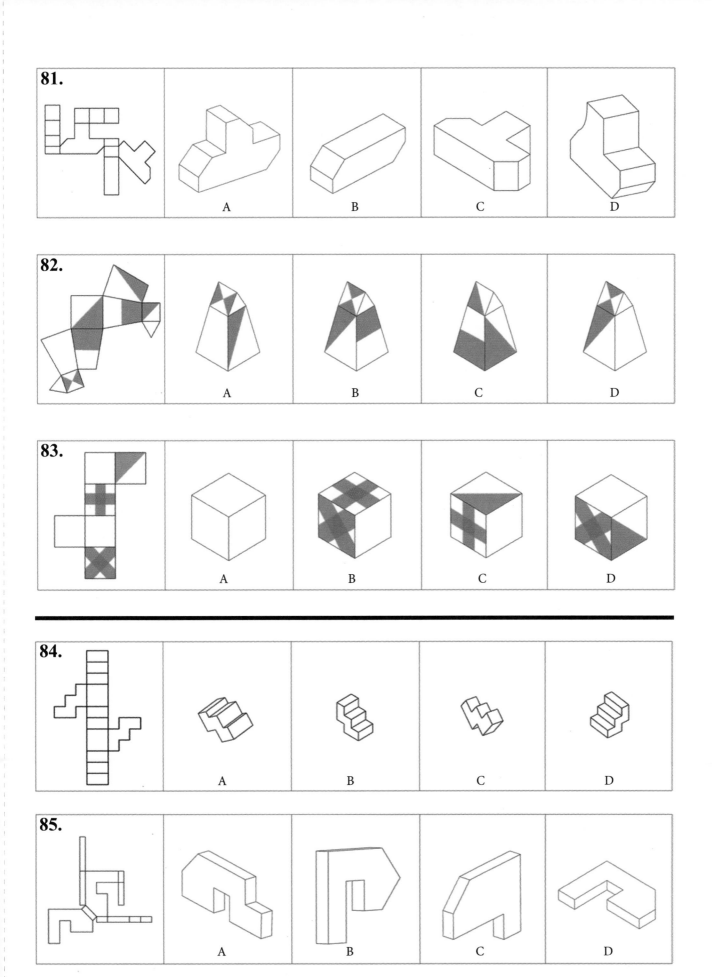

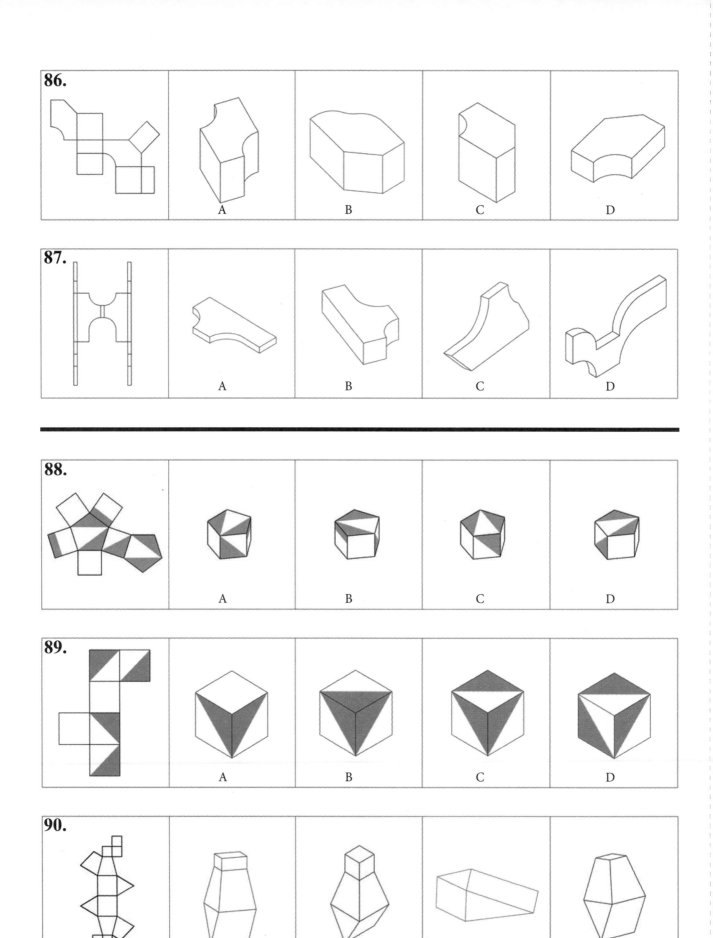

Passage 1

Cosmic Rays

(1)   The earliest telescopes were optical telescopes, allowing astronomers to view the Universe in visible light. In the 20th century, astronomers extended the range of telescopes to cover the entire electromagnetic spectrum, from radio and infrared regions, into the ultraviolet, X ray, and gamma ray bands. However, electromagnetic radiation isn't the only sort of particle that falls from the sky: ionized atomic nuclei hit the Earth's atmosphere continuously, with such "cosmic rays" providing hints on energetic processes in the Universe. Since the middle of the 20th century, astronomers have been setting up instrument systems to help determine the origin of cosmic rays.

(2)   After the discovery of radioactivity at the beginning of the 20th century, scientists then discovered that there seemed to be a pervasive background radiation that was present almost everywhere. The radiation was believed to be coming from the Earth itself. In 1910, a Jesuit pries named Theodor Wulf (1868 – 1946) went up the Eiffel Tower in Paris to measure radiation levels with an "electroscope." This was a simple device consisting of a sealed gas-filled globe with a metal rod inserted in the top, connected to two thin gold leaves inside the globe. A static electric charge could be used to form the two leaves to spread apart; any radiation passing through the globe would ionize the gas, causing the charge on the leaves to discharge so that they would gradually fall back together.

(3)   If the radiation was actually coming from the Earth, it would be weaker at the top of the tower – but the radiation levels were surprisingly high. Wulf suggested that this mysterious radiation might be coming from the upper atmosphere or space. He suggested that balloon flights might be conducted to confirm this notion.

(4)   In 1911 – 1912 an Austrian physicist named Victor Hess (1883 – 1964) made a series of ten balloon flights with an electroscope to investigate. Hess did discover that radiation increased with altitude. There was widespread skepticism over his findings, but a German researcher named Werner Kollhoerster made five Time flights of his own and provided confirmation. Kollhoerster's last flight was on 28 June 1914; that was the day Serbian extremists assassinated the heir to the throne of the Austro-Hungarian Empire, setting off World War I, which put pure scientific research on the back burner until the end of the war in 1918.

(5)   After the conflict in 1922, the American experimental physicist Robert Millikan (1868 – 1953) conducted studies of his own on the matter, launching automated balloons from Texas and performing studies from the top of tall Pike's Peak in Colorado. He reported no rise in the level of radiation; his findings were correct, but it turned out that the level of cosmic radiation in those regions was unusually low. Hess and Kollhoerster hotly contested Millikan's findings; although Millikan was not noted for being flexible in his judgments, he was very thorough, and so he conducted further studies in the mountains of California in 1925. He was forced to concede that the radiation did exist, naming it "cosmic rays."

(6)   That would prove to be his only really positive contribution to the debate. Millikan insisted that cosmic rays were high-energy gamma rays, but in 1929 Kollhoerster and his colleague Walter Boethe built a "coincidence counter," using two proportional counter tubes that would go off when a single particle passed through both. After recording the passage of cosmic-ray particles through the two tubes, they placed a slab of gold between them, assuming it would block the cosmic rays. It would have if they had been photons; but it didn't, meaning they were charged particles with mass.

(7)   Millikan insisted that their experiment was in error. Kollhoerster and Boethe suggested that if cosmic rays were charged particles, not photons, then they would be deflected by the Earth's magnetic field, with the cosmic-ray flux strongest at the poles and weakest at the equator. Studies by various researchers, including Millikan, were afflicted by equipment and other problems and gave ambiguous results, but in 1932 one of Millikan's ex-students, Arthur Holly Compton (1892 – 1962), announced the results of a careful series of observations to show that cosmic rays did vary with latitude as would be expected if they were charged particles. Millikan bitterly attacked Compton's results and then, confronted with new evidence that confirmed Compton's conclusions, abruptly reversed himself, claiming that he and Compton were (and had been) in complete agreement.

(8)   The entire subject of cosmic rays ended up being an embarrassment to Millikan. Although he could be hidebound, he was still one of the finest experimental physicists of his generation. He was simply off his game when it came to cosmic ray studies, and he would hardly mention them in his memoirs. There was a widespread belief for a time that he had discovered cosmic rays, but Hess's work was well documented, and Hess received the Nobel Prize for physics in 1936 for the discovery.

(9) A consensus emerged that cosmic rays were generally charged atomic nuclei moving at a high velocity through space that strike the Earth's atmosphere, generating a "cascade" of a million to a billion secondary particles known as an "air shower," with the particles scattered over an ellipse hundreds of meters wide when it hits ground. The particles in the air showers proved to be a gold mine for particle physicists, since the cascades contained short-lived particles not easily found in the laboratory. In the postwar period, up to the early 1950s, cosmic rays were investigated with balloons that carried stacks of photographic emulsions to high altitude to record the traces of these particles.

(10) Cosmic rays hit the Earth at a rate of about one thousand a second per square meter, and their energies don't seem to have any upper bound, though their numbers do unsurprisingly fall off as the energy level increases. About 90% are hydrogen nuclei (protons), 9% are helium nuclei (alpha particles), and the remaining 1% are (mostly) various heavier nuclei. Since they are charged particles, their paths through space are scrambled by galactic magnetic fields, making it difficult to determine the location of their origin.

(11) There are two classes of cosmic rays, those with energies below 10^{16} electron-volts (eV) and those above that level up to 10^{20} eV or more. Astronomers believe the two classes arise from separate processes. The low energy cosmic rays are common, while the more interesting high energy cosmic rays are rare, with the entire Earth intercepting one about once every second. The low energy cosmic rays are not seen as particularly mysterious: the great Italian – American physicist Enrico Fermi suggested that ordinary charged particles could be accelerated to such energies over long periods of time by magnetic fields in our Galaxy. They are also produced by the solar wind from the Sun. Low energy cosmic rays are also not seen as particularly interesting and for the most part, users of modern cosmic ray observatories regard them as "background noise" that has to be screened out.

(12) In contrast, nobody has any clear idea of where the superpowerful cosmic rays come from. They are so powerful that they have been said to have energies comparable to a brick thrown through a plate glass window; pretty impressive performance for a submicroscopic particle. They are generally referred to as "ultra-high energy cosmic rays (UHECRs)". Galactic magnetic fields aren't strong enough to push them around, and since they hit the Earth from all directions instead of along the plane of the Milky Way in our sky, they appear to be produced by extragalactic sources, possibly by supernovas or other "cosmic catastrophes" – though some physicists have suggested they may arise from exotic processes, such as the decay of "magnetic monopoles."

(13) As earlier mentioned, about 1% of cosmic rays are "mostly" relatively heavy nuclei. However, that 1% includes a thin flux of very high-energy gamma rays, in the 10^{12} eV range, that cause air showers very similar to those created by cosmic rays, with about one gamma-ray event for every 100,000 cosmic ray events. Millikan's assertion that cosmic rays were gamma rays wasn't completely wrong – but it was very close to completely wrong. These gamma rays aren't diverted by galactic magnetic fields and so can be traced back to a source by mapping the geometry of the air shower.

(14) There are four ways to observe cosmic rays: by observing the track of faint blue "Cerenkov radiation" left by the air shower particles using something similar to a reflecting telescope; by picking up the "footprint" of the air shower using an array of particle detectors, including proportional counter tubes, scintillation detectors, and wire chambers (Somewhat confusingly, some particle detectors also observe Cerenkov light, though with the light created by passage of particles through a sealed tank of water instead of the atmosphere.); by sensing the faint fluorescence (more properly "luminescence", but the term "fluorescence" has stuck) of atmospheric nitrogen gas in the wake of the air shower; and, by picking up the radio energy generated by the air shower. This is not a popular approach, but the LOFAR low-frequency radio telescope mentioned previously has been used for this purpose.

(15) It is of course possible to build "hybrid" detector systems that use more than one of these methods. Particle detector and radio detector systems work round the clock; air Cerenkov and fluorescence detectors can only really work on clear, moonless nights.

1. Cosmic rays are considered to be:

    A.   footprints of the air shower.
    B.   random gamma rays.
    C.   ionized atomic nuclei.
    D.   short-lived particles.
    E.   magnetic monopoles.

2. Which of the following devices was first designed to measure radiation?

    A.   Balloon flights
    B.   Optical telescope
    C.   Electroscope
    D.   Wire chamber
    E.   Coincidence counter

3. Which of the following scientists is credited with beginning research on cosmic rays?

A. Victor Hess
B. Werner Kollhoerster
C. Walter Boethe
D. Arthur Holly Compton
E. Theodor Wulf

4. Which of the following represents the number of times that balloon flights were conducted manually?

A. 4
B. 7
C. 16
D. 15

5. Who of the following was awarded the Noble Prize for the discovery of cosmic rays?

A. Theodor Wulf
B. Robert Millikan
C. Arthur Holly Compton
D. Werner Kollhoerster
E. Victor Hess

6. Cosmic rays hit the Earth at which of the following rates?

A. One million a second per square meter
B. One thousand a second per square meter
C. One hundred a second per square meter
D. Varies with magnetic field
E. One billion a second per square meter

7. Which of the following statements are true about the composition of cosmic rays?

A. About 90% are hydrogen nuclei (alpha particles), 9% are helium nuclei (protons), and the remaining 1% are (mostly) various heavier nuclei.
B. About 90% are hydrogen nuclei (protons), 9% are helium nuclei (alpha particles), and the remaining 1% are (mostly) various heavier nuclei.
C. About 90% are hydrogen nuclei (protons), 9% are helium nuclei (alpha particles), and the remaining 1% are (mostly) various lighter nuclei.
D. About 90% are helium nuclei (protons), 9% are hydrogen nuclei (alpha particles), and the remaining 1% are (mostly) various heavier nuclei.
E. About 9% are hydrogen nuclei (protons), 90% are helium nuclei (alpha particles), and the remaining 1% are (mostly) various heavier nuclei.

8. How do users of modern cosmic ray observatories regard low energy cosmic rays?

A. Similar to a laminar flow
B. Background noise
C. Constituent of alpha particle dispersion
D. Proton particle dispersions

9. From where do ultra-high energy cosmic rays most possibly originate?

A. Cosmic dispersion and flow
B. Supernovas, cosmic catastrophes, or decay of magnetic poles
C. Scattering cascades that hit the ground
D. Solar wind from the sun
E. Intergalactic star and sun events

10. Of the 1% of relatively heavy nuclei found in cosmic rays, a thin flux is comprised of which of the following?

A. Alpha particles
B. Magnetic monopoles
C. Protons
D. Neurons
E. Gamma rays

11. Between approximately what years were cosmic rays investigated using balloons that carry photographic emulsions and record traces of particles in air showers?

A. 1918 – 1950
B. 1922 – 1950
C. 1910 – 1914
D. 1910 – 1915
E. 1922 – 1925

12. What does the LOFAR telescope measure?

A. Gamma rays
B. Alpha particles
C. Supernovas
D. Radio energy generated by the air shower
E. Protons

13. Which of the following declarations by Millikan was very close to being completely wrong?

A. Supernovas are one cause of cosmic rays.
B. Alpha particles account for all of cosmic rays.
C. Cosmic Rays are gamma rays.
D. There is a divided mix between protons and alpha particles within the nuclei.
E. Air showers are caused by magnetic mono poles.

14. Which of the following best typifies the two classes of cosmic rays?

A. Those with energies below 10^{13} electron-volts (eV) and those above that level up to 10^{20} eV or more
B. Those with energies below 10^{16} electron-volts (eV) and those above that level up to 10^{22} eV or more
C. Those with energies below 1^{16} electron-volts (eV) and those above that level up to 10^{20} eV or more
D. Those with energies below 10^{16} electron-volts (eV) and those above that level up to 10^{20} eV or more
E. Those with energies below 10^{14} electron-volts (eV) and those above that level up to 10^{20} eV or more

15. Particle detectors are able to pick up Cerenkov radiation and "footprints" of the air shower.

The LOFAR low-frequency radio telescope is used to detect the fluorescence of atmospheric nitrogen gas from air shower.

A. Both statements are true.
B. Both statements are false.
C. The first sentence is true while the second sentence is false.
D. The first sentence is false while the second sentence is true.

Passage 2

Artificial Neural Networks

(1) Artificial Neural Networks are a tool for computation that is based on the neuron's interconnection in the human brain's nervous system as well as that of other organisms. It is also called neural nets, artificial neural nets, or simply ANN.

(2) An artificial neural net is a non-linear type of processing system which is made to perform various kinds of tasks, especially those that do not have an exact algorithm. ANN strives to simulate the firing of synapses. Hence, artificial neural nets can be designed to solve problems based on sample data and teaching methods fed to it, which it uses as a basis for computation and output. With regards to the received training, various tasks can be operated by means of utilizing artificial neural networks that are constructed identically. Just as long as there are proper training modes, a sort of logical generalization is possible in the use and function of artificial neural networks. Generalization is the capability to recognize patterns and similarities among various inputs. Noise-corrupted patterns can also be recognized by generalization. Naturally, the equivalence of an Artificial Neural Network is BNN, which means Biological Neural Networks.

(3) One important factor of neural networks is the neural nets. Commonly, the term "neural net" pertains solely to artificial systems like artificial neural networks. However, the biological variants of neural net cannot be taken for granted because these exist apart from the artificial variant of neural net. Neural nets are not linear mathematically speaking. They cannot be described as a straight arrow, nor a simple cause-effect, stimulus-response type of relationship or model. They can be thought of as layered spatially with a linear type of effect or result of processing. Each layer has something to do with the layer it follows or is imbricated with. There is a representation of combinations of multiplicity. This makes the net a complex system.

(4) Of course, the most complex system is the biological neural system. A common neural system of a human body or that of another organism has billions of cells that interconnect with every neuron. This aspect cannot be achieved by even the latest artificial system; this multitude of complexity is why it is not likely to produce an exact reproduction of biological systems behavior.

(5) The neuron is the basic foundation from which the network systems are constructed for both Biological Neural Networks and Artificial Neural Networks. Every neuron is a system that handles signals out of inputs since it is a MIMO system (multiple-input, multiple-output). After receiving the signal, a resultant signal is produced, and then the signal is transmitted to all of the outputs. The neurons that can be found in an artificial neural network are formed into layers. The first layer is known as the input layer, which functions with interaction with the environment in order to handle input. On the other hand, the final layer is called the output layer, which handles the output in order to tender the data that has been processed. Those layers that do not have any kind of interaction with the input or the output (or the environment in general) are known as hidden layers as these lie in the layers between the output layer and the input layer. These hidden layers make the system complex due to their multiplicity and non-linear relationship, though combined in unique packets or interactions with each other.

(6) Neurons are commonly known as PE or Processing Elements as these can have different forms. The term Processing Elements is used in order to treat it differently from the biological equivalents. There is a certain network pattern into which the Processing Elements are linked. When it comes to artificial systems, PE are only electrical unlike the biological neurons that are chemical. PE may be analog, digital, or hybrid. Analog elements move in time, so to speak, while digital elements move in space, while hybrid elements simulate both temporal and spatial movements. But then again, in order to duplicate the synapse effect, there are multiplicative weights assigned to the connections. Calibration of these weights is necessary to tender the right system output. We can think of weights as the amount of information fed through multiple inputs.

(7) Two equations that define the key concept of Processing Elements represent the McCulloch-Pitts model of a neuron. The simple input and output relationship

known as the McCulloch-Pitts neuron, the linear system and the step activation function are characterized by the Perceptron. However, there were some people who did not feel the early success of this work as well as the research for artificial neural networks in general. Among them were Seymore Papert and Marvin Minsky. They had a book entitled Perceptrons, published in 1969 and this was utilized for the discrediting of the artificial neural networks research. One point that Papert and Minsky highlighted was that Perceptron did not classify the non-linear patterns that can be separated from the input space.

(8) There are two main alternative uses of artificial neural nets: algorithmic solution and expert system. Algorithmic solution is raised when there is enough information regarding the data as well as the underlying theory. Unknown solutions can be directly calculated through analyzing the data as well as the data's theoretical relationship. For ease of calculation, ordinary von Neumann computer applications can be utilized. Expert system, on the other hand, is utilized when there is not enough theoretical background and data needed for the creation of any form of reliable problem model. This can be considered a stochastic model. It represents random distributions or patterns, which may bring generalizations or results that can be further tested or refined with guided assumptions or theories.

(9) Moreover, the use of artificial neural networks can be maximized in instances where there is abundant data but little amount of underlying theory, guidance or direction, if you will. When it comes to neural networks, a priori assumptions for the problem space, as well as information regarding the statistical distribution, are not required. Assumptions characterized by patterns are not needed by the neural networks. They can produce results without a distributive framework. Even so, the use of a priori information can still aid on speeding the training when used as statistical distribution of the input space.

(10) Overtraining usually becomes an issue when there are too many training examples and the system is overwhelmed to the extent of not using the useful generalizations. Overtraining can also transpire when there are so many neurons within the network, and the computation capacity exceeds its limit. Despite what sounds like high tech artificial intelligence gibberish or slang, artificial neural networks are used in many contexts. Artificial Neural Networks have been used in sales forecasting, industrial process control, customer research, and data validation, risk management and target marketing. They have also been used in medicine in diagnostics and as you might have guessed, in software games as AI. Though seemingly artificial, there are a number of scientists who believe that artificial neural networks may

someday be "conscious," –resembling some of the popular media stereotypes, which we have all seen in helpful robots, cars, and "friendly" space ship computers.

(11) A historical view of ANN and BNN can be summarized as follows:

Late 1800's. There were attempts of scientific study pertaining to how the brain of human beings works. These were usually philosophical works of logic and rationalism.

1890. The first work regarding the activity pattern of the human brain was published by William James.

1943. A neuron model was developed by Warren McCulloch and Walter Pitts. This model, which is broken into a summation over weighted inputs and sum output function, is still utilized these days in the field of artificial neural networking.

1949. The Organization of Behavior was published by Donald Hebb. This work shows an outline of a law for the learning of synaptic neurons. As a commemoration of his work, this law was later renamed as Hebbian Learning.

1951. The first Artificial Neural Network was made by Marvin Minsky while he was at Princeton.

1958. It was one year after the death of John von Neumann when The Computer and the Brain was published. His work showcased propositions about several radical changes in the means, which researchers use to model the brain.

1958. Frank Rosenblatt created the Mark I Perceptron computer at Cornell University. It was an attempt to utilize the techniques of neural network for recognition of characters.

1960. Frank Rosenblatt created the book entitled Principles of Neurodynamics. This contained his ideas and researches about brain modeling.

1974. Paul John Webros discovered the backpropagation algorithm.

1986. The backpropagation algorithm was rediscovered by David Rumelhart, Geoffrey Hinton, and R. J. Williams through their book Learning Internal Representation by Error Propagation. As a gradient descent algorithm, backpropagation is utilized for the purpose of curve-fitting and finding weights that minimize errors in artificial neural networks.

1987. Slated for artificial neural networks researches, the Institute of Electrical and Electronics Engineers (IEEE) began its annual international ANN conference. The INNS or the International Neural Network Society was created.

1988. The INNS Neural Networking journal began its publication.

16. Which of the following CANNOT be performed by ANN?

  A.   Analyze data
  B.   Solve problem
  C.   Recognize patterns among assorted inputs
  D.   Replicate exact biological systems behavior
  E.   Calculate unknown solutions

17. Stochastic generalizations from ANN are produced from random patterns.
  ANN do not require a priori information.

  A.   Both statements are true.
  B.   Both statements are false.
  C.   The first sentence is true while the second sentence is false.
  D.   The first sentence is false while the second sentence is true.

18. ANN strives to simulate:
  A.   systems of complexity.
  B.   transmission of input-output information.
  C.   data collation.
  D.   computer logic.
  E.   algorithms.

19. The Neural Net is:
  A.   linear.
  B.   causal.
  C.   effects-oriented.
  D.   layered.
  E.   cause-oriented.

20. What produces complexity within the neural net?

  A.   Imbrications of variance
  B.   Hidden layers
  C.   Multitudinal velocities
  D.   Multiple inputs
  E.   Complex interactions

21. MIMO stands for:

    A.   Multitude Inertia, Mass Organization
    B.   Main Inertia, Mass Organization
    C.   Multiple Inputs, Multiple Outputs
    D.   Main Inputs, Main Outputs
    E.   Mass Internalization, Multiple Inertia

22. ANN utilizes algorithms. ANN strives to emulate BNN.

    A.   Both statements are true.
    B.   Both statements are false.
    C.   The first sentence is true while the second sentence is false.
    D.   The first sentence is false while the second sentence is true.

23. The following network patterns in artificial systems are linked with neurons. Which one is the exeption?

    A.   Electrical
    B.   Temporal
    C.   Digital
    D.   Analog
    E.   Hybrid

24. Hybrid PE tend to move:

    A.   in time.
    B.   in conjunction with layers.
    C.   in space.
    D.   in time and space.
    E.   in a linear fashion.

25. Overtraining is the result of:

    A.   exceeding the maximum computation capacity.
    B.   too much data but not enough underlying theory.
    C.   too many useful generalizations.
    D.   expert systems using a priori assumptions.
    E.   algorithmic complexity.

26. ANN utilizing "Expert Systems" represent models that are:

    A.   guided by theory.
    B.   lacking in statistical data.
    C.   trained by a priori assumptions.
    D.   overtrained.
    E.   random and stochastic.

27. Which factor characterizes both the Artificial and the Biological Neural Networks?

    A.   The linear system
    B.   Multiplicative weights
    C.   The neuron as basic foundation
    D.   Processing Elements
    E.   The step activation function

28. Which of the following best describes the use of backpropagation?

    A.   Finding errors in a learning application
    B.   Minimizing error functions in neural nets
    C.   Limiting training to a priori assumptions
    D.   Introducing feedback loops
    E.   Propagating errors to increase learning

29. Which of the following is NOT true concerning the history of ANN?

    A.   Minsky created the first ANN.
    B.   Papert and Minsky created the Perceptron.
    C.   The law for the learning of synaptic neurons was renamed after Donald Hebb.
    D.   McCullogh and Pitts created the neuron model.
    E.   The book Learning Internal Representation by Error renewed interest in backpropagation algorithm.

30. The weighted functions in PE can be thought of as:

    A.   resultant outputs from data.
    B.   the quantity of data into multiple inputs.
    C.   hidden layers of complexity.
    D.   theory or a priori assumptions.
    E.   calibrated generalizations.

31. Based on usage in this passage, which of the following refers to "a priori"?

    A.   Inherent mental structures
    B.   Assumed theories
    C.   Guided training
    D.   Expert systems
    E.   Overtrained generalizations

32. The best results from ANN are produced with the use of:

    A.   much theory, little data.
    B.   much data, little theory.
    C.   much data and theory.
    D.   non-linear patterns.

33. Analog Processing Elements can be thought to work in:

    A.   expert systems.
    B.   space.
    C.   layers.
    D.   time.
    E.   generalized patterns.

34. The difference between algorithmic and expert systems basically concerns:

    A.   the amount of data.
    B.   the amount of training.
    C.   the amount of theory.
    D.   the amount of generalization.
    E.   the amount of neurons.

35. ANN can generalize the following EXCEPT:

    A.   noise.
    B.   similarities among assorted inputs.
    C.   linear computations.
    D.   random patterns.
    E.   complex distributions.

Passage 3

Music and Mathematics

(1) Many music theorists use mathematics to understand music. Indeed, musical sounds seem to display an inherent order of number properties. Although the ancient Chinese, Egyptians and Mesopotamians are known to have studied the mathematical principles of sound, the Pythagoreans of ancient Greece are the first researchers known to have investigated the expression of musical scales in terms of numerical ratios, particularly the ratios of small integers.

(2) The Greek octave had only five notes, coinciding with the principle of perfect fifths. Pythagoras discovered that differences in the ratio of the length between two strings create variations in pitch. The ratio 2:3 creates the musical fifth, 3:4 the fourth, and so on. Moreover, the ancient Greeks learned that a note with a given frequency could only be combined and played harmoniously with other notes whose frequencies were integer multiples of the first. These would eventually signify the ratio of the wavelength or frequency of a given note to another and thus, the creation of chords.

(3) In addition, Pythagoras pointed out that each note is a fraction of a string. Thus, if a musician had a string that played an A, then the next note is 4/5 the length (or 5/4 the frequency) which is approximately a C. The rest of the octave has the fractions 3/4 (approximately D), 2/3 (approximately E), and 3/5 (approximately F), before reaching 1/2 which is the octave A. With a guitar, the octave is the 12th Fret, and in terms of distance, mathematically it should be half the distance between the bridge at the lower end of the guitar and the nut where the strings cross over at the top of the guitar. Shortening the length between the two produces a higher pitch or tone – envision the strings in a piano, which range from the lower tones-longer strings to the higher tones-shorter strings.

(4) In the Western system of musical notation, the frequency ratio 1:2 is generally identified as the octave. Two different notes in this relation are often considered as fundamentally the same and only vary in pitch but not in character. Octaves of a note occur at 2n times the frequency of that note (where n is an integer), such as 2, 4, 8, 16, etc. and the reciprocal of that series. For example, 50 Hz and 400 Hz are one and two octaves away from 100 Hz because they are ½ (or 2 -1) and 4 (or 22) times the frequency, respectively. Hence, notes an octave apart are given the same note name – the name of a note an octave above A is also A. This is called octave equivalency, the assumption that pitches one or more octaves apart are musically equivalent in many ways, leading to the convention "that scales are uniquely defined by specifying the intervals within an octave."

(5) The application of mathematical concepts to music did not merely involve notes and harmony. The attempt to structure and communicate new ways of composing and hearing music has led some composers to incorporate the golden ratio and Fibonacci numbers into their work.

(6) In mathematics and the arts, two quantities are in the golden ratio if the ratio of the sum of the quantities to the larger quantity is equal to the ratio of the larger quantity to the smaller one. The Fibonacci numbers are the numbers in the following integer sequence: 0,1,1,2,3,5,8,13,21,34, 55,89,144. By definition, the first two Fibonacci numbers are 0 and 1, and each subsequent number is the sum of the previous two. The most important feature in the sequence of Fibonacci ratios – the ratio of a Fibonacci number with its bigger adjacent – is that it converges to a constant limit known as the golden ratio of 0.61803398...

(7)   The golden section is employed by musicians to generate rhythmic changes or to develop a melody line. James Tenney reconceived his piece For Ann (rising), which consists of up to twelve computer-generated upwardly glissandoing tones , having each tone start with the golden ratio (in between an equal tempered minor and major sixth) below the previous tone, so that the combination tones produced by all consecutive tones are a lower or higher pitch already, or soon to be, produced.

(8)   In Béla Bartok's Music for Strings, Percussion and Celesta, the xylophone progression occurs at the intervals 1:2:3:5:8:5:3:2:1 – a sort of bell curve of a golden ratio. French composer Erik Satie used the golden ratio in several of his pieces, including Sonneries de la Rose+Croix. The golden ratio is also apparent in the organization of the sections in the music of Debussy's Reflets dans l'eau (Reflections in Water), from Images (1st series, 1905), in which "the sequence of keys is marked out by the intervals 34, 21, 13 and 8, and the main climax sits at the phi position."

(9)   Also, many works of Chopin, mainly Etudes (studies) and Nocturnes are formally based on the golden ratio. This results in the biggest climax of both musical expression and technical difficulty after about 2/3 of the piece. The mathematician Michael Schneider analyzed the waveform of the Amen break and found that the peaks are spaced at intervals in the golden ratio.

(10)   An emerging and modern connection between music and mathematics is being made from the relationship of fractals and the generation of melodic form. Fractals are visual representations of certain mathematical functions, which show increasing detail upon magnification. A very important phenomenon of fractals is that they manifest self-similarity at all scales. Benoit Mandelbrot, one of the fathers of fractal geometry (and the man who coined the term fractal), loosely defines fractals as "shapes that are equally complex in their details as in their overall form. That is, if a piece of a fractal is suitably magnified to become of the same size as the whole, it should look like the whole, either exactly, or perhaps only slightly deformed." Today, we see fractal imagery all over the net in graphic design. Its self-replicating form is also found in nature: imagine broccoli, or even the circulatory system as fractal. Composers are also taking this idea to music.

(11)   One would expect that the construction of such complex shapes would require complex rules, but in reality, the algorithms (equations) that generate fractals are typically extraordinarily simple. Their visual results, however, show great richness. The seeming paradox is easily demystified: these algorithms involve "loops."

(12)   The key to the richness of detail that fractals exhibit is something that mathematicians call iteration. Most equations that we learned in school are linear – that is, the input is proportional to the output. For example, the equation $x2 - 1 = 0$ is a linear equation. The equations that generate fractals, however, are nonlinear. Nonlinear equations involve iteration, which means that the solution of the equation is repeatedly fed back into itself. It is an arresting thought that something produced from a purely mathematical procedure can be so aesthetically pleasing.

(13)   Algorithms (or, at the very least, formal sets of rules) have been used to compose music for centuries; the procedures used to plot voice-leading in Western counterpoint, for example, can often be reduced to algorithmic determinacy. The term is usually reserved, however, for the use of formal procedures to make music without human intervention, either through the introduction of chance procedures or the use of computers.

(14)   Many algorithms that have no immediate musical relevance are used by composers as creative inspiration for their music. Algorithms such as fractals, L-systems, statistical models, and even arbitrary data (e.g. census figures, GIS coordinates, or magnetic field measurements) are fair game for musical interpretation. The success or failure of these procedures as sources of "good" music largely depends on the mapping system employed by the composer to translate the non-musical information into a musical data stream.

(15)   There is no universal method to sort different compositional algorithms into categories. One way to do this is to look at the way an algorithm takes part in the compositional process. The results of the process can then be divided into music composed by computer and music composed with the aid of computer. Music may be considered composed by computer when the algorithm is able to make choices of its own during the creation process.

(16).   Another way to sort compositional algorithms is to examine the results of their compositional processes. Algorithms can either provide notational information (sheet music) for other instruments or provide an independent way of sound synthesis (playing the composition by itself). There are also algorithms creating both notational data and sound synthesis.

(17).   Algorithmic techniques have also been employed in a number of systems intended for direct musical performance, with many using algorithmic techniques to generate infinitely variable improvisations on a predetermined theme. An early example was the 1982 computer game Ballblazer of Lucasfilm Games, where the computer improvised on a basic jazz theme composed by the game's musical director Peter Langston; later in the life of that company, now rechristened LucasArts, an algorithmic iM-USE engine was developed for their flagship game, Dark Forces. Similar generative music systems have caught the attention of noted composers. Brian Eno has produced a number of works for the Koan generative music system, which produces ambient variations for web-pages, mobile devices, and for standalone performance.

36. In a musical scale, 13 notes separate each octave of 8 notes. The 5th note and 3rd note comprise the basic foundation of the chords. These are based on the whole tone, which is two steps from the 1st note of the scale. The pattern represents:

A. The Greek octave.
B. The Fibonacci sequence.
C. Fractals.
D. An algorithmic technique.
E. The golden section.

37. Which of the following phenomena in Nature would NOT resemble the self-replicating form of a fractal?

A. Snow flakes
B. Lightning
C. Circulatory system
D. Wind
E. Broccoli

38. In terms of tone, the middle point on a string in a guitar is known as:

A. a half-tone.
B. the middle 5th.
C. C Major.
D. an octave.

39. Which of the following statements is the best interpretation of the principle of the golden ratio?

A. Each two measures add up to make the next one sequentially proportionate to the lower measure.
B. The length of a whole relates to its large part in the same way that the large part relates to the small part.
C. The proportion of the smaller parts is exponentially derivative to the larger parts.
D. The whole is an expanding sequence of the smaller parts.

40. The key to the richness of details exhibited by fractals are what mathematicians call:

A. non-linear equations.
B. iteration.
C. loops.
D. regeneration.
E. magnified details.

41. The paradox of fractals is stated to be that:

A. its algorithms involve loops.
B. the richness of fractals is self-replicating.
C. the construction of complex shapes requires extraordinarily simple equations.
D. something produced from a purely mathematical procedure can be so aesthetically pleasing.
E. their visual results show great richness.

42. In Béla Bartók's Music for Strings, Percussion and Celesta, the xylophone progression demonstrates:

A. the Fibonacci numbers inverted.
B. a bell curve of a golden ratio.
C. he harmonic ratios of the Pythagoreans.
D. the golden ratio starting at phi and going downwards.
E. a combination of the golden ratio and the Fibonacci numbers.

43. The ancient Greeks measured notes and harmony using frequency ratios. Modern musicians use the golden section to generate rhythmic changes or to develop a melody line.

A. Both statements are true.
B. Both statements are false.
C. The first statement is true, the second statement is false.
D. The first statement is false, the second statement is true.

44. Based on statements in the passage, if one note has a frequency of 400 Hz, the note an octave below it, would be which of the following frequencies?

A. 200 Hz
B. 400 Hz
C. 600 Hz
D. 800 Hz
E. All of the above

45. What makes fractals an important phenomenon in musicology?

- A. Their algorithms are very simple.
- B. They can produce pleasant music from a purely mathematical procedure.
- C. Composers use them as creative inspiration for their music.
- D. They manifest self-similarity at all scales.

46. What is the main idea of the passage?

- A. Math can be found in all music.
- B. Music can be defined using mathematical techniques.
- C. Either the golden ratio or the Fibonacci numbers occur in all music.
- D. There is an intricate yet measurable relationship between music and math.
- E. The form and content of music and mathematics are essentially the same.

47. Algorithms in music usually refer to:

- A. formal procedures to make music without human intervention.
- B. formal sets of rules that produce fractals.
- C. equations.
- D. the mapping system of a composer.
- E. notational data and sound synthesis.

48. The name of a note an octave above A is also A because a note with a given frequency could only be combined with another note whose frequency is an integer multiple of the first.

- A. Both the statement and reason are correct and related.
- B. Both the statement and the reason are correct but NOT related.
- C. The statement is correct but the reason is NOT.
- D. The statement is NOT correct, but the reason is correct.
- E. NEITHER the statement NOR the reason is correct.

49. Which of the following would be the best conclusion for the closing paragraph?

- A. Indeed, such developments serve to prove that mathematics is as much an art as it is a science.
- B. Still, whatever connects music with mathematics, both of them remain two different disciplines.
- C. Over the years, mathematics and music do not form such strong opposites as they are commonly considered to do; after all, certain connections and similarities between them explain why some musicians like mathematics and why mathematicians generally love music.
- D. Although a less popular notion, mathematical applications have indeed greatly contributed to the world's reservoir of beautiful musical creations.

50. The Pythagoreans investigated musical scales in terms of:

- A. mathematical iterations.
- B. ratios of small integers.
- C. harmonic proportions.
- D. rough trigonometry.
- E. basic fractions.

1. Stephen is 4ft tall, and he is growing ½ in. every two months. John is 3ft 10in and is growing 1in. every three months. If these rates remain constant, how tall will Stephen and John be when they are the same height?

- A. 4ft 6in
- B. 4ft 10in
- C. 5ft
- D. 5ft 6in
- E. 6ft

2. Which of the following are possible values of x if $x^2 - 7x + 5 = -7$?

- A. -3
- B. 3
- C. 4
- D. A and C
- E. B and C

3. What is the mean value of the set {7, 7, 8, 10, 13}?

- A. 7
- B. 8
- C. 9
- D. 10
- E. 11

4. If an equilateral triangle has a base of length 3, what is the measure of the angle between the base and the left side?

- A. 60°
- B. 45°
- C. 30°
- D. 90°
- E. Insufficient information to draw a conclusion

5. If a six-sided die is rolled three times, what is the probability that every roll will turn up an even number?

- A. 3/2
- B. 1/2
- C. 1/6
- D. 1/8
- E. 1/16

6. If f is a function that satisfies $f(x) = 2f(x)$ for all real numbers x, which of the following must be true of $f(1)$?

- A. $f(1) = 2$
- B. $f(1) = 1$
- C. $f(1) = 0$
- D. Either $f(1) = 1$ or $f(1) = 0$
- E. Insufficient information to draw a conclusion

7. A certain blueberry bush can produce a maximum of 400 berries in a season. If one year it produces only 30% of its maximum yield and the next year it produces 85%, how many berries does it produce over the two-year period?

- A. 200
- B. 340
- C. 400
- D. 460
- E. 600

8. If 2 km is equal to 1.2 miles, then 3.5 miles is approximately equal to how many km?

- A. 2.7
- B. 4.75
- C. 5.4
- D. 5.8
- E. 12

9. Which of the following is the value of $\cot\left(\dfrac{7\pi}{6}\right)$?

- A. -1
- B. -1/2
- C. $\sqrt{2}$
- D. $\sqrt{3}$
- E. $\dfrac{\left(\sqrt{3}\right)}{2}$

10. Consider the point p with coordinates (5 , 1) in the Cartesian plane. What is sin θ where θ is the angle between the x-axis and the line from the origin to p?

A. 1/50

B. $\dfrac{1}{\sqrt{26}}$

C. 1/5

D. 1/2

E. $\dfrac{\sqrt{3}}{2}$

11. If a cup of sand has a mass of 360 g, about how many cups are in 20 kg of sand?

A. .06
B. 18
C. 55.6
D. 100
E. 720

12. Which of the following is the best approximation for $\dfrac{\left[\left(7.2\times10^3\right)\left(4.61\times10^8\right)\right]}{\left(2.23\times10^7\right)}$?

A. 1.5×10^{-4}
B. 1.5×10^{-2}
C. 1.5×10^{3}
D. 1.5×10^{4}
E. 1.5×10^{5}

13. What is the length of a diagonal of a rectangle with sides length 3 and 5?

A. 4

B. $\sqrt{15}$

C. $\sqrt{34}$

D. 8

E. 15

14. Three days, 14 hours, and 26 minutes is equal to how many minutes?

A. 3266
B. 4026
C. 4826
D. 5126
E. 5186

15. Which of the following is the length of each side of a square inscribed in a circle with a radius of 3?

A. 3
B. $3\sqrt{2}$
C. 5.2
D. 6
E. 9

16. 3x is to 6y as 5xy is to:

A. 10x
B. 10y
C. 10x/y
D. $10x^2$
E. $10y^2$

17. Which of the following is the value of x if $(3x + 2)2 - x = 6$?

A. 1/5
B. 2/5
C. 1
D. 2/3
E. 2/7

18. Which of the following is the length of the side labeled S in the right triangle below?

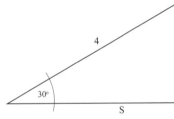

A. 1/2

B. $\dfrac{\sqrt{3}}{2}$

C. $\sqrt{2}$

D. 2

E. $2\sqrt{3}$

19. Which of the following is equal to $\sin x$ if $\csc x = \dfrac{2}{\sqrt{3}}$ and if $\dfrac{3\pi}{2} < x < 2\pi$?

A. $-\dfrac{\sqrt{3}}{2}$

B. $-1/2$

C. $1/2$

D. $\dfrac{\sqrt{3}}{2}$

E. $\dfrac{1}{\sqrt{2}}$

20. If $(2/x) + 3 > 5 - (1/x)$, then which must be true?

A. $(1/x) > (2/3)$
B. $(1/x) < (2/3)$
C. $(3/2) > x$
D. $(3/2) < x$
E.   A and C

21. A cylinder has a height of 10 cm and a base diameter of 6 cm. Which of the following is the best approximation of the total surface area, in cm^2?

A.   245
B.   220
C.   180
D.   120
E.   60

22. A car is travelling at 65 mph. What fraction of an hour will it take for the car to travel 25 miles?

A.   1/4
B.   5/13
C.   1/2
D.   2/3
E.   23/30

23. While shopping for clothing John purchases three pairs of pants at $39.99 each, four shirts at $15.75 each, and a dozen socks at $3.00 a pair. Which of the following best approximates John's total purchase?

A. $60
B. $200
C. $220
D. $240
E. $300

24. Which of the following is 75% of 7/2?

A.   11/6
B.   21/8
C.   5/2
D.   3
E.   13/4

25. If the planet Earth has a mass of 5.97×10^{24} kg, and the planet Jupiter has a mass of 1.90×10^{27} kg, approximately how many times more massive is Jupiter than Earth?

A. 3.2×10^{-3}
B. 3.2×10^{1}
C. 3.2×10^{2}
D. 3.2×10^{3}
E. 3.2×10^{51}

26. How many pounds does 4.5 kg equal if 1 kg is equal to 2.2 pounds?

A.   2
B.   4.5
C.   7.2
D.   9
E.   9.9

27. Which of the following represents the distance between the points (-2 , 1) and (10 , 6) in the Cartesian plane?

A. $2\sqrt{3}$
B. $2\sqrt{11}$
C.   13
D.   17
E. $12\sqrt{5}$

28. Taylor has a container with 12 blue marbles and 8 yellow marbles. If she draws two marbles in a row without replacement, what is the probability that both marbles are yellow?

  A.   14/95
  B.   14/57
  C.   4/19
  D.   5/19
  E.   1/3

29. Which of the following equations describe a line passing through points (-1 , 3) , (1 , 0) and (5 , -6) in the Cartesian plane?

  A. $y = -(3/2)x + 1$
  B. $y = (3/2)x + 3/2$
  C. $3y + 3x = 5$
  D. $y + 2x = 2/3$
  E. $2y + 3x = 3$

30. Which of the following is equivalent to the fraction

$$\frac{\left[2 - \left(\dfrac{6}{5}\right)\right]}{\left[1 + \left(\dfrac{2}{5}\right)\right]} ?$$

  A.   1
  B.   1/2
  C.   4/7
  D.   11/5
  E.   2

31. In a college classroom of 143 students the ratio of women to men was 4 to 7. How many of the students were male?

  A.   13
  B.   36
  C.   52
  D.   81
  E.   91

32. Which of the following is smallest?

  A. $\dfrac{1}{\sqrt{3}}$

  B.   11/23
  C.   2/3
  D.   3/5
  E.   7/13

33. Which of the following is equal to x if
$$\left(\frac{.06}{2.7}\right)\left(\frac{81}{x}\right) = 5.4 ?$$

  A.   1/3
  B.   1
  C.   2
  D.   9/5
  E.   20/3

34. A tree that is 4 meters tall will grow in height by a maximum of 40% for every subsequent year. Which of the following represents the best approximation of the maximum increase in height the tree can have over the next 3 years?

  A.   1.6
  B.   4.8
  C.   6.4
  D.   7.0
  E.   11.0

35. Which of the following is the value of x if $x \neq -2$, $x \uparrow 3$, and $\dfrac{2}{[3(x+2)]} + \dfrac{3}{(x-3)} = \dfrac{(5x-1)}{(x^2 - x - 6)} ?$

  A.   3/4
  B.   15/4
  C.   15
  D.   -2
  E.   -6

36. To the nearest multiple of 10, which of the following best approximates 17.4×9.7?

  A.   100
  B.   160
  C.   170
  D.   180
  E.   200

37. On a trip to and from the grocery store Sid travelled at an average speed of 28 mph. If it took him 18 minutes to get to the store and 12 minutes to get back home, what was his average speed on the way home?

  A.   20 mph
  B.   24 mph
  C.   28 mph
  D.   30 mph
  E.   35 mph

38. A jar contains 3 green balls and 6 red balls. If 3 balls are drawn without replacement, what is the probability that the first 2 will be green and the third will be red?

A. 1/11
B. 1/12
C. 1/13
D. 1/14
E. 1/15

39. If 2 cups of water, 1 cup of 90% apple juice and 3 cups of 60% apple juice are mixed, what is the percentage of apple juice in the mixture?

A. 45%
B. 50%
C. 60%
D. 75%
E. 90%

40. On a math quiz, 1/3 of the 36 students in the class scored a 10, 1/12 scored a 9, ¼ scored an 8, and the rest scored a 7. What was the median quiz score?

A. 10
B. 9.5
C. 9
D. 8
E. 7

Answer Keys & Solutions

Answer Document

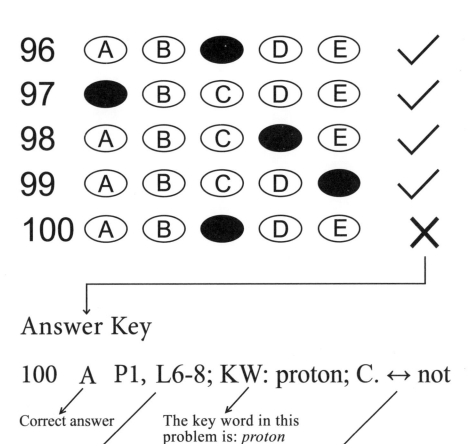

Answer Key

100   A   P1, L6-8; KW: proton; C. ↔ not

Correct answer

The key word in this
problem is: *proton*

Paragraph 1, lines 6 to 8,   Choice C. is wrong
is where the answer   because of the word "*not*"
can be found

GS-1: Natural Sciences Test

Cross-reference

1. C BIO 15.5
2. A BIO 7.5, 8.3
3. E BIO 12.4
4. B BIO 15.1, 15.3
5. E BIO 17.1, 17.2 , 17.2.3
6. C BIO 17.1, 17.2
7. B BIO 14.5.1
8. E BIO 2.2, BIO 16.6.4
9. A BIO 6.3.3, 5.4.4
10. A BIO 4.1, CHM 9.7; CHM 9.7
11. C BIO 14.5
12. E BIO 19.7
13. E BIO 7.2, 7.3, 7.5.1
14. B BIO 7.5.2, 10.3
15. C BIO 4.3, 2.5, 2.5.1
16. B BIO 4.1, 15.7, Chapter 15 Appendix
17. B BIO 1.2.2, BIO 3, BIO 20.5
18. E BIO 15.2
19. C BIO 6.2.3
20. E BIO 1.4.1, 17.6.4
21. C BIO 1.1.3
22. D BIO 1.1.1, 4.1
23. D BIO 2.2, BIO 16.6.4
24. D BIO 19.2
25. E BIO 1.1, 5.1.1, 5.1.3
26. D BIO 14.2
27. C BIO 4.4
28. E BIO 14.3
29. B BIO 4.2
30. C BIO 14.2
31. E BIO 1.2.2, 3.0
32. D BIO 2.2
33. A BIO 9.4.1
34. D BIO 17.6.3, 17.6.6
35. E BIO 4.1, 4.7; CHM 8.2, 10.1, 10.2

Cross-reference

36. E BIO 20.2.2
37. E BIO 7 Appendix
38. B BIO 16.3, 19.2-19.4 and Appendix
39. E BIO 16.4.2, 17
40. A BIO 11.3, 11.3.3
41. A CHM 8.3, 1.4
42. E CHM 3.4, 6.1
43. D CHM 1.4
44. E CHM 5.3.1
45. A CHM 6.6, 6.5
46. A CHM 1.3, 1.5
47. B CHM 10.1
48. C CHM 2.3
49. A CHM 4.2, 4.3.2
50. C CHM 4.2, ORG 10.1
51. B CHM 4.1.7
52. E CHM 11.4
53. D CHM 11
54. B CHM 10.1, 10.2
55. D CHM 5.3.2
56. D CHM 3.5
57. E CHM 2.4, 2.4.1
58. C CHM 1.1-1.5
59. B CHM 2.3
60. D CHM 10.4
61. E CHM 6.9
62. E CHM 1.5.1, 5.2, 6.2, 6.9.1
63. C CHM 2.1, 2.2, 2.3
64. B CHM 6.1
65. D E; CHM 8.10
66. E CHM 8.7
67. A CHM 5.1.1, 5.1.2
68. A CHM 4.1.2, 4.1.8
69. C CHM 9.3
70. A CHM 12.3.1
71. A ORG 2.1, 2.2, 2.3
72. E ORG 1.6, 7.1, 8.1, 9.4

Cross-reference

73. A CHM 6.3, ORG 1.6, 4.2.1, 6.2.4, 11.1.1
74. D ORG 4.2, 7.1, 8.1, 14.1
75. D ORG 1.1, 8.1
76. B CHM 6.3, ORG 5.2.2, 10.2
77. C ORG 7.2.2
78. D ORG 13.3, CHM 12
79. B CHM 3.5, ORG 3.3, 10.1
80. C ORG 7.1
81. A ORG 13.2.1
82. A ORG 12.1.2
83. C ORG 14.2
84. E ORG 3.1, 4.1
85. C ORG 13
86. C ORG 2.1, 2.2, 2.3
87. E ORG 6.2.4
88. E ORG 7.2.3
89. A ORG 2.3.1, 2.3.2, 2.3.3
90. B ORG 4.2.1
91. C CHM 9.5, 9.7, 9.8, 9.10, ORG 6.2.1
92. C CHM 8.2, 8.10, 9.5
93. E ORG 3.3, 12.3.2 F
94. C CHM 3.5; ORG 1.2, 1.3
95. B ORG 4.2.4
96. A ORG 4.2.2, 6.1, 9.4, 13.1; CHM 12
97. E CHM 3.5; ORG 1.2, 1.3, 4.1, 4.2
98. E ORG 5.1.1
99. D ORG 1.6, 5.2, 5.2.1, 5.2.2, 6.2.2, 7.2.3
100. C CHM 3.5; ORG 1.2, 1.3

To estimate your standard score, sign in to dat-prep.com then click Tests in the top Menu. Cross-references above refer to subsections from chapters in the Gold Standard Book Set.

GS-1: Perceptual Ability Test

1.	E	24.	A	47.	E	70.	B
2.	D	25.	D	48.	B	71.	C
3.	D	26.	B	49.	D	72.	B
4.	B	27.	B	50.	A	73.	E
5.	A	28.	A	51.	B	74.	C
6.	E	29.	A	52.	C	75.	C
7.	B	30.	B	53.	D	76.	B
8.	D	31.	D	54.	A	77.	C
9.	C	32.	C	55.	D	78.	D
10.	A	33.	B	56.	D	79.	B
11.	C	34.	D	57.	B	80.	B
12.	D	35.	A	58.	E	81.	C
13.	B	36.	D	59.	C	82.	A
14.	A	37.	B	60.	A	83.	D
15.	E	38.	A	61.	D	84.	B
16.	B	39.	D	62.	E	85.	D
17.	C	40.	C	63.	B	86.	C
18.	D	41.	B	64.	C	87.	A
19.	A	42.	C	65.	D	88.	C
20.	B	43.	A	66.	B	89.	A
21.	C	44.	B	67.	A	90.	B
22.	C	45.	A	68.	E		
23.	D	46.	C	69.	D		

GS-1: Reading Comprehension Test

1.	C	18.	B	35.	C
2.	C	19.	D	36.	B
3.	E	20.	B	37.	D
4.	D	21.	C	38.	D
5.	E	22.	A	39.	B
6.	B	23.	B	40.	B
7.	B	24.	D	41.	C
8.	B	25.	A	42.	B
9.	B	26.	E	43.	A
10.	E	27.	C	44.	A
11.	B	28.	B	45.	D
12.	D	29.	B	46.	D
13.	C	30.	B	47.	A
14.	D	31.	B	48.	C
15.	C	32.	B	49.	D
16.	D	33.	D	50.	B
17.	A	34.	C		

GS-1: Quantitative Reasoning Test

		Cross-reference			Cross-reference			Cross-reference
1.	A	QR 3.2, 3.2.1, 8.2, 8.2.1	14.	E	QR 3.1, 3.1.1			5.1.1
2.	E	QR 4.6, 4.6.1	15.	B	QR 5.2, 5.2.3, 6.3, 6.3.3	28.	A	QR 7.1, 7.1.2
3.	C	QR 7.2, 7.2.2	16.	E	QR 2.4, 2.4.2	29.	E	QR 4.5, 4.5.4
4.	A	QR 5.2, 5.2.2	17.	B	QR 4.1, 4.1.1, 4.3, 4.3.1	30.	C	QR 2.4, 2.4.2
5.	D	QR 7.1				31.	E	QR 2.6
6.	C	QR 4.1, 4.1.4	18.	E	QR 6.1, 6.1.2	32.	B	QR 2.4, 2.4.1
7.	D	QR 2.4.3, 8.3	19.	A	QR 6.1, 6.1.4, 6.2, 6.2.1	33.	A	QR 2.4, 2.41, 2.4.2
8.	D	QR 2.6				34.	D	QR 8.2, 8.2.3
9.	D	QR 6.1, 6.1.4, 6.2, 6.2.1	20.	A	QR 4.2, 4.2.2	35.	B	QR 4.3, 4.3.1, 4.3.3
			21.	A	QR 5.3, 5.3.3	36.	C	QR 2.2, 2.2.1
10.	B	QR 5.1, 5.1.1, 5.2, 5.2.2, 6.1, 6.1.1	22.	B	QR 2.6	37.	E	QR 3.1, 3.1.1, 8.2, 8.2.2
			23.	C	QR 2.2, 2.2.3			
11.	C	QR 2.6, 3.2, 3.2.1	24.	B	QR 2.4, 4.2	38.	D	QR 7.1, 7.1.2
12.	E	QR 2.5, 2.5.2	25.	C	QR 2.5, 2.5.2	39.	A	QR 2.4.3, 8.3, 8.3.3
13.	C	QR 5.2, 5.2.2, 6.3, 6.3.3	26.	E	QR 2.6	40.	D	QR 7.2, 7.2.2
			27.	C	QR 4.5, 4.5.2, 5.1,			

To estimate your standard score, sign in to dat-prep.com then click Tests in the top Menu. Cross-references above refer to subsections from chapters in the Gold Standard Book Set.

GS-1
SOLUTIONS

Question 1   C

See: BIO 15.5

Mutations are rare, inheritable, random changes in the genetic material (DNA) of a cell. Mutations are much more likely to be either neutral (esp. silent mutations) or negative (i.e. cancer) than positive for an organism's survival. Nonetheless, such a change in the genome increases genetic variability. Only mutations of gametes, and not somatic cells, are passed on to offspring. The following are some forms of mutations:

- Point mutation is a change affecting a single base pair in a gene

- Deletion is the removal of a sequence of DNA, the regions on either side being joined together

- Inversion is the reversal of a segment of DNA

- Translocation is when one chromosome breaks and attaches to another

- Duplication is when a sequence of DNA is repeated.

- Frame shift mutations occur when bases are added or deleted in numbers other than multiples of three. Such deletions or additions cause the rest of the sequence to be shifted such that each triplet reading frame is altered.

Question 2   A

See: BIO 7.5, 8.3

The spleen contains white pulp and red pulp. While the white pulp contains leukocytes (including antigen presenting cells) which filter red blood cells as well as foreign particles, the red pulp stores erythrocytes. It does not, however, produce platelets which are formed from fragments of large bone marrow cells or megakaryocytes.

Question 3   E

See: BIO 12.4

Inspiration is active and requires the contraction of the diaphragm by the phrenic nerve. The diaphragm will thus move downward, while the thoracic cage is pushed outwards increasing the volume of the chest cavity. This will thus cause a negative internal pressure which will allow air to enter the lungs. Hence, only answer choice **E.** is correct.

Question 4   B

See: BIO 15.1, 15.3

The reaction indicates that the allele for the normal and abnormal gene exists in the mother (Aa) and 2 abnormal alleles exist in the father (aa). As such, a Punnett square can be produced for this couple.

A = chromosome with normal gene

a = chromosome with abnormal gene

	a	**a**
A	Aa	Aa
a	aa	aa

Hence, 50% of boys will manifest the disease: boys (actually either sex since this is not sex-linked) could be either Aa or aa.

Question 5   E

See: BIO 17.1, 17.2 , 17.2.3

The vascular bundle is scattered in monocots. In dicot stems, it is common that the xylem and phloem tissues are present on the same radius and just opposed to each other in conjoint vascular bundles (ring patterned). Depending on the number and position of phloem group, conjoint vascular bundles can be of two types: collateral type and bi-collateral type.

Collateral vascular bundles are very common and seen in stems of dicotyledons (with some exceptions). Cambium may be present or absent in between xylem and phloem patches making the vascular bundle open or closed, respectively.

Bi-collateral vascular bundles contain two (= bi) patches of phloem on either sides of the xylem on the same radius. The outer phloem or external phloem remains towards the periphery of the central cylinder and the inner or internal phloem remains towards the center.

Question 6   C

See: BIO 17.1, 17.2

The cuticle is a continuous layer of waxy substances covering the outer surfaces of the epidermis of plants, it contains cutin and protects against water loss (or gain) and other damage. The term is also used for the hard outer covering or case of certain organisms such as arthropods and turtles.

The epidermis is a single-layered group of cells that covers plants' leaves, flowers, roots and stems.

Stomata, the plural of stoma, refers to the minute pores in the epidermis of the leaf or stem of a plant that allows movement of gases in and out of the intercellular spaces.

Even if you had never heard of bulliform cells, you should have gotten the answer correct by knowing the preceding plant structures.

Bulliform cells are large, bubble-shaped, empty-looking, colorless epidermal cells that occur in groups on the upper surface of the leaves of many grasses. During drought, the loss of moisture through vacuoles leads the leaves of many grass species to close as the two edges of the grass blade fold up toward each other. Once adequate water is available, these bulliform cells enlarge and the leaves open again.

Question 7   B

See: BIO 14.5.1

First off, it is important to know that a blastomere represents the first week of cell replication. The point at which a blastomere is committed to becoming a germ cell is different from the point at which the germ cell actually starts to function as a germ cell (i.e. producing cell-specific proteins). Determination is the point at which a cell is committed to becoming a particular type of cell, although it may not display any specific characteristics that would yet identify it as a specific type of cell. After determination, a cell will differentiate into a particular type of cell, and the fully differentiated cell is called *specialized*. Determination is the crucial point at which the fate of the blastomere is decided.

Question 8   E

See: BIO 2.2, BIO 16.6.4

Protists are a diverse group of eukaryotic microorganisms thus they have nuclei. The protists do not have much in common besides a relatively simple organization - either they are unicellular, or they are multicellular without specialized tissues. This simple cellular organization distinguishes the protists from other eukaryotes, such as fungi, plants and animals.

Question 9   A

See: BIO 6.3.3, 5.4.4

Osteoclasts are responsible for the release of calcium to the blood.

Question 10   A

See: BIO 6.3.3, 5.4.4; CHM 9.7

The equilibrium of a catalyzed reaction remains constant (constant amount of reactants and products); the rate at which equilibrium occurs increases.

Question 11   C

See: BIO 14.5

Implantation of the developing embryo into the uterine lining occurs during blastulation whereby the embryo has developed into a blastocyst.

Question 12   E

See: BIO 19.7

The tree line is the ecological boundary between forest and tundra and thus does not divide the tundra. Tundra can be further subdivided into alpine, arctic or Antarctic (frozen). Tundra is known for permafrost and short growing seasons but "frozen" or "antarctic" tundra is incapable of supporting vegetation because it is too cold and dry. Most of Antarctica (the continent) is covered by ice fields.

Question 13   E

See: BIO 7.2, 7.3, 7.5.1

Oxygen from lungs → <u>pulmonary vein</u> → heart → aorta → arteries to body tissues → body tissues (capillaries) → veins from body tissues (includes renal) → vena cava → heart → pulmonary arteries → lungs. Note that a portal system or portal vein shuttles blood from one capillary bed to another.

Question 14   B

See: BIO 7.5.2, 10.3

Blood (or hydrostatic) pressure is proportional to the filtration rate.

Question 15   C

See: BIO 4.3, 2.5, 2.5.1

There are two main differences between Trials 1 and 2 in Table 1: (1) the [inhibitin] is increased by a relatively small amount (approx. 10^{-6} mmol/L); (2) the [trypsin] is increased by a relatively large amount (by a factor of 10). Answer choices **B**. and **D**. cannot account for the constant rate observed for the two reactions since a significant increase in inhibitor, or decrease in enzyme should cause a decrease in the reaction rate. However, a significant increase in [trypsin] (difference #2) with a concomitant minor increase in [inhibitin] could allow the enzyme to overcome the effects of the inhibitor, resulting in a constant rate of reaction.

Question 16   B

See: BIO 4.1, 15.7, Chapter 15 Appendix

This question requires knowledge of the definition of anabolism and catabolism. A catabolic reaction involves the breakdown of macromolecules, whereas an anabolic reaction involves the synthesis of macromolecules from individual building blocks (BIO 4.1). PCR entails the synthesis (amplification) of a new DNA strand using a DNA template and free nucleotides, therefore, it is an anabolic reaction that synthesizes new DNA strands.

Background: The polymerase chain reaction (PCR) is a powerful biological tool that allows the rapid amplification of any fragment of DNA without purification. In PCR, RNA primers are made to flank the specific DNA sequence to be amplified. These RNA primers are then extended to the end of the DNA molecule with the use of a heat-resistant DNA polymerase. The newly synthesized DNA strand is then used as the template to undergo another round of replication.

Question 17   B

See: BIO 1.2.2, BIO 3, BIO 20.5

The question states that AZT is an analog of thymidine and differs from thymidine in that it lacks the 3'–OH group. This OH group is crucial in the synthesis of DNA strands because it is required to form the 5'–3' phosphodiester linkage which holds the DNA backbone together (BIO 1.2.2). Consequently, since there is a 3'–N$_3$

rather than a 3'–OH, once this nucleotide analog is incorporated into the DNA, synthesis of the DNA strand will be blocked as no subsequent nucleotide will be able to form a bond with the 3' carbon atom. Moreover, the retroviral RNA must be converted to DNA in a process known as reverse transcription. In this case, the RNA strand will serve as a template to generate a single strand of DNA. Hence, it is reverse transcription of the viral RNA that will be disrupted by AZT. Recall that conventional transcription uses uridine instead of thymidine, and so AZT would not affect the conversion of DNA to RNA (BIO 3).

Question 18   E

See: BIO 1.2.2, BIO 3

An antibody-antigen interaction involving serum and red blood cells leads to clumping or agglutination. Type O blood is the "universal donor" because the red blood cells have no antigens. However, type O serum contains anti-A and anti-B antibodies. I, II and III contain red blood cells with either some A or B or both antigens, thus resulting in antibody-antigen interaction with type O serum.

Question 19   C

See: BIO 6.2.3

The semicircular canals, which are found in the inner ear, are responsible for maintaining a sense of equilibrium.

Question 20   E

See: BIO 1.4.1, 17.6.4

In multicellular plants, the structural functions of cell junctions are provided for by cell walls. The analogues of communicating cell junctions in plants are called plasmodesmata (BIO 17.6.4). 1. Communicating junctions, like gap junctions in animal cells, are narrow tunnels which allow the free passage of small molecules and ions. One gap junction channel is composed of two connexons (or hemichannels) which connect across the intercellular space (BIO 1.4.1).

Question 21   C

See: BIO 1.1.3

Receptor-mediated endocytosis is mediated by clathrin-coated vesicles (CCVs). Exocytotic vesicles are usually not clathrin coated, most of them have no coat at all.

In exocytosis, the transient vesicle fusion with the cell membrane forms a structure shaped like a pore (= *porosome*). Porosomes contain many different types of protein including chloride and calcium channels, actin, and SNARE proteins that mediate the docking and fusion of vesicles with the cell membrane. The primary role of SNARE proteins is to mediate vesicle fusion through full fusion exocytosis or open and close (= "kiss-and-run fusion") exocytosis.

Question 22   D

See: BIO 1.1.1, 4.1

Answer choices **A** and **C** are consistent with simple diffusion. Answer choice **C** is equivocal. Answer choice **D** suggests the presence of a transporter (carrier mediated transport) because there must be a limited number of carriers, if the concentration of dopamine gets too high, the carriers would be saturated thus the rate of crossing the membrane would level off (plateau).

Question 23   D

See: BIO 2.2, BIO 16.6.4

The Archaea (AKA archeabacteria) are a domain of single-celled microorganisms. These microbes have no cell nucleus or any other membrane-bound organelles. Initially, archaea were termed "extremophiles" because of their ability to live in harsh or extreme environments, but they have since been found to also live in a broad range of habitats.

Protobionts are systems that are considered to have possibly been the precursors to prokaryotic cells.

Question 24   D

See: BIO 19.2

J-shaped curves are a classic representation of exponential growth. The J-shaped curve is characteristic of populations that are introduced into a new or unfilled environment, or alternatively, whose numbers have been drastically reduced by a catastrophic event and are rebounding.

Question 25   E

See: BIO 1.1, 5.1.1, 5.1.3

The question essentially provides the following information: (i) the concentration of potassium (the only cation) on both sides of the membrane is equal; (ii) the concentration of the anions on side X (Cl^- and $Prot^-$) must be equal to side Y (Cl^- alone). Therefore:

$$Cl^-_x + Prot^-_x = Cl^-_y$$

Thus:

$$Cl^-_x < Cl^-_y$$

Since $[Cl^-]_y > [Cl^-]_x$, there exists a chemical gradient for diffusion (BIO 1.1.1) from Y to X (i.e. answer choice **A**. is incorrect). The electrical gradient depends on the membrane potential (BIO 5.1.3). The electrical and chemical gradients balance at an equilibrium which is dynamic (answer choice **E**.; other answer choices do not take into account the dynamic equilibrium).

Note: The Gibbs–Donnan effect (also known as the Donnan effect or Gibbs–Donnan equilibrium) is the name for the behavior of charged particles near a semi-permeable membrane to sometimes fail to distribute evenly across the two sides of the membrane.

Question 26   D

See: BIO 14.2

Spermatogonia (diploid) are male germ cells which can produce primary spermatocytes.

Each primary spermatocyte duplicates its DNA and eventually undergoes meiosis I to produce two haploid secondary spermatocytes. Each of the two secondary spermatocytes further undergo meiosis II to produce two spermatids (haploid). Thus 1 primary spermatocyte produces 4 spermatids. The spermatids then undergo spermiogenesis to produce spermatozoa.

Question 27   C

See: BIO 4.4

Glucose (from glycogen) is the first and most common source to produce ATP. Amino acids, which requires the breakdown of protein in muscle which would be fed into the Krebs cycle, would only be used when all else fails.

Question 28   E

See: BIO 14.3

You must be familiar with the graph of the menstrual cycle in order to know which curve is referring to which hormone. There are four hormones involved: luteinizing hormone (LH), follicle stimulating hormone (FSH), estrogen and progesterone. If the menstrual cycle is understood well, you should immediately know that both estrogen and progesterone are secreted by the corpus luteum which came from the ovary. Alternatively, if the pituitary hormones are known, it is easy to eliminate LH and FSH because they are secreted by the anterior pituitary. Notice the LH surge before ovulation (III) which remains low in the 2nd part of the menstrual cycle.

Question 29   B

See: BIO 4.2

In this case, the inhibitor (I) binds the active site of the enzyme (E) reversibly and thus, it can be displaced by the substrate (S). Therefore, if [S] is gradually increased for a given [I], the inhibitor will be displaced from the active site of the enzyme and the effect of the inhibitor will be overcome as the enzyme reaches its normal maximal velocity (V_{max}). On the other hand, the K_m of the enzyme, which represents the [S] at half V_{max} should increase. In our example, the same V_{max} for the enzyme will be reached if enough S is added, however, this increase in [S] needed to overcome the effect of the inhibitor will raise the K_m accordingly. You should be aware that the larger the K_m, the less efficient the enzyme because a higher [S] is required to reach a given velocity of the reaction.

Question 30   C

See: BIO 14.2

Down's syndrome, or trisomy 21, is caused by the presence of triplicate copies of chromosome 21 in the afflicted individual. Since a normal genotype consists of two chromosome 21s, the overall number of chromosomes in a Down's syndrome patient is increased by one (46 + 1 = 47N). In both meiosis and mitosis, the separation of chromosomes (in meiosis I) or sister chromatids (in mitosis and meiosis II) occurs during anaphase, thereby eliminating answer choices **A**. and **B**. Recall that meiosis is divided into two steps. During the reduction division, the homologous chromosomes pair at the equatorial plate and separate to form two daughter cells consisting of a haploid (N) number of chromosomes. During the second meiotic division, the chromosomes line up at the center of the cell (just as they would in mitosis) and the sister chromatids separate to form two daughter cells of a haploid number of chromosomes. Since the homologous chromosomes pair up only in meiosis 1, we expect that the failure of chromosomes 21 to separate will occur, with a greater likelihood, in Anaphase I.

Question 31   E

See: BIO 1.2.2, 3.0

You must know that A pairs with T and C pairs with G. However, the question is asking about RNA, not DNA. In RNA, T is replaced by U. Therefore, the complementary sequence of CAG is GUC.

Question 32   D

See: BIO 2.2

The question is asking for a feature that *eukaryotes* have that *prokaryotes* (i.e. bacteria) do not have. A cell wall is listed, however, a cell wall is a feature that the *prokaryote* has that some eukaryotes have (i.e. plants and fungi).

One of the major differences between *prokaryotes* and *eukaryotes* is that *prokaryotes* contain no membrane bound organelles. Therefore, a *eukaryote* would have lysosomes, while a *prokaryote* would not.

Question 33   A

See: BIO 9.4.1

This is very simple question. You should know that the liver produces bile and the gallbladder stores it.

Question 34   D

See: BIO 17.6.3, 17.6.6

During dark phase (= dark stage/reaction = light independent stage/reaction), the reduced $NADPH_2$ transfers its hydrogens to CO_2 which is reduced to carbohydrate. The dark stage takes place in the stroma of the chloroplast. Unlike the light stage, the dark stage is controlled by enzymes and therefore affected by temperature. The enzyme is ribulose bisphosphate carboxylase oxygenase (RUBISCO).

Question 35   E

See: BIO 4.1, 4.7; CHM 8.2, 10.1, 10.2

Endergonic is defined as "absorbing energy in the form of work." In metabolism, an endergonic process is anabolic (energy is stored) which is usually coupled with ATP. Reduction is defined as a gain in electrons (GERC: Gain Electrons Reduction Cathode). Anabolic reactions refers to the set of metabolic pathways that construct molecules from smaller units using energy. Activation energy can be defined as the minimum energy required to start a chemical reaction. It's relationship to entropy is nowhere as clear as the other answer choices.

Question 36   E

See: BIO 20.2.2

The primary structure refers to the amino acid linear sequence of the protein held together by covalent peptide bonds. Keep in mind that the primary structure is the order of the amino acids in the protein. For this reason, even post-translational modifications such as disulfide formation, phosphorylations and glycosylations are considered a part of the primary structure (these are all types of covalent bonding).

The dipeptide cystine is composed of two cysteine amino acids joined by a disulfide bond (= bridge) and can help to stabilize the tertiary structure and to some degree, the quaternary structure of proteins (and rarely involved in secondary structure). H-bonding, which is non-covalent, is prominent in secondary and tertiary protein structures.

Question 37   E

See: BIO 7 Appendix

Even if you had forgotten the equation, because EF is a fraction (often given as a %), it has no units, so the numerator and denominator must have the same unit.

EF = stroke volume / end diastolic volume

Cardiac output = stroke volume × heart rate

Question 38   B

See: BIO 16.3, 19.2-19.4 and Appendix

The question discusses evolution within two different species. Within a species, the passage distinguishes between "local" populations and "other" populations which suggests that the populations live apart (= *allopatric*; BIO 16.3). Since the local population evolves differently (i.e. "*more capable of attacking the host . . .*"), genetic drift may be implicated. Recall that genetic mutations are usually either negative or neutral with regard to the organism's survival (BIO 15.5). Note: interspecific means 'between different

species' whereas intraspecific means 'within the same species'.

Question 39   E

See: BIO 16.4.2, 17

Answer choice **E** is both irrelevant and untrue since plant cells have both chloroplasts and mitochondria.

Question 40   A

See: BIO 11.3, 11.3.3

Some common relations in brackets: carpals (wrist), metacarpals (palm), phalanges (fingers), tarsals (ankle), metatarsals (foot), phalanges (toes).

Question 41   A

See: CHM 8.3, 1.4

From Table I we are not given ΔH formation; rather, we are provided with a different parameter which the table describes as the enthalpy of combustion ΔHc of carbon. The end product of combustion (the oxide) of carbon is carbon dioxide. Now we can use Hess's Law knowing that the ΔHc for $C_{graphite}$ = −393.3 kJ mol^{-1} and for $C_{diamond}$ = −395.1 kJ mol^{-1}. We can summarize the process as follows:

$C_{graphite} \rightarrow CO_2$ ΔHc = −393.3 kJ mol^{-1}

$CO_2 \rightarrow C_{diamond}$ ΔHc = 395.1 kJ mol^{-1}

$C_{graphite} \rightarrow C_{diamond}$ ΔHc = 1.8 kJ mol^{-1}

{Notice the change in direction of the equation for $C_{diamond}$ was necessary in order to cancel the CO_2; thus the sign for ΔHc was changed from negative to positive}

Question 42   E

See: CHM 3.4, 6.1

By definition, a Lewis acid is a chemical species which accepts an electron pair (CHM 3.4). Answer choice **A.** is the Bronsted-Lowry definition of an acid (CHM 6.1).

Question 43   D

See: CHM 1.4

The relative atomic mass of O is ≈ 16; that of H is 1.0; and that of S is ≈ 32. Thus the relative molecular mass of H_2SO_3 is (2 × 1.0) + 32 + (16 × 3) = 82. The mass of the molecular oxygen (16 × 3 = 48) is more than half of 82. There is only one answer choice (**D.**) which is greater than 0.5! Alternatively, you can do it the old fashioned way: 48/82 + calculate!

Question 44   E

See: CHM 5.3.1

On the Surface:

x = molarity of $Mg_3(PO_4)_2 \rightarrow$ Solve for x

$(.005M\ Mg^{2+})\ (.005\ L) + (3x)(.015\ L) = (.05M\ Mg^{2+})(.02\ L)$

Note the 3 in front of x because there are 3 potential Mg^{2+} generated from each $Mg_3(PO_4)_2$ in aqueous solution. Solve for x:

$(3x)(.015\ L) = (.05M\ Mg^{2+})(.02\ L) - (.005M\ Mg^{2+})(.005\ L)$

$x = [(.05)(.02) - (.005)(.005)] / (0.045)$

Thus $x = 0.022$ M.

Going Deeper: a detailed calculation follows . . .

Let's begin with the total number of moles of Mg^{2+} present in the final solution: 0.05 moles/L $\times$ 0.02 L = 0.001 moles of Mg^{2+}. Next, let's look at the number of moles of Mg^{2+} obtained from $MgCl_2$: 0.005 moles/L $\times$ 0.005 L = 0.000025 moles of Mg^{2+}. Now we know the number of moles of Mg^{2+} we need supplied from $Mg_3(PO_4)_2$: (0.001 − 0.000025) moles = 0.000975 moles. Thus from the 15 mL of $Mg_3(PO_4)_2$ we need 0.000975 moles of Mg^{2+}. But each mole of $Mg_3(PO_4)_2$ contains 3 moles of Mg^{2+} Therefore, the concentration of $Mg_3(PO_4)_2$ = [(0.000975 moles)/(0.015 L)] $\times$ 1/3 = 0.022 mol L^{-1} = 2.2×10^{-2} M.

Sometimes on the real DAT, they will not calculate the answer; they will just confirm that you know how to set up the solution such as the answer choices in this question.

Question 45   A

See: CHM 6.6, 6.5

Using $K_b = ([X^+][OH^-]) / [XOH]$; X is most probably a Group I metal since it is monovalent (= univalent = a valence of one).

Assuming that $[X^+] = [OH^-]$ approximately

$K_b = [OH^-]^2 / [XOH]$, where XOH approximates 1.0 M at equilibrium, thus:

$1.0 \times 10^{-6} = [OH^-]^2 / 1$

$[OH^-]^2 = 1.0 \times 10^{-6}$

$[OH^-] = 1.0 \times 10^{-3}$ mol dm^{-3}

$pOH = -\log[OH^-] = -\log(1.0\ x\ 10^{-3}) = -(-3) = 3$

Using pH + pOH = 14, we get:

$pH = 14 - pOH = 14 - 3 = 11$

Question 46   A

See: CHM 1.3, 1.5

Using Number of moles = (Mass)/(Relative molecular mass)

For PCl_3: Number of moles = (68.75 g)/[(31.0 + 35.5 × 3) g mol^{-1}] = 68.75/137.5 = 1/2

Equation: $P_4\ (s) + 6Cl_2 \rightarrow 4PCl_3$

Thus, Number of moles of P_4 = 1/4 × Number of moles PCl_3 = 1/4 × 1/2 mole = 1/8 mole

Using 1 mole of particles = 6.0×10^{23} particles (Avogadro's # = 6.023×10^{23} particles/mole)

1/8 mole P_4 = 1/8 × 6.0×10^{23} = 3/4 × 10^{23} = 0.75×10^{23} P_4 molecules

Question 47   B

See: CHM 10.1

The reduced species of the electrochemical equilibrium with the most negative E° value is the strongest reducing agent (CHM 10.1). Memory aside (!), it is of value to note that a reducing agent reduces the other substance, thus <u>a reducing agent is oxidized</u>. Note that only answer choices **B**. and **C**. are oxidized (= *lose electrons*). When you write the two relevant equations as oxidations, instead of reductions like the table provided, you will note that only answer choice **B**. has a positive E° value indicating the spontaneous nature of the reaction. The table provided demonstrates <u>half-reactions</u> written as <u>reduction potentials</u>. In order to write the oxidation, simply reverse the reaction and change the sign of E°:

Oxidation: $Cr^{2+} \rightarrow Cr^{3+} + e^-$ E° = 0.410

Question 48   C

See: CHM 2.3

As one moves across the periodic table, the atomic radius decreases as a result of the increasing effective nuclear charge (*without an increase in the number of atomic orbitals*). In other words, the nucleus becomes more and more positive from left to right on the periodic table resulting in the drawing of negatively charged orbital electrons nearer and nearer to the nucleus. As a result, atoms will accept electrons more readily as we go across the periodic table and the electron affinity (EA) becomes more negative (*less positive*). For example, halogens have very negative EA values because of their strong tendencies to form anions. Alkaline earths have positive EA values.

Question 49   A

See: CHM 4.2, 4.3.2

Any dipole-dipole interaction (ie, due to the separation of charges or difference in electronegativities between H and Cl) present requires energy to be broken before the HCl can enter the gaseous phase, thereby making HCl more difficult to boil (*i.e. the boiling point is elevated*). Neither Cl_2 nor H_2 have a separation in charge. Note that for the molecule HF, the boiling point is even greater due to H-bonding which is an even stronger intermolecular force than simple dipole-dipole interactions.

Question 50   C

See: CHM 4.2, ORG 10.1
Ethers possess a highly electronegative atom (*oxygen*), but no hydrogen atom is directly bonded to an oxygen or any other electronegative atom. As a result, another molecule with an electropositive hydrogen (i.e. water) can form hydrogen bonds with the oxygen atom of an ether, but the ether's hydrogen atoms will not be involved in hydrogen bonding.

Question 51   B

See: CHM 4.1.7
Keep in mind that: Partial pressure = Mole fraction × Total pressure

Since the total pressure is 100 atm, the mole fraction of 0.40 for HCl represents 40 atm; we are given 35 atm for Cl_2, thus $100 - (40 + 35) = 25$ atm.

Question 52   E

See: CHM 11.4

Using Fraction of activity remaining = (Final activity)/(Initial activity)

Fraction of activity remaining = $(10.8$ dpm g$^{-1})/(43.0$ dpm g$^{-1}) = 1/4$, approximately

Using Fraction of activity remaining = $(1/2)^{\text{number of half-lives}}$

$1/4 = (1/2)^x$, thus $x = 2$

Question 53   D

See: CHM 11
Recall that an alpha particle is a helium nucleus ($^4_2$He) and a beta particle is an electron ($^0_{-1}$e$^-$).

Equation I: $^{238}_{92}$U $\rightarrow ^x_y$Z $+ 3^4_2$He $+ 2^0_{-1}$e$^- + 3$ (gamma rays)

Since the sum of the atomic numbers and mass numbers on either side of the equation must be equal:

$238 = x + (3 \times 4) + (2 \times 0) + (3 \times 0)$

$x = 226$

$92 = y + (3 \times 2) + (2 \times -1) + (3 \times 0)$

$y = 88$

Thus, from the answer choices, Z = Ra; note that gamma rays are a form of electromagnetic radiation (CHM 11) and thus have no charge and no mass.

Question 54   B

See: CHM 10.1, 10.2
Written as standard reduction potentials, we get:

$O_2 + 2H_2O + 4e^- \leftrightarrow 4OH^-$ E° $= +0.401$ V Cathode (gain of electrons)

$2Fe^{2+} + 4e^- \leftrightarrow 2Fe$ E° $= -0.440$ V Anode (loss of electrons)

$E°_{\text{reaction}} = E°_{\text{reduction}} - E°_{\text{oxidation}}$

$E°_{\text{reaction}} = +0.401 - (-0.440) = +0.841$ V

Question 55   D

See: CHM 5.3.2
Equation: $FeX_2 \leftrightarrow Fe^{2+} + 2X^-$

Solubility s can be calculated using the above equation and $K_{sp} = [Fe^{2+}] [X^-]^2$:

$K_{sp} = (s) (2s)^2 = 4s^3$

Thus $s^3 = (K_{sp}/4) = (5.0 \times 10^{-16})/4 = (1.25 \times 10^{-16})$
$\qquad = 0.125 \times 10^{-15} = 1/8 \times 10^{-15}$

$s = [\text{cube root } (1/8)] \times [\text{cube root } (10^{-15})] = 1/2 \times 10^{-5}$
$\quad = 5.0 \times 10^{-6}$ mol L^{-1}

The calculation can be done in under a minute without a calculator.

Question 56   D

See: CHM 3.5
P: 3 bonds

Phosphorus is in Group V. It can therefore either have a valency of 3 or 5 (*you can memorize this or determine it through VSEPR modeling*). Answer choice **D.**, which has three bonds to each phosphorous, is the only answer which fulfils this requirement.

Question 57   E

See: CHM 2.4, 2.4.1
Metals have high melting points and densities. They are excellent conductors of heat and electricity due to their valence electrons being able to move freely. This fact also accounts for the major characteristic properties of metals: large atomic radius, low ionization energy, high electron affinities and low electronegativity. Groups IA and IIA are the most reactive of all metal species. Of course, metals tend to be shiny and solid (with the exception of mercury, Hg, a liquid at STP). They are also ductile

(they can be drawn into thin wires) and malleable (they can be easily hammered into very thin sheets). Metals form positive ions by losing electrons.

Metalloids (or semimetals) conduct better than nonmetals but not as well as metals.

Question 58   C

See: CHM 1.1-1.5

Let us use the process of elimination. Answer choice **A**. is false because it would support a lighted splint (*translation: fire burns in the presence of oxygen!*). Answer choice **B**. (molecular weight or MW = 28 g/mol) is somewhat lighter than air which is mostly nitrogen (78%, MW = 28 g/mol) with oxygen (21%, MW = 32 g/mol). Answer choice **D**. is really an anion (*carbonate*) not a gas (P2) and answer choice **E**. is a solid. Thus we are left with carbon dioxide (MW = 44 g/mol) which is heavier than air and does not support a lighted splint.

Question 59   B

See: CHM 2.3

Lithium only has one valent electron (Group I, PT; CHM 2.3). Therefore, one would expect only one covalent bond per lithium atom with no extra valent electrons on the lithium (that is, no lone pairs nor single electrons).

Question 60   D

See: CHM 10.4

A is the positively charged electrode i.e. anode in the diagram so the electrolyte used is irrelevant.

Question 61   E

See: CHM 6.9

Since the pH is less than the pK_a of the indicator, the undissociated form predominates.

$pH = 2$; $pK_a = -\log K_a = -\log (4 \times 10^{-4}) = 4 - \log(4) > 2$

{for the math see CHM 6.5.1, and the end of CHM 6.6.1}

Since the pH of the solution is less than the pK_a of the indicator, reduced pH means increased [H$^+$], looking at Reaction I and remembering Le Chatelier's Principle, if the stress is on the right side of the equilibrium (i.e. increased [H$^+$]), the reaction shifts to the left which gives the red color (i.e. increased [HMe]).

Going Deeper: Note that from the math described, we know that the pK_a of methyl orange must be between 3 and 4 which suggests that if the pH of the solution is 2, it must be red, if it a pH of 5 (for example), it must be yellow. However, if the pH is between 3 and 4, the color would be a combination of yellow and red which would mean orange. Normally, indicators switch between their 2 colors (i.e. red and yellow in this example) over a pH range of about 2.

Question 62   E

See: CHM 1.5.1, 5.2, 6.2, 6.9.1

Answer choice **A**. can be eliminated since the oxidation numbers of the atoms in the reactants and products remain constant (CHM 1.6). A neutralization (answer choice **B**.) would involve an acid/base reaction, however, only acid is present in the equation. The precipitation of sulfur involves the replacement of the chlorine atoms with sulfur (CHM 1.5.1; cf. CHM 5.2, 6.2, 6.9.1) to form FeS(s), and, the replacement of sulfur atoms with chlorine to form HCl (= double replacement; CHM 1.5.1, also called *metathesis*).

Question 63   C

See: CHM 2.1, 2.2, 2.3

The roman numerals of the Group A atoms (which include the metals; see CHM 2.3F) indicate the number of electrons in the outer shell of the atom. In this case, both answer choices **B**. and **C**. have 2 valence electrons; however, answer choice **B**. represents the structure of He, a nonmetal. Answer choice **E**. has a d orbital. Keep in mind that in general, a transition metal is one which forms one or more stable ions which have incompletely filled d orbitals. Thus answer choice **E**. is Cr (not a Group II metal) but the more stable state would have the d orbital half filled thus $3d^5$, $4s^1$.

Question 64   B

See: CHM 6.1

K_{a2} is the expression describing the further dissociation of the conjugate base from the K_{a1} expression; in other words, the dissociation of the second proton. For the reaction:

$HS^- \rightarrow H^+ + S^{2-}$

$K_{a2} = $ [products] / [reactants] $ = $ [H$^+$][S^{2-}] / [HS$^-$].

Question 65   D

See: E; CHM 8.10
$\Delta G = \Delta H - T\Delta S$

"The sublimation of carbon dioxide occurs quickly at room temperature" means that it is spontaneous and so ΔG must be negative (by definition). Sublimation means:

Solid CO_2 + heat $\rightarrow$ vapor

Entropy (randomness) is clearly increasing (thus positive ΔS) because we are moving from a structured, ordered solid to randomly moving gas particles. Heat is required so it is endothermic meaning ΔH is positive. The question is asking about the reverse reaction so all 3 signs are reversed: ΔG is now positive; ΔH is now negative; ΔS is now negative.

Going deeper: Notice that a negative ΔS multiplied by a $-T$ (see the Gibbs free energy equation) creates a positive term which overshadows the effect of the negative ΔH and thus ΔG is still positive. Also, please keep in mind that sometimes the real DAT will provide the Gibbs free energy equation but sometimes they won't.

Question 66   E

See: CHM 8.7
The easiest way to objectively answer the question is to round the figures which can be done because the values of the specific heats are so far apart thus: 4 J/g•°C for water and 1 J/g•°C for glass. Using dimensional analysis (paying attention to the units):

Water: (40 J)/(4 J/g•°C) = 10 °C for 1 gram.

Glass: (40 J)/(1 J/g•°C) = 40 °C for 1 gram.

Question 67   A

See: CHM 5.1.1, 5.1.2
This question tests your understanding of *colligative properties*. From the equation

$T_b = K_B m$, where K_B is constant, or the molality is the factor to be considered. Recall that m = (Number of moles solute)/(1000 g solvent) and number of moles = (Mass of substance present)/(Relative molecular mass). Since glucose has a smaller relative molecular mass than sucrose, there will be a greater number of moles of glucose present when equal masses of the two substances are used. Therefore, the molality of glucose is greater and hence the boiling point elevation is greater.

Question 68   A

See: CHM 4.1.2, 4.1.8
A gas most closely approaches ideality at very low pressures (*thus making the relative volume that the gas particles occupy and the attractive forces between them negligible*) and at high temperatures (*so that the energy loss in inelastic collisions is negligible*). {*Plow and Thigh !*}

Question 69   C

See: CHM 9.3
By looking at Table 1, we can see that when the concentration of X is quadrupled (factor of 4^1) while [Y] is unchanged (Exp. 1 and 3), the rate is increased by a factor of $4 = 4^1$. Thus the order of the reaction with respect to X is 1. When the concentration of Y is doubled (factor of 2^1) while [X] remains the same (Exp. 1 and 2), the rate of reaction is quadrupled (factor of $4 = 2^2$). Thus, the order of reaction with respect to Y is 2. The rate equation is Rate = [X][Y]^2.{*Notice that the stoichiometric coefficients are not relevant*}

Question 70   A

See: CHM 12.3.1
A buret would be better but a graduated cylinder is by far the best on the list.

Question 71   A

See: ORG 2.1, 2.2, 2.3
A chiral carbon or stereogenic carbon center (or stereocenter) must be bonded to 4 different substituents. For this reason, ignore

all carbons with double bonds (notice double bonds in the rings labeled A and C) and ignore all carbons bonded to hydrogen twice (some in rings B and E). We are left with 5 centers of chirality which are all in rings B and C (C5, C6, C9, C13 and C14; note that 13 is not labeled in the diagram but it is clearly in ring B between 12 and 14).

Question 72   E

See: D; ORG 1.6, 7.1, 8.1, 9.4
Keep in mind that alkyl lithiums and Grignard reagents (i.e. RMgBr) general partially negative carbons which will be attracted to partially positive carbons thus creating carbon-carbon bonds.

First identify the compound as 4-propyl-4-octanol and consider quickly sketching it in a way that resembles the tertiary alcohol in the mechanism provided so that you can more easily compare the various R groups. Doing so reveals 2 propyl groups attached to the central carbon meaning that there is either a propyl lithium or propyl MgBr (Grignard) being used. The 4-propyl-4-octanol also has a butyl group (R') which must originate from the ester thus it must be pentanoate. The nature of R" is irrelevant since it is part of the leaving group and thus is not found in the product.

The General Reaction Mechanism:

In case you were tripped up by nomenclature, here is hexyl pentanoate:

Question 73   A

See: CHM 6.3, ORG 1.6, 4.2.1, 6.2.4, 11.1.1

A base can be defined as a proton (H^+) acceptor. The strongest base would more likely carry a negative charge (opposites attract) and would create the most stable product. Alkanes are very stable and it is extremely difficult to remove a proton. Furthermore, primary anions (I) are extremely unstable thus it strongly wants a proton. This is followed by an ethoxide group (II) and then a compound that does not even have a negative charge (III; it has an electronegative N which would not be as attractive for a proton as a negatively charged O or C).

Question 74   D

See: ORG 4.2, 7.1, 8.1, 14.1

This question tests your memory of a couple of the IR absorption peaks. The absolute minimum to memorize are the bands for an alcohol (OH, 3200 – 3650) and that for the carbonyl group (C = O, 1630 – 1780) because these are the two most encountered functional groups in DAT organic chemistry.

Bottle II has a peak at 1710 (carbonyl) 3333 - 3500 (hydroxyl) = carboxylic acid (i.e. benzoic acid). Bottle IV has a peak at 3333 so it must be the alcohol. Without doing anything else, there is only one possible answer, **D**.

{For fun, draw the structures of the four compounds; allyl, ORG 4.2, add -OH to make it an alcohol; benzoic acid - ORG 8.1; the four carbon ketone 2-butanone (= methyl ethyl ketone) and the four carbon aldehyde butyraldehyde (= butanal) - ORG 7.1}

Question 75   D

See: ORG 1.1, 8.1

Formic acid (HCOOH) is a carboxylic acid whose structure is shown by answer choice **D**. Note that answer choices **A.**, **B**. and **E**. can be quickly discounted because carbon needs to form 4 bonds to be neutral (ORG 1.1). Similarly, oxygen needs 2 bonds to be neutral, eliminating answer choice **B**.

Question 76   B

See: CHM 6.3, ORG 5.2.2, 10.2

When a compound becomes more acidic, Ka increases (CHM 6.3) thus pKa decreases because pKa = – log Ka. That's all!

The following information is for the curious minded (!) but was certainly not needed in order to answer the question: (i) substituents affect the acidity of phenols (ORG 10.2); (ii) halides (i.e.

Br) are weakly deactivating groups but they are O-P Directors (ORG 5.2.2); (iii) activating groups (O-P Directors except halides) decrease the acidity of the phenol (ORG 10.2); (iv) in summary, where EDG = electron donating group and EWG = electron withdrawing group, we get:

EDG	EWG	EWG: Halogens
activates the ring	deactivates the ring	weakly deactivating
O/P Directing	Meta Directing	O/P Directing
i.e. alkyl groups	i.e. nitro ($-NO_2$)	i.e. bromine
acid weakening	acid strengthening	acid strengthening
increase pKa	decrease pKa	decrease pKa

The Reasoning: Electron withdrawing groups can stabilize the negative charge on oxygen which encourages oxygen to lose a proton (i.e. become more acidic). One more time for fun! When a compound becomes more acidic, Ka increases (CHM 6.3) thus pKa decreases because pKa = – log Ka. That's all!

Question 77   C

See: ORG 7.2.2

This question provides us with only one answer which could possibly have the correct geometry! Nonetheless, let's work through the mechanism.

The story goes something like this: The catalyst (H^+), being the most charged substance is implicated first. Thus the electrons from the electronegative oxygen (O in the carbonyl, C = O) are attracted to the proton (H^+) and bonds. To remain neutral oxygen loses its pi bond with carbon, leaving only a single bond and secondary carbocation. The δ – charge on the oxygen from the *diol* (= a compound with 2 alcohol – OH – groups) attacks the positively charged carbocation. The extra hydrogen on the oxygen which now attaches to carbon is kicked out as a proton (regenerating our catalyst). Now we have our "*hemi-ketal*": the ketone has been converted into a hydroxyl group and the diol (*minus one hydrogen*).

Next, the proton strikes again! It can be attracted to the hydroxyl group which falls off as water (*a great leaving group*), thus we have a secondary carbocation, again. Now we have a partial negative charge (the oxygen of the free arm of the diol) and a positive charge (the carbocation) in close proximity in the same molecule! In a very fast *intra*molecular reaction, the nucleophile meets the carbon nucleus and regenerates the proton catalyst. The product is answer choice **C**., a ketal.

Question 78   D

See: ORG 13.3, CHM 12

Overheating may destroy the pure compounds or increase the percent impurities. Some of the methods which are classically used to prevent overheating include boiling slowly, the use of boiling chips (= ebulliator, which makes bubbles) and the use of a vacuum which decreases the vapor pressure and thus the boiling point. A nucleophile could only create unwanted products and thus prevent the isolation of a pure product from the original mixture.

Going Deeper: Boiling chips, or boiling stones, are small chunks of inert material. A few are added to a liquid before it is heated and they tend to promote steady, even boiling. In theory, a liquid should boil when it is heated at its boiling point. The temperature should remain constant because the excess heat is dissipated in overcoming the heat of vaporization required to move liquid molecules into the gas phase. In practice, spontaneous formation of gas bubbles within the liquid can be slow which could lead to super-heating and ultimately, large violent bubbles. Boiling chips produce small gas bubbles where the liquid molecules can evaporate and initiate boiling at a steady even rate.

Question 79   B

See: CHM 3.5, ORG 3.3, 10.1

Since epoxides are by definition 3-membered rings, they will have the same geometry as cyclopropane. Hence, their bond angles should be 60° (ORG 3.3).

Question 80   C

See: ORG 7.1

The α carbon is the carbon adjacent to the carbon of the carbonyl group of the molecule and it has increased acidity because of the resonance stabilization of the anion.

Note that the carboxylic acid hydrogen is the most acidic hydrogen of this molecule but that hydrogen is not directly bonded to a carbon.

Question 81   A

See: ORG 13.2.1

If the material in the GLC absorbs each compound equally well, then they cannot be separated by this method.

Note that GLC is similar to fractional distillation - both processes separate the components of a mixture primarily based on boiling point (or vapor pressure) differences. Fractional distillation is usually used to separate components of a mixture on a large scale, whereas GLC can be used on a much smaller scale. Neither is directly dependent on the melting point.

Question 82   A

See: ORG 12.1.2

This is a common type of DAT question. You should be familiar with the concept of isoelectric point from the organic chemistry review.

The isoelectric point is defined as the pH at which an amino acid is immobile in an electric field due to the neutrality of the molecule (note that the negative charge on the carboxyl group cancels out the positive charge on the amino group). If we are in a medium which is more acidic (= lower pH) than the isoelectric point, the carboxyl group will become protonated to give a molecule with an overall positive charge. At a pH greater than the isoelectric point, the amino group will lose its proton and give a negatively charged methionine.

Note that the acidic component ($-COOH$) of the amino acid acted like an acid by donating a proton (and becoming $-COO^-$). The basic component of the amino acid ($-NH_2$) acted like a base and received a proton ($-NH_3^+$). But overall, being the isoelectric point, the molecule is neutral.

Question 83   C

See: ORG 14.2

Observe that the ^{1}H NMR spectrum has 3 groups of lines or peaks; thus there are 3 groups of chemically equivalent protons. Additionally, since the relative areas of the peaks is 3:2:3, the number of protons in the groups is in the ratio 3:2:3.

Next, there is spin-spin splitting in two of the peaks. One peak is a triplet, indicating the presence of 2 adjacent non-equivalent protons. The other peak is a quadruplet, indicating the presence of 3 adjacent non-equivalent protons. Since the 3rd peak is not split, the protons that caused it must not be adjacent to any non-equivalent protons. The only choice consistent with these requirements is $CH_3CH_2COOCH_3$.

Question 84   E

See: ORG 3.1, 4.1

$CH_3CH_2CH(CH_3)CH(CH(CH_3)_2)CH_2CH=C(CH_3)_2$

- Eliminate **D** by noticing at the right end of the molecule there is a double bond followed by a **C** with 2 methyl groups attached. The location of the double bond also helps to orient the direction of the molecule and avoid potential traps.

- In the middle of the molecule, there are 2 methyl groups attached to a CH which is in turn attached to a CH so this eliminates answer **C**: $CH(CH(CH_3)_2)$

- And finally, to the far left, **A** and **B** start as though the molecule has 2 methyl groups attached to a CH which is incorrect since the molecule begins with 1 methyl: CH_3CH_2

- Of course, you can come to the solution any way you are comfortable but this is one systematic way to avoid traps.

Question 85   C

See: ORG 13

All of the answer choices are useful to help an extraction to occur except answer choice **C**. Ideally, a solvent dissolves the solute (for example, when you add salt in water) but you do not expect nor would the objective be to create a molecule between the water and the solute because that would change the nature of the solute (i.e. salt or caffeine, etc).

Aside: it is important to note that it is more efficient to perform several small extractions using a small amount of solvent each time rather than one extraction using a large amount of solvent.

Question 86   C

See: ORG 2.1, 2.2, 2.3

Two of the structures below are (Z)–2–butene and (E)–2–butene which are stereoisomers of each other, not structural isomers. They have the same molecular formula, same connectivity, but different spatial arrangement. These would constitute stereoisomers thus there would be only 5 structural isomers in all. See isomers below:

1. (E) and (Z) 2–butene;

2. 1–butene;

3. 2–methyl–propene;

4. cyclobutane; and,

5. methyl–cyclopropane (not illustrated)

Question 87   E

See: ORG 6.2.4

This is Elimination 1ˢᵗ order, E1, meaning that: (a) 2 atoms will be <u>eliminated</u> from the original molecule (turning a single bond into a double bond); and (b) the "1" means that the rate determining step depends on the concentration of 1 molecule. The rate determining step (RDS) is the slowest step in a reaction mechanism.

1. FAST: the proton is attracted to the partial negative charge on oxygen in –OH forming a great leaving group (water). Answer **B**.

2. SLOWEST: the oxygen in the water substituent pulls electrons away from the central carbon to get rid of its formal positive charge and now neutral water leaves the tertiary carbocation. Answers **A** and **D**.

3. FAST: electrons in a neighboring C–H bond are attracted to the carbocation forming a C = C bond and kicking out the proton which is regenerated (= catalyst).

Question 88   E

See: ORG 7.2.3

This is a typical imine formation, which involves the nucleophilic attack of the amino hydrogen on the central carbonyl carbon of the reactant on the left, followed by a dehydration. Since H_2O is being removed, this reaction is considered a dehydration, not a decarboxylation (= loss of CO_2). In addition, answer choice **C**. is incorrect because cleavage would consist of the reverse reaction (i.e. the formation of two molecules from one, through the breaking of bonds). The N and C in the imine are sp^2 hybridized, eliminating answer choice **D**. An enamine is formed when a secondary amine is used but the reaction in this problem uses a primary amine.

Question 89   A

See: ORG 2.3.1, 2.3.2, 2.3.3

A stereogenic or chiral carbon is a carbon atom which is asymmetric which means that it is attached to four different atoms or groups. Having a chiral carbon is usually a prerequisite for a molecule to have chirality, though the presence of a chiral carbon does not necessarily make a molecule chiral (i.e. a meso compound). A meso compound has an internal plane of symmetry which bisects the molecule and thus it displays no optical activity.

The 1st and 4th molecules happen to be named pentane-2,3,4-triol or 2,3,4-pentanetriol. Notice the position of the chiral carbons (asterix *) as well as the absence of an internal plane of symmetry. Notice that if the molecule was folded along the dotted line, the top part would not match the bottom part: no symmetry within the molecule.

Going Deeper: the following information would not affect your answer but it will help to train your eyes. Keep in mind that a Fisher projection is a 2D way to represent 3D molecules in which all horizontal lines are actually pointing towards the viewer. Notice the perspective of the viewer we placed above the 3D image of the molecule. Notice that the first OH group is to the left of the viewer which you can see in the Fisher projection also. It is also easy to see why the 3rd OH group is to the right of the viewer. But notice the 2nd OH group (on carbon–3) in the 3D representation of the molecule is pointing away from the viewer. But in order to do a Fisher projection, the horizontal groups must point towards the viewer. The only way to do this is to rotate the bond 180 degrees so that they point towards the viewer but, of course, the 2nd OH now ends up on the right side.

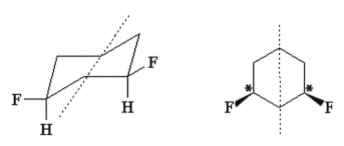

The second molecule happens to be named 1,3–difluorocyclohexane. Notice the position of the chiral carbons (asterix *) as well as the internal plane of symmetry (meso compound). Notice that each chiral carbon is attached to: (1) **H**; (2) **F**; (3) a carbon attached to a carbon attached to **F**; (4) a carbon attached to a carbon that is not attached to **F**.

The 3rd molecule has 2 chiral carbons * but has an internal plane of symmetry (meso). Notice that the ring has a double bond on the right side but none on the left: this fact is important to understand how the 2 carbons became chiral.

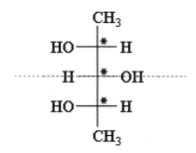

The fourth molecule (pentane-2,3,4-triol) shows an internal plane of symmetry with chiral carbons noted *.

Question 90   B

See: ORG 4.2.1
This question asks us to remember 'Mark's rule': alkene + acid → under ionic conditions (i.e. no: uv, hf, increased energy/heat), hydrogen adds preferentially to where its buddies are (= *the greatest number of other H's at the double bond* = a simplification of Markovnikoff's rule. Thus answer choice **B**. is the major product and **A**. is the minor product.

Question 91   C

See: CHM 9.5, 9.7, 9.8, 9.10, ORG 6.2.1
This question tests your understanding of a catalyst: they speed up the rate of a reaction (kinetics), they decrease the activation energy, they do not affect K_{eq}, they are not used up in a reaction, and finally, they do not affect thermodynamics, $\Delta G°$ (CHM 9.5, 9.7, 9.8, 8.10). If you're interested in dehydration of alcohols (!) see ORG 6.2.1.

Question 92   C

See: CHM 8.2, 8.10, 9.5
When a compound reacts with the solvent, the process is referred to as a *solvolysis* reaction.

Because of the stability of tertiary compounds, one compound is in rate-determining step: t–butyl bromide in solution can simply dissociate into Br⁻ and the stable t–butyl .

Now a nucleophile would be happy to *quickly* mate with the positive carbocation (*nucleophilic substitution, first*** order* = S_N1). If the nucleophile is hydroxide, or water, then the product would be the tertiary alcohol tert–butanol $(CH_3)_3C$-OH {*note –OH substituted –Br*}. If the nucleophile is ethoxide, or ethanol, then the product would be the ether $(CH_3)_3$C-OCH_2CH_3. {*The preceding product can be named t–butyl ethyl ether, or, ethoxy t–butane*; see ORG 10.1}

The solvolysis reaction occurs spontaneously, which means $\Delta G < 0$, which also means that the great likelihood is that $\Delta H < 0$. The latter is called an *exothermic* reaction. Since energy is released, the reactants must have a higher energy and the products must have a lower energy. The only possible answers are **A**. and **C**. However, the intermediate in **A**. has a low energy which indicates stability implying that any further reaction is not likely to be spontaneous (from the mechanism just described we know this to be false, untrue and unpleasant to hear!). Answer choice **C**. suggests a higher energy intermediate which would be happy to engage in a further reaction to create a low energy, very stable final product.

Question 93   E

See: ORG 3.3, 12.3.2 F
This question tests two concepts.

1.   Just like atoms or molecules, groups attached to a ring have electrons in their outermost shells. Like charges

repel. Thus *electron shell repulsion* means substituents want to be maximally apart.

2.   There are two positions for substituents of a ring: *axial* and *equatorial*. <u>Equatorial substituents are maximally apart</u>.

Question 94   C

See: CHM 3.5; ORG 1.2, 1.3

C1 is the first carbon in cyclic coniine which is the carbon in the ring attached to the propyl substituent (or ligand). It has 4 bonds: 1 to propyl, one to N, one to the carbon in the ring 'above' and one bond to H which is not shown in the structure but assumed to be there in this neutral molecule. Thus 4 bonds to carbon (1s + 3p) must be 4sp^3 hybridized bonds.

For your interest: notice that C1 is the only chiral carbon in coniine.

Question 95   B

See: ORG 4.2.4

The Diels–Alder reaction is a cycloaddition reaction between a conjugated diene and a substituted alkene (= the dienophile) to form a substituted cyclohexene system.

Diene + dienophile = cyclohexene

All Diels-Alder reactions have four common features: (1) the reaction is initiated by heat; (2) the reaction forms new six-membered rings; (3) three π bonds break and two new C–C σ bonds and one new C–C π bond are formed; (4) all bonds break and form in a single step.

The Diels Alder diene must have the two double bonds on the same side of the single bond in one of the structures, which is called the s-cis conformation (s–cis: cis with respect to the single bond). If double bonds are on the opposite sides of the single bond in the Lewis structure, this is called the s-trans conformation (s-trans: trans with respect to the single bond).

Answer choices **C** and **D** can gain the correct s–cis conformation by rotation about a C–C bond. Here is an example:

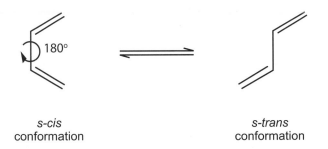

s-cis
conformation

s-trans
conformation

{Side Note: in the preceding equilibrium, 98% would be in the more stable s-trans conformation of 1,3–butadiene (answer choice **D**) in order to minimize electron shell repulsion. Nonetheless, both conformations are possible.}

Notice that the diene in answer choice **B** can never gain the correct conformation because the C–C bond between the alkenes is constrained within the ring. In fact, answer choice **B** is unreactive in a Diels-Alder reaction because 3 methylenecycloxenene is 100% s-trans:

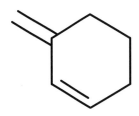

On the other hand, notice that answer choice A, cyclopentadiene, is constrained by the ring and is thus 100% s–cis (i.e. both double bonds are 'permanently' on the same side of the single bond between them):

Question 96   A

See: ORG 4.2.2, 6.1, 9.4, 13.1; CHM 12

Distillation is the process by which compounds are separated based on differences in boiling points. Alcohols (1–butanol) have a partially negatively charged oxygen and a partially positively charged hydrogen which can engage in hydrogen bonding which increases the boiling point. Esters (ethyl acetate) have a partially negative oxygen but no partially positive hydrogen so no hydrogen bonding with itself. For this same reason, esters are more volatile than carboxylic acids of similar molecular weight.

Question 97   E

See: CHM 3.5; ORG 1.2, 1.3, 4.1, 4.2

Consider the structure of allene and review the answer choices.

Notice that the 2 carbons at the end of the molecule are in the center of a triangle: trigonal planar 120° sp^2 hybridization with neighboring atoms (ORG 1.2,1.3; CHM 3.5). Notice that the C in the center of allene is in the middle of a line: linear 180° sp hybridization.

Note that dienes can be divided into 3 classes, depending on the relative location of the double bonds:

1. Cumulated dienes, like allene, have the double bonds sharing a common atom.

2. Conjugated dienes, like 1,3–butadiene, have conjugated double bonds separated by one single bond.

3. Unconjugated dienes (= isolated dienes) have the double bonds separated by two or more single bonds. They are usually less stable than isomeric conjugated dienes.

Question 98   E

See: ORG 5.1.1
If a compound does not meet all the following criteria, it is likely not aromatic.

1. The molecule is cyclic.

2. The molecule is planar.

3. The molecule is fully conjugated (p orbitals at every atom in the ring).

4. The molecule has $4n + 2$ π electrons.

Notice that the number of π delocalized electrons must be even but NOT a multiple of 4. So $4n + 2$ number of π electrons, where $n = 0, 1, 2, 3$, and so on, is known as Hückel's Rule.

Thus the number of pi electrons can be 2, 6, 10, etc.

Of course, benzene is aromatic (6 electrons, from 3 double bonds), but cyclobutadiene is not, since the number of π delocalized electrons is 4. However, the cyclobutadienide (2−) ion is aromatic (6 electrons).

A, **B**, **C** and **D** are all cyclic and planar. **A**, **B** and **D** have positive charges that will attract the negative pi electrons from neighboring carbons creating resonance forms delocalizing the pi electrons over all carbons in the ring. Answer choice **C** has an extra pair of p orbital electrons and thus, again, all carbons would be involved in the delocalization of pi electrons. In terms of the total number of electrons for each molecule, **A** has 2 π electrons (i.e. 1 double bond), **B** has 6 π electrons, **C** also has 6 π electrons (2 double bonds and 1 lone pair) and **D** has 2 π electrons (i.e. 1 double bond).

Question 99   D

See: ORG 1.6, 5.2, 5.2.1, 5.2.2, 6.2.2, 7.2.3
Note that Me = methyl = CH_3.

Step 1: Friedel Crafts acylation using aluminium chloride produces acetophenone (other names: phenyl methyl ketone, phenylethanone). It is the simplest aromatic ketone.

Step 2. When an aldehyde or a ketone reacts with a primary amine, an imine (Schiff base) is formed. Thus the primary amine $MeNH_2$ condenses with acetophenone to form an N-methylimine [Ph(Me)C=NMe] and water as the inorganic by-product.

Step 3. Sodium borohydride, a mild reducing agent compared to lithium aluminium borohydride, reduces the imine turning the double bond into a single bond to give the secondary amine.

Question 100   C

See: CHM 3.5; ORG 1.2, 1.3
First, let's number the carbons in the ring. Oxygen is attached to C1 and so N is attached to C3. So in the original molecule, we see that there are double bonds in the ring between C2 = C3 and C5 = C6. All of the answer choices follow the rules of drawing resonance structures except answer choice **C**. Let's carefully follow the electrons for answer choice **C** and thus we can understand what went wrong.

Our starting material:

Keep in mind that oxygen is the most electronegative atom in the molecule and thus 'wishes' to withdraw electrons to itself.

1. The nitrogen is positively charged because it contributed its lone pair of electrons to carbon.

2. Carbon's double bond with the 2nd nitrogen breaks and thus nitrogen has a negative charge and an extra lone pair (note: this describes answer choice **B**.).

5) We just worked out why answer choice **E** is correct. Well, the only difference between **E** and **C** is that **E** correctly has the double bond C5 = C6 like the starting material but answer choice C incorrectly places the double bond at C4 = C5. That would only be possible if C6 had a + charge and C4 had a − charge.

3. Nitrogen's lone pair bonds with C3 which breaks C3 = C2 so now C2 has a lone pair and a formal negative charge (C2 is secondary carbanion and this describes answer choice **D**).

6) And finally, answer choice **A** is like the starting material except, instead of oxygen pulling electrons from nitrogen along 'the top' (!!) of the molecule, oxygen pulls electrons from the C5 = C6 double bond creating a C6 = C1 double bond, a lone pair on oxygen and a secondary carbocation at C5 (because it lost its bond).

4. Remember that oxygen wants the electrons more than any other atom in this molecule. C2's lone pair bonds with C1 as C = O breaks so now oxygen has the lone pair and the formal negative charge (this describes answer choice **E**).

PART 1

Question 1   E

First: *Scan the choices*. The choices seem to show that the object is viewed from either the front or the rear, so focus on these sides. You may also rotate the object at different angles. You will instantly identify the correct answer **E**, which is the rear side.

Second: *Check the largest surface area and its details*. Notice that the bottom right, outer curved edge and inner diagonal of the front side becomes the bottom left of the rear side. This eliminates **A**, **B** and **C** choices. Furthermore, the upper left outer diagonal and inner curved edge of the front side becomes the upper right of the rear side. You can now eliminate **D** from the choices.

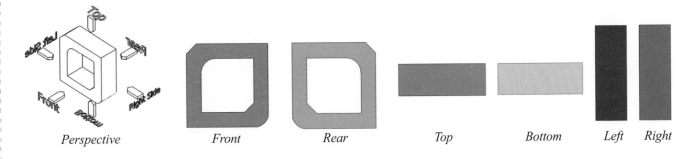

Perspective   *Front*   *Rear*   *Top*   *Bottom*   *Left*   *Right*

Question 2   D

First: *Focus on the outline of the object.* You can immediately get rid of **C** and **E** since the center hole of the 3D object is obviously a small circle.

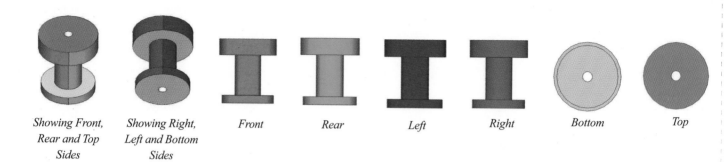

Showing Front, Rear and Top Sides   *Showing Right, Left and Bottom Sides*   *Front*   *Rear*   *Left*   *Right*   *Bottom*   *Top*

Second: *Check the details.* Observe that the thickness of the bottom cylinder is approximately half of the upper cylinder. The diameter of the hole at the center is about one-eighth of the upper cylinder. You can now readily eliminate choices **A** and **B**, leaving **D** as the answer.

Question 3   D

First: *Consider the standard views.* Examine the 3D object carefully and recognize that it has straight edges. Visualize how the object would look from different standard views. The following illustrations will show that the object's front view is just a mirror image of the rear view. The same with right-left views and bottom-top views.

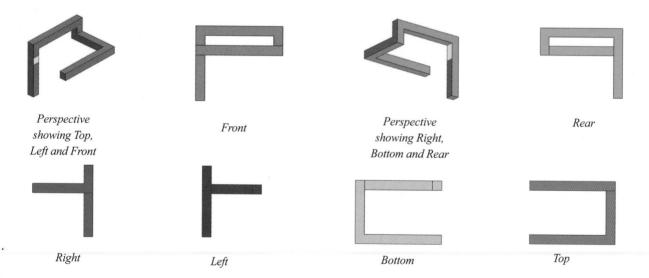

Perspective showing Top, Left and Front   *Front*   *Perspective showing Right, Bottom and Rear*   *Rear*

Right   *Left*   *Bottom*   *Top*

Second (Optional): *Focus on the outline of the 3D object.* You can also look at the outline of the perspective since it is composed of straight lines. Visually trace the continuous straight lines of the object to figure out its outline from different views. You may also try to draw the different views through this outline. At this point, you can spot **D** as the correct answer.

Question 4   B

First: *Determine or estimate the largest part (volume) of the 3D object*. This will aid you in figuring out the main component of the object. From this, associate the other details to the main component which are the smaller ones.

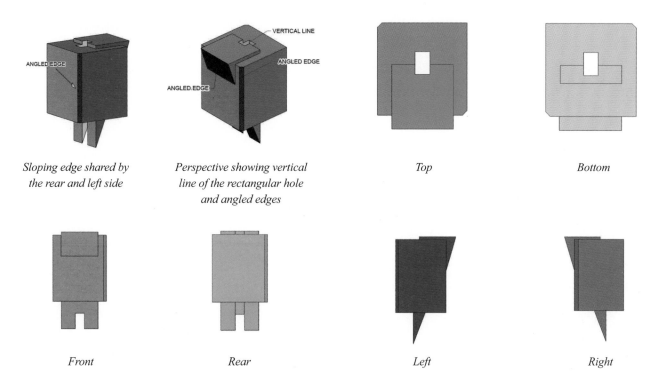

Sloping edge shared by the rear and left side

Perspective showing vertical line of the rectangular hole and angled edges

Top

Bottom

Front

Rear

Left

Right

Second: *Observe the details*. Do not ignore the smaller components because these are most important. Notice that the main component has a total of six corners and two of them have small dimensions. Another detail appearing is the horizontal area between the two feet-like components at the bottom. Also, the box at the center passes all the way through the 3D object, so it should be reflected in the top and bottom view. The correct answer is **B**.

Question 5   A

First: *Look for slopes*. As observed, there are sloped and curved parts from the top to the rear. These areas should appear on both the rear and left views. It may not be obvious but you have to be observant of the other curve from top to the left side of the 3D object. Other slopes play insignificant roles since there are wider areas behind that cover them.

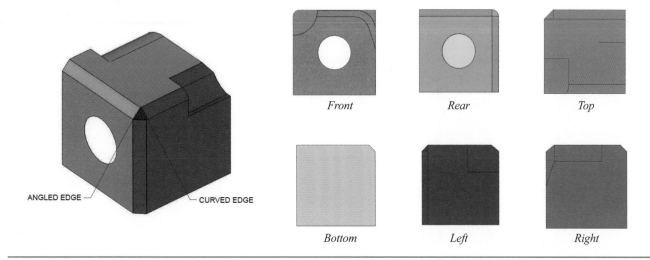

Front

Rear

Top

Bottom

Left

Right

Second: *Follow the outline of the whole 3D object*. Make sure to include the outline of the hole.

Front Outline

Rear Outline

Top Outline

Bottom Outline

Left Outline

Right Outline

Third: *Check the choices*. If you look at **A**, it has a hole in the center, which means it is either viewed from the front or rear.

Take note that the curve in **A** is located at the upper right, which is the same in the rear view and therefore, the correct answer.

Question 6   E

First: *Scan the choices*. All of the choices have overlapping holes within; therefore, you can narrow down your standard views into two: the left and the right sides.

Second: *Sketch or imagine the standard sides*. Remember that if

there are sloping edges in the front view, the angled plane should be seen on both the top and left sides or top and right sides. Furthermore, the edges of this shared area are straight when viewed on right and left.

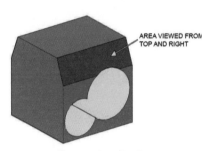

Perspective showing angled areas and hole

Right

Left

Third: *Compare the choices*. Bear in mind that there are no angled edges on either the right or left side views, which makes Options **C** and **D** wrong. Next, consider the location of the hole

with regard to the corners of the right and left views. You can instantly spot the correct match to the left side, which is **E**.

Question 7   B

First: *Focus on the outer outline of the 3D object*. You can start by counting the number of corners which is nine, and the number of

sides which is eight. Notice that one of the edges is curved.

Front

Top

Bottom

Left

Rear

Right

Second: *Compare the choices*. Option **A** is obviously out since the curved edge does not appear. Option **C** is too thin when compared to the left, front, rear and right sides. Options **B** and **D**

are quite similar except that the curved portion appears in Option **B**, which makes it the correct answer.

Question 8   D

First: *Be attentive to the holes of the 3D object*. There are two circles passing all the way through the right and left sides of the 3D object. The two rectangles, on the other hand, are passing through the front and the rear.

Second: *Study the sloping edges*. Three edges shaded in black are sloping which means that these areas are visible from at least two standard sides.

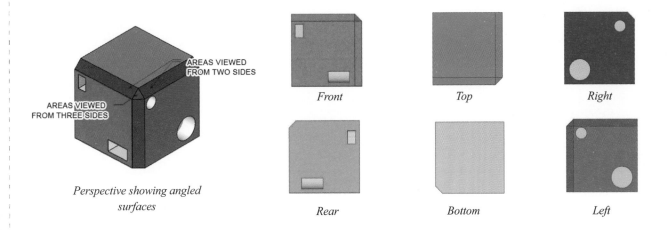

Perspective showing angled surfaces

Front   *Top*   *Right*

Rear   *Bottom*   *Left*

Third: *Compare the standard views with the choices*. Focusing on the outlines of these different views, only one edge is angled in all six views. Associate this angled edge with the holes within the

3D object and notice its position. Option **D** is the correct answer because one of its sides is angled and the positions of the (squared) holes are correctly placed.

Question 9   C

First: *Sketch the six sides of the 3D object*. Be keen with the details such as the hole, slopes and curves within the object. Also, try to

rotate the object that would fit the aperture.

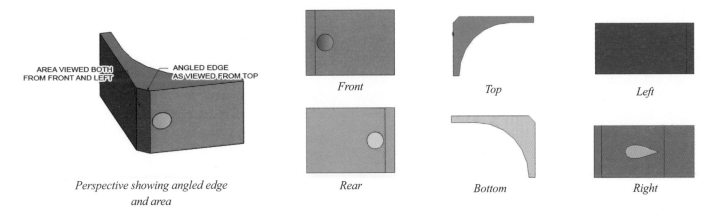

Perspective showing angled edge and area

Front   *Top*   *Left*

Rear   *Bottom*   *Right*

Second: *Check the choices*. Option **A** is viewed from the top and is incorrect since the lower left should be angled and not curved. Option **B** is also incorrect because the hole is placed too near from the left edge. Remember that an angled edge showed from the top

will still be shown both from the front and rear views. In Option **C**, there is enough space which is the angled area between the hole and the left edge. Therefore, **C** is the correct answer.

Question 10   A

First: *Concentrate on the largest surface of the 3D object*. Count the number of corners and determine the two smallest edges. Note that these two smallest edges are located alternately. The circular hole is located on the upper left from the front view and the rectan-

gular hole is on the lower right when viewed from the front.

Second: *Sketch the six standard views*. This is important because the choices project any of the six sides of the 3D object.

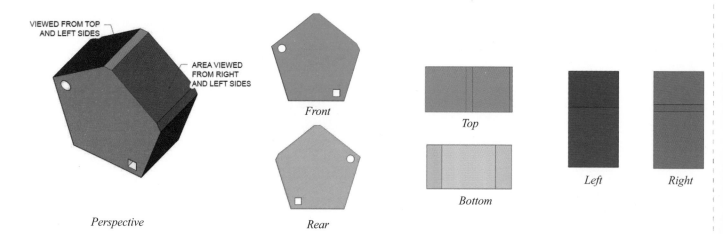

Perspective

Front

Rear

Top

Bottom

Left

Right

Third: *Check the choices*. You can instantly compare the rear standard view with Option **A** and thus, the correct answer.

Question 11   C

First: *Identify the holes*. From here, you can immediately get rid of choices **B** and **D** because both do not have square holes. Option **A** may also be tricky but if you look closely, the inner oval is posi- tioned vertically which affects the distance from the square holes. This makes **A** an incorrect answer. There are also smaller elliptical holes through the sides of the 3D object.

Front

Rear

Top

Bottom

Left

Right

Second: *Check other options*. You can easily identify the correct answer, which is **C** representing the top/bottom view. Option **E** has straight edges but does not provide for the whole in the middle, which is incorrect.

Question 12   D

First: *Be observant on the number of the protruding compo- nents and the distances between them*. There are three triangles protruding and each does not cover up one another even when viewed from any standard sides.

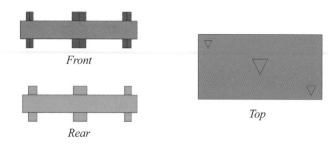

Front

Rear

Top

Bottom

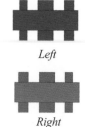

Left

Right

Second: *Be keen on the sizes of the components*. Small discrep- ancy in sizes and distances make a big outcome on the aperture. In addition, the sizes of these triangles are different, the center being the biggest and the upper left triangle viewed on top being the smallest. By this, you can readily eradicate Options **A**, **B**, **C**, and **E**. The correct answer is **D**.

Question 13   B

First: *Scan the choices*. The options seem to be viewed from the different angles, so you may need to determine the six standard views.

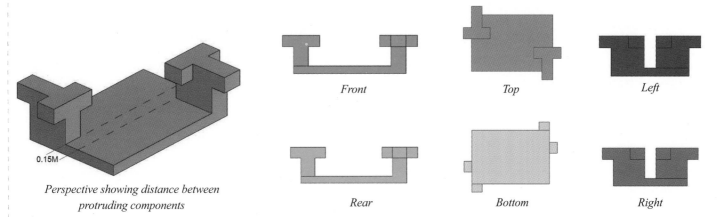

Perspective showing distance between protruding components

Front

Top

Left

Rear

Bottom

Right

Second: *Focus on the protruding components of the 3D objects*. There are recognizable shapes in the 3D object. In this problem, there are two letter Ts protruding upwards. Two other Ts are seen from the front and rear views. Estimate the lengths and widths of the two protrusions. You can also map out and extend the lines of the base of Ts to further clarify the distance between the two protrusions.

Third: *Compare the choices*. Neither Option **A** nor **D** is correct because the other part of the T is not reflected on the front or rear or from the right or left view of the 3D object. Option **E** is also incorrect because another part of the T is not seen as compared to the top and bottom view. Option **C** is incorrect as well because of the circular hole in the center. Therefore, **B** is the only correct answer as viewed from the right or left side.

Question 14   A

First: *Focus on the largest part of the 3D object*. The largest part may not be always the one with the largest surface. In this case, it is the base of the 3D object. It is the bottom square with a circular hole in the center.

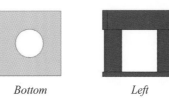

Front

Rear

Top

Bottom

Left

Right

Second: *Compare the choices*. Take into account that the circular shape on the top portion passes all the way through it. Checking

Option **A**, it really fits to the base of the 3D object and thus the correct answer.

Question 15   E

First: *Observe the characteristics of the 3D object*. The 3D object has a total of seven holes all over it. Now, focus on the largest flat surface of it and determine its outline.

Second: *Compare the choices*. Options **A** and **C** are apparently incorrect given that its outlines have bigger spaces and far different from that of the 3D object. There are no way that Options **B** and **D** can pass through it also because **B** is too small and **D** has no hole in it. The correct answer is **E**.

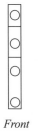
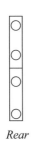

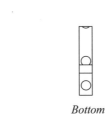

Front

Rear

Top

Bottom

Left

Right

PART 2

Question 16   B

This is an easy question. All of the choices have similar shapes. The thing that matters within these options are the number of solid and dotted lines. Remember that the FRONT VIEW is directly along the TOP VIEW and so, they should have the same measurements and distances. Then, count the number of solid lines which are instantly seen from the TOP. Also, count the number of hidden lines which are represented by dotted lines as viewed from the TOP VIEW. By closely observing the FRONT VIEW, there are a total of eight solid lines and 2 dotted ones. The correct answer is **B**.

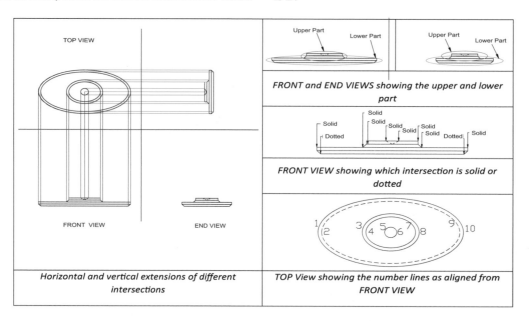

Question 17   C

This is an average question. Similar to number 16, rotate the END VIEW 90 degrees counterclockwise and project all intersecting lines horizontally to the TOP VIEW area. Also extend lines vertically from the intersection on the FRONT VIEW to the area of the TOP VIEW. Mark the intersections and verify each line. Imagine this object to be a table with two trapezoidal feet. These feet are located below the table top and so, it should be hidden from the TOP VIEW. The right answer is **C**.

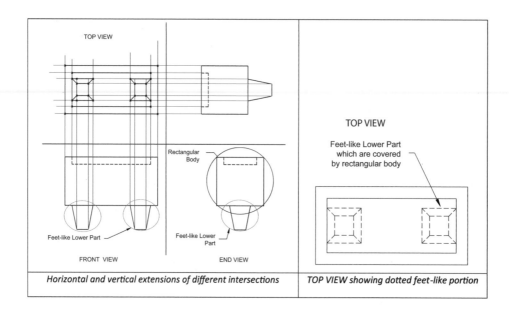

Question 18   D

This poses as a difficult question. First, rotate the TOP VIEW 90 degrees clockwise. Then, draw vertical lines from each intersection of the rotated TOP VIEW towards the END VIEW area. Also,

draw horizontal lines from intersections at the FRONT VIEW to the END VIEW. Next, mark its intersections and clarify which lines are solid and dotted ones. The correct answer here is **D**.

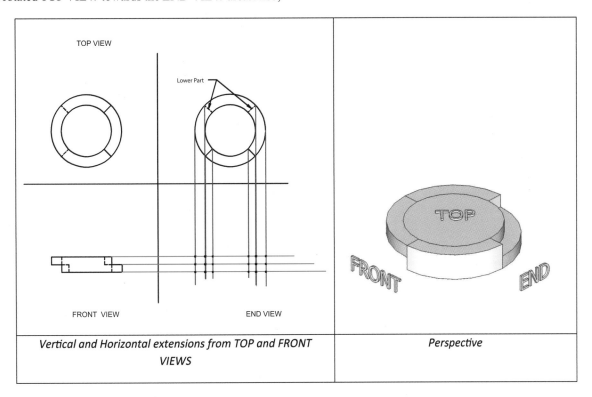

Vertical and Horizontal extensions from TOP and FRONT VIEWS	Perspective

Question 19   A

This question is easy. Similar to Question 18, rotate the top view 90 degrees clockwise. Then, create lines from all intersections at the TOP VIEW in a downward direction. Next, draw lines from each intersection at the FRONT VIEW and extend it horizon-

tally until it reaches or intersects with the vertical ones. Mark each intersection but be aware that not all intersections are part of the END VIEW.

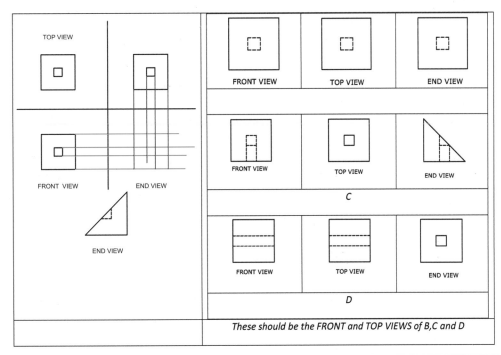

You can also check each of the choices. Option **A** is the right answer because the small inner square reflects as solid lines in both the TOP and FRONT views. Option **B**, on the other hand, is wrong since the dotted small square represents a hole that passes all the way through the object. **C** is also incorrect because the dotted lines extend downwards to the edge of the square, which is not shown from the FRONT VIEW.

Question 20   B

This item is quite easy. You can start by instantly eliminating the wrong choice. One thing that is crucial to identify is the distance between the upper portion and its middle portion. Option **A** is incorrect because it is heavier on the right than the left side. **B**, on the other hand, has a heavier left part than the right one and so, it is the correct answer. Options **C** and **D** are both wrong because a circular shape viewed from the TOP should not appear circular from the FRONT.

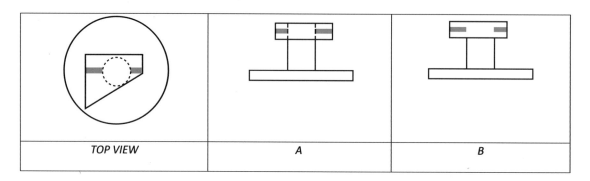

Question 21   C

This question has average difficulty. For a complicated looking object, you may want to go directly over the choices. It may be tricky because square and circle shapes from TOP both have straight edges from FRONT and END views. You can start by closely observing the solid and dotted lines at the END VIEW and especially at the FRONT VIEW since its lines are directly aligned with the TOP VIEW. Then count the number of solid and dotted lines and its sequence when viewed from the TOP. **C** is the right answer.

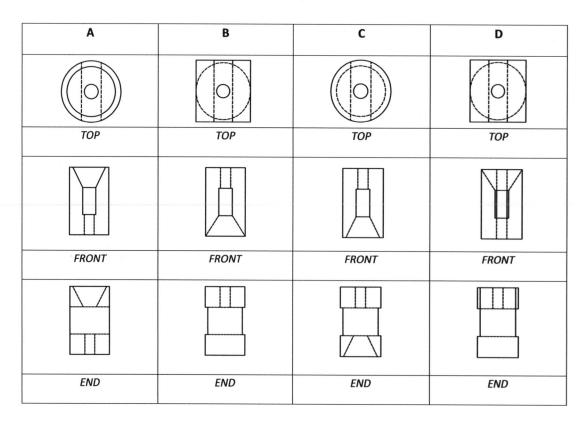

Question 22   C

To aid you in imagining the 3D object, you may need to label the different parts of it. The object seems like it has an upper and a lower plate with a cylindrical middle part. As obeserved in the END VIEW, the three circular holes pass all the way through the upper and lower plates of the object. The option that best reflects these characteristics is **C**. Option **D** is obviously wrong because its width is the same as that from the END VIEW. Option **A** is also wrong since the holes should be located more to the right than to the left of the plate. The cylindrical portion should be viewed in solid lines from the FRONT VIEW, which makes **B** – showing it in dashed lines (implying that it is hidden) – incorrect.

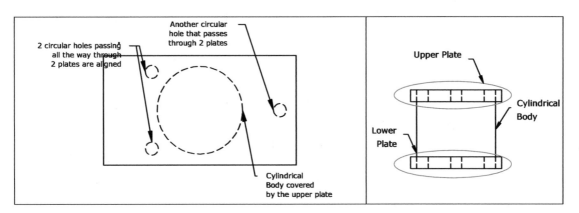

Question 23   D

This question is average in difficulty. Imagine that the object is like a computer monitor. It has a screen, a support, and a base. Now imagine if the monitor is viewed from top. You can start by rotating the END VIEW 90 degrees counterclockwise and leaving the FRONT VIEW as is. Then project horizontal lines from the intersections of the rotated END VIEW and vertical lines from intersections at the FRONT VIEW. Next, mark the created significant intersections.

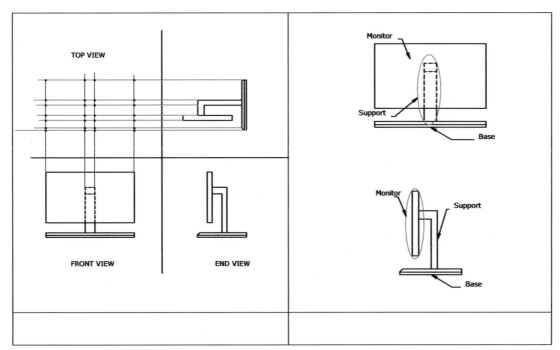

Also, take note of the sequence of the dotted and the solid lines. You can instantly delete **A** from the choices since the monitor is placed at the rear, which is incorrect. **B** is also incorrect because the slope on the base is not seen. **C** is wrong because the monitor seems to be outside the base, which is not true as seen from the END VIEW. **D** is the correct answer. Only the part of the suppport should be seen dotted from the TOP VIEW.

Question 24   A

This question may look complicated but it is actually easy. Keenly observe the characteristics of the object by verifying its form from the TOP to the FRONT VIEW, and vice versa. It is evident that there is a circular hole passing all the way through the 3D object. This "inner" hole should be seen dotted from the END VIEW. The only choice that best reflects this is **A**.

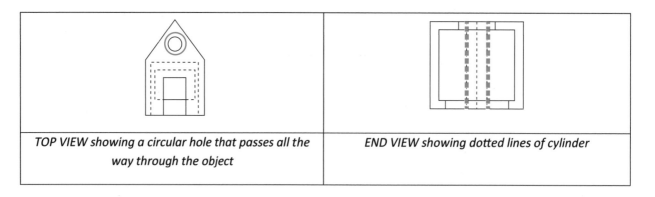

TOP VIEW showing a circular hole that passes all the way through the object	*END VIEW showing dotted lines of cylinder*

Question 25   D

Based on the choices, there are three equally sized circles within the 3D object. As observed from the END VIEW, the middle circle is dotted while the other two circles, which form as the cylinders are solid ones. Yet when viewed from the TOP, a rectangular piece or plate covers the other two holes of the cylinder, which are located at the front and rear. Therefore, the only solid circle should be the one at the center because it passes all the way through the two rectangular pieces while the top and bottom circles are located between two plates or rectangular pieces. The correct answer is **D**.

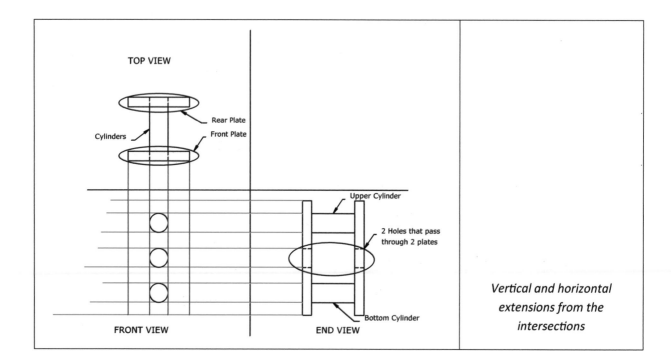

Question 26   B

This should be an easy one. If you rotate the TOP VIEW 90 degrees in a clockwise direction, you will realize that there is a rectangular portion at the left of the circle. Only **B** has a rectangular shape at its left part and so, it is absolutely the correct answer.

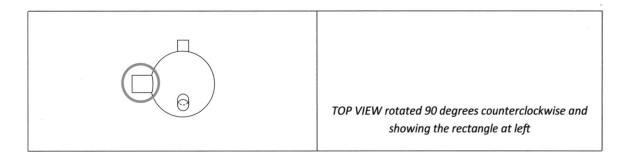

TOP VIEW rotated 90 degrees counterclockwise and showing the rectangle at left

Question 27   B

If you think that the question poses difficuty because of the several intersections in the object's outline, you may directly go over the choices. **A** is wrong simply because it has a line or intersection at the center. Option **B** is the correct answer because it does not have a line at the center but rather, it is curved. **C** has several dotted lines, which are unnecessary. All lines should have been shown from the TOP VIEW. Lastly, **D** is incorrect since it only shows an outer line when it is obvious that there are angled lines from the front and end views.

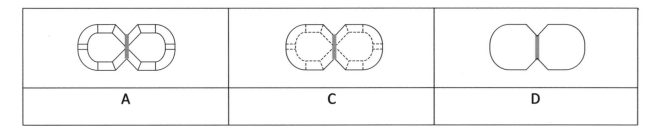

| A | C | D |

Question 28   A

Here, you can conclude instantly that there are two intersecting cylindrical shapes within the 3D object. These cylinders pass all the way through it, which means that they should be hidden from view and therefore, represented by dotted lines. What you need to check are its sizes and position when viewed from the FRONT. Always remember that the TOP VIEW is always aligned with the FRONT VIEW. And so, the vertical cylinder should be bigger than the horizontal one. **A** is the correct answer.

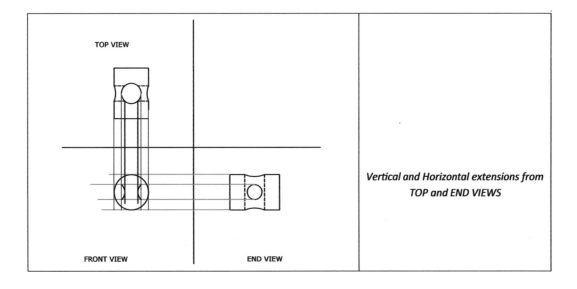

Vertical and Horizontal extensions from TOP and END VIEWS

Question 29   A

This object is kind of symmetrical in the sense that it has four parts, which intersects at the center, so you need to take note of the shapes of each part. It is clear that one part is cylindrical as a circle is spotted from FRONT VIEW. Another obvious shape is the square from the END VIEW which creates a tube. The upper part is bigger than the rest. The bottom part is a smaller tube.

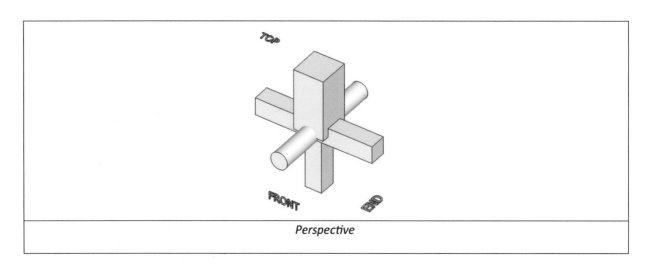

Perspective

With these noted characteristics, you can check each of the choices. **A** is the correct answer because the bottom tube, the bit parts of the cylinder, and the bigger tube should be dotted from the TOP VIEW. **B** and **C** are both incorrect because they show all solid lines. Option **D** is incorrect because its center is not the biggest part of the object.

Question 30   B

Rotate first the END VIEW 90 degrees counterclockwise and retain the FRONT VIEW. Then mark the intersections of the extended vertical and horizontal lines created from the two given views. The FRONT VIEW is similar with the END VIEW with three solid squares/cubes and three dotted ones; they only differ on the locations of the square/cubes. You will realize that the object is a large cube with small cubes as its corners. The dotted lines shown in the FRONT VIEW are cubes located at the rear or the opposite face of the front. The dotted cubes seen in the END VIEW are located at its opposite face. The correct answer is **B**.

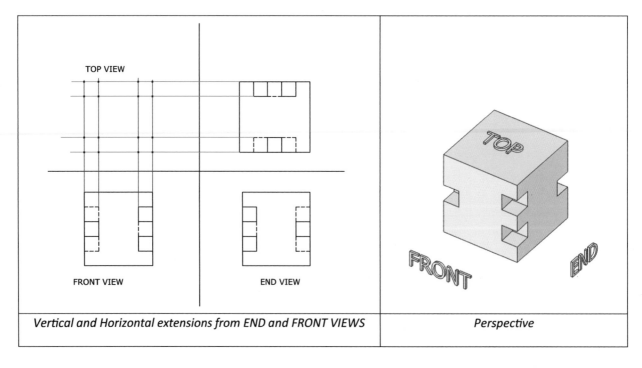

Vertical and Horizontal extensions from END and FRONT VIEWS   *Perspective*

PART 3

Question 31 D

This may be a very tricky question. The angles are directed in different ways, and you need to be very keen in observing the inner portion of each angle. Another crucial point is to find the smallest angle because some angles may differ for only a few degrees. At first glance, you can choose the one with the smallest angle. From here, compare the angle of your choice with the other options and check the given sequence if it fits. The correct answer is **D**.

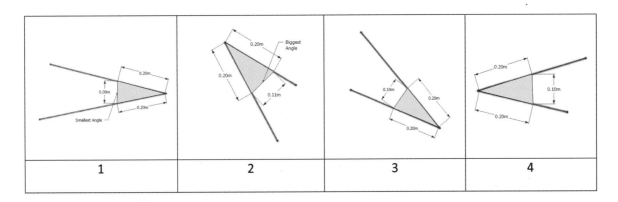

Question 32   C

Some angles are difficult to distinguish from others due to very small differences. 1, 2 and 3 may truly be confusing but you should realize that 4 has the smallest angle of all. Based on the choices, only **C** begins at 4 and so, it is the correct answer.

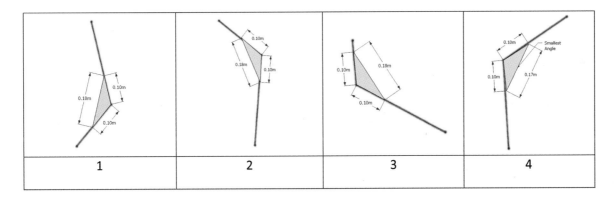

Question 33   B

Similar to Question 32, you need to identify first the option with the smallest angle. First, Keep on comparing each angle with one another until you can determine that 1 is the smallest. The next bigger angles are no longer necessary once you distinguish the smallest because none in the given options repeats 1 as the first in the sequence.

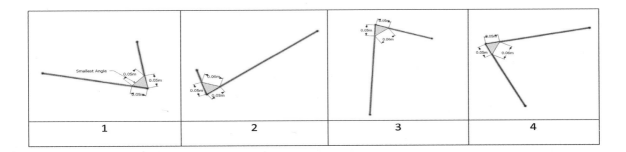

Question 34   D

For items that have very small angles, observe first the ones with the "darkest" angle. At first scan, the smallest may be 3 or 4. In this case, you can instantly eliminate options **A** and **B**. Next,

closely compare 1 and 2 – 2 is slightly bigger than 1. The correct answer is **D**.

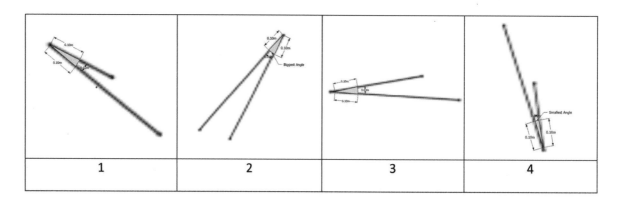

Question 35   A

All of the given angles resemble the letter L. It is easier if you compare the given angles to a letter L, which is a right angle. Determine first the smallest angle and observe that 1 is a bit

smaller than 4. You may now delete **C** from your options. **A** here is the right answer because you already know that 4 is the next bigger angle to 1.

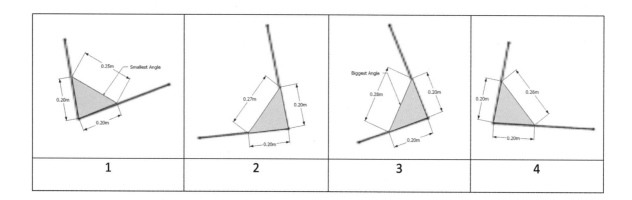

Question 36   D

Do not be deceived with the variations of the angle's rays in this question. Just focus on the bend of the angles. If you are unsure

which angle is bigger, for example between 3 and 4, proceed to other angles to compare. The correct answer is **D**.

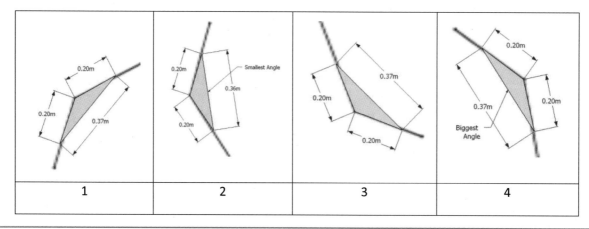

Question 37   B

First, compare the angles that are pointed in a similar direction. In this item, these are 2 and 3. Now notice that 2 is remarkably smaller than 3. Also, note that 1 and 4 have shorter rays than the others, and these are simply created to confuse you. The correct sequence should be 2-3-1-4, which is **B**.

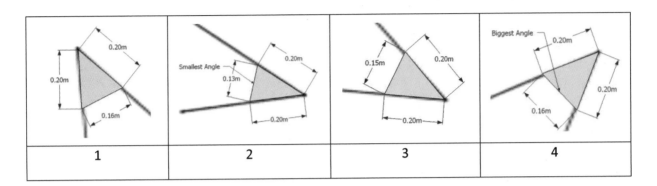

Question 38   A

Compare first 1 and 2 since they look similar. Between 1 and 2, 1 is smaller. On the other hand, between 3 and 4, it is 3 that is smaller. Next, compare 1 and 3, and see that 3 is smaller. Take note of the significant initial sequence and check it with the given choices. The correct answer is **A**.

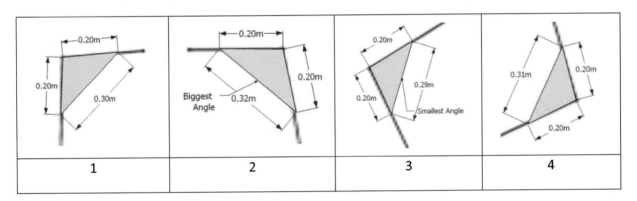

Question 39   D

For obtuse angles, the straighter the angle the bigger it is. Both 1 and 4 are bent to the right. Observe that 4 might look wide but it is 1 that is actually wider. Again, sizes of angles might deceive you and you need to be careful on that. 3 has the most bent leg and therefore, it is the smallest. The correct answer is **D**.

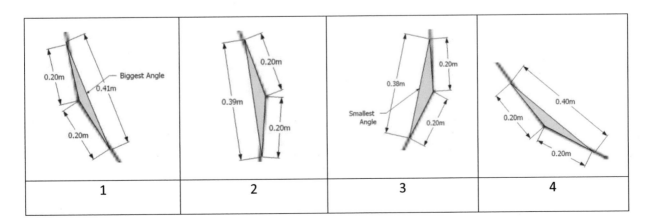

Question 40   C

At initial glance, 1 may be the smallest in size, but it is not the smallest angle. Next, proceed to compare 2 and 3 which seem to be alike. The most important thing is to determine the smallest angle, and it is 4. **C** is the correct answer.

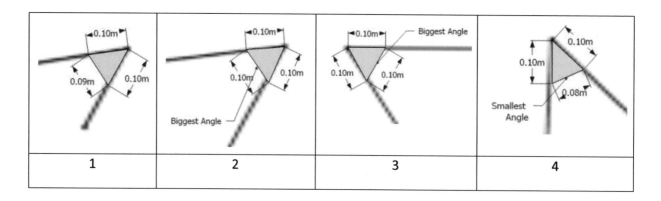

Question 41   B

Comparing 1 and 4 may be difficult since they are quite similar. However, you can observe that 1 is a bigger angle than 2 while 2 is a bit bigger than 3. The only sequence that can justify this is **B** which is 3-2-4-1.

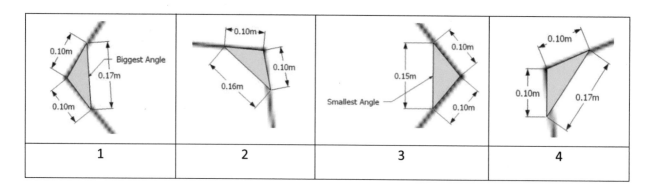

Question 42   C

Distinguishing smaller from bigger angles, which are closer to a line, is easy. In this item, 1 is the most bent among any other angles. 3 and 4 are closer to being straight lines. The correct answer is **C**.

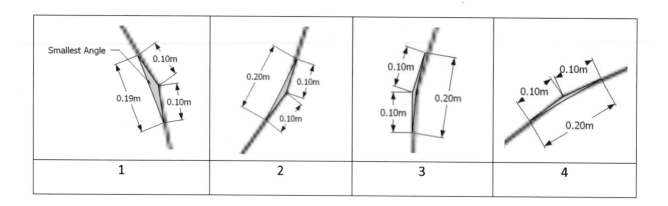

Question 43   A

In this question, you just have to try concentrating on each of the angle created by the same length of legs. This makes obvious that 4 is the smallest angle. Next, compare the angles between 1 and 2 and evidently, 1 is smaller. With at least the first 2 sequence determined which is 4-1, you can already choose the correct answer, and it is **A**.

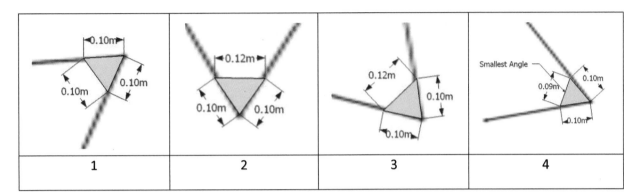

Question 44   B

Again, the angles in this question are like the letter L. The closer angle to be a letter L or a right angle is the smallest. 2 is best close to L and so, it should be the first on the sequence. Among the choices, only **B** starts with 2, therefore it is the correct answer.

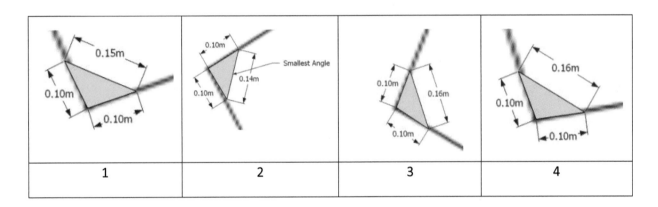

Question 45   A

This is an easy question. The most bent angle is 3 while, the one that is closest to being a line is 2. The correct sequence is 3-1-4-2. The correct answer is **A**.

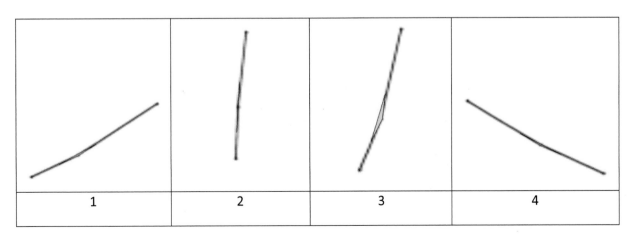

PART 4

Question 46   C

First: *study the foldings and count the number of layers of paper for each hole*. Start counting the layers of paper from Fold 1 then, count the layers on Fold 2. One hole is punched in 2 layers while the other is punched in 4 layers. The total number of holes should be 6.

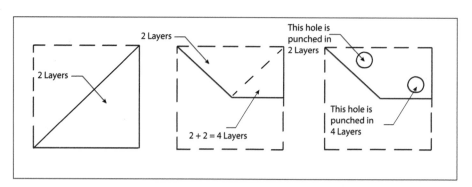

Second: *narrow down the choices*. Given that there should be 6 holes in total, the correct answer is **C**. It is the only option that has 6 holes.

Question 47   E

First: *study the number of layers in each of the holes*. You need to trace back the folding and determine how many folds there are for a hole. In total, there should be 5 punched holes.

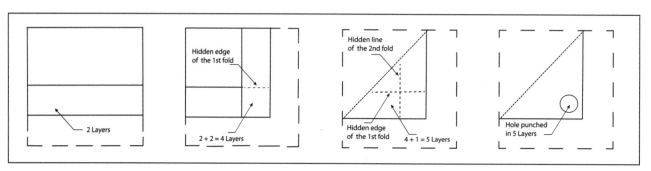

Second: *narrow down the choices*. **A**, **B** and **C** are all obviously incorrect. Take note that the last fold, which is a single layer was taken from the first quadrant. Therefore, this part should only have 1 punched hole while the fourth quadrant should have 4 punched holes. The correct answer is **E**.

Question 48   B

First: *First:study the number of layers in each of the holes.* Closely observe the process of folding and count each layer where the hole is punched. In this question, the two holes are both punched in 4 layers and so, the total number of holes should be 8.

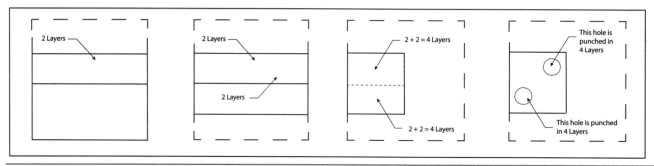

Second: *narrow down the choices*. Options **C**, **D** and **E** are all incorrect because they only have 6 to 7 holes. Be observant on the pattern of the fold. If the fold is symmetrical, then the punched holes should also be symmetrical. In this case, **B** is correct because the folding is symmetrical or a mirror image of the other. On the other hand, **A** has irregular placement of punched holes.

Question 49   D

First: *study the number of layers in each of the holes*. Carefully follow the folding and count the number of total layers where the hole was punched. The total number of layers is 8 and so should the number of the punched holes.

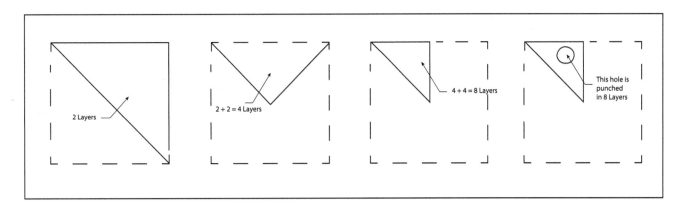

Second: *narrow down the choices*. **A** and **B** are both wrong because they have 6 holes. **E** has only 4, which is also incorrect. Narrowing down our choices to **C** and **D**, be keen on observing the location of the holes. You can start with the layer that was not moved. It is apparent that a mirror image pairing of holes should be present (similarly positioned at 1-2).   Only option **D** has the 1-2 holes on each side. Therefore, it is correct.

Question 50   A

First: *study the number of layers in each of the holes*. One of the holes is punched in 4 layers and the other hole is punched in only 2 layers. Hence the total number of punched holes should be 6.

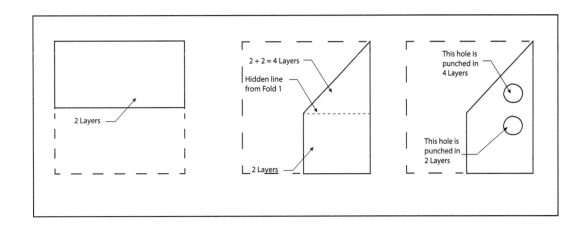

Second: *narrow down the choices*. Options **B** and **E** are incorrect because they only have 4 holes. **C** is also wrong because it has 8 punched holes. Take note of the retained portion of the layer, which is the lower right half of the second quadrant. 2 holes should result from this fold: one on this side and another one on its opposite side (or the second hole from the upper left edge). In addition, please remember that the punched hole on the upper-right half of the paper was folded twice. 4 holes should result from this: 1 on the initial position of the punched hole, 1 on the third hole from the upper left edge, and 2 in the middle of the lowermost part of the paper. **A** is the right answer.

Question 51   B

First: *study the number of layers in each of the holes*. Be careful in excluding the layers that are not covered by the punched hole. Take note that the hole was punched on the inner center of the folded paper. This portion does not include the layer or the fold shown in the second quadrant. Therefore, the hole should result to only 4.

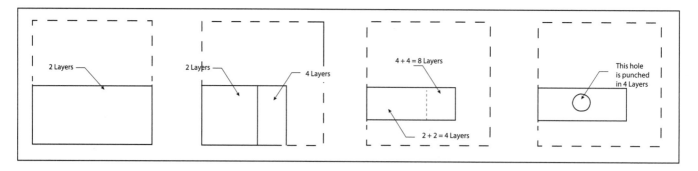

Second: *narrow down the choices*. You can easily eliminate **D** and **E** since they have 7 and 2 punched holes, respectively. The critical part here are the locations of the holes. You will determine this by mentally unfolding the layers one by one while taking note of the holes in the process. Finally, the holes are positioned vertically along the first and third quadrants. Here, **B** is the correct answer.

Question 52   C

First: *study the number of layers in each of the holes*. One by one, add each layer as they are folded to the next. Notice that one of the holes is punched in only 1 layer. Immediately, imagine this hole to be placed on the uppermost right corner of the paper when unfolded. Next, take note that the other hole is punched in 3 layers. So the total number of punched holes should be 4. You can now delete **A**, **B** and **D** from the choices.

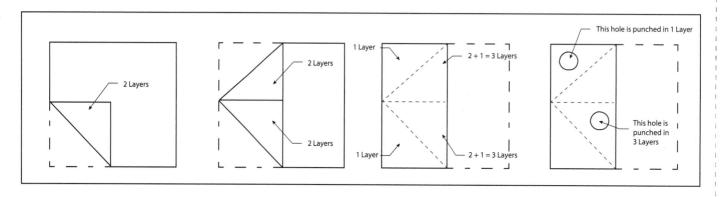

Second: *determine the correct placement of the holes*. Again, remember that the bottom hole is punched in 3 layers. If you unfold it, you will see that there should be a hole mirroring it (just beside it on the right). Next, look at the second quadrant to visualize where the fourth hole should go. It should be placed on the lowest left edge of the paper. Option **C** shows the correct answer.

Question 53   D

First: *study the number of layers in each of the holes*. This is an easy one since you can disregard the last fold. There is no punch hole in the last fold. Clearly, there should only be 2 punched holes.

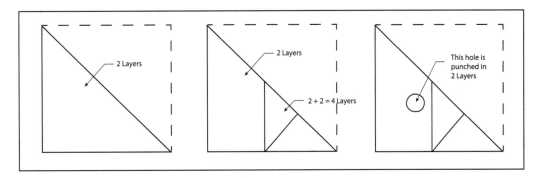

Second: *narrow down the choices*. You can effortlessly eradicate **A** from the choices. As observed, the third quadrant stays as is. With this information, further eliminate options **B** and **E**.

Since the sheet is divided in two diagonally, the holes should be symmetrical showing the 3-2 and 2-3 positions. The correct answer is **D**.

Question 54   A

First: *study the number of layers in each of the holes*. Pay attention to the process of folding. You may even need to sketch out hidden edges and folds of the previous folding. The top and

bottom holes are both punched in 2 layers while the middle one is punched in 4 layers. The total number of punched holes should be 8.

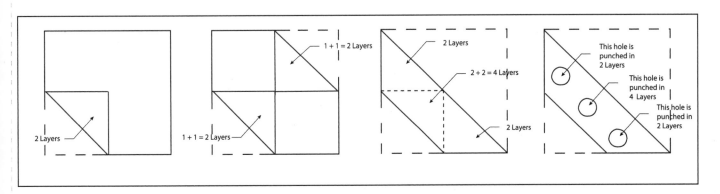

Second: *narrow down the choices*. **B** and **D** are both incorrect because they only have 6 holes. What you need to clarify now is the location of each hole. Through a representation of each hole with respect to its quadrant, it is easier to locate symmetrical

holes. The bottom halves of quadrants 1 and 4 and the upper half of quadrant 3 are retained. Therefore, there should have holes 1-3, 3-2, and 4-3. Given these 3 holes, you will realize that **A** is the correct answer.

Question 55   D

First: *study the number of layers in each of the holes*. Drawing the hidden edges behind the fold greatly helps in determining the number of punched holes. Do not forget that each portion of the

sheet has a different number of layers. In this question, the upper hole is punched in 3 layers and the bottom one is punched in 2 layers. There should be a total of 5 punched holes.

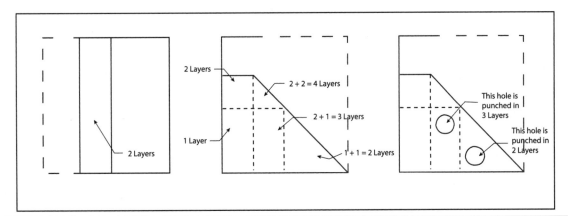

Second: *narrow down the choices*. Three of the choices which are **A**, **B** and **C** are readily eliminated. Subsequently, it is quite impossible to have hole 4-1 because diagonally, the opposite hole of 4-3 is 4-2. This makes **D** the correct answer.

Question 56   D

First: *study the number of layers in each of the holes*. The critical part here is Fold 2 in determining the number of layers where the holes are punched. There are 4 punch holes in total.

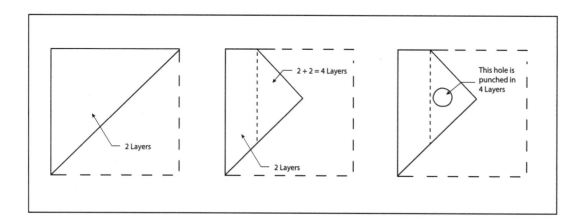

Second: *narrow down the choices*. **B** has 6 and **E** has 3 holes, so these are both incorrect. Do not forget that if you unfold starting in Fold 2, the hidden line would be the upper edge of the plain square sheet. This means that there should be a hole in 2-2. Among the remaining choices, only **D** has the hole 2-2. Therefore, it is the correct answer.

Question 57   B

First: *study the number of layers in each of the holes*. Closely follow the folding in each step. The upper hole is punched in 6 layers while the lower hole is punched in 2 layers. Therefore, the total number of punched holes should be 8.

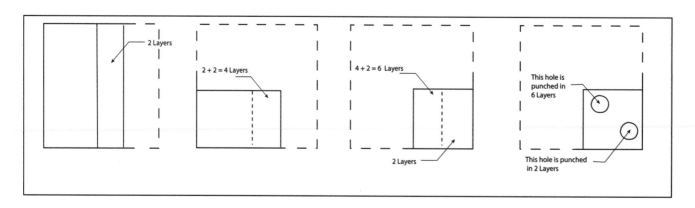

Second: *narrow down the choices*. Options **C**, **D** and **E** are all wrong. Next, notice that the only portion, which is not moved is the left half of the fourth quadrant. However, both **A** and **B** has hole 4-1. The next hole to study is the one which is punched in 2 layers. Through mentally unfolding the 2 layers, you will see that these holes are 3-3 and 1-1. Still **A** and **B** have 3-3 and 1-1. By critically observing the holes in 6 layers and unfolding the hidden parts, you will find that there should be holes 3-4 and 4-2. The option that has these holes is **B**, therefore, the right answer. Another quick way to determine the correct answer is recognizing that the second hole from the lowest right corner does not correspond to the postion of either of the two hole punches. Without further visualizing the postion of the other punched holes, you can immediately choose **B** as the best option.

Question 58   E

First: *study the number of layers in each of the holes*. Imagine the folding process starting from Fold 1. If you have trouble picturing things out, try sketching the edges behind the fold and represent them with dashed lines. The upper hole is punched in 4 layers and the bottom hole is punched in 2 layers. Therefore, the total punched holes should be 6.

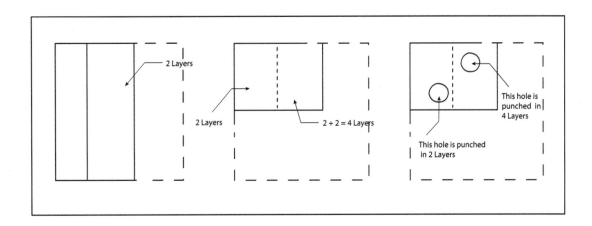

Second: *narrow down the choices*. Since there should be 6 punched holes, options **A**, **B** and **D** can now be eliminated. Both remaining options have holes 1-3 and 2-1. What you need to focus on are the holes punched in 4 layers. You would see that this hole is located on the upper right corner, which is hole 2-2. Option **C** does not have hole 2-2 and so, **E** is the right answer.

Question 59   C

First: *study the number of layers in each of the holes*. The unusual folding pattern shown in this question can be initially scary. However, this is, in fact, an easy question. You can draw the hidden edges and folds in order to avoid getting confused with the layers of the folds. These will serve as your clue in determining the exact location of the hole within the sheet: on the second column and second row from the left side of the paper. For this single punch, 1 hole is punched in 4 layers. This also results to 4 punched holes.

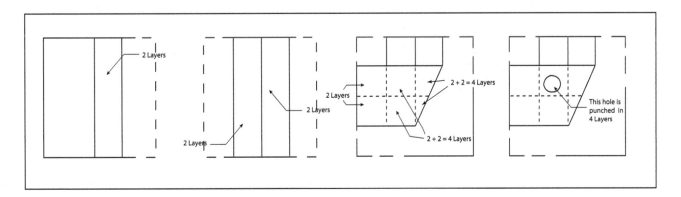

Second: *narrow down the choices*. Of the five options, only **B** does not have 4 holes. Now note that the right half of the first quadrant is not moved, so the position of the hole is 1-4. With this, **A** is automatically wrong. The next hole should be 4-1 since it is the opposite of 1-4 if you unfold Fold 3. This eliminates Option **D**. Finally, if you spread the remaining folds on both sides, holes 1-3 and 4-2 should be apparent, which are all positioned at the edge of the sheet. The correct answer is **C**.

Question 60   A

First: *study the number of layers in each of the holes*. The dashed lines will greatly help you in knowing the different areas of the fold. Knowing the number of layers of each part of the folding would greatly help as well. Through this, it would be clear that the 2 holes are both punched in 3 layers. Hence, the total number of punch holes is 6.

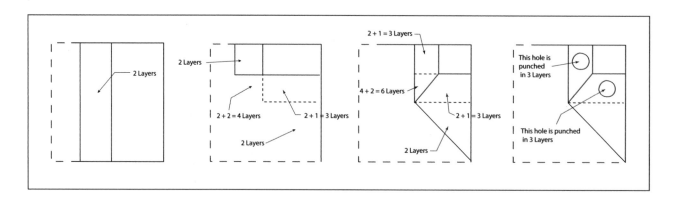

Second: *narrow down the choices*. You can now confidently exclude **B**, **C** and **D** as possible answers. The whole second quadrant remains and it should have holes 2-1 and 2-4. Both **A** and **E** have these holes so you need to proceed with evaluating the other holes. The 3 layers where the upper hole is punched is folded from the left and because of that, there should be other holes in the first quadrant namely, 1-1 and 1-2. **A** is the correct answer.

PART 5

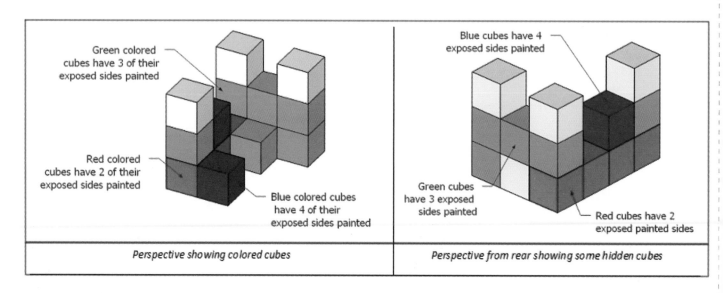

| Perspective showing colored cubes | Perspective from rear showing some hidden cubes |

Question 61   D

When a cube is attached to 3 other cubes excluding the base where it rests, the total number of exposed sides should be 2. The red colored cubes are the ones with 2 exposed sides painted. These cubes are usually located at the bottom or in the middle and often hidden by the other cubes. Hence, there are 4 cubes with 2 exposed sides painted. The answer is **D**.

Question 62   E

On the other hand, the green colored cubes represent those that have 2 other cubes attached to its sides. Remember that the base of the cube is always covered and thus not included in the count as an exposed side. This means that the exposed sides left should be 3. There are a total of 6 green cubes; therefore, the right answer is **E**.

Question 63   B

This question asks for the number of cubes with 4 exposed sides painted. In this case, there are 2 cubes which are connected to only 1 other cube. These are the blue-colored cubes. The correct answer is **B**.

You may also want to designate a number on each of the cube

to prevent confusion. Then you can use the formula,which we have dicussed in the chapter lessons on cube counting: number of attached cubes + base of the cube itself = total number of hidden sides; 6 (total number of sides of a cube) – total number of hidden sides = number of exposed sides / painted

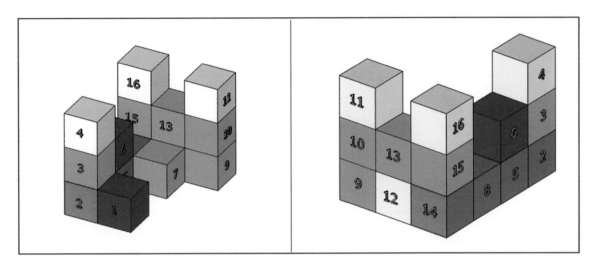

To answer Question 61, you need to look for cubes that have 3 other cubes attached to it. The attached cubes could be stacked to 3 of its sides, or 1 of them is on top of the cube. Do not consider those that are stacked under a cube because these merely serve as the base:

1. Cube 2 has 3 attached cubes, which are cubes 1 and 5 on its sides and cube 3 on its top. So, 3 + 1(base) = 4. Hence, 6 - 4 = 2 exposed sides painted.

2. Cube 5 has 3 attached cubes, which are cubes 2 and 8 on its sides and cube 6 on top. So, 3 + 1(base) = 4. Hence, 6 - 4 = 2 exposed sides painted.

3. Cube 8 has 3 cubes attached to its 3 sides, which are cubes 5, 7, and 14. So, 3 + 1(base) = 4. Hence, 6 - 4 = 2 exposed sides painted.

4. Cube 14 has 3 cubes attached to it, which are cubes 8 and 12 on its sides and cube 15 on its top. So, 3 + 1(base) = 4. Hence, 6 - 4 = 2 exposed sides painted.

In Question 62, since you are required to look for cubes that have 3 sides exposed, you will have to locate those that have 2 other cubes attached to it – either on 2 of its sides or 1 on its side and 1 on top. Again, discount the cube stacked under it because it simply serves as the base:

1. Cube 3 has 2 cubes attached to it, which are cube 4 on its top and cube 6 on one of its sides (cube 2 is not counted because it only serves as a base). So, 2 + 1(base, which is cube 2) = 3. Hence, 6 - 3 = 3 exposed sides painted.

2. Cube 7 has 2 cubes attached to 2 of its sides, which are cubes 8 and 12. So, 2 + 1(base) = 3. Hence, 6 - 3 = 3 exposed sides painted.

3. Cube 9 has 2 cubes attached to it, which are cube 10 on its top and cube 12 on one of its sides. So, 2 + 1(base) = 3. Hence, 6 - 3 = 3 exposed sides painted

4. Cube 10 has 2 cubes attached to it, which are cube 11 on top and cube 13 on one of its sides (cube 9 is not counted since it acts as the base). So, 2 + 1(base, which is cube 9) = 3. Hence, 6 - 3 = 3 exposed sides painted.

5. Cube 13 has 2 cubes attached to its sides: cubes 10 and 15. So, 2 + 1 (base, which is cube 12) = 3. Hence, 6 - 3 = 3 exposed sides painted.

6. Cube 15 has 2 cubes attached to it, which are cube 13 on one of its sides and cube 16 on its top. So, 2 + 1 (base, which is cube 14) = 3. Hence, 6 - 3 = 3 exposed sides painted.

For Question 63, look for cubes that have 4 other cubes attached to it (except the one acting as base):

1. Cube 1 has only 1 cube attached to one of its sides, which is cube 2. So, 1 + 1(base) = 2. Hence, 6 - 2= 4 exposed sides painted.

2. Cube 6 has only 1 cube attached to one of its sides, which is cube 3. Cube 5 only serves as a base, so this should not be counted as an attachment. So, 1 + 1(base, which is cube 5) = 2. Hence, 6 - 2 = 4 exposed sides painted.

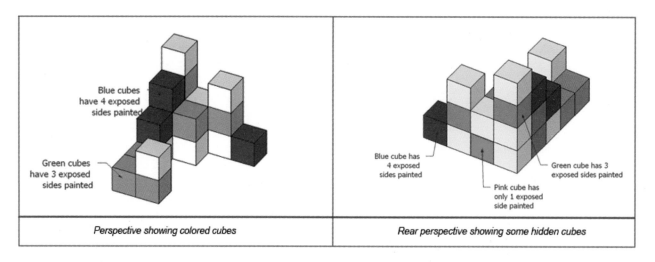

| Perspective showing colored cubes | Rear perspective showing some hidden cubes |

Question 64   C

A cube that has only 1 exposed side should have the most number of attached cubes. As illustrated, the pink colored cubes are surrounded with other cubes on 3 of its sides and 1 on top of it. As a result, only 1 side is seen. There are 3 pink-colored cubes. The correct answer is **C**.

Question 65   D

Since this question is looking for the number of cubes with 3 exposed sides, try locating cubes with 2 other cubes attached to it. Through a keen observation of each cube, you will find 6 cubes with 3 of its exposed sides painted. These are indicated as green cubes in the illustration. **D** is the correct answer.

Question 66   B

Lastly, the blue-colored cubes in the illustration are the ones with 4 of their sides exposed and painted. Always remember that only 1 should be attached to this kind of cube – a cube stacked under it is not counted because it serves as its base. These cubes are often located at the edge of the group. In this case, only 3 cubes in the diagram have 3 of their exposed sides painted. Hence, the correct answer is **B**.

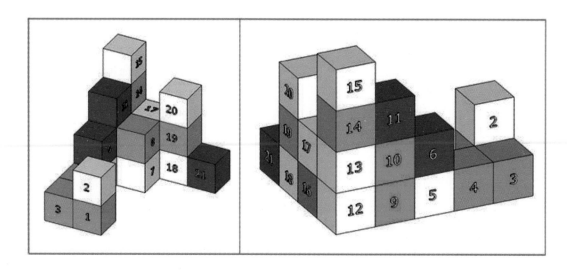

Again, if you are quick in math, you may want to focus on the number of attached cubes to each cube. You can simply subtract the number of cube/s attached to it to 5, which is the total number of sides exposed on each cube, excluding its base. With such information, in addition to assigning a number on each cube, you can note the number of exposed sides of each cube.

To answer Question 64, you need to look for cubes that has the most number of attached cubes (usually 4):

1.   Cube 9 has 4 cubes attached to it, which are cubes 12, 5, 7 and 10. So, 4 + 1(base) = 5. Hence , 6 - 5 = 1 exposed side painted.

2. Cube 10 has 4 cubes attached to it, which are cubes 6, 13, 11 and 8. So, 4 + 1(base, which is cube 9)= 5. Hence , 6 - 5 = 1 exposed side painted.

3. Cube 16 has 4 cubes attached to it, which are cubes 7, 12, 18 and 17. So, 4 + 1(base)= 5. Hence , 6 - 5 = 1 exposed side painted.

For Question 65, remember that cubes with 2 other cubes attached to it have 3 of their exposed sides painted:

1. Cube 1 has 2 cubes attached to it, which are cubes 2 and 3. So, 2 + 1(base)= 3. Hence, 6 - 3 = 3 exposed sides painted.

2. Cube 3 has 2 cubes attached to it, which are cubes 1 and 4. So, 2 + 1(base) = 3. Hence , 6 - 3 = 3 exposed sides painted.

3. Cube 4 has 2 cubes attached to it, which are cubes 3 and 5. So, 2 + 1(base) = 3. Hence , 6 - 3 = 3 exposed sides painted.

4. Cube 8 has 2 cubes attached to it, which are cubes 17 and 10. So, 2 + 1(base) = 3. Hence , 6 - 3 = 3 exposed sides painted.

5. Cube 14 has 2 cubes attached to it, which are cubes 11 and 15. So, 2 + 1(base, which is 13) = 3. Hence , 6 - 3 = 3 exposed sides painted.

6. Cube 19 has 2 cubes attached to it which are cubes 17 and 20. So, 2 + 1(base which is 18) = 3. Hence, 6 - 3 = 3 exposed sides painted.

In Question 66, you need to look for cubes, which have only 1 cube attached to it on the side. Do not consider the cube that acts as a base. Start evaluating those that are located on the edges of the diagram:

1. Cube 6 has only cube 10 attached to it, so 1 + 1(base, which is cube 5) = 2. Hence , 6 - 2 = 4 exposed sides painted.

2. Cube 11 has only cube 14 attached to it , so 1 + 1(base which is cube 10) = 2. Hence , 6 - 2 = 4 exposed sides painted.

3. Cube 21 has only cube 18 attached to it, so 1 + 1(base) = 2. Hence , 6 - 2 = 4 exposed sides painted.

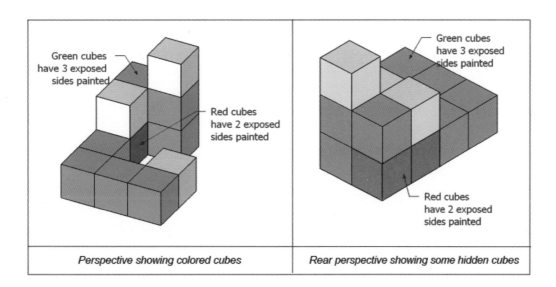

| Perspective showing colored cubes | Rear perspective showing some hidden cubes |

Question 67   A

For questions requiring you to look for for cubes with 2 of their exposed sides painted, you need to focus on the cubes located on the inner portion of the figure. These cubes are colored red in the illustration, and as observed, they are situated at the bottom. There are only 2, so the correct answer is **A**.

Question 68   E

Closely observe that cubes with 3 of their exposed sides painted are mostly seen at the edge of the figure and have 2 cubes attached to it (except those that serve as bases). The green-colored cubes in the illustration represent those with three exposed side. The correct answer is 7 – option **E**.

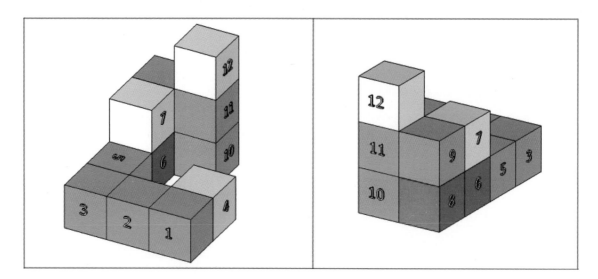

Alternative method: designating numbers or names on each cube, and then adding the number of attached cube/s to a constant 1 (which is the cube's base). The sum is subtracted to 6. The difference is the number of exposed side/s.

To answer Question 67, look for cubes that have 3 other cubes attached except that which acts as its base:

1. Cube 6 has 3 cubes attached to it – cubes 5, 7and 8. So, 3 + 1(base) = 4. Hence, 6 - 4 = 2 exposed sides painted.

2. Cube 8 has 3 cubes attached to it – cubes 6, 9 and 10. So, 3 + 1(base) = 4. Hence, 6 - 4 = 2 exposed sides painted.

In Question 68, your objective is to identify cubes that have 2 other cubes attached to it, except those that serve as their bases:

1. Cube 1 has 2 cubes attached to it – cubes 2 and 4. So, 2 + 1(base) = 3. Hence, 6 - 3 = 3 exposed sides painted.

2. Cube 2 has 2 cubes attached to it – cubes 1 and 3. So, 2 + 1(base) = 3. Hence , 6 - 3 = 3 exposed sides painted.

3. Cube 3 has 2 cubes attached to it – cubes 2 and 5. So, 2 + 1(base) = 3. Hence , 6 - 3 = 3 exposed sides painted.

4. Cube 5 has 2 cubes attached to it – cubes 3 and 6. So, 2 + 1(base) = 3. Hence , 6 - 3 = 3 exposed sides painted.

5. Cube 9 has 2 cubes attached to it – cubes 11 and 7. So, 2 + 1(base) = 3. Hence , 6 - 3 = 3 exposed sides painted.

6. Cube 10 has 2 cubes attached to it – cubes 8 and 11. So, 2 + 1(base) = 3. Hence , 6 - 3 = 3 exposed sides painted.

7. Cube 11 has 2 cubes attached to it – cubes 9 and 12. So, 2 + 1(base, which is cube 10) = 3. Hence , 6 - 3 = 3 exposed sides painted.

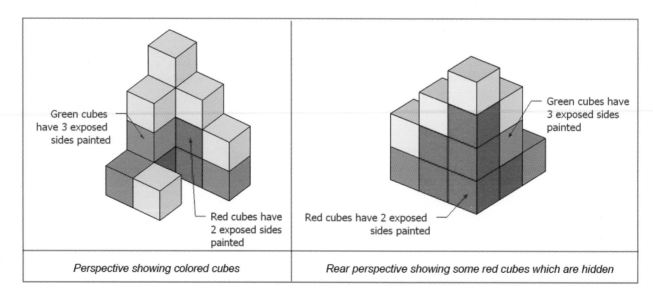

Perspective showing colored cubes   *Rear perspective showing some red cubes which are hidden*

Some cubes are hidden from view in the given perspective of the figure. Just keep in mind that for every cube visible on a second layer, a cube at the bottom of it, which may not be visible, serves as the support base.

Question 69   D

This question asks you to look for cubes with 2 of their sides exposed. These cubes are colored red in the illustration, and there

are 6 of them. Thus, the correct answer is **D**.

Question 70   B

This question asks for cubes having 3 of their sides exposed and painted. To aid you in determining these, look for cubes at the corners and edges of the figure with only 1 layer. You will see that

these three cubes are colored green in the illustration. The right answer is **B**.

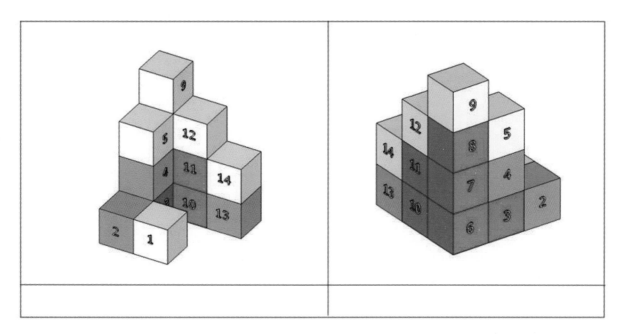

In Question 69, you are asked to determine how many cubes in the figure would have 2 of its sides exposed. The tricky part in this question is understanding that the topmost cube (cube 9) represents another layer of hidden cubes stacked under it. Cubes of these types, whether placed on the corner or in between the stacks, have 3 other cubes attached to it (on its top and on 2 of its sides) :

1. Cube 3 has 3 cubes attached to it, which are cubes 2, 4 and 6. So, 3 + 1(base) = 4. Hence, 6 - 4 = 2 exposed sides painted.

2. Cube 6 has 3 cubes attached to it, which are cubes 3, 7 and 10. So, 3 + 1(base) = 4. Hence, 6 - 4 = 2 exposed sides painted.

3. Cube 7 has 3 cubes attached to it, which are cubes 4, 8 and 11. So, 3 + 1(base which is cube 6) = 4. Hence, 6 - 4 = 2 exposed sides painted.

4. Cube 8 has 3 cubes attached to it, which are cubes 5, 9 and 12. So, 3 + 1(base which is cube 7) = 4. Hence, 6 - 4 = 2 exposed sides painted.

5. Cube 10 has 3 cubes attached to it, which are cubes 6, 11and 13. So, 3 + 1(base) = 4. Then, 6 - 4 = 2 exposed sides painted.

6. Cube 11 has 3 cubes attached to it, which are cubes 7, 12 and 14. So, 3 + 1(base which is cube 10) = 4. Then, 6 - 4 = 2 exposed sides painted.

Question 70 asks you to count the number of cubes that have 3 sides exposed. These cubes are placed on the edges of the figure. Look for cubes that have 2 other cubes attached either 1 on top and another 1 on one of its sides or on any 2 of its sides:

1. Cube 2 has 2 cubes attached to it, which are cubes 1 and 3. So, 2 + 1(base) = 3. Hence, 6 - 3 = 3 exposed sides painted.

2. Cube 4 has 2 cubes attached to it, which are cubes 5 and 7. So, 2 + 1(base which is cube 3) = 3. Hence, 6 - 3 = 3 exposed sides painted.

3. Cube 13 has 2 cubes attached to it, which are cubes 10 and 14. So, 2 + 1(base) = 3. Hence, 6 - 3 = 3 exposed sides painted.

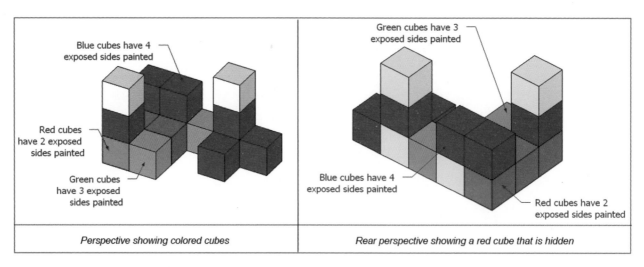

Perspective showing colored cubes | Rear perspective showing a red cube that is hidden

Question 71   C

To quickly determine cubes that have only 2 of its sides exposed, look at all corner and bottom cubes. Check whether 3 other cubes are attached on its sides or 2 other cubes are placed on its sides while another 1 is on top of it.

In the illustration, cubes that have 2 of their exposed sides are painted red. There are 3 other cubes attached to the red ones. It is as well evident that a corner cube below another cube has 2 of their exposed sides painted. There are a total of 4 red cubes and so, the right answer is **C**.

Question 72   B

The green-colored cubes in the illustration have 3 of their exposed sides painted. There are only 2 cubes that have this characteristic in the given figure. Hence, the correct answer is B.

Question 73   E

On the other hand, there are 6 cubes that have 4 of their exposed sides, and these are painted in blue in the illustration. The correct answer is **E**.

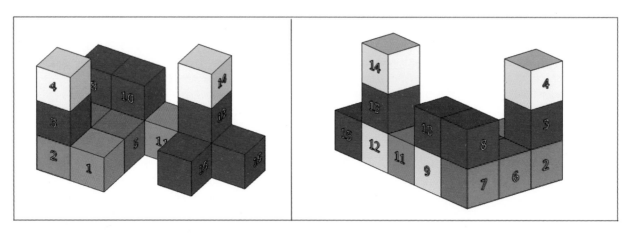

In Question 71, looking for cubes with 2 exposed sides would require you to consider those that have 3 other cubes attached to it:

1. Cube 2 has 3 cubes attached to it, which are cubes 1 and 6 on its sides and cube 3 on top. So, 3 + 1(base) = 4. Hence, 6 - 4 = 2 exposed sides painted.

2. Cube 5 has 3 cubes attached to 3 of its sides: cubes 1, 9 and 6. So, 3 + 1(base) = 4. Hence, 6 - 4 = 2 exposed sides painted.

3. Cube 6 has 3 cubes attached to it on 3 sides: cubes 5, 2 and 7. So, 3 + 1(base) = 4. Hence, 6 - 4 = 2 exposed sides painted.

4. Cube 7 has 2 cubes attached to its sides, which are cubes 6 and 9, and 1 on top, which is cube 8. So, 3 + 1(base) = 4. Hence, 6 - 4 = 2 exposed sides painted.

Question 72 requires you to look for cubes with 2 other cubes attached to it in order to determine those with 3 exposed sides:

1. Cube 1 has 2 cubes attached to its sides, which are cubes 2 and 5. So, 2 + 1(base) = 3. Hence, 6 - 3 = 3 exposed sides painted.

2. Cube 11 has 2 cubes attached to its sides, which are cubes 9 and 12. So, 2 + 1(base) = 3. Hence, 6 - 3 = 3 exposed sides painted.

In Question 73, you need to look for cubes that have only 1 cube attached to determine that these have 4 exposed sides:

1. Cube 3 has only 1 cube attached on its top, which is cube 4. So, 1 + 1(base, which is cube 2) = 2. Hence , 6 - 2 = 4 exposed sides painted.

2. Cube 8 has only 1 cube attached to it which is cube 10. So, 1 + 1(base, which is cube 7) = 2. Hence , 6 - 2 = 4 exposed sides painted.

3. Cube 10 has only 1 cube attached to it, which is cube 8. So, 1 + 1(base, which is cube 9) = 2. Hence , 6 - 2 = 4 exposed sides painted.

4. Cube 13 has only 1 cube attached on its top, which is cube 14. So, 1 + 1(base which is cube 12) = 2. Hence , 6 - 2 = 4 exposed sides painted.

5. Cube 15 has only 1 cube attached to it, which is cube 12. So, 1 + 1(base) = 2. Hence , 6 - 2 = 4 exposed sides painted.

6. Cube 16 has only 1 cube attached to it, which is also cube 12.   So, 1 + 1(base) = 2. Hence , 6 - 2 = 4 exposed sides painted.

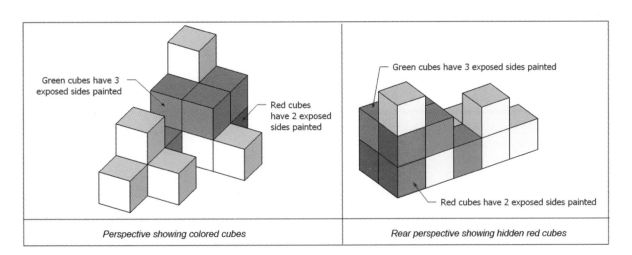

Perspective showing colored cubes   *Rear perspective showing hidden red cubes*

Question 74   C

Cubes that have 2 of their exposed sides painted are frequently seen at the bottom corner of a figure. These cubes are colored red in the illustration. There are a total of 3 red cubes. Thus, the correct answer is **C**.

Question 75   C

This question asks for the number of cubes that have 3 of their exposed sides painted. The green-colored cubes in the illustration are the ones with these characteristics. **C** is the correct answer because there should be 4 cubes with 3 exposed sides.

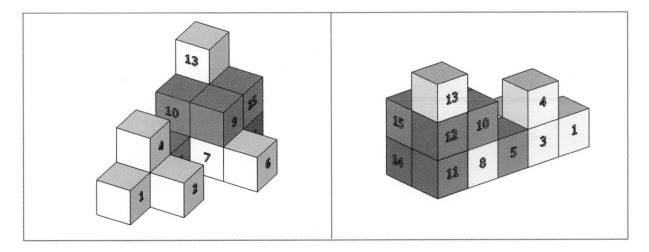

In Question 74, looking for cubes with 2 exposed sides would require you to calculate for those that have 3 other cubes attached to them:

1. Cube 11 has 3 cubes attached to it, which are cubes 14 and 8 on two of its sides and cube 12 on its top. So, 3 + 1(base) = 4. Hence, 6 - 4 = 2 exposed sides painted.

2. Cube 12 has 3 cubes attached to it, which are cubes 10 and 15 on two of its sides and cube 13 on its top. So, 3 + 1(base, which is cube 11) = 4. Hence, 6 - 4 = 2 exposed sides painted.

3. Cube 14 has 3 cubes attached to it, which are cubes 11 and 7 on two of its sides and cube 15 on its top. So, 3 + 1(base) = 4. Hence, 6 - 4 = 2 exposed sides painted.

In Question 75, you need to look for cubes that have 2 other cubes attached to it to confirm that these have 3 exposed sides:

1. Cube 5 has 2 cubes attached to it, which are cubes 8 and 3.

So, 2 + 1(base) = 3. Hence, 6 - 3 = 3 exposed sides painted.

2. Cube 9 has 2 cubes attached to it, which are cubes 10 and 15. So, 2 + 1(base) = 3. Hence , 6 - 3 = 3 exposed sides painted.

3. Cube 10 has 2 cubes attached to it, which are cubes 9 and 12. So, 2 + 1(base, which is cube 8) = 3. Hence , 6 - 3 = 3 exposed sides painted.

4. Cube 15 has 2 cubes attached to it which are also cubes 9 and 12. So, 2 + 1(base, which is cube 14) = 3. Hence, 6 – 3 = 3 exposed sides painted.

PART 6

Question 76   B

First: *scan the choices.* This question is somewhat tricky because all the choices are angled in the same direction. However, what really matters here are the locations of the lines. Quite significantly, all options are pentagon-shaped.

Second: *establish the BASE.* Notice that only two parts of the figure are wider than the rest and both are pentagon-shaped. This means that one of them is the base and the corresponding shape is

the top. What you need to focus now are the lines on each square (the smaller parts) as you fold the components.

Third: *rotate the folded figure.* You may need to flip the 3D object, making the base become the top portion. You can also put numbers in each component so you do not get confused. The correct answer is **B**.

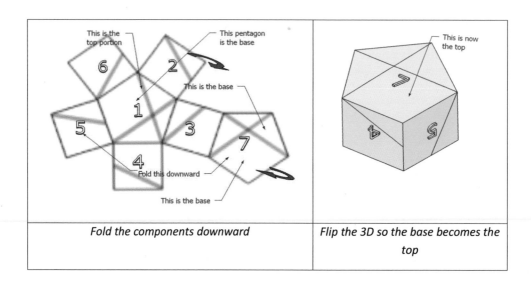

Fold the components downward	Flip the 3D so the base becomes the top

Question 77   C

In this question, the options are presented in different perspectives. The shapes of each component in every option varies.

First: *identify the essential features of the object.* Identify the geometric shapes of the object's components: squares and triangles. Notice that the squares are connected to the bigger/longer triangles on both ends and then the smaller triangles on one side each. There are 8 components in total. With these observations,

you may be able to examine each option.

Second: *evaluate the options.* **A** is wrong because the smaller triangles are not visible. **B** is also wrong because it has a total of nine components. **C** has 8 components, and each shape from the unfolded figure is represented. **D** is wrong because although it also has 8 components, it shows the rectangle shape on two of its components. Thus, **C** is the correct answer.

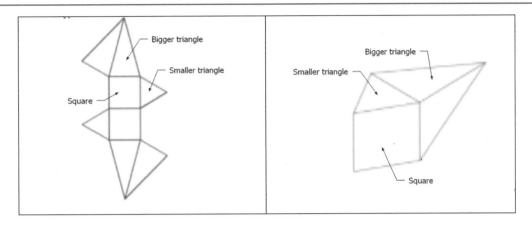

Question 78   D

The figure is just a simple cube. When figures have shadings or lines, you simply fold the components in a downward direction.

First: *compare each option*. Check the orientation of the shades in relation to each other. In option **A**, the position of the triangular obtuse shades should be sideways, not top and bottom, to the rectangular shade on the top face of the cube. In **B**, the positions of the rectangular shade on top and triangular shapes below it are correct. However, the horizontal rectangular shade on the

center of the cube's right face should not be there. It should be on the other side and should be positioned in a vertical orientation. **C** has the correct orientation of the triangular and linear shades. However, a closer look at the triangular shades would reveal that their angles are neither obtuse nor equilateral. This leaves **D** as the correct answer.

Second: *visualize the folding process*. To double-check, simply visualize folding the figure continuously downward.

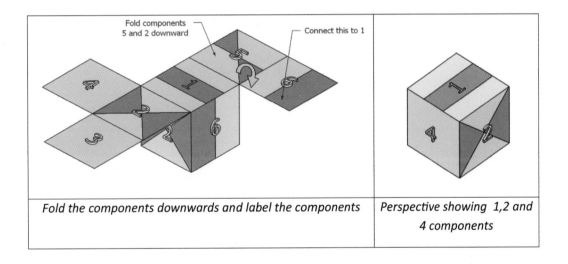

Fold the components downwards and label the components | Perspective showing 1,2 and 4 components

Question 79   B

First: *establish the BASE. At first glance, all the options are quite similar*. The tricky part is that they are all angled from different views. As seen in the unfolded figure, the biggest area has six sides and is located at the center portion. The rectangular components represent the depth or thickness of the object.

Second: *compare the options*. Immediately, you can eliminate **D** because its rectangular components are significantly wide.

Between **A** and **B**, the sharply angled protrusion is longer in **A** than in the original figure. This is incorrect. Next, take note that the unfolded figure shows right angle corners on the opposite side of the nose-like protrusion. **C** has a right angle on one corner and a 135^0 angle on the other corner. Option **B** is the correct answer since its base follows the same shape as the unfolded figure.

Question 80   B

First: *establish the BASE and count the components*. All of the options resemble a stair-like object. With this, you may choose the biggest area on the unfolded figure where many other components are connected. The dashed lines mean that the edges of some components are connected to it. Moreover, it is necessary to know that there are 13 components in total including the base.

Second. *Compare the options*. Option **A** is incorrect because there is a big rectangular piece on it and there are only 12 components. Options **C** and **D** are both wrong because **C** has only 10 components while **D** has 16. The correct answer is **B**.

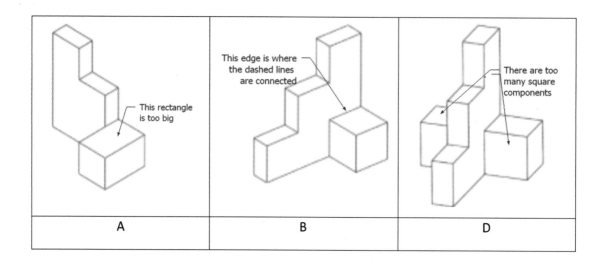

Question 81   C

First: *establish the BASE and then count the components*. For figures with a base that has a highly irregular shape, you have to take extra note of the details such as the number of slopes and the adjacency of the edges. In this case, the base has 2 sloping sides which are opposite to each other. The number of components totals 12.

Second: *compare the choices*. Keenly observe that there are 3 sloping sides on the base of option **A**, so this can be eliminated. **B** has only 8 components, which is wrong. Option **D** has a curved edge towards the top of the figure, which is also incorrect. This leaves **C** as the correct answer.

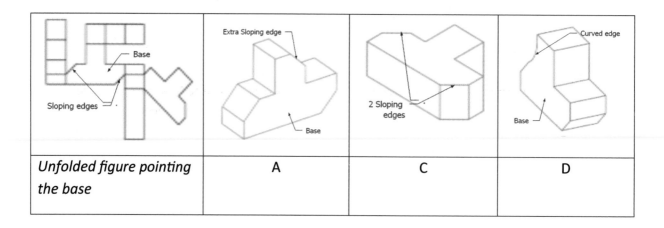

Question 82   A

First: *establish the BASE and count the components*. Assign numbers to each component as shown in the following illustration.

There are 9 components in the figure. Mentally fold the components surrounding the square base in a downward direction. You would realize that component 7 should be connected to components 1 and 3. By twisting the 3D figure, you will see that A is the correct answer.

Second: *compare the choices*. Keenly observe that components 8 and 7 are always connected to each other. Options **B** and **D** are both incorrect because the orientation of the shadings on component 8 and 7 do not correspond to the patterns shown on the unfolded figure. Option **C** is also incorrect since the shading of component

2 should be adjacent to that of component 4.

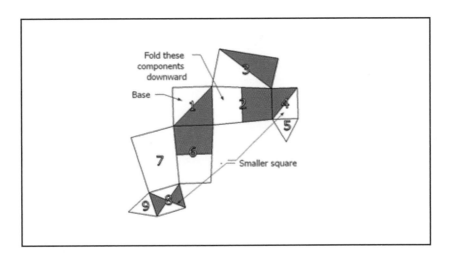

Question 83   D

This is another 3D figure, which is just a cube. Because a cube has a very basic, clean outline, you can directly go over each of the options and compare them with the patterns on the unfolded figure. Option **A** is obviously wrong because there is no way that the 3 unshaded sides would be directly adjacent to each other

when attached. **B** is also incorrect because an unshaded side comes in between components 1 and 3, so they cannot be adjacent to each other either. **C** is wrong as well because the shaded part of component 6 should be inverted as shown on the unfolded figure. Therefore, **D** is the correct answer.

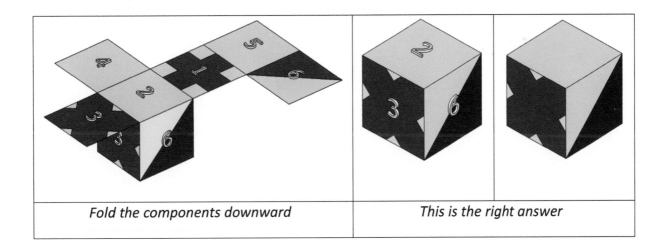

| *Fold the components downward* | *This is the right answer* |

Question 84   B

First: *establish the BASE*. All given choices look very similar in form, which is like a staircase. Counting the components will not work here because all options have 12. You must then carefully examine the base of the unfolded figure and focus on the differences in the dimensions of the components of the four options.

Second: evaluate each option. You can see that **A** has wider "steps" compared to the components of the unfolded figure. **B** has the most exact shapes and sizes of all the parts. Option **C** on the other hand, has square components which are obviously incorrect. Lastly, **D** is rectangular but they are narrower. This means **B** is the best answer.

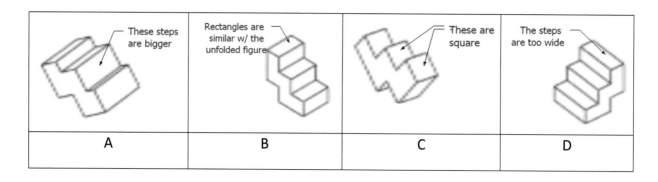

Question 85   D

First: *establish the BASE and count the components.* Again, choose the most unique and biggest component as the base. In this item, the base has 8 straight sides and 1 sloping side. In total, there are 11 components.

Second: *compare the choices.* If you twist option **A**, it has an "extra" 90⁰ angled cut on its ledge, opposite the sloping side. Another wrong answer is **B** because it has 2 sloping sides instead of just 1. Next, observe that **C** has the widest surface for the base and lacks the inner angled cuts on the figure. This leaves **D** as the correct answer.

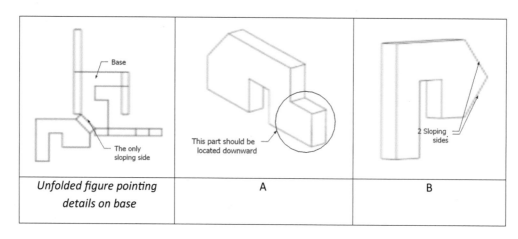

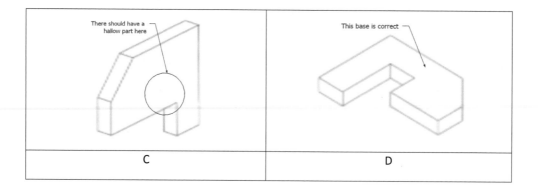

Question 86   C

First: *establish the BASE and count the components.* In this question, you have to keep in mind that the squares and the rectangles represent the thickness of the 3D object. Notice that the base has 4 straight sides, 1 sloping side, and 1 curved side.

Second: *compare the choices.* If you scan the options, **D** is clearly wrong because it is too thin and the square component is not present. Options **A** and **B** are also incorrect because they have 2 curved sides. The correct answer is **C**.

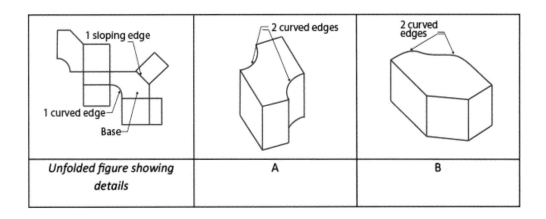

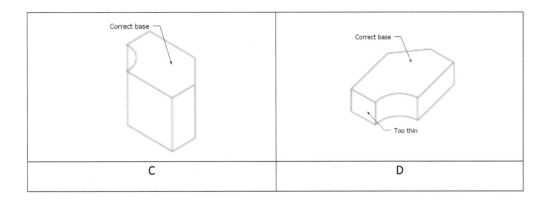

Question 87   A

This is an easy one. By simply comparing the largest surface and the thickness of the other rectangular components to each of the choices, you will realize that **A** is the correct answer. **B** has a thicker rectangular piece, which makes it a wrong choice. Options **C** and **D** have too different bases compared to the base of the unfolded figure. **A** is the best choice.

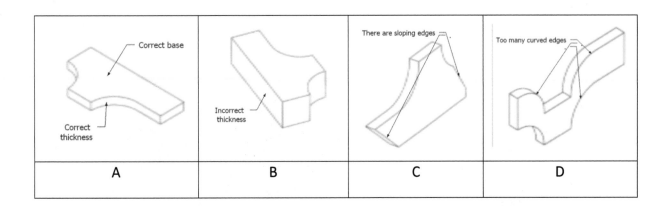

Question 88   C

First: *establish the BASE*. Choose the base where you can fold the other components around it. In this case, it is the pentagon shape with 2 triangular shades. Start folding the other components. A rough sketch will help here a lot. You can also put numbers on each side for easy distinction.

Second: *keenly compare the shading patterns in each option.*

Take careful note of the adjacent components and use your numbering. If nothing seems to match, try to visually twist or rotate the 3D figure. In Option **A**, the position of the 2 triangular shades on top (component 1) is reversed, therefore, incorrect. **B** has the correct orientation of the shadings in components 1, 2 and

3. However, component 4 should have the rectangular shade at the bottom. Option **B** shows a diagonal or triangular one, hence incorrect. **C** shows the shading orientation of components 7, 6 and 2 to be correct. **D** shows the incorrect pattern of the shadings when the figure is folded.

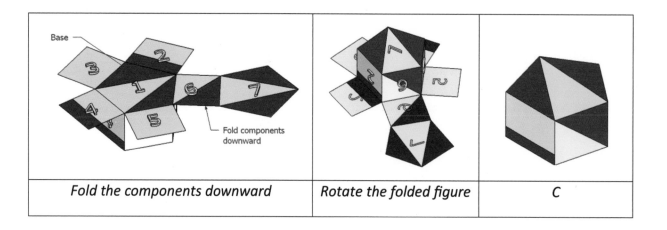

Fold the components downward	Rotate the folded figure	C

Question 89   A

First: *number each component.* Similar to Question 83, assigning a number on each side of the figure makes remembering the adjacent and attached sides easier. After folding the components in a downward direction, you can start comparing the different options.

Second: *evaluate the choice that shows the only different pattern.* Since options, **A**, **B**, and **C** all show the same orientation of the triangular shadings of 2 adjacent components, starting with **D** would be much easier. Components 2 and 3 would show two right triangles facing opposite each other and forming a white "V" in between as shown in **D**'s pattern. No other possible "combinations" seems to show the white "V" pattern. Now look at the possible third/adjacent face, which is component 4 and should be blank. **D** is definitely wrong.

Third: *compare the choices with similar patterns.* Next, consider the 3 options left. Look at the unfolded figure and imagine how

the 4 components with the triangular shadings (2, 3, 5, and 6) show when "combined" once the figure is folded. You should visually twist and rotate the 3D figure.

A combination of components 3 and 6 would show a shaded "V" at the center (similar to the pattern shown on **A**, **B**, and **C**). Now look at the possible third component. An adjacent, third component would be 2. However, the resulting pattern would show an inverted shaded "V". None of the three options shows this pattern. Next, consider component 5. The resulting pattern is similar to option **A**.

To double-check, components 3 and 5 also show the pattern of a shaded "V." A third, adjacent face would be component 4, which has a blank face. None of **A**, **B**, or **C** shows this pattern.

No other combination or pattern seems possible. This confirms **A** as the correct answer.

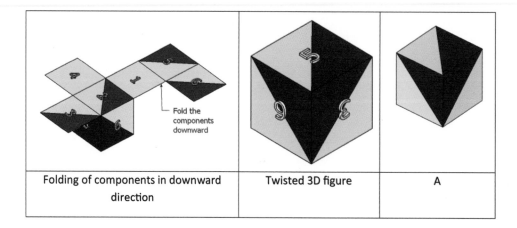

Folding of components in downward direction	Twisted 3D figure	A

Question 90   B

For this question, you need to count the number of components, which totals to 13. The unfolded figure does not have any unique component or part, so keep in mind that all geometric shapes must be equally important. The shapes that are found here are squares, trapezoids, and triangles. Take note that there should be smaller square components in the 3D figure. Only option **B** has this feature. Hence **B** is the correct answer.

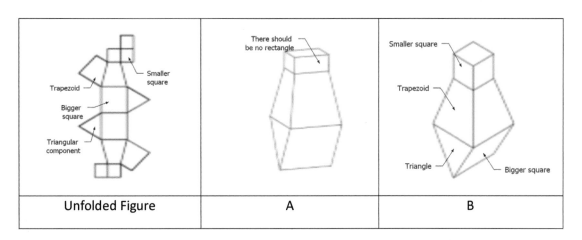

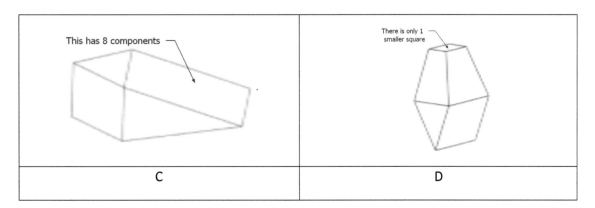

Question 1.   C

Question Type: Recall
Strategy: SI; prior knowledge; P1 S3

This question can be somewhat tricky to a non-science candidate. The term "cosmic ray" is slightly mentioned in Paragraph 1 without any explicit reference to its meaning or scientific label. However, in Sentence 3, we can infer from the following line that "cosmic rays" pertain to the ionized atomic nuclei hitting the Earth's atmosphere: "ionized atomic nuclei hit the Earth's atmosphere continuously, with such 'cosmic rays' providing hints on energetic processes . . ."

The other answers are merely distractions. Option **A** is a typical decoy in the DAT RC, wherein one of the options is mentioned in one of the last two paragraphs. Indeed, the idea of "footprints of the air shower" is indicated in Paragraph 14. However, such elements are only one of the means to track cosmic rays. Paragraph 9 denotes the same idea pertaining to "short-lived particles." This makes **D** also incorrect.

The hypothesis that cosmic rays are gamma rays was put forward by Robert Millikan, but it is conclusively eliminated in Paragraph 13. **B** is thus incorrect. Finally, in Paragraph 12, some physicists suggested "the decay of magnetic monopoles" to generate cosmic rays – they are not cosmic rays themselves. This eliminates **E**.

Question 2 C

Question Type: Recall
Strategies: SaL, PoE; P2 S3 and S4

Question 3 E

Question Type: Recall
Strategies: SaL, attention to details; P2 S2 to S3
This question can be confusing because several names of scientists are mentioned within the passage. The main strategy here is to locate either the very first scientist who was named in the passage or the scientist whose work was associated to the earliest date. Fortunately, you only have to look for the one who was first mentioned in Paragraph 2:

"In 1910, a Jesuit priest named Theodor Wulf (1868 – 1946) went up the Eiffel Tower in Paris to measure radiation levels with an 'electroscope'."

The work of the other scientists came at later dates. Paragraph 4 identifies (A) Victor Hess as the physicist who made a series of ten balloon flights with an electroscope to investigate the phenomenon in 1911 to 1912. (B) Werner Kollhoerster is the German researcher who confirmed Hess' findings by conducting his own flights sometime in 1914. (C) Walter Boethe entered the picture only in 1929 when, together with Kollhoerster, he built a "coincidence counter" to study the real nature of cosmic rays (P6). Paragraph 7 would prove that (D) Arthur Holly Compton conducted his own studies in 1932.

E is the best answer.

Question 4 D

Question Types: Recall; Math-related
Strategies: SaL, attention to details; P4 S1 to S3
In 1911-1912, Victor Hess made a series of 10 balloon flights with an electroscope to investigate Wulf's suggestion that the radiation might be coming from the upper atmosphere or space. On the other hand, the German researcher named Werner Kollhoerster made 5 flights of his own, the last of which was on June 28, 1914 Thus, a total of 15 balloon flights were conducted manually.

Question 5 E

Question Type: Recall
Strategy: SI; P8, S4
Hess received the Nobel Prize for Physics in 1936 for discovering cosmic rays; although there was a widespread belief for a period of time that Robert Millikan discovered cosmic rays.

Question 6 B

Question Type: Recall
Strategy: SaL; P10, S1

Question 7 B

Question Type: Recall
Strategies: SaL, attention to details; P10, S2

Question 8 B

Question Type: Recall
Strategies: SaL or SI, attention to details in P11
This is a very easy question, although you need to make a careful reading of Paragraph 11 in order to weed out the other keywords and confirm "background noise" as the correct answer.

Question 9 B

Question Type: Recall
Strategies: SaL and SI
This question can only be confusing because of the other valid-sounding keywords. Also, option **B** is verbatim of the elements mentioned in Paragraph 12, which seems too easy and can make you suspicious if this is indeed the correct answer. Nevertheless, **B** is the best choice.

Question 10 E

Question Type: Recall
Strategies: SaL, PoE; P13, S1

Question 11 B

Question Type: Recall
Strategies: SI, attention to details; P5 S1, P9 S1 and last sentence
This question looks as though you would need to do a careful reading and then take note of specific dates from Paragraph 4 to Paragraph 7. However, the correct answer can be simply inferred from the last sentence of Paragraph 9:

"In the postwar period, up to the early 1950s, cosmic rays were investigated with balloons that carried stacks of photographic emulsions to high altitude to record the traces of these particles."

The postwar period is indicated in the passage to have begun in 1922 when Robert Millikan started conducting studies by launching automated balloons. This is stated in Sentence 1 of Paragraph 5. This confirms B (the period between 1922 and 1950) to be the best answer.

Question 12 D

Question Type: Evaluation Question (Implication)
Strategies: SI, PoE; P14, last sentence.
This question requires you to carefully understand and infer the relevance of the LOFAR telescope to the information discussed in Paragraph 14.

In the last sentence of Paragraph 14, it is mentioned that "the LOFAR low frequency radio telescope has been used for this purpose." As to the exact purpose, we can refer to the last part of Sentence 1 in the same paragraph where the detection of radio energy generated by the air shower is mentioned as the purpose for using LOFAR low-frequency radio telescope.

You may also opt to eliminate the other options by checking if any mention of the LOFAR telescope in relation to gamma rays, alpha particles, supernovas, or protons is mentioned.

Question 13   C

Question Type: Recall
Strategy: SaL; P13, S3

Question 14   D

Question Type: Recall
Strategy: Sal; P11, S1

Question 15   C

Question Type: True False Statements (Two Statements)
Strategies: SI; P14, S1
The first two measures of observing cosmic rays mentioned in Sentence 1 of Paragraph 14 prove the first statement to be true. On the other hand, the last sentence of the same paragraph indicates that the LOFAR low-frequency radio telescope is used to pick-up the radio energy generated by the air shower.

Question 16   D

Question Type:Exception/Negative Question; Evaluation Question
Strategies: SI, attention to details; P2, P4, P8

While this question asks you to select what is NOT a quality of ANN, the terms used in the different options are not verbatim of the descriptions used in the passage. Hence, identifying the best answer requires inferring from the relevant paragraph.

First, you need to locate the part of the passage that discusses the various functions of ANN, which is Paragraph 2. Next, evaluate the statements within the paragraph. Sentence 3 pertains to the functions specified in **A**, **B**, **E**. Sentence 5 pertains to **C**.

Alternatively, you can look at Paragraph 8 to infer that (A) analyzing data, (B) solving problems, (C) recognizing patterns, and (E) calculating unknown solutions can be performed by the ANN. This leaves **D** as the only option, which is not mentioned.

Paragraph 4 does denote that ANN cannot replicate exact biological systems behavior. Therefore, **D** is the correct answer.

Question 17   A

Question Type: True False Statements (Two Statements)
Strategy: SI; P8 last sentence, P9 S2

In the last sentence of Paragraph 8, the first statement is found to be true while the latter is supported by Sentence 2 in Paragraph 9.

Question 18   B

Question Type: Evaluation Question (Implication)
Strategies: SI, attention to details; P5, S1 to S2
This question tests your interpretation of the first two sentences of Paragraph 5:

"The neuron is the basic foundation from which the network systems are constructed for both Biological Neural Networks and Artificial Neural Networks. Every neuron is a system that handles signals out of inputs since it is a MIMO system (multiple-input, multiple-output)."

Question 19   D

Question Type: Recall
Strategies: SI, PoE; P3, P5
This is another question that requires you to recall and infer information at the same time on particular parts of the passage. You may combine the process of elimination and careful understanding of information to narrow down the best choice.

In Paragraph 3 Sentences 4 and 5, the passage is clear in eliminating the neural net as (A) linear, (B) causal or (E) cause-oriented, and (C) effects-oriented. To further confirm your answer, going over the discussions in Paragraph 3 Sentence 6 and Paragraph 5 Sentence 4 would support the idea that the neural net is layered. The correct answer is **D**.

Question 20   B

Question Type: Recall
Strategy: SaL; P5 last sentence

Question 21   C

Question Type: Recall
Strategy:SaL; P5, S2

Question 22   A

Question Type: True False Statements (Two Statements); Evaluation Question (Implication)
Strategies: SaL, SI; P8 S1
This question combines an assessment of your recall and inference skills. The first statement can be easily confirmed with Paragraph 8 Sentence 1.

On the other hand, the second statement is generally implied in the passage. Some clues can be found in Paragraph 1 (". . . is based on the neuron's interconnection in the human brain's nervous system"), in Paragraph 2 ("ANN strives to simulate the firing of synapses."), and in Paragraph 11("The first work regarding the activity pattern of the human brain was published by William

James." and "The Computer and the Brain . . . showcased propositions about several radical changes in the means, which researchers use to model the brain.")

Question 23   B

Question Type: Exception/Negative Question
Strategies: SaL, never lose sight of the question; P6 S4 to S5
(A) Electrical is stated in Paragraph 6 Sentence 4 while (C) digital, (D) analog and (E) hybrid are stated in Sentence 5 of the same paragraph. Although (B) temporal is also stated, this time in Sentence 6, it refers to the simulation of hybrid elements and not by the neurons. Therefore, the correct answer is **B**.

Question 24   D

Question Type: Recall
Strategies: SI, never lose sight of the question; P6 S6
Although this is a recall question, it also requires simple inference since the correct option does not use the exact same terms used in the passage.   Moreover, the other choices tend to trick you with qualities that are associated with either the neurons or the ANN. Take note that the question asks for a characteristic of the hybrid PE (Processing Element).

From Paragraph 6 Sentence 6, "hybrid elements simulate both temporal and spatial movements." Temporal means time while spatial means space. **D** is thus the best option.

Question 25   A

Question Type: Recall
Strategy: SaL; P10 S2

Question 26   E

Question Type: Recall
Strategies: SI; P8 S5 to S7
This is another type of recall question that also compels you to do a little inference because of the way the question stem and the choices are reworded from the passage.   The answer is a paraphrase from Paragraph 8 Sentences 5 to 7.

Question 27   C

Question Type: Evaluation Question (Main Idea)
Strategy: SI; P5 S1
This question measures your overall comprehension of the similarities and differences discussed between ANN and BNN. The best support for this question can be found in Sentence 1 of Paragraph 5. The best answer is **C**.

Question 28   B

Question Type: Recall
Strategy: SI; P11 (1986) S2
This question needs you to be quick in locating the required information within the passage. At the same time, you need to carefully understand the brief description in order to match the paraphrased options.

Paragraph 11 is the summarization of the historical view of ANN and BNN. Under the 1986 data in Sentence 2, the purpose of back-propagation is stated as minimizing error functions in neural nets.

Question 29   B

Question Type: Exception/Negative Question
Strategies: SaL, PoE, attention to details; P7 S4 to S5, P11 (1958)
This question mixes up two significant points in the development of the ANN research:

1.   The 1958 data denotes that "Frank Rosenblatt created the Mark I Perceptron computer at Cornell University."

2.   Reviewing Paragraph 7, Sentences 4 and 5 tell us that Papert and Minsky wrote a book entitled Perceptrons discrediting the ANN research.

This means that the statement in B, which says "Papert and Minsky created the Perceptron," is incorrect.   They wrote and published Perceptrons, not the Perceptron.   It was Frank Rosenblatt who created the Perceptron.

Indeed, you need to pay close attention to the subtle differences in the information as you eliminate each option in order to determine the best answer.

A is supported by Paragraph 11 in the 1951 history of the ANN: "The first Artificial Neural Network was made by Marvin Minsky while he was at Princeton."

C and **D** are also explicitly stated in Paragraph 11 in the 1949 and the 1943 data of the ANN history, respectively.

For option **E**, you can infer from the 1986 overview in Paragraph 11 that this statement is also correct.

The best answer to this question is, therefore, **B**.

Question 30   B

Question Type: Recall
Strategies: SaL, attention to details; P6 last sentence

Question 31   B

Question Type: Evaluation Question (Implication)
Strategies: SI, attention to details; P9, P10
In this question, you will need to use contextual clues in order

to determine the best option. Paragraph 9 repeatedly emphasizes a priori as unnecessary in the processing of data with artificial neural networks. This idea is expressed using different terms such as "little amount of underlying theory" and "assumptions characterized by patterns are not needed by the neural networks." The closest answer is **B**.

(A) "Inherent mental structures" is not really mentioned in Paragraph 9. (C) "Guided training and (D) "expert systems" are mentioned in Paragraph 8, but they are not associated with a priori assumptions. (E) "Overtraining" and "generalizations" are also mentioned in the immediately following paragraph, but they are two separate albeit contextually associated concepts.

Question 32   B

Question Type: Recall
Strategy: SI; P9 S1
The answer to this question is a paraphrase of the first sentence in Paragraph 9.

Question 33   D

Question Type: Recall
Strategy: SaL; P6 S6

Question 34   C

Question Type: Evaluation Question (Implication)
Strategies: SI, PoE; P8
This question requires your understanding of the concepts discussed in Paragraph 8 and distinguish them from the succeeding information presented in the succeeding paragraphs. While algorithmic solutions are used when there is enough information and underlying theory, expert systems are useful when there is not enough theoretical background and data. The difference in the use of the two systems clearly relies on the amount of available data that they have to process.

(A) Analysis, (B) training, and (D) generalization are tasks that can be performed by the ANN, based on the amount of data fed to the network. (E) Neurons form as the basic framework of the ANN. This confirms C as the correct answer.

Question 35   C

Question Type: Exception/Negative Question
Strategy:SI; P2 S1, S6 and S7, P8 last sentence
Sentence 1 of Paragraph 2 states that ANN is a non-linear type of system. The last sentence cites the capacity of neural networks to generalize and recognize (A) noise-corrupted patterns and (B) similarities among assorted inputs. In the last sentence of Paragraph 8, artificial neural networks are also known to generalize (D) random patterns and (E) complex distributions. These narrow down our option to C as the exception to ANN's generalization

capabilities.

Question 36. Answer: B

Question Type: Application Question
Strategies: SI, attention to details; P6 S2
By just looking at the pattern of the musical scale given in this question, you will find the numbers 1, 2, 3, 5, 8, and 13 coinciding with the Fibonacci sequence of 0, 1, 1, 2, 3, 5, 8, 13 discussed in Paragraph 2. This makes **B** as the best answer.

A is wrong because, as Sentence 1 of Paragraph 2 indicates, the Greek octave has only 5 notes while the question specifies an octave of 8 notes. **C** is too general to be the best match for this question. Fractals, according to Paragraph 10, are visual patterns that show a replicating sequence, which could be based on the Fibonacci numbers or ANY OTHER system.

D sounds off: the question describes a musical scale, which does not equate a technique. On the other hand, **E** sounds like a probable option. However, you must remember that determining whether the golden section is observed or not in a musical composition requires looking at the ratio of the various rhythmic scales or melodic lines. You would not be able to tell if a golden section is present or not by taking just a single musical scale into account.

Question 37   D

Question Type: Exception/Negative Question
Strategies: SaL, prior knowledge, attention to details; P10 S7
The quickest way to answer this question is to consider which of the options would not have visible traits and patterns. Only the (D) wind has a gaseous property and therefore, difficult to visually observe any pattern. Moreover, it can exhibit erratic traits such as direction and speed to create any regular, self-replicating form.

In the second to the last sentence of Paragraph 7, the passage names the (C) circulatory system and (E) broccoli as examples of fractals in nature. From common knowledge, (A) snowflakes are known examples of fractals while (B) lightning does exhibit some sort of a repeating pattern.

Question 38   D

Question Type: Evaluation Question (Implication)
Strategies: SI, paraphrasing, attention to details; P3 S4
This question requires your ability to interpret the information given in Paragraph 3. Sentence 4 of this paragraph specifically states that the octave in a guitar "should be half the distance between the bridge at the lower end of the guitar and the nut where the strings cross over at the top of the guitar." This essentially implies the octave to be the middle point on a string in a guitar. The best answer is **D**.

The other answers are meant to mislead you to either draw from or assume that you need prior knowledge in music in order to answer this question.

Question 39   B

Question Type: Evaluation Question (Main Idea)
Strategies: SI, PoE; P6 S1
In Paragraph 6, the golden ratio is defined as two quantities having a ratio of the sum of to the larger quantity equaling the ratio of the larger quantity to the smaller one. This clearly eliminates **C**: no mention is made about the quantities being raised to an exponent.

A is a probable paraphrase except that it uses the term "sequentially" while the passage's definition implies equality. The same is the case in **D**: the golden section does not necessarily require an "expanding sequence" although this is usually a resulting pattern. The closest choice is **B** as the phrase "in the same way that" connotes an equal correspondence of the quantities.

Question 40   B

Question Type: Recall
Strategies: SaL, PoE; P12 S1

Question 41   C

Question Type: Evaluation Question (Main Idea)
Strategy: SI; P11, P12
This question requires your comprehension of Paragraph 11's main idea. Knowing the meaning of the word "paradox" would also help you determine the answer accurately.

"Paradox" means self-contradictory or contrary to common opinion. This is already indicated in Paragraph 11 Sentence 1: "One would expect that the construction of such complex shapes would require complex rules, but in reality, the algorithms (equations) that generate fractals are typically extraordinarily simple." Option C rephrases this idea.

Option **A**, although verbatim from Paragraph 11 as well, cannot be the correct answer. The statement that the algorithms of fractals involve loops is simply a confirmation – not a paradox – that the repeating equations ('loops"), albeit simple, can produce such visually-rich results. This is further confirmed in Paragraph 12 Sentence 5.

B, **D**, and **E** do not also state a paradox. Rather, these either describe or support the mechanics behind fractals.

Question 42   B

Question Type: Recall
Strategy: SaL; P8 S1

Question 43   A

Question Type: True False Statements (Two Statements)
Strategies: SaL; P2 S4, P7 S1

Question 44   A

Question Type: Application Question
Strategies: SI, attention to details; P4
In Sentence 1 of paragraph 4, musical notation in the Western system, "the frequency ratio 1:2 is generally identified as an octave." This means that the note an octave below 400Hz is 200Hz while the note above it is 800 Hz. The answer is A.

Question 45   D

Question Type: Recall
Strategies: SaL, SI, P10, S3

Question 46   D

Question Type: Evaluation Question (Main Idea)
Strategies: PoE, OA, SI; P1, P5, P14, P15
A quick way to deal with this question is to eliminate the most obvious wrong answers first. A is quite absolute in stating that math can be found in ALL music. Paragraph 14 notes, "Many algorithms that have no immediate musical relevance are used by composers as creative inspiration for their music." This means that mathematics is not really present in all music, but they merely serve as springboard for some – but not all – musicians.

C, on the other hand, is too specific. The passage does not solely discuss about the golden ratio or the Fibonacci numbers. **E** sounds somewhat possible. Still, nothing in the passage confirms the duplication of music and math in terms of content, at the very least. This leaves our possible choices between **B** and **D**.

The passage has indeed demonstrated that musical compositions and structures can be analyzed through the (B) use of mathematical patterns. However, this concept can also be included in the more encompassing statement found in option **D** – that is, "an intricate yet measurable relationship between music and math" has been observed and is being utilized by some composers through the use of math principles and algorithms. The best answer is **D**.

Question 47   A

Type of Question: Recall
Strategy: SaL; P13 S2

Question 48   C

Question Type: True False Statements (Statement and Reason)
Strategies: Sal and SI; P4
The first statement "The name of a note an octave above A is also A" is verbatim of Sentence 5 in Paragraph 4. However, the reason for this has to do with octave equivalency, which considers two notes an octave apart (for example, an octave above A) basically the same except in pitch. Hence, notes an octave apart are given the same note name (in the given example, also named A).

The reason given in the question, that the duplication in a note's name has to do with its combination with another note, is therefore, wrong.

Question 49   D

Question Type: Evaluation Question (Main Idea)
Strategies: PoE, OA, attention to details; P17
Similar to Question 46, the correct answer can be easily determined through a process of elimination. In addition, you have to note that the question specifically asks for the most possible closing statement for the last paragraph of the passage. This means that you also have to consider both the general idea of the passage AND the last few statements that will best connect to the given options.

The phrasing of Option **A** makes this choice wrong because it emphasizes math as the main subject of the passage. The passage, as well as the last paragraph, revolves around the relationship between math and music.

B is a true-sounding statement, but this is not mentioned anywhere in the passage or the last few paragraphs.

In Option **C**, the first half of the statement sounds applicable to the main idea of the passage. However, the second idea about mathematicians and musicians liking the other's discipline is not clearly suggested in the passage or the last paragraph.

This leaves **D** as the only best choice. Indeed, the last paragraph refers to certain mathematical applications or algorithms being employed to create beautiful music. This statement also applies to the idea of the passage in general.

Question 50   B

Type of Question: Recall
Strategy: SaL; P1 last sentence

Question 1   A

See: QR 3.2, 3.2.1, 8.2, 8.2.1
This is a rate problem with two initial values and two rates of growth. These can be combined into two expressions, one of Stephen's height and one of John's height. Let t be a variable for time in months:

Stephen: 4 ft   +   (.5 in/2 mo) t

John: 3 ft 10 in + (1 in/3 mo) t

Keeping track of units of measurement is very important in this kind of problem! Let's simplify these expressions by converting feet to inches. Remember, 12 inches to a foot. This gives:

Stephen: 48 in + t (1/4) in/mo

John: 46 in   + t (1/3) in/mo

To find the time when their heights will be the same, simply set these expressions equal to each other and solve for t:

$$48 \text{ in} + t(1/4) \text{ in/mo} = 46 \text{ in} + t(1/3) \text{ in/mo}$$

$$2 \text{ in} = (t/12) \text{ in/mo}$$

$$t = 24 \text{ mo}$$

Finally, to find the height they will both be after 24 months, plug 24 back into the original expressions:

Stephen: 4 ft   + (.5 in/2 mo) 24 = 4ft + 6in

John: 3ft 10 in + (1in/3 mo) 24   = 4ft + 6 in

Note: Evaluating both expressions is a quick way to check your work. If they aren't equal, something is wrong with your solution.

Question 2   E

See: QR 4.6, 4.6.1
First add 7 to both sides to set the quadratic equation equal to zero:

$$x^2 - 7x + 12 = 0 .$$

Next, check if you can factor the quadratic equation easily. In this case, you can:

$$(x - 3)(x - 4) = 0$$

$$(x - 3) = 0 \text{ or } (x - 4) = 0$$

$$x = 3 \text{ or } x = 4$$

Question 3   C

See: QR 7.2, 7.2.2
Remember, the "mean" is the average value of the set of numbers. Add the numbers together and divide by how many there are:

$$(7 + 7 + 8 + 10 + 13)/5 = 9 .$$

Question 4   A

See: QR 5.2, 5.2.2
Read the question carefully! It says this is an equilateral triangle, which means all of the sides are the same length and all of the angles are 60°.

Question 5   D

See: QR 7.1
First we need to find the probability that a single roll will turn up an even number. There are three possible even numbers (2, 4, and 6) out of six total possible outcomes. So the probability of rolling an even number once is:

$$p = 3/6 = 1/2.$$

Now to find the odds of rolling three even numbers in a row, multiply:

$$(p)(p)(p) = (1/2)(1/2)(1/2) = 1/8.$$

Question 6   C

See: QR 4.1, 4.1.4
We can treat $f(x) = 2f(x)$ as an algebraic equation with $f(x)$ as the variable. All we need to do is solve for $f(x)$. Subtracting $f(x)$ from both sides gives:

$$0 = f(x)$$

The function is equal to zero, no matter what x we put in. So $f(1) = 0$ is the solution.

Question 7   D

See: QR 2.4.3, 8.3
We are looking for the amount of berries produced over the course of two years. All we need to do is find the number produced in the first year and add it to the number produced in the second year. Let x be the number produced in year 1 and y be the number produced in year 2. Then:

$$x = .30\,(400) = 120$$

$$y = .85\,(400) = 340$$

$$\text{Total} = x + y = 120 + 340 = 460.$$

Question 8   D

See: QR 2.6
We are given the identity 2 km = 1.2 mi. We want to find an identity for 3.5 mi. If we divide both sides by 1.2, the right hand side will be 1 mi and we can then multiply by 3.5 to obtain:

$$(3.5/1.2)\,2\text{ km} = 3.5\text{ mi}$$

The expression on the left is the solution we are looking for. Since the problem asks for an approximation, there are many ways we can approach it. Here is a simple one. Start with $(3.5/1.2)\,2 = 7/1.2$. Now convert 1.2 to the fraction 6/5.

$$7/1.2 = 7/(6/5) = (7 \times 5)/6 = 35/6$$

All we need to do now is approximate 35/6. Notice:

$$35/6 = (36/6) - (1/6) = 6 - 1/6$$

But 1/6 is just a bit less than $1/5 = .2$, so we can approximate the expression by:

$$6 - .2 = 5.8.$$

Question 9   D

See: QR 6.1, 6.1.4, 6.2, 6.2.1
Remember the definition of cotangent as cosine/sine. Also notice that $7\pi/6$ is in the lower left quadrant of the unit circle, where both cosine and sine are negative. These negatives will cancel and cotangent will be positive, the same as it is in the upper right quadrant. So:

$$cot(7\pi/6) = cot\,(\pi/6)$$

$$= cos\,(\pi/6)/sin\,(\pi/6)$$

$$= (\sqrt{3}\,/2)\,/\,(1/2)$$

$$= \sqrt{3}$$

Question 10   B

See: QR 5.1, 5.1.1, 5.2, 5.2.2, 6.1, 6.1.1
The key in this problem is to think of the line from the origin to the point (5 , 1) as the hypotenuse of a right triangle with legs of length 5 (along the x-axis) and 1. Then we can use the identity $sin\,\theta$ = opposite/hypotenuse. The opposite leg has length 1. We can use the Pythagorean Theorem to find the length of the hypotenuse:

$$5^2 + 1^2 = c^2$$

$$c^2 = 26$$

$$c = \sqrt{26}$$

Therefore $sin\,\theta = 1/\sqrt{26}$.

Question 11   C

See: QR 2.6, 3.2, 3.2.1
We are given the identity 1 cup = 360 g. We want to know how many cups are in 20 kg, so the first thing to do is convert grams to kilograms. Remember, 1 kg = 1000 g, so:

$$1\text{ cup} = (360/1000)\text{ kg} = 0.36\text{ kg}$$

Now set up the ratios, cross multiply, and solve for the unknown variable:

$$0.36\text{kg}/1\text{cup} = 20\text{kg}/x\text{ cups}$$

$$0.36x = 20$$

$$x = 20/0.36 = 2000/36 = 500/9$$

We can avoid finding the exact solution to this if we just notice that 500/9 is a little more than 500/10 = 50. The only solution close to 50 is 55.6.

Question 12   E

See: QR 2.5, 2.5.2

Since the solution options are all multiples of 1.5, we only need to figure out the order of magnitude. First consider the powers of 10:

$$(10^3 \times 10^8)/10^7 = 10^{11}/10^7 = 10^4$$

Now consider the multipliers. They approximately equal $(7 \times 4)/2$ = 14. So we have:

$$14 \times 10^4 = 1.4 \times 10^5$$

Therefore the correct answer is 1.5×10^5.

Question 13   C

See: QR 5.2, 5.2.2, 6.3, 6.3.3

The diagonal of a rectangle forms the hypotenuse of a right triangle. The legs are the sides of the triangle, in this case of length 3 and 5. To find the length of the diagonal, use the Pythagorean Theorem:

$$c^2 = 3^2 + 5^2 = 9 + 25 = 34$$

$$c = \sqrt{34}.$$

Question 14   E

See: QR 3.1, 3.1.1

We can convert the hours and the days to minutes separately, and add all of the resulting minutes together to get the total:

Total = 26 min + 14 hr (60 min/1 hr) + 3 days (24 hr/1 day)(60 min/1 hr)

= 26 min + 14 (60 min) + 3 (24)(60 min)

= 26 min + 840 min + 4320 min

= 5186.

Question 15   B

See: QR 5.2, 5.2.3, 6.3, 6.3.3

The key in this problem is that the diagonal of a square inscribed in a circle is the diameter of the circle.

Diameter = $2 \times$ radius = 2×3 = 6

The sides of any rectangle and its diagonal are related by the Pythagorean Theorem. Since all sides of a square are the same length a, we can use b = a, c = 6:

$$6^2 = a^2 + a^2$$

$$36 = 2a^2$$

$$18 = a^2$$

$$a = \sqrt{18} = 3\sqrt{2}.$$

Question 16   E

See: QR 2.4, 2.4.2

This problem translates to an equation with fractions on either side:

$$3x/6y = 5xy/Z$$

Z is the value we are looking for. We can reduce the fraction on the left, and then cross multiply:

$$x/2y = 5xy/Z$$

$$Zx = 10xy^2$$

$$Z = 10y^2.$$

Question 17   B

See: QR 4.1, 4.1.1, 4.3, 4.3.1

First we want to get rid of the parentheses by distributing the 2:

$$(3x + 2)2 - x = 6$$

$$6x + 4 - x = 6$$

Next, combine like terms:

$$5x + 4 = 6$$

Next isolate the x term on one side:

$$5x = 2$$

Finally we want a single x on the left, so divide both sides by 5:

$$x = 2/5.$$

Question 18   E

See: QR 6.1, 6.1.2

Use the trigonometric identity $cos\ \theta$ = Adjacent / Hypotenuse. This gives:

$$cos\ 30° = S/4$$

$$\sqrt{3}/2 = S/4$$

$$S = 2\sqrt{3}.$$

Question 19   A

See: QR 6.1, 6.1.4, 6.2, 6.2.1

Since cosecant = 1/sine, we know that:

$$1/(sin\ x)\ =\ 2/\sqrt{3}$$

$$sin\ x\ =\ \sqrt{3}/2$$

Since we are given that $3\pi/2 < x < 2\pi$ we know x is in the lower right quadrant. Therefore sin x = $-\sqrt{3}/2$

Question 20   A

See: QR 4.2, 4.2.2

Before we worry about the different options given, let's isolate the *x* terms on one side and the constants on the other:

$$(2/x)\ +\ 3\ >\ 5\ -\ (1/x)\ =\ (3/x) >\ 2\ =\ (1/x)\ >\ (2/3)$$

Now be careful. It is tempting to multiply through by *x* to try and clear the denominator, but we don't know whether *x* is negative or positive. If it is negative, the direction of the inequality will change. We cannot tell whether (c) or (d) is the correct inequality. Therefore we can only say that (a) must be true.

Question 21   A

See: QR 5.3, 5.3.3

The surface area of a cylinder is:

  A = (circumference of its base) × (height) + 2(area of base)

$$A\ =\ (2\pi r)(h)\ +\ 2(\pi r^2)$$

The radius of the base *r* = diameter *x* ½ = 3.

$$A\ =\ (6\pi\ cm)(10\ cm)\ +\ 18\pi\ cm^2\ =\ 78\pi\ cm^2$$

To approximate this value, let $\pi = 3.1$

$$A\ =\ 78 \times 3.1\ cm^2\ \approx\ 242$$

So the best approximation given is 245.

Question 22   B

See: QR 2.6

This is a ratio problem. You can think of it as asking, 65 miles is to 1 hour as 25 miles is to *x* hours. Mathematically, set it up like this:

$$65mi/1hr\ =\ 25mi/x$$

All we have to do now is cross multiply and solve for x.

$$65x\ =\ 25$$

$$x\ =\ 25/65\ =\ 5/13\ .$$

Question 23   C

See: QR 2.2, 2.2.3

Since this is an approximation problem, we can save time by rounding the given values to the nearest integer before doing any operations. $39.99 becomes $40 and $15.75 becomes $16. Then the total spent is approximately:

$$3(\$40)\ +\ 4(\$16)\ +\ 12(\$3)$$

$$=\ \$120\ +\ \$64\ +\ \$36$$

$$=\ \$220\ .$$

Question 24   B

See: QR 2.4, 4.2

Convert 75% to a fraction, then multiply the two fractions together:

$$75\%\ =\ 3/4$$

So 75% of 7/2 is:

$$(3/4)(7/2)\ =\ 21/8\ .$$

Question 25   C

See: QR 2.5, 2.5.2

This question is asking the value of *y* in the equation:

$$(5.97 \times 10^{24})\,y\ =\ 1.90 \times 10^{27}$$

Since this is an approximation problem, it will make things easier if we round $5.97 \approx 6$ and $1.90 \approx 2$. Then:

$$y \approx (2 \times 10^{27})/(6 \times 10^{24})$$

$$=\ (1/3) \times (10^3)\ \approx\ .33 \times 10^3$$

$$=\ 3.3 \times 10^2$$

Our approximation is slightly different than the solution given due to different rounding, but clearly the correct answer is 3.2×10^2.

Question 26   E

See: QR 2.6

This is a ratio problem. We can write it in equation form like this:

$$2.2lb/1kg\ =\ x\ lb/4.5kg$$

Now cross multiply and solve for *x*:

$$x\ =\ (2.2)(4.5)\ =\ 9.9\ .$$

Question 27   C

See: QR 4.5, 4.5.2, 5.1, 5.1.1
We can use the properties of right triangles to solve this problem. Simply think of the line segment connecting the two points as the hypotenuse of a right triangle. Drawing a picture can help you visualize this. The lengths of two legs of the triangle are the horizontal and vertical distance between the points given:

$$x = 10 - (-2) = 12 \text{ and } y = 6 - 1 = 5$$

Now we can use the Pythagorean theorem to find the hypotenuse:

$$c^2 = 12^2 + 5^2 = 144 + 25 = 169$$

$$c = 13.$$

Note: this is a 5-12-13 triangle. If you memorize this relationship, you can save time by skipping the last calculation.

Question 28 A

See: QR 7.1, 7.1.2
First add the number of blue and yellow marbles to find the total, 20 marbles in the container. The probability of the first ball drawn being yellow is:

$$(\# \text{ yellow})/(\text{total } \# \text{ of marbles}) = 8/20 = 2/5$$

Since the problem specifies that there is no replacement the probability of the second ball being yellow is:

$$(\text{new } \# \text{ yellow})/(\text{new total } \#) = 7/19$$

The odds of both events happening is equal to the product of their individual probabilities:

$$P = (2/5)(7/19) = 14/95.$$

Question 29 E

See: QR 4.5, 4.5.4
To define a line we only need 2 points in a plane, so the problem gives more information than is necessary. We can pick 2 of the 3 points to use. To make calculations easier, choose any point with 0's or 1's first, then opt for points with integers closest to 0. In this case let's use $(1, 0)$ and $(-1, 3)$ to find an equation for the line in slope-intercept form:

$$y = (\text{slope})x + (y\text{–intercept})$$

Remember, slope = rise/run:

$$\text{slope} = (0 - 3)/[1 - (-1)] = -(3/2)$$

$$y = -(3/2)x + b$$

To find b, plug a point into this equation (the point $(1, 0)$ will be easiest to use):

$$0 = -(3/2)1 + b$$

$$3/2 = b$$

So the final equation is:

$$y = -(3/2)x + (3/2)$$

But this doesn't appear as a solution option, so we need to try putting (c) (d) and (e) in slope-intercept form. It makes since to start with (e) since there are 2's and 3's as coefficients in it. When we rearrange, we see that (e) is in fact correct.

Question 30 C

See: QR 2.4, 2.4.2
First convert the integers to fractions with denominator 5, then combine:

$$[2 - (6/5)] / [1 + (2/5)]$$

$$= [10/5 - (6/5)] / [5/5 + (2/5)]$$

$$= (4/5) / (7/5)$$

$$= 4/7.$$

Question 31 E

See: QR 2.6
Since there are 7 men to every 4 women, 7 out of every 11 students are men. So 7/11 of the students are men. Multiplying this by the total number of students, we get:

$$(7/11)(143) = (7)(13) = 91.$$

Question 32 B

See: QR 2.4, 2.4.1
Options (c) (d) and (e) are easy to rule out since they are all greater than 1/2, whereas (b) is less than 1/2. The tricky one is (a). Here is a shortcut: using the fact that $\sqrt{3} < \sqrt{4} = 2$, we know that $1/\sqrt{3} > 1/2$. So the only solution less than 1/2 is 11/23.

Question 33 A

See: QR 2.4, 2.41, 2.4.2
First get rid of all decimals because the fractions are easier to work with. Multiply the left side by (100/100) and both sides by 10:

$$(60/270)(81/x) = 54$$

Now cancel common factors and solve:

$$(2/9)(81/x) = 54$$

$$(2)(9/x) = 54$$

$$1/x = 3$$

$$x = 1/3.$$

Question 34   D

See: QR 8.2, 8.2.3

This is essentially a compound interest problem. We have a present value of 4 meters, and a growth rate of 1.4 per year. So after three years:

$$\text{Future Height} = 4(1.40)3 = 10.976 \approx 11$$

But the problem is asking for the change in height, not the height itself. Therefore the solution is:

$$\text{Future Height} - \text{Present Height} = 11 - 4 = 7.$$

Question 35   B

See: QR 4.3, 4.3.1, 4.3.3

Notice that there are a lot of binomials hanging around this equation. First look for ways to cancel whole binomials, since that would simplify the equation quickly. Before we do that, though, we need to factor $(x^2 - x - 6)$. We need a two numbers whose sum is -1 and whose product is -6. -3 and 2 work. So:

$$(x^2 - x - 6) = (x - 3)(x + 2)$$

Multiplying the equation through by this factorization we get:

$$2(x - 3)/3 + 3(x + 2) = (5x - 1)$$

Distribute the coefficients and combine like terms, then solve for x:

$$(2x - 6)/3 + 3x + 6 = 5x - 1$$

$$(2x - 6)/3 = 2x - 7$$

$$2x - 6 = 6x - 21$$

$$15 = 4x$$

$$x = 15/4.$$

Question 36   C

See: QR 2.2, 2.2.1

Round 9.7 up to 10 and round 17.4 down to 17. Since we rounded one value up and the other down, at least a portion of the error will cancel itself out, but to be sure we are obtaining a close enough approximation (and assuming you have enough time) you can always multiply the original numbers for an exact solution.

$$10 \times 17 = 170.$$

Question 37   E

See: QR 3.1, 3.1.1, 8.2, 8.2.2

The total trip was 18 min + 12 min = 30 min long. Over these 30 minutes, the average speed was 28 mph. First find the total distance travelled, then divide by 2 to get the one-way distance from the house to the store:

$$(28 \text{ mph})(30 \text{ min}) = (28 \text{ mph})(1/2 \text{ hr}) = 14 \text{ miles}$$

$$14 \text{ miles} \div 2 = 7 \text{ miles}$$

Now we can solve for the value we are looking for. We know the distance (7 miles) and the amount of time it took to cover that distance (12 min):

$$x = (7 \text{ miles})/(12 \text{ min})$$

$$= (7 \text{ miles})/(1/5 \text{ hr})$$

$$= (7)(5) \text{ mph}$$

$$= 35 \text{ mph}.$$

Question 38   D

See: QR 7.1, 7.1.2

There are three events in this problem: the first green ball drawn, the second green ball drawn, and finally a red ball drawn. The probability of all three of them happening is equal to their individual probabilities multiplied together. Remember, the second and third events are dependent on the previous ones because the problem specifies that the balls are not replaced:

$$P(\text{1st ball is green}) = 3/9$$

$$P(\text{2nd ball is green, given the 1st was green}) = 2/8$$

$$P(\text{3rd ball is red, given the 1st and 2nd were green}) = 6/7$$

$$P(\text{all three}) = (3/9)(2/8)(6/7) = 1/14.$$

Question 39   A

See: QR 2.4.3, 8.3, 8.3.3

To find the percentage of juice in the mixture we need to find the weighted average of the ingredients:

$$[(0)2\text{cups} + (0.9)1\text{cup} + (0.6)3\text{cups}]/6 \text{ cups}$$

$$= 2.7/6$$

$$= 0.45 = 45\%.$$

Question 40   D

See: QR 7.2, 7.2.2

A good strategy for this problem is to convert all the fractions so they have the same least common denominator. In this case, 12:

4/12 got a 10

1/12 got a 9

3/12 got an 8

The rest $= (12 - 8)/12 = 4/12$ got a 7

Now we can think of the class as having 12 students total in it. Then the score breakdown is:

$$\{10, 10, 10, 10, 9, 8, 8, 8, 7, 7, 7, 7\}$$

To find the median, count 6 from either side and draw a line:

$$\{10, 10, 10, 10, 9, 8 \mid 8, 8, 7, 7, 7, 7\}$$

The median is the average of the two numbers on either side of the line, in this case 8 and 8. So the median is 8.

The Gold Standard DAT

Answer Document 1

Test GS-1

CANDIDATE'S NAME ————————————————   STUDENT ID ———————————

Mark one and only one answer to each question. Be sure to use a soft lead pencil and completely fill in the space for your intended answer. If you erase, do so completely. Make no stray marks.

Survey of the Natural Sciences

1 (A) (B) (C) (D) (E)	35 (A) (B) (C) (D) (E)	69 (A) (B) (C) (D) (E)
2 (A) (B) (C) (D) (E)	36 (A) (B) (C) (D) (E)	70 (A) (B) (C) (D) (E)
3 (A) (B) (C) (D) (E)	37 (A) (B) (C) (D) (E)	71 (A) (B) (C) (D) (E)
4 (A) (B) (C) (D) (E)	38 (A) (B) (C) (D) (E)	72 (A) (B) (C) (D) (E)
5 (A) (B) (C) (D) (E)	39 (A) (B) (C) (D) (E)	73 (A) (B) (C) (D) (E)
6 (A) (B) (C) (D) (E)	40 (A) (B) (C) (D) (E)	74 (A) (B) (C) (D) (E)
7 (A) (B) (C) (D) (E)	41 (A) (B) (C) (D) (E)	75 (A) (B) (C) (D) (E)
8 (A) (B) (C) (D) (E)	42 (A) (B) (C) (D) (E)	76 (A) (B) (C) (D) (E)
9 (A) (B) (C) (D) (E)	43 (A) (B) (C) (D) (E)	77 (A) (B) (C) (D) (E)
10 (A) (B) (C) (D) (E)	44 (A) (B) (C) (D) (E)	78 (A) (B) (C) (D) (E)
11 (A) (B) (C) (D) (E)	45 (A) (B) (C) (D) (E)	79 (A) (B) (C) (D) (E)
12 (A) (B) (C) (D) (E)	46 (A) (B) (C) (D) (E)	80 (A) (B) (C) (D) (E)
13 (A) (B) (C) (D) (E)	47 (A) (B) (C) (D) (E)	81 (A) (B) (C) (D) (E)
14 (A) (B) (C) (D) (E)	48 (A) (B) (C) (D) (E)	82 (A) (B) (C) (D) (E)
15 (A) (B) (C) (D) (E)	49 (A) (B) (C) (D) (E)	83 (A) (B) (C) (D) (E)
16 (A) (B) (C) (D) (E)	50 (A) (B) (C) (D) (E)	84 (A) (B) (C) (D) (E)
17 (A) (B) (C) (D) (E)	51 (A) (B) (C) (D) (E)	85 (A) (B) (C) (D) (E)
18 (A) (B) (C) (D) (E)	52 (A) (B) (C) (D) (E)	86 (A) (B) (C) (D) (E)
19 (A) (B) (C) (D) (E)	53 (A) (B) (C) (D) (E)	87 (A) (B) (C) (D) (E)
20 (A) (B) (C) (D) (E)	54 (A) (B) (C) (D) (E)	88 (A) (B) (C) (D) (E)
21 (A) (B) (C) (D) (E)	55 (A) (B) (C) (D) (E)	89 (A) (B) (C) (D) (E)
22 (A) (B) (C) (D) (E)	56 (A) (B) (C) (D) (E)	90 (A) (B) (C) (D) (E)
23 (A) (B) (C) (D) (E)	57 (A) (B) (C) (D) (E)	91 (A) (B) (C) (D) (E)
24 (A) (B) (C) (D) (E)	58 (A) (B) (C) (D) (E)	92 (A) (B) (C) (D) (E)
25 (A) (B) (C) (D) (E)	59 (A) (B) (C) (D) (E)	93 (A) (B) (C) (D) (E)
26 (A) (B) (C) (D) (E)	60 (A) (B) (C) (D) (E)	94 (A) (B) (C) (D) (E)
27 (A) (B) (C) (D) (E)	61 (A) (B) (C) (D) (E)	95 (A) (B) (C) (D) (E)
28 (A) (B) (C) (D) (E)	62 (A) (B) (C) (D) (E)	96 (A) (B) (C) (D) (E)
29 (A) (B) (C) (D) (E)	63 (A) (B) (C) (D) (E)	97 (A) (B) (C) (D) (E)
30 (A) (B) (C) (D) (E)	64 (A) (B) (C) (D) (E)	98 (A) (B) (C) (D) (E)
31 (A) (B) (C) (D) (E)	65 (A) (B) (C) (D) (E)	99 (A) (B) (C) (D) (E)
32 (A) (B) (C) (D) (E)	66 (A) (B) (C) (D) (E)	100 (A) (B) (C) (D) (E)
33 (A) (B) (C) (D) (E)	67 (A) (B) (C) (D) (E)	
34 (A) (B) (C) (D) (E)	68 (A) (B) (C) (D) (E)	

The Gold Standard DAT

Answer Document 2

Test GS-1

CANDIDATE'S NAME _____   STUDENT ID _____

Mark one and only one answer to each question. Be sure to use a soft lead pencil and completely fill in the space for your intended answer. If you erase, do so completely. Make no stray marks.

Perceptual Ability Test

#	Answer	#	Answer	#	Answer
1	Ⓐ Ⓑ Ⓒ Ⓓ Ⓔ	31	Ⓐ Ⓑ Ⓒ Ⓓ Ⓔ	61	Ⓐ Ⓑ Ⓒ Ⓓ Ⓔ
2	Ⓐ Ⓑ Ⓒ Ⓓ Ⓔ	32	Ⓐ Ⓑ Ⓒ Ⓓ Ⓔ	62	Ⓐ Ⓑ Ⓒ Ⓓ Ⓔ
3	Ⓐ Ⓑ Ⓒ Ⓓ Ⓔ	33	Ⓐ Ⓑ Ⓒ Ⓓ Ⓔ	63	Ⓐ Ⓑ Ⓒ Ⓓ Ⓔ
4	Ⓐ Ⓑ Ⓒ Ⓓ Ⓔ	34	Ⓐ Ⓑ Ⓒ Ⓓ Ⓔ	64	Ⓐ Ⓑ Ⓒ Ⓓ Ⓔ
5	Ⓐ Ⓑ Ⓒ Ⓓ Ⓔ	35	Ⓐ Ⓑ Ⓒ Ⓓ Ⓔ	65	Ⓐ Ⓑ Ⓒ Ⓓ Ⓔ
6	Ⓐ Ⓑ Ⓒ Ⓓ Ⓔ	36	Ⓐ Ⓑ Ⓒ Ⓓ Ⓔ	66	Ⓐ Ⓑ Ⓒ Ⓓ Ⓔ
7	Ⓐ Ⓑ Ⓒ Ⓓ Ⓔ	37	Ⓐ Ⓑ Ⓒ Ⓓ Ⓔ	67	Ⓐ Ⓑ Ⓒ Ⓓ Ⓔ
8	Ⓐ Ⓑ Ⓒ Ⓓ Ⓔ	38	Ⓐ Ⓑ Ⓒ Ⓓ Ⓔ	68	Ⓐ Ⓑ Ⓒ Ⓓ Ⓔ
9	Ⓐ Ⓑ Ⓒ Ⓓ Ⓔ	39	Ⓐ Ⓑ Ⓒ Ⓓ Ⓔ	69	Ⓐ Ⓑ Ⓒ Ⓓ Ⓔ
10	Ⓐ Ⓑ Ⓒ Ⓓ Ⓔ	40	Ⓐ Ⓑ Ⓒ Ⓓ Ⓔ	70	Ⓐ Ⓑ Ⓒ Ⓓ Ⓔ
11	Ⓐ Ⓑ Ⓒ Ⓓ Ⓔ	41	Ⓐ Ⓑ Ⓒ Ⓓ Ⓔ	71	Ⓐ Ⓑ Ⓒ Ⓓ Ⓔ
12	Ⓐ Ⓑ Ⓒ Ⓓ Ⓔ	42	Ⓐ Ⓑ Ⓒ Ⓓ Ⓔ	72	Ⓐ Ⓑ Ⓒ Ⓓ Ⓔ
13	Ⓐ Ⓑ Ⓒ Ⓓ Ⓔ	43	Ⓐ Ⓑ Ⓒ Ⓓ Ⓔ	73	Ⓐ Ⓑ Ⓒ Ⓓ Ⓔ
14	Ⓐ Ⓑ Ⓒ Ⓓ Ⓔ	44	Ⓐ Ⓑ Ⓒ Ⓓ Ⓔ	74	Ⓐ Ⓑ Ⓒ Ⓓ Ⓔ
15	Ⓐ Ⓑ Ⓒ Ⓓ Ⓔ	45	Ⓐ Ⓑ Ⓒ Ⓓ Ⓔ	75	Ⓐ Ⓑ Ⓒ Ⓓ Ⓔ
16	Ⓐ Ⓑ Ⓒ Ⓓ Ⓔ	46	Ⓐ Ⓑ Ⓒ Ⓓ Ⓔ	76	Ⓐ Ⓑ Ⓒ Ⓓ Ⓔ
17	Ⓐ Ⓑ Ⓒ Ⓓ Ⓔ	47	Ⓐ Ⓑ Ⓒ Ⓓ Ⓔ	77	Ⓐ Ⓑ Ⓒ Ⓓ Ⓔ
18	Ⓐ Ⓑ Ⓒ Ⓓ Ⓔ	48	Ⓐ Ⓑ Ⓒ Ⓓ Ⓔ	78	Ⓐ Ⓑ Ⓒ Ⓓ Ⓔ
19	Ⓐ Ⓑ Ⓒ Ⓓ Ⓔ	49	Ⓐ Ⓑ Ⓒ Ⓓ Ⓔ	79	Ⓐ Ⓑ Ⓒ Ⓓ Ⓔ
20	Ⓐ Ⓑ Ⓒ Ⓓ Ⓔ	50	Ⓐ Ⓑ Ⓒ Ⓓ Ⓔ	80	Ⓐ Ⓑ Ⓒ Ⓓ Ⓔ
21	Ⓐ Ⓑ Ⓒ Ⓓ Ⓔ	51	Ⓐ Ⓑ Ⓒ Ⓓ Ⓔ	81	Ⓐ Ⓑ Ⓒ Ⓓ Ⓔ
22	Ⓐ Ⓑ Ⓒ Ⓓ Ⓔ	52	Ⓐ Ⓑ Ⓒ Ⓓ Ⓔ	82	Ⓐ Ⓑ Ⓒ Ⓓ Ⓔ
23	Ⓐ Ⓑ Ⓒ Ⓓ Ⓔ	53	Ⓐ Ⓑ Ⓒ Ⓓ Ⓔ	83	Ⓐ Ⓑ Ⓒ Ⓓ Ⓔ
24	Ⓐ Ⓑ Ⓒ Ⓓ Ⓔ	54	Ⓐ Ⓑ Ⓒ Ⓓ Ⓔ	84	Ⓐ Ⓑ Ⓒ Ⓓ Ⓔ
25	Ⓐ Ⓑ Ⓒ Ⓓ Ⓔ	55	Ⓐ Ⓑ Ⓒ Ⓓ Ⓔ	85	Ⓐ Ⓑ Ⓒ Ⓓ Ⓔ
26	Ⓐ Ⓑ Ⓒ Ⓓ Ⓔ	56	Ⓐ Ⓑ Ⓒ Ⓓ Ⓔ	86	Ⓐ Ⓑ Ⓒ Ⓓ Ⓔ
27	Ⓐ Ⓑ Ⓒ Ⓓ Ⓔ	57	Ⓐ Ⓑ Ⓒ Ⓓ Ⓔ	87	Ⓐ Ⓑ Ⓒ Ⓓ Ⓔ
28	Ⓐ Ⓑ Ⓒ Ⓓ Ⓔ	58	Ⓐ Ⓑ Ⓒ Ⓓ Ⓔ	88	Ⓐ Ⓑ Ⓒ Ⓓ Ⓔ
29	Ⓐ Ⓑ Ⓒ Ⓓ Ⓔ	59	Ⓐ Ⓑ Ⓒ Ⓓ Ⓔ	89	Ⓐ Ⓑ Ⓒ Ⓓ Ⓔ
30	Ⓐ Ⓑ Ⓒ Ⓓ Ⓔ	60	Ⓐ Ⓑ Ⓒ Ⓓ Ⓔ	90	Ⓐ Ⓑ Ⓒ Ⓓ Ⓔ

The Gold Standard DAT

Answer Document 3

Test GS-1

CANDIDATE'S NAME ——————————————— STUDENT ID ———————————————

Mark one and only one answer to each question. Be sure to use a soft lead pencil and completely fill in the space for your intended answer. If you erase, do so completely. Make no stray marks.

Reading Comprehension Test

1 Ⓐ Ⓑ Ⓒ Ⓓ Ⓔ		26 Ⓐ Ⓑ Ⓒ Ⓓ Ⓔ	
2 Ⓐ Ⓑ Ⓒ Ⓓ Ⓔ		27 Ⓐ Ⓑ Ⓒ Ⓓ Ⓔ	
3 Ⓐ Ⓑ Ⓒ Ⓓ Ⓔ		28 Ⓐ Ⓑ Ⓒ Ⓓ Ⓔ	
4 Ⓐ Ⓑ Ⓒ Ⓓ Ⓔ		29 Ⓐ Ⓑ Ⓒ Ⓓ Ⓔ	
5 Ⓐ Ⓑ Ⓒ Ⓓ Ⓔ		30 Ⓐ Ⓑ Ⓒ Ⓓ Ⓔ	
6 Ⓐ Ⓑ Ⓒ Ⓓ Ⓔ		31 Ⓐ Ⓑ Ⓒ Ⓓ Ⓔ	
7 Ⓐ Ⓑ Ⓒ Ⓓ Ⓔ		32 Ⓐ Ⓑ Ⓒ Ⓓ Ⓔ	
8 Ⓐ Ⓑ Ⓒ Ⓓ Ⓔ		33 Ⓐ Ⓑ Ⓒ Ⓓ Ⓔ	
9 Ⓐ Ⓑ Ⓒ Ⓓ Ⓔ		34 Ⓐ Ⓑ Ⓒ Ⓓ Ⓔ	
10 Ⓐ Ⓑ Ⓒ Ⓓ Ⓔ		35 Ⓐ Ⓑ Ⓒ Ⓓ Ⓔ	
11 Ⓐ Ⓑ Ⓒ Ⓓ Ⓔ		36 Ⓐ Ⓑ Ⓒ Ⓓ Ⓔ	
12 Ⓐ Ⓑ Ⓒ Ⓓ Ⓔ		37 Ⓐ Ⓑ Ⓒ Ⓓ Ⓔ	
13 Ⓐ Ⓑ Ⓒ Ⓓ Ⓔ		38 Ⓐ Ⓑ Ⓒ Ⓓ Ⓔ	
14 Ⓐ Ⓑ Ⓒ Ⓓ Ⓔ		39 Ⓐ Ⓑ Ⓒ Ⓓ Ⓔ	
15 Ⓐ Ⓑ Ⓒ Ⓓ Ⓔ		40 Ⓐ Ⓑ Ⓒ Ⓓ Ⓔ	
16 Ⓐ Ⓑ Ⓒ Ⓓ Ⓔ		41 Ⓐ Ⓑ Ⓒ Ⓓ Ⓔ	
17 Ⓐ Ⓑ Ⓒ Ⓓ Ⓔ		42 Ⓐ Ⓑ Ⓒ Ⓓ Ⓔ	
18 Ⓐ Ⓑ Ⓒ Ⓓ Ⓔ		43 Ⓐ Ⓑ Ⓒ Ⓓ Ⓔ	
19 Ⓐ Ⓑ Ⓒ Ⓓ Ⓔ		44 Ⓐ Ⓑ Ⓒ Ⓓ Ⓔ	
20 Ⓐ Ⓑ Ⓒ Ⓓ Ⓔ		45 Ⓐ Ⓑ Ⓒ Ⓓ Ⓔ	
21 Ⓐ Ⓑ Ⓒ Ⓓ Ⓔ		46 Ⓐ Ⓑ Ⓒ Ⓓ Ⓔ	
22 Ⓐ Ⓑ Ⓒ Ⓓ Ⓔ		47 Ⓐ Ⓑ Ⓒ Ⓓ Ⓔ	
23 Ⓐ Ⓑ Ⓒ Ⓓ Ⓔ		48 Ⓐ Ⓑ Ⓒ Ⓓ Ⓔ	
24 Ⓐ Ⓑ Ⓒ Ⓓ Ⓔ		49 Ⓐ Ⓑ Ⓒ Ⓓ Ⓔ	
25 Ⓐ Ⓑ Ⓒ Ⓓ Ⓔ		50 Ⓐ Ⓑ Ⓒ Ⓓ Ⓔ	

The Gold Standard DAT

Answer Document 4

Test GS-1

CANDIDATE'S NAME _____   STUDENT ID _____

Mark one and only one answer to each question. Be sure to use a soft lead pencil and completely fill in the space for your intended answer. If you erase, do so completely. Make no stray marks.

Quantitative Reasoning Test

#	A B C D E		#	A B C D E
1	Ⓐ Ⓑ Ⓒ Ⓓ Ⓔ		21	Ⓐ Ⓑ Ⓒ Ⓓ Ⓔ
2	Ⓐ Ⓑ Ⓒ Ⓓ Ⓔ		22	Ⓐ Ⓑ Ⓒ Ⓓ Ⓔ
3	Ⓐ Ⓑ Ⓒ Ⓓ Ⓔ		23	Ⓐ Ⓑ Ⓒ Ⓓ Ⓔ
4	Ⓐ Ⓑ Ⓒ Ⓓ Ⓔ		24	Ⓐ Ⓑ Ⓒ Ⓓ Ⓔ
5	Ⓐ Ⓑ Ⓒ Ⓓ Ⓔ		25	Ⓐ Ⓑ Ⓒ Ⓓ Ⓔ
6	Ⓐ Ⓑ Ⓒ Ⓓ Ⓔ		26	Ⓐ Ⓑ Ⓒ Ⓓ Ⓔ
7	Ⓐ Ⓑ Ⓒ Ⓓ Ⓔ		27	Ⓐ Ⓑ Ⓒ Ⓓ Ⓔ
8	Ⓐ Ⓑ Ⓒ Ⓓ Ⓔ		28	Ⓐ Ⓑ Ⓒ Ⓓ Ⓔ
9	Ⓐ Ⓑ Ⓒ Ⓓ Ⓔ		29	Ⓐ Ⓑ Ⓒ Ⓓ Ⓔ
10	Ⓐ Ⓑ Ⓒ Ⓓ Ⓔ		30	Ⓐ Ⓑ Ⓒ Ⓓ Ⓔ
11	Ⓐ Ⓑ Ⓒ Ⓓ Ⓔ		31	Ⓐ Ⓑ Ⓒ Ⓓ Ⓔ
12	Ⓐ Ⓑ Ⓒ Ⓓ Ⓔ		32	Ⓐ Ⓑ Ⓒ Ⓓ Ⓔ
13	Ⓐ Ⓑ Ⓒ Ⓓ Ⓔ		33	Ⓐ Ⓑ Ⓒ Ⓓ Ⓔ
14	Ⓐ Ⓑ Ⓒ Ⓓ Ⓔ		34	Ⓐ Ⓑ Ⓒ Ⓓ Ⓔ
15	Ⓐ Ⓑ Ⓒ Ⓓ Ⓔ		35	Ⓐ Ⓑ Ⓒ Ⓓ Ⓔ
16	Ⓐ Ⓑ Ⓒ Ⓓ Ⓔ		36	Ⓐ Ⓑ Ⓒ Ⓓ Ⓔ
17	Ⓐ Ⓑ Ⓒ Ⓓ Ⓔ		37	Ⓐ Ⓑ Ⓒ Ⓓ Ⓔ
18	Ⓐ Ⓑ Ⓒ Ⓓ Ⓔ		38	Ⓐ Ⓑ Ⓒ Ⓓ Ⓔ
19	Ⓐ Ⓑ Ⓒ Ⓓ Ⓔ		39	Ⓐ Ⓑ Ⓒ Ⓓ Ⓔ
20	Ⓐ Ⓑ Ⓒ Ⓓ Ⓔ		40	Ⓐ Ⓑ Ⓒ Ⓓ Ⓔ